D0555900

Lincoln Journal Star presents

A Salute to Nebraska's
TOM OSBORNE

Officially Endorsed by Tom Osborne

Sports Publishing Inc.
Champaign Illinois

©1998 Lincoln Journal Star
All Rights Reserved.

Coordinating Editor: Julie Koch
Production Manager: Susan M. McKinney
Book and Dustjacket Design: Michelle R. Dressen
Photo Editor: Ted Kirk

All photos courtesy of the Journal Star Library

ISBN: 1-57167-230-3

Printed in the United States

ACKNOWLEDGMENTS

Many thanks to Mike Pearson of Sports Publishing Inc. for the opportunity to compile this book, SPI's Susan McKinney and Michelle Dressen for the layout and design, Lincoln Journal Star publisher Bill Johnston, editor David Stoeffler and sports editor John Mabry for supporting this project, the writers on the Journal Star sports staff for their stories and advice, Ted Kirk, Randy Hampton, Gail Folda, Ian Doremus, Robert Becker and the rest of the Journal Star photo staff, and especially, Journal Star head librarian Pat Sloan, photo librarian Judy Foreman and Susan Steider for their help in finding the stories and photos for this book.

Julie Koch

Coordinating Editor

A Salute to Nebraska's Tom Osborne

Coach Devaney opened the door and put together a dynasty, and Coach Osborne improved on it. When you get to the highest level, it's difficult to maintain, but Coach Osborne did it for 25 years because of his integrity and his stability.

Dave Rimington
Two-time Outland Trophy winner at
Nebraska and Omaha native

Not the victory but the action;
Not the goal but the game;
In the deed the glory

Memorial Stadium
Lincoln, Nebraska

CONTENTS

The Greatest

by Ken Hambleton
Lincoln Journal Star

Jan. 12, 1998

Two more coaches added their names to the list of Tom Osborne admirers in 1997.

Tennessee Coach Phil Fulmer and Texas A&M Coach R.C. Slocum joined the list that includes Penn State's Joe Paterno, Florida State's Bobby Bowden, Florida's Steve Spurrier, the entire Big Eight, and now the Big 12, roster of coaches over the last 25 years.

"Nebraska gives you more to prepare for than any team in the country," said Fulmer, whose team fell to the Huskers 42-17 in the January 2, 1998 Orange Bowl. "I asked around and I heard it from everybody I talked to—so many variables on offense, you just can't account for them all, and enough speed and aggressiveness on defense, you're bound to get into trouble."

Even Bowden, who had a 6-2 record head-to-head with Osborne, said he learned more from the Nebraska coach than from almost anyone else he ever coached against.

"When you get your defense ready for Nebraska, you just hope you get the basics covered and get them to make a mistake or two," he said. "The last couple of years, they didn't even make the mistakes and they beat just about everybody they played."

Three losses in Osborne's last five years as coach was all.

Actually, Osborne's offensive alacrity dates back to his days of playing at Hastings High School, then Hastings College and eventually with the Washington Redskins and San Francisco 49ers of the NFL.

"Football is always my favorite sport," Osborne said. "I guess for a number of reasons. One is that my dad loved football and he played it. Another is that I loved the contact. I wasn't always built for it, but I tried my best and had a lot of fun playing. I have come to love the strategy of the game and the subtle changes that can change an entire game."

Simple enough. So simple it led to one of the most productive college offenses in the last 30 years and possibly the most consistent and most potent of all time.

"I borrow from everybody, everywhere and try to see what will work here," Osborne said. "I'm sure that as we borrow here, people borrow from us. I watch a lot of film and trade a lot of film. And if I've got the time, I'll watch any game that's on television.

"I enjoy the strategy. I enjoy the time I spend on Xs and Os."

Until his retirement, Osborne still took home game films and videotapes seven nights a week, 50 weeks a year.

"He would even scribble plays, formations, whatever, on cocktail napkins, scraps of paper, even on some tablecloths by accident," said Nancy Osborne. "It never ends. But he enjoys it and he's pretty good at it."

Coach Tom Osborne watches intently while others on the Husker sideline celebrate Kareem Moss' interception late in the 1995 Orange Bowl game against Miami. The interception on Miami's last play preserved NU's 24-17 victory and gave Osborne his first national championship. (Gail Folda, Journal Star Library).

Osborne picked up the game early as a player, then as a graduate assistant under Bob Devaney. Osborne's first exposure to college football coaching was the full-house backfield on offense and the 5-2 front on defense.

He explained that the full-house backfield Devaney used for the Nebraska offense and the Wyoming offense in the late 1950s and early 1960s was a derivative of the same offense used by Duffy Daugherty at Michigan State, where Devaney was an assistant.

"The full-house backfield that Bob Devaney used was a version of the wishbone," Osborne said. "The only difference was that you moved the fullback up a bit and ran it from there. In the 1930s, there was a version of the full-house backfield. We've seen teams go from full-house to two-backs to one-back sets, and then go back again. Some things become popular and then they fall by the wayside in favor of something else."

When Nebraska suffered back-to-back 6-4 seasons in 1967 and 1968, Osborne was charged with helping revamp the Husker offense.

Devaney, who died in May 1997, said in a 1990 interview, "Tom helped convince me that we should change from our unbalanced line offense to the I-formation. We didn't call him the offensive coordinator, but that's what he was. He was very instrumental in the success we had through 1972."

The office number on Tom Osborne's door changed with every victory. (Ted Kirk, Journal Star Library)

In 1969, Nebraska bounced back with a 9-2 season and trip to the Sun Bowl. In 1970 and 1971, the Huskers won national championships and strung together 32 games without a loss.

"I know we wouldn't have won the two national championships without Tom," Devaney said. "He added things, took risks as an assistant and I tried to keep to the conservative side. But what he was doing for our offense was right and it worked."

Osborne was later perceived as being too conservative. Devaney explained, "Head coaches tend to get that way and assistants tend to be the daring ones."

Osborne said that he was calling the same plays in 1973, when he became head coach, as he was as an assistant in the press box on the headphones with Devaney. "The difference was, we didn't have Johnny Rodgers in 1973 and that made a big difference," he said.

Osborne had his defensive assistant coaches stick with the 5-2, and he tried to incorporate more passing into the Nebraska offense.

He recruited Dave Humm and Vince Ferragamo, among others, and had offenses that led the Big Eight in passing. "But we didn't beat Oklahoma for a long time (Osborne's first five years) and we felt we had to change again."

Osborne then recruited option quarterbacks and incorporated the option into the offense. It was a concession to the great wishbone teams of Oklahoma, but it was also the path to winning more games.

"We figured if we could beat Oklahoma, then we'd be in the national picture as well because they were always on top," he said. "We made the decision to recruit speed at quarterback rather than throwing ability. It seemed Oklahoma always had a quarterback hurting us with the run late in the game. It seemed like a good idea to try the same thing."

The changes took awhile, but finally reached a pinnacle when Osborne recruited Turner Gill out of Texas. From 1981 through 1983, Nebraska beat Oklahoma, won the Big Eight title and challenged for the national title all three years. In 1983, Nebraska was just a two-point conversion away from beating Miami for the national title.

The option was in, and Nebraska settled into a wide-open ground attack. "The option offense tends to distort the secondary on the defense," Osborne said. "It does present a lot of problems that other offenses don't. The drawback is you have to keep the timing of the option exact and you have to have the people to be able to practice it extensively every day in practice."

There was still a string of bowl losses, seven in a row, that kept the picture from becoming complete.

"People complained we didn't have offense, but I thought the key was the

Coach Osborne reacts after a roughing the kicker penalty during the Texas Tech game September 12, 1993. (Ted Kirk, Journal Star Library)

teams we played in those bowls had the defense," Osborne said. "It didn't matter if Miami passed or Florida State was a passing team. What mattered was that they played great defense. When you play defense like that, you can play any offense you want."

Still, there were complaints that Nebraska didn't pass enough, was too pre-dictable on offense and the dinosaur running game was being passed by the passing game.

"You can't run a program on what people think or what they seem to want," Osborne said. "We do what we think we can do to win with our personnel and the weather we have. Philosophically, all we're doing is looking at what it takes to win. Go back 20 years, 30 years, you have to see that defense makes the difference. Miami had the best defense and had the best record in the 1980s and early 1990s. "If you can stop the other team, get the ball back to the offense more often, and occasionally get a turnover, then you have a chance. Defensive coaches like the running game because it keeps them off the field, gives them better field position, control of the ball, and so we feel it's important to helping our defense by running. Obviously, some balance in offense is good. But if throwing is suspect, then you should run."

Osborne began to finish the championship product when the Huskers recruited Brian Washington, Brian Davis, Charles Fryar, Tim Jackson, Reggie Cooper, Tyrone Byrd and a host of other defensive backs in the mid-to-late 1980s. Defensive backs at Nebraska in the past were usually converted running backs, former receivers or former quarterbacks. Nebraska now targeted defensive backs as a recruiting goal.

"You see pro teams reading on defense, and you see college teams taking all of the ball they can get—attacking the gaps, not reading as much," Osborne said. "There is a variety in college and pros. For years, the pros were a four-man

front, then an odd-man front, following the colleges. We made a shift here, and we've seen how it worked out."

The result was the Huskers were playing more man-to-man pass coverage and were able to gamble more with the pass rush.

"Once we got the dime package (two extra pass defenders) and found we could stop the run with that defense as well, we went to the 4-3 defense in 1992," Osborne said. "We recruited people who could cover man-to-man, went to smaller, quicker defensive people up front and made the switch away from the 5-2 defense for the first time in almost 30 years."

The result was a devastating defense that helped Nebraska capture three national titles and come within a field goal of a fourth in Osborne's last five years as head coach.

"When you can pressure on defense, get the ball back to your offense, you can

do a lot of things with the offense," Osborne said.

"We've taken this 4-3 for a full-time defense after we dabbled in it for a few years. It helps your coaches to play the 4-3 against different offenses and get through it enough to know what the problems are. You're able to adjust quicker, and that helps. You can add a few wrinkles here and there and the learning process speeds up."

The same went for the offense. Nebraska got better at the option and got better people to run it. None was better than Tommie Frazier of Bradenton, Florida, and Scott Frost of Wood River, Nebraska.

Frazier made the option offense the most dangerous it's ever been. Frost excelled in the option and became the first Husker to pass and run for 1,000 yards in each category in the same season.

It got to the point where it didn't

Tom Osborne became known as a very good tactician, able to switch his offense to adapt to what the defense was giving it. (Ted Kirk, Journal Star Library).

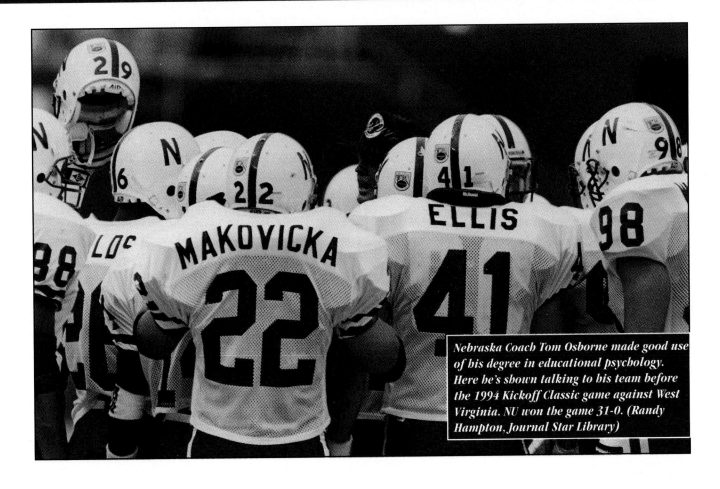

Nebraska Coach Tom Osborne made good use of his degree in educational psychology. Here he's shown talking to his team before the 1994 Kickoff Classic game against West Virginia. NU won the game 31-0. (Randy Hampton, Journal Star Library)

matter who the Huskers were playing, they worried only about their own plans on offense.

"We choose the plays based on the tendencies of our opponent's defense, but we have enough to go against just about any defense," Osborne said.

Each week, Osborne would select more than 75 plays to use depending on the down and distance. He also scripted the first 25 plays of each game, allowing for audibles to change the direction of the play or the blocking scheme.

The entire playbook was in Osborne's head. When an assistant coach would ask about a particular slant or stunt by an upcoming defense, Osborne could rattle off in 15 seconds at least 12 plays to adjust to the attack. In another minute, he'd have the diagram of each play on the board.

The same went for game time.

Osborne and his staff earned the reputation as the best halftime coaches in the business.

They devised a pass coverage scheme at halftime of the 1997 Missouri game, using a plan not used in 11 years. The second half of the 1998 Orange Bowl was an example of the Husker offense adjusting to Tennessee's defensive scheme that forced the Huskers to pass in the first half. The result was 227 yards rushing and three touchdowns in the third quarter alone in the 42-17 victory.

"We do have a lot of experience and we share all our ideas," Osborne said. "It would be hard to think of something we haven't tried or had tried on us.

"But nobody has seen it all or done it all. There are limits to things you can do, but there are always variations. Football runs in cycles. Things that were used 20-30 years ago are coming back. We just

tried to keep in mind what worked in the past and what might work in the future."

Osborne also kept up with the changes in the rules.

"The biggest change in the game has been the way offensive linemen can use their hands," he said. "You used to have to keep both fists inside the cylinder of your body. If you opened you hands or extended them, that was illegal use of hands. Now, offensive linemen have all kinds of freedom. At one time, playing offensive line was very difficult. Now, they've made that much easier. And they've made it more difficult to play defensive football.

"They liberalized the pass-blocking techniques, keep a guy out of there for three seconds, and that's why there's more passing.

"Some passing and running is geographical. If you're in an area with a lot of wind, it's hard to pass a lot. If you're in warm weather, it's easier to throw. We threw quite a bit in the 1970s. We led the league in passing and didn't win like we wanted to. Oklahoma beat us often.

"It seems like whatever you're not doing is what people talk about. Miami and Oklahoma have complained about not running the ball like they once did. Here you hear about not passing enough. We showed it's difficult to go in with four practices and play against the option."

Nebraska added the double-wing formation and used it exclusively in a 67-yard drive that took 62 seconds to tie Missouri and send the 1997 game into overtime. The Huskers reverted to wingback-around plays with Bobby Newcombe and Shevin Wiggins, reminiscent of plays for Rodgers and Kenny Brown in the 1970s. The double-slant offense threw the Texas A&M defense into a panic in NU's 54-15 romp in the Big 12 championship game in 1997.

The Huskers picked up the shotgun offense in the early 1990s. It was nothing new, Osborne said. "The shotgun is a throwback to the single-wing," Osborne said. "Florida State capitalized on it because they had a guy, a good thrower with great running ability. Of course, they didn't have the buck lateral or the spinner."

Still borrowing and still adapting through the last game of his coaching career, Osborne said he loved the planning almost as much as the game itself.

Every day at 7 a.m., for all but two weeks a year, the Nebraska coaching staff met and worked on football. The coaches went home about 10 p.m. during the season. Osborne left about 11 p.m.

"This is what I love doing," Osborne said. "It's not a hardship. It's enjoyable."

He had reasons for his intense preparation.

"You don't want to go into a game and not have the answers," Osborne said. "The other is, preparation is fun.

"The game itself is a little more intense than the preparation. Preparation is obviously more time-consuming. We spend 50 to 60 hours a week for each particular game. Behind that, there's another 70-80 hours in preparation for the game with practices, meetings, and weight room work. There is a lot of time spent with the coaching staff, picking out plans, strategies and plays, then that is passed along to the players. They play the game and there's not much you can really do once the game is going. The work is done in preparation."

So the 41-pitch that is so famous for all Nebraska I-backs may get a wrinkle in blocking or the depth of the pitch. The 41-pitch may be left alone except for a different variable for the quarterback to call.

It's always in flux, even though it's always a constant.

"Football can change so much with just a little bit of change," Osborne said. "A new blocking scheme, a new pattern, can give the defense problems. That's the idea behind the offense. That's the strategy that I enjoy. That keeps the game interesting and fresh to me.

"I've enjoyed it all." ■

Osborne's Honors

- In 25 years, Osborne had a 255-49-3 record
- Three national championships in last four years
- Five Osborne teams finished regular season unbeaten
- Last five teams combined for 60-3 record
- Highest winning percentage among active coaches
- All 25 of his teams won at least nine games a season
- First coach to reach 200 wins in 21seasons and first to win 250 games in 25 seasons
- Nebraska leads country in Academic All-Americans and the Big 12 Conference in football player graduation rates

- Nebraska has played in a bowl game 29 consecutive years, including 17 major bowls, both NCAA records
- Osborne's record in 25 bowl games was 12-13
- NU has been ranked in the final Associated Press poll in each of Osborne's seasons
- Osborne's teams won 12 Big Eight Conference titles and one Big 12 crown
- Nebraska has 39-game conference regular-season winning streak and 63-2 record at Memorial Stadium in last 10 years NCAA-record 220 straight sell-outs at Memorial Stadium

- Honored as coach of the year in 1994 by AFCA and Chevrolet in 1995
- Received Giant Steps Award from Northeastern University Center for the Study of Sport in Society
- Received 1995 National Football Foundation and College Hall of Fame Distinguished American Award
- Established The Osborne Endowment for Youth's Husker Teammates program and Osborne Legacy Project at Hastings College
- With wife Nancy received 1995 Father Flanagan Award for Service to Youth ■

Tom Osborne addresses his players before practice in the fall of 1995. (Randy Hampton, Journal Star Library)

For These Coaches, God is the Goal

by Don Walton

Lincoln Journal Star

Sept. 16, 1995

There is more to life for Tom Osborne than football. Far more.

Osborne publicly and clearly identifies his Christian belief and values as the dominant force in his life, as do a number of his assistant coaches on the national championship Husker football team.

Although there are additional Christian coaches on the Nebraska staff, Osborne and two of his assistants, Ron Brown and George Darlington, have been highly visible in expressing their faith.

"I attempt to honor God with what I'm given. That doesn't mean that I don't sometimes fail," Osborne said. "But that is the goal that is most meaningful to me in my life.

"If my only mission was to win football games, I don't think you could ever win enough to find fulfillment."

Brown, the receivers' coach, said the same thing in another way: "I'm going to seek God's applause, not man's."

Darlington, who coaches the defensive backs, said, "Not any of us (coaches) will still be here if our football team wins five or six games. We know we'll be out the door.

"So why not be more concerned with things more ultimately important?"

Those are direct words that might make some Nebraska football fanatics who have elevated the Huskers to a transcendent place in their lives a tad uncomfortable. But not to worry: All three coaches want to develop excellent football players and superior teams. All want to win. Excellence in their work is part of their Christian values, too.

The proof is in the pudding: These are the defending national champions who have won 15 games in a row, and 26 of their last 27, you know.

The issue is one of priority and perspective. What is more important: Victory in today's football game or victory in living a Christian life? A season of triumph on the football field or salvation and eternal life?

"Christianity calls me to a life of service, less to be self-serving, more called to serve God. That's my sense of what a Christian mission is," Osborne said.

With a Christian perspective, "I've noticed that life has greater meaning and purpose," he says. "But like everyone on a spiritual journey, there have been bumps in the road."

Although he grew up in a Christian home, Osborne believes he can trace his commitment to faith to a Fellowship of Christian Athletes meeting in Estes Park, Colorado, when he was about 20.

"I believe I heard Christianity articulated in a way I clearly understood by people I could relate to. That's when I made a mature step of faith."

Osborne said he tries to engage in daily "personal devotionals" of prayer and Scripture reading, usually in the morning.

"It is helpful to me in terms of spiritual strength and energy. I think it is important to start the day focused in a spiritual sense."

The early morning meeting of the coaching staff also begins with a Biblical verse or prayer. Coaches who do not wish to participate are urged to show up five minutes late.

How do his Christian belief and values impact Osborne's work?

"I think they make a difference in how you treat a recruit, how you conduct yourself on the sidelines, how you deal

Nebraska Coaches Ron Brown (left), Tom Osborne and George Darlington acknowledge that their faith is the dominant force in their lives. (Gail Folda, Journal Star Library)

with fellow coaches," he said. "I know that means that people are always looking for signs of hypocrisy or insincerity. That sometimes makes it a little uncomfortable to be scrutinized heavily.

"I think it is important that when you tell a young person that things will be done a certain way that you do it. I believe strongly in the work ethic. There is no place in athletics for lazy people. You have to pay a price to improve.

"I believe strongly in perseverance. People who hang in there succeed. In most cases the race doesn't go to the swiftest, it goes to the person with staying power.

"In the end, I hope to make a difference in a few people's lives."

One obvious place that is occurring is in a program Osborne started for at-risk youths. It provides mentors, tutors, summer jobs and ultimately a college education for those who persist. In addition to the money they raise, Osborne and his wife, Nancy, give $10,000 to the program every year.

Osborne said he does not preach to his football players "or try to make them believe as I do. However, I want our players to feel there's an opportunity there. It's important to examine your spiritual life while you're in college."

There's a chapel service for those who wish to participate before every game and a silent prayer in the locker room before and after each game.

One issue Osborne said he wrestles with is the question of time commitment.

"You can argue that your commitment is where you spend the most time. I spend a lot of time on football, 70 to 80 hours a week," he says. "But my faith is never very far away."

Brown said he considers football to be "part of my ministry."

"My faith in Christ and the ministry God has given me outweighs the football aspect. I want to honor God in every aspect of coaching that I do." His primary goal, he said, is "to remind people who Jesus Christ is."

He does that primarily through a crowded schedule of public speaking and teaching.

Brown said he tells his players up front that he's a Christian.

"I tell them that I want to honor God, and if I'm ever out of line in terms of respect or fairness you need to let me know. I never want to lie. I want to be held accountable, even by players."

While "I'm not a perfect man," Brown said, "I want people to see something of the Lord Jesus living in me. We always need to be alert to the fact that we're witnessing, whether we are speaking or not."

Like Osborne, Brown engages in early morning prayer and Bible reading, and he likes to do it again before he goes to bed at night.

And he too is active in youth work. Brown and a high school coach in Baltimore operate five Christian camps for lower-income youths.

Brown said his leap of faith occurred about the time of his graduation from college.

"I decided to cash in everything else and follow Jesus Christ. I intellectually knew who Jesus was, but I had never trusted Jesus as my Lord. I decided I have come to an end of myself. All of a sudden, I had a passion for God."

Darlington said he tries to always remember that "every man is accountable

before God for his life and how he lives.

"The Bible teaches me about my job and my relationship to the kids. It teaches that there is no dominant person, that everyone is of tremendous value. That's true in my job whether they're tremendous football players or average football players.

"The clear example in the Bible of equality in God's eye is that Christ died for the sins of mankind."

Darlington too engages in daily devotionals, reading through the Bible once a year. He said he "really came to grips with the fact that I was a sinner" during his junior year in high school and came to the belief that "Christ came to earth to pay the penalty for my sins."

To Darlington, the book of Ephesians clearly outlines the path of salvation: "For by grace you have been saved through faith–and this is not your own doing, it is the gift of God–not because of works, lest any man should boast."

"If you try to be perfect," he said, "you're going to fail."

Like Osborne and Brown, Darlington has been active in youth work, including Pioneer Girls Camp.

His highest-visibility activity as a Christian has been in efforts that would affect public schools.

"Teachers may need more pay and more responsibility," he says. "And there are books that are perceived by some of us to be of less value as opposed to others. We really got labeled and branded for saying that. What we are saying is open up the attitude toward Christian values, not burn or censor books."

Still, the bottom line, Darlington said, is that "parents need to be involved." ■

Tom Osborne Timeline

- **Feb. 23, 1937—** Born to Charles and Erma Osborne in Hastings.

- **1955—** Graduates from Hastings High School.

- **1959—** For the second straight year, is named the Lincoln Journal Star State College Athlete of the Year after a standout career as a quarterback on the football team and a standout basketball player for Hastings College.

- **1959—** Chosen in the 18th round of the NFL draft by the San Francisco 49ers, and spends season on taxi squad.

- **1960—** Released by San Francisco; picked up by the Washington Redskins.

- **1961—** Retires from professional football.

- **1962—** Joins Bob Devaney's staff at Nebraska as a graduate assistant coach.

- **Aug. 4, 1962—** Marries the former Nancy Tederman.

- **1963—** Earns his master's degree at Nebraska.

- **1965—** Earns his Ph.D. in educational psychology. Serves at Nebraska as instructor of educational psychology in the Teacher's College and a part-time coach under Devaney.

- **1967—** Joins Devaney's staff as a full-time coach. During his first full season on the coaching staff, becomes the Huskers' receivers coach.

- **Jan. 17. 1972—** Devaney announces he will step down as Nebraska's coach following the 1972 season and handpicks the 34-year-old Osborne as his successor. Osborne is named the assistant head coach and director of recruiting for Devaney's final season at Nebraska.

- **Dec. 9, 1972—** Is awarded a five-year contract as Nebraska head coach. First salary is $23,000.

- **Jan. 2, 1973—** The day after Devaney coaches his last game at Nebraska—a 40-6 victory against Notre Dame in the Orange Bowl—Osborne becomes the 25th head football coach in school history.

- **Sept. 8, 1973—** Nebraska opens the Osborne era with a 40-13 win against UCLA.

- **Oct. 13, 1973—** Nebraska suffers its first loss under Osborne when Missouri beats the Huskers 13-12 at Columbia, Mo.

- **Jan. 1, 1974—** Nebraska wins its first bowl game under Osborne with a 19-3 decision over Texas in the Cotton Bowl.

- **Nov. 23, 1974—** Nebraska faces a No. 1 team for the first time with Osborne as the head coach. The Huskers lose to Oklahoma 28-14, the second of five straight losses to the Sooners.

Tom Osborne offers a sheepish grin while being interviewed by NBC announcer John Dockery after the Huskers defeated Miami in the 1995 Orange Bowl to give Osborne his first national championship. (Journal Star Library)

• **Sept. 11, 1976—** Nebraska opens the season as The Associated Press top-ranked team in the country, the first time the Huskers have been atop one of the major polls under Osborne. A 6-6 tie with unranked Louisiana State causes Nebraska to drop to No. 8.

• **Sept. 11, 1977—** Nebraska drops out of the AP poll for the first time under Osborne after a 19-10 loss to Washington State in the season opener at Memorial Stadium.

• **Nov. 11, 1978—** After losing to Oklahoma five straight years, Osborne finally beats the Sooners when the Huskers claim a 17-14 victory at NU's Memorial Stadium. The win against the Barry Switzer-coached Sooners gave Nebraska its first Big Eight title and first Orange Bowl berth under Osborne.

• **Sept. 25, 1982—** The only thing standing between Nebraska and a national championship was a 27-24 loss to Penn State. The Huskers finished the season 12-1 and ranked third.

• **Sept. 24, 1983—** Nebraska wins its 100th game under Osborne when the Huskers beat UCLA 42-10 at Memorial Stadium.

• **Oct. 8, 1983—** Osborne becomes the all-time winningest coach in Nebraska history when the Huskers give him his 102nd career victory with a 14-10 defeat of Oklahoma State. With the win, Osborne passes Devaney, who led Nebraska to 101 wins.

• **December, 1983—** Nebraska's Mike Rozier becomes Tom Osborne's first and only Heisman Trophy winner. Rozier rushed for a school-record 2,148 yards in leading the "Scoring Explosion" offense to a 12-0 record during the regular season.

• **Jan. 2, 1984—** Nebraska, playing for the national championship, loses to Miami 31-30 when Turner Gill's pass to Jeff Smith on a two-point conversion is foiled with 48 seconds left. Smith scored on a 24-yard run to cut Miami's lead to one point, and Osborne elected to go for two instead of settling for a tie.

• **Feb. 5, 1985—** Undergoes coronary double-bypass surgery at Bryan Memorial Hospital.

• **Sept. 24, 1988—** Gets 150th victory at Nebraska with a 47-16 win against Arizona State.

• **Oct. 7, 1993—** Wins 200th game at Nebraska with a 27-13 win against Oklahoma State.

• **Jan. 1, 1995—** Nebraska wins its first national championship under Osborne, and the first at the school since 1971, when the Huskers beat Miami 24-17 at the Orange Bowl.

• **Jan. 2, 1996—** Nebraska wins its second straight national title when it beats No. 2 Florida 62-24 in the Fiesta Bowl.

• **Nov. 1, 1997—** Nebraska gives Osborne his 250th victory with a 69-7 whipping of Oklahoma at Memorial Stadium.

• **Dec. 6, 1997—** Nebraska beats Texas A&M 54-15 as the Huskers win their first Big 12 Conference championship under Osborne. It's the 13th conference title (12 were in the Big Eight) during Osborne's 25 years at the school.

• **Dec. 10, 1997—** Announces retirement, effective after the Jan. 2 Orange Bowl.

• **Jan. 2, 1998—** Coaches his final game, a 42-17 victory against No. 3 Tennessee in the Orange Bowl, giving him a 255-49-3 record in 25 years.

• **Jan. 3, 1998—** NU wins its third national championship in four years when the coaches vote the Huskers No. 1.

Family Background Molds Osborne's Character

by **Randy York**

Lincoln Journal Star

Jan. 27, 1985

If there's a football coach in America more steeped in his state's tradition than Nebraska's Tom Osborne, I'd like to meet him.

To understand Tom Osborne, the man, you have to know the late Thomas Osborne, his grandfather. And you have to know the late Charles Osborne, his father.

Thomas Osborne played on the first Hastings College football team at the turn of the century.

He went into the seminary and his first pastorate was in Wayne, perched high in the northeastern corner of Nebraska.

Thomas Osborne had homesteaded some land near Bayard in the Panhandle. But he wasn't aware until after he filed his claim that you had to live on that land for a certain number of months.

So, he left his wife and two small children (including Charles) in a sod house in Bayard while he preached the gospel in Wayne.

When Thomas Osborne returned to the Panhandle, where you could, and still can, travel 60 miles between homesteads, he committed himself to a mission.

He was a prairie preacher, taking the pulpit from his horse to anyone willing to listen.

"He moved around a lot in the Alliance, Bayard and Scottsbluff area," related NU's head coach. "He was a pretty good athlete. He played a lot of tennis and spoke a lot of languages. He was fairly fluent in Spanish and spoke Sioux Indian. He even spoke a little German and a little Russian."

Thomas Osborne was a popular man among ranchers and early settlers in the Panhandle. They often asked him to officiate at their funerals, even though a lot of them never really went to church.

Thomas was such an effective communicator that he eventually won a seat in the State Legislature.

Then, in the 1930s, he lost his voice and had to give up preaching and take up farming. "Learning to farm in midlife is pretty tough," Tom said. "There were some hard years when the Depression hit."

But Thomas Osborne persevered and when his voice recovered, he returned to preaching.

"He was struck by lightning and killed when he was 65, when I was 6 or 7," Tom said. "Because he lived in the western part of the state, I was only around him four or five times. But he was

Tom Osborne adapted to Nebraska's changing weather just like he adapted to being in the spotlight as Nebraska's head football coach. (Ian Doremus, Journal Star Library)

a guy I certainly looked up to. I guess I looked up to him more from what I knew of him, than how I actually knew him. He was a well-respected man and I admired him."

Tom Osborne also admired his father, Charles, who died last year.

Charles Osborne appeared to love football more than he appeared to embrace religion. He played high school football in Bayard and played center for Hastings College.

Charles Osborne was interested in all kinds of history. "But mostly, he was interested in the history of the West—the fur trade, the Oregon Trail and Nebraska history," Tom said. "I often thought he would have enjoyed being a history professor. We encouraged him many times to write a book. I think he could have put it together better than most historians."

Charles Osborne was active in the Nebraska State Historical Society in Lincoln. But he also had this other passion—football.

"He told me once that when he finished college, he carried a football suit around in the trunk of his car," Tom related.

"He traveled in his job and when he'd get to a town where he knew the high school coach, he'd go over and talk to him. If that high school was having a scrimmage that day, my dad would get the suit out of his car and scrimmage with them. I don't know why he did that, but he did it for a couple years. He just loved football, I guess."

Charles Osborne "was a guy who liked to have a good time," Tom said. "He was kind of a practical joker. I think he reacted strongly to being a preacher's kid. He didn't want anybody to feel he was pious. He worked pretty hard all his life, convincing people that he wasn't."

At times, Tom Osborne's passion for football and religion may seem incongruous. But if you know his background, the combination makes perfect sense. ■

Tom Osborne may not have believed it, but his 1976 Nebraska team was considered the best in the country before the season. (Randy Hampton, Journal Star Library)

The Stabilizing Influence

by Randy York
Sunday Journal and Star

April 15, 1979

Easter Sunday seems appropriate to check with one of this state's most influential citizens on a most influential subject—the religion of Tom Osborne.

Nebraska's head football coach, a former lay leader at St. Paul's United Methodist Church, has maintained a low-key religious stance since becoming Nebraska's foremost public figure.

"My faith is very important to me because it gives me the stability I need in a precarious business," Osborne said, "but it's always difficult for me to talk about because it is so personal.

"I don't like wearing religion on your sleeve, so I guess I almost bend over backward to make sure it goes the other way. I don't believe in a preachy attitude."

Nevertheless, Tom Osborne's background and thoughts on this religious holiday seem worth sharing.

"I'm not one who can say I became a Christian at 10 o'clock on the morning of April 3 and since then, there have been no problems," Osborne said.

But he can say he became a Christian sometime between his sophomore and junior years in college after attending the second conference ever of the Fellowship of Christian Athletes (FCA) in Estes Park, Colorado.

Early Christian training in the Presbyterian Church was significant, but Osborne never really tried to put everything into perspective until he attended that conference in 1957.

"Ironically, a great number of University of Oklahoma players influenced me," he said. "They helped bring everything home to me. It was the major personal change in my life. Whatever maturity I gained as a Christian began to develop there in Estes Park."

Preparing to become a coach, Osborne didn't like the logic of basing his life in terms of wins and losses on a football field.

"The impact for me was the realization that you are not called in life to be a success, but called to be faithful," Osborne said. "As far as coaching, your only obligation is to do the very best you can with whatever you have without violating your principles.

"That should enable you to live with yourself no matter what happens. For me, Christianity hasn't been a panacea making life easy, but it has made it more meaningful."

Coaching is such an up-and-down profession, Osborne said, that he's learned how to handle both the good and the bad times.

"A Christian realizes that not only is he not a total failure when he loses, but neither is he perfect when he wins. It's easy to get a false impression of your own importance when you win. You need to realize how temporary and transitory that importance is."

Even though Osborne tries to stay low key, he says it's impossible not to carry his religious faith over into his coaching.

"One of the basic tenets of religion is that every person is worthwhile . . . every person is important in God's eyes," he said. "I hope I get this across to my players. Whether they're first team or fifth

Nebraska's Tom Osborne was honored in November 1971, with an Admiralship in the Great Nebraska Navy. Army veteran Ralph Peacock (left) presents Osborne with his certificate. (Journal Star Library)

team, I care about them."

Positive feedback is not always immediate.

"Sometimes," Osborne said, "it takes five to 10 years to bear fruit."

For Jeff Kinney, who sat in a boat at Branched Oak Lake fishing with Osborne until 2 a.m. Saturday, spiritual reality struck when his marriage was suffering while playing for the Kansas City Chiefs.

"Jeff got to the point where his back was against the wall," Osborne said. "I think everybody gets to that point in their own way. I've always thought Jeff was a great guy, but if you knew him before and after he became a Christian, you'd appreciate how it changed his life. He's a different guy . . . a happier guy."

Osborne said he and his wife, Nancy, "try to let our children know how important our faith is. But we don't impose it on them. Their faith can't be our faith. They'll have to discover their own."

That discovery may not necessarily come in church, either, Osborne said.

"I must admit," he added, "I miss church a few times myself . . . during fishing season." ■

Humanitarian Osborne

My memory of Tom Osborne I would like to share is not Tom Osborne the coach but Tom Osborne the humanitarian.

Twelve years ago today, December 15, I received the gift of life with a pancreas transplant. Due to a non-payment by our insurance, we were forced to ask for donations to help pay for the surgery.

When asked to help a stranger and someone he didn't know, he took time from his busy schedule to volunteer to host a fund-raising dance and speak of faith, adversity and hope. He reached out later to help promote organ donor awareness in Nebraska for all transplant patients.

His generosity will always be remembered and he will always be cherished as each day I celebrate my health and this gift of life I am so very grateful for. Thanks again, Tom. The world is a better place because of you.

-Bonnie Smith
Lincoln

With his partner, John McEnroe, taking it easy, Nebraska Football Coach Tom Osborne prepares to return a volley during an exhibition match July 23, 1985. (Gail Folda, Journal Star Library)

As head coach of the Cornhuskers, Tom Osborne was a popular figure at the team's photo day. (Journal Star Library)

Generosity Remembered

everal years ago, a friend and I went to Val's for lunch.

As the hostess seated us, I glanced at the two gentlemen sitting at the next table, probably 18 inches away from us. The gentleman facing me looked up, smiled and gently acknowledged me with a nod of his head. It was Tom Osborne.

As lunch progressed, the autograph seekers were steady and he gently signed each one and thanked them. After several autographs, he said he'd sign for the young boy if he also had his lunch companion sign. The boy did so and left smiling.

I told my husband about it and he wanted to know who the companion was. I didn't know at that time, but later that evening on TV they were showing the coaches' workshop that was held in town, and guess who the other coach was? It was Bobby Bowden.

—Betty Swenson
Lincoln

Florida State Coach Bobby Bowden was a guest speaker at a 1994 fund-raising banquet honoring Tom Osborne for his 200th victory. (Journal Star Library)

A Lot of Giving

Osborne leaving game with many goals to go

by Ken Hambleton
Lincoln Journal Star

The player wiped his nose and listened.

"I want you to know it was nothing you did or didn't do," the coach said. "We value your contributions to the team. But we have to cut about 10 guys for the trip to the Orange Bowl this year."

The coach said that budget cutbacks had forced the decision. He repeated that the player had done nothing wrong.

The player paused. Then he dug into a shopping bag and pulled out a football, a hat and a jersey.

"Coach? Could you sign these? I'm giving them as Christmas gifts."

Tom Osborne signed the items and shook the player's hand.

The player, a walk-on who had sweated and toiled for months to get a bowl trip, smiled and thanked his coach.

"Don't worry about me," the player said. "I'll get down to the bowl. I hope we win."

As it turns out, the player is in south Florida preparing for the Orange Bowl. The Cornhuskers didn't leave anyone behind.

In 25 years as Nebraska's head football coach, Osborne has tried very hard not to leave anyone behind.

When Tom Osborne packs up his trophies, awards, pictures, the famous mounted walleye ("I've got a few bigger") and heads home from the office for the last time as Nebraska's head football coach, he'll create an emptiness in Cornhusker football never felt before.

Nebraska supporters will be losing more than just a master tactician on the field, they also will be losing a man who served as a moral bellwether for the thousands of football players he came in contact with during his 25 years as head coach.

Those young men came into Osborne's program raw and left knowing a lot more about discipline, teamwork, charity and the importance of getting a degree.

They learned from a man who has a Ph.D. in educational psychology, is a strict vegetarian, runs three miles a day, rises at dawn to meditate for 30 minutes and then puts in a 15-hour day.

The Orange Bowl will be Osborne's last game as Nebraska's head football coach. It will not be the end of his commitment to helping others.

While the players seek refuge in Osborne's replacement, Frank Solich, the community of charity and care will be able to count on Osborne as much, if not more, than ever.

"I feel that if I would go forward at this time, I could not feel good about the spiritual aspect of my life," Osborne said. "All I can say about my faith is my intuition that where you are and where you need to go sometimes takes a change. If I stayed on I would violate a trust."

That "trust" involves a Christian pledge to his community and the youth of the city, state and country, said his wife Nancy Osborne. "Tom and I both see this as resigning and not retiring. He's got a lot of energy and talent in a lot of areas. And he will, we will work as long as he can."

Osborne said his interests in charity and Bible study began at an early age.

"I taught Sunday school when I was only a year or two older than the students in the class," he said. "My faith is important to me and I believe strongly in the Gospel. I have seen it make a lot of difference in many people's lives. It is impor-

Tom Osborne was a players' coach. At the last home game of each season, the Husker seniors are introduced. Here, on November 5, 1994, Kareem Moss gives his coach a hug. (Ian Doremus, Journal Star Library)

tant to give your time and effort to others. Sometimes the frustration is that your job can take you away from doing as much as you should."

Some of his future work will involve the Fellowship of Christian Athletes. Osborne helped found the FCA chapter at the University of Nebraska, and he and Nancy founded the Teammates Program, which originally matched NU players with junior-high students. The program now matches business and academic professionals–as well as players–with junior-high students.

"I see this program going a lot further than it has gone already because it does reach young people and it does make a difference," Osborne said.

Osborne regularly stopped his press conferences to introduce Special Olympics, the Lincoln Food Bank and the Red Cross and advocates for a dozen other causes. He serves on the boards of at least 20 different charity organizations. His name is gold for any charity seeking funds.

He also turns some of his individual projects into charitable fund-raisers. Profits from his book, *On Solid Ground,* go to charity. The money from his shoe contract goes to his assistant coaches. All the funds raised through the sale of items commemorating his 25th year as head coach at Nebraska go to charity.

Tom Osborne has been more than a football coach.

At various times he has been the spotlight spokesman for anti-alcohol groups, anti-pornography groups, anti-gambling groups, fund-raising groups, players' rights, student-athlete

forums and a large number of amateur athletic organizations.

The parade of requests never ends.

"The problem with most of those things is that from August to March I couldn't do much because my No. 1 responsibility was to coach the football team," Osborne said. "I think I will be able to pick up the pace in many of the causes I believe in."

He sided with student-athletes in gaining full payment of Pell Grant funds previously awarded only to non-athletes. He has backed legislation to protect athletes by requiring sports agents to be registered in Nebraska. He even supported Sen. Ernie Chambers' idea of paying players. While he didn't agree completely with Chambers, Osborne said the idea was solid and some sort of stipend should be granted to those who create the millions of dollars in revenue.

Governors, mayors and state legislators have counted on and, in some cases, counted against Osborne.

Now, nobody–not even Osborne–knows who will pick up those advocacy

roles. Frank Solich, who will take over as head coach after the Orange Bowl game against Tennessee, will assume some of Osborne's public-relation tasks–tasks that come with being the driving force behind the state's most-publicized and most-recognizable product since 1962.

But Osborne will remain in the public eye.

Osborne and his family have paid a heavy toll for his career as head coach. Nancy was left to raise the children except for the two months Tom was not coaching or recruiting. At his resignation press conference, he apologized to Nancy and recognized the effort she made.

There were other challenges for the family of the head coach.

Nancy said she was surprised at negative reactions when the Huskers failed to cover a big spread or, heaven forbid, lost. In 1973, when Nebraska fell to Missouri 13-12 in Osborne's first year as head coach, she told the papers, "I never thought one lousy point would mean that much."

A string of losses to Oklahoma–five

NU's Tom Osborne always made time to acknowledge Husker fans. (Gail Folda, Journal Star Library)

in a row to open his coaching career–created so much pressure that Osborne considered taking the head-coaching job at Colorado. He told his Nebraska players one reason he didn't take the Colorado job was that he couldn't figure a way to say good-bye to the players he recruited.

Opportunities kept coming his way. The NFL's Houston Oilers and Denver Broncos, among others, made offers. Osborne's name crept onto a long list of rumored college coaching changes.

But he stayed. For 25 years he's been head coach of the most successful program in college football.

In that time, Osborne said he went from the "guy who couldn't win the big one to the coach who won at all costs." He explained that he was probably neither and probably both.

The coach who couldn't win the big one enjoyed an 18-16 loss to Florida State in the January 1, 1994, Orange Bowl as much as any game. That loss set the stage for national championships the next two years. Since the 1993 season, Osborne's teams are 59-3 and have been ranked in the Top 10 every week.

Osborne made changes. He helped the NU defense adopt the attacking 4-3 style, in place of the 5-2 Eagle Nebraska had used the previous 30 years. He made more changes in option and power football than anybody had in the last half century.

Meanwhile, he managed to hold on to some of the best assistant coaches in the business and turned recruiting into a science as NCAA rules changed. He found ways to compete with Miami, Florida and Florida State after those schools finally discovered they had the best talent in the country right in their own backyards.

When Nebraska, despite injuries to quarterbacks Tommie Frazier and Brook Berringer, maneuvered its way to the national championship in 1994 and blasted its way to the title in 1995, the message to the colleges of the country was clear–Osborne was on top of the game.

He also became the focus of attacks for his support of players Lawrence Phillips, Irving Fryar, Riley Washington, Christian Peter, Abdul Muhammad, Tyrone Williams and others.

Phillips' attack of a former girlfriend in September 1995 was marked as Osborne's ethical undoing. He brought Phillips back to the team after a six-game suspension because he thought it was best for Phillips. Osborne still does not regret any part of that decision, although almost every national column about his resignation mentioned that the Phillips case stained his legacy.

"I have no regrets because I thought it was best for everybody that Lawrence Phillips return to the team," Osborne said.

Even the victim's attorney said it was best because it would increase her chances of receiving a financial settlement and that further punishment of Phillips would be in nobody's best interest.

Osborne stuck with all his players, and the loyalty paid off. Peter eventually signed with the New York Giants, Fryar became a preacher and prominent spokesman for children's causes and Phillips is with the Miami Dolphins.

Beyond the football field, Osborne's direct influence will continue as long as he lives, his wife said.

Once he leaves coaching, Osborne will devote more time and attention to fulfilling his lifelong personal pledge to help youth–a pledge, he said, that drives him as much as anything else.

"I think because I see so many young people in football, through recruiting and other ways, that I have a good understanding of what is going on," he said. "More than half of the recruits I visit are in one-parent families. The father isn't around and, too often, the mother isn't around much either. Yet, we hold these young people to 1950s standards of two parents.

"If you think about it, some of these young people, if they are from a neighborhood of no serious, constant adult influence, violence, drugs and promiscuity, are doing pretty well if they aren't in trouble all the time.

"And I don't believe that theory that we can't build jails fast enough and put enough people away. That doesn't seem like a complete answer. The private sector needs to pick up the pace and I think that's where Nancy and I can come in."

Osborne has been recognized as a major contributor to Lincoln and Nebraska. Examples include the Osborne Legacy Project, a $15 million program for his alma mater, Hastings College, and a dozen of other community projects.

Though he earned coach-of-the-year honors, Osborne is prouder of the 1994 Giant Steps Award, sponsored by the Northeastern University Center for the Study of Sports in Society, and the Father Flanagan Award for Service, given in memory of the founder of Boys Town.

"We have seen the first 20 kids in the Teammates Program go on and 18 of them graduated with a high school degree," Osborne said. "I think 16 of them have gone on to higher education of some sort, too. That is important. If left alone, I think their counselors would say those same young people would have had a 25 percent graduation rate and even less would have gone on to higher education.

"I try to stay sensitive to the fact you can't hit people over the head with your beliefs, but you can use the platform you have to influence people and educate people to some needs they may not know about.

"I have tried to make sure the issues I stood for were appropriate within the bounds of being the football coach here. Some might say, 'Coach the team and shut up.'

"But you shouldn't be ashamed to speak up for what you believe, either."

■

Tom Osborne appears relaxed and ready as he addresses members of the media before the 1996 season. (Randy Hampton, Journal Star Library)

A Players' Coach

by **Mark Derowitsch**

Lincoln Journal Star

Jan. 12, 1998

Steve Taylor remembers being impressed with Tom Osborne the first time they met.

Taylor was a senior at Lincoln High School in San Diego in 1984 when he first met Osborne, who was in California recruiting. During his visit with Taylor, Osborne didn't spend time telling the young quarterback how great he was or making elaborate promises.

But his few words made a lasting impression on Taylor, who ended up attending Nebraska in the fall of 1985 and taking over as quarterback for Osborne's Cornhuskers the following season.

"A lot of coaches promise recruits a lot of things that just won't happen. But all Coach Osborne told me was, if I came to Nebraska I'd have a chance to get a solid education and a chance to play quarterback," said Taylor, who now is a real estate agent in Lincoln.

"He didn't try to sweet talk me or anything. I trusted him immediately and decided right there that I was going to Nebraska. I took four other recruiting trips, but I did it just to have a good time. From the time I met him, I knew I was going to Nebraska."

Taylor made the most of his opportunity. He started for three seasons and is sixth on the school's career passing chart with 2,815 yards and 16th on the rushing list with 2,125 yards. Taylor also rushed for 32 touchdowns and threw for 30 more.

Success came easy and early for Taylor. He won the starting quarterback's job as a sophomore and led the Huskers to a 31-6 record his final three years.

Yet Taylor said Osborne reminded him almost daily not to think too highly of himself.

"He used to walk up to me during our daily quarterback meetings and pat me on the back and say, 'When things are going great they'll love you, when things aren't going so great, they won't love you.'

"I think he did that to keep me thinking about the team. It's a team game, and he made sure to remind you that no one individual is more important than the team."

Taylor was a fly-by-the-seat-of-his-pants quarterback, often scrambling and throwing on the run, or tucking the ball away and taking off.

He was exciting. A playmaker.

Osborne didn't discourage Taylor's improvisation. Whether a play worked or failed, Osborne's response was always the same.

Even after big games—whether Nebraska blew out UCLA or lost a heartbreaker to Oklahoma—Osborne's demeanor never changed.

"He was a cool coach," Taylor said. "No matter what happened, he was always the same, always in control. He didn't let himself get too excited or too down. That kind of attitude, he was easy to play for."

Osborne still had ways of getting af-

Quarterback Steve Taylor celebrates a touchdown against Oklahoma State. Taylor lettered at NU from 1985-88. (Ted Kirk, Journal Star Library)

ter his team, especially after a lackluster performance.

Dave Rimington, who played center from 1979-82, said Osborne appeared upset with the Huskers just once during Rimington's career. It was the fourth game of the 1981 season, Rimington's junior year, and the Huskers found themselves trailing Auburn at halftime in Lincoln. The Huskers were 1-2 on the season, and another loss could have proven fatal.

Rimington came into the locker room and was joking around with friend and teammate Tony Felici, like they normally did.

"But Coach Osborne came in and started yelling at us," Rimington said. "Tony gave me a look that said, 'Do you believe this is happening.' Usually, it would be pretty quiet in the locker room, but Coach had had enough. He tossed a few 'dadgumits' around and it definitely got us fired up."

The Huskers came back to beat Auburn 17-3 and went on to win the Big Eight championship.

Osborne's outbursts were a rare occurrence during his 25 years as head coach. A number of athletes who played for Osborne looked up to the coach as a role model. However, some didn't realize it until they had left the program.

Wide receiver Irving Fryar, who lettered at Nebraska from 1981-83, just finished his 14th season in the NFL. Early in his professional career, Fryar's personal life was a mess. In fact, his name was in the news more often for his off-field problems than it was for his football accomplishments.

He was involved in a domestic dispute in 1986, and he was picked up on weapons charges twice during the next four seasons.

But six years ago, Fryar turned his life around. He was ordained as a minister, and he credits the time he spent with Osborne for causing the turnabout.

"He was always a calming force," Fryar said. "I had to try and get my act together and steady myself as a man—be like Tom."

Osborne affected players on the field, too. In 25 seasons, 49 players earned All-America honors, 35 were named academic All-Americans, one earned the Heisman Trophy, four won the Lombardi Award and five won the Outland Trophy.

In addition, 175 of Osborne's players at Nebraska were selected in the NFL draft, including 20 who were first-round picks.

Taylor, who played eight seasons in the Canadian Football League, said when players left Nebraska, they were ready for the next level.

"He knows the game inside and out and he's a great teacher," Taylor said of Osborne. "He has his philosophies of football and he believes in them. I've never been around a better Xs and Os coach."

Could Osborne have been a successful coach in the professional ranks? Taylor says yes.

"No doubt about it, but he was never going to put himself into that kind of situation," he said. "In the pros, a lot of coaches tend to put themselves before the players and that's not Coach Osborne's style.

"Plus, he likes to mold players, to teach them the game. When you're a professional coach, you do a lot of babysitting and it's hard to get through to players who are making millions of dollars a year. It's totally different, but I think if that was something that interested him, he would have been successful."

Even though Taylor has been away from the Nebraska football program for nine seasons, he still talks with Osborne.

"Mostly, he asks me about the real estate business," Taylor said. "He's always interested in what I've been doing."

Many former Nebraska players claim that playing for Osborne was like having a second father, but Taylor disagrees.

He said Osborne never pushed himself on the players as something he was not.

"He was our coach, our friend," Taylor said. "That doesn't mean the players weren't close to him. When I was thinking about playing in Canada, he was the first person I talked to about the situation. I wanted his advice because I respected him as a man, not as a father figure.

"Even today, if I had a problem or if I needed someone to talk to, I wouldn't hesitate to go to Coach Osborne."

When you ask other Husker players about Osborne, the same words keep popping up: integrity, loyalty, fair, truthful.

Osborne, over the years, has gotten a reputation for only caring about winning. He won three national championships during his last four seasons, but Taylor believes he could have walked away from the game just as content if he had never won the big one.

"That was our goal every year, but he wasn't obsessed with it," he said.

No, most Huskers agree Osborne cared primarily about his players.

And his players cared for him, too.

"The man stands for everything right," said Jason Peter, who played for Osborne the last four years. "And what he does on the field is just a small part of it." ■

Walk-ons: A Story of Success

by Ryly Jane Hambleton

Lincoln Journal Star

Jan. 12, 1998

Just like everything else in nature, the Nebraska walk-on program evolved under the watchful eye of Tom Osborne.

Although some aspects have changed, the idea of the program remains the same.

"The walk-on program is the foundation of the program," said George Darlington, the only Nebraska assistant who was with Osborne all 25 years. "With good walk-ons, you are in better shape if kids you offer scholarships don't come through like you thought or if you have injuries.

"Recruiting is an inexact science. How can you predict what an 18-year-old will be like as a 22-year-old? With walk-ons, you don't drop from good to poor at a position. If you drop, it's to above-average and that's what keeps a program from having terrible years."

The walk-on program offers an opportunity to young men who aren't offered a scholarship to prove themselves.

"In my eyes, it gave me a chance to play football at Nebraska. Playing at Nebraska was always a dream of mine," said

Nebraska quarterback Matt Turman, a walk-on from Wahoo Neumann High School, fulfilled his fantasy in helping the Huskers past Kansas State in 1994. (Gail Folda, Journal Star Library).

former Nebraska quarterback Matt Turman. "Coach (Turner) Gill was my idol. Without the walk-on program, I never would have had a chance to fulfill my dream. Most of the walk-ons are from Nebraska and grew up dreaming about playing for the Huskers."

The Nebraska walk-on program didn't have many rules in the early years. Basically, anyone who wanted to go out for the team could.

"We had a freshman team that was playing five or six games a year, so all those players would have a chance to participate," said Darlington. "They had the opportunity, they had good coaches, they had a lot of fun and they were part of the program."

There were problems, however.

"It almost became too much of a good thing. Sometimes, we'd have six, eight or even 10 deep at a position," said Darlington. "We had a young man who walked on and was way down the depth chart. He got discouraged and transferred to UNO. By the time he was done, he was drafted in the second round of the NFL draft. (Actually, Dan Fulton, who became an All-America receiver at UNO, was drafted in the third round by the Buffalo Bills.)

"We decided it was time to re-evaluate the program because, if we had so many players that we couldn't even work with a player with NFL potential, then we needed to do a better job."

The evaluation led to putting limits on the walk-on program. Players had to be invited by Nebraska coaches to be walk-ons.

"All of a sudden, we had some very irate mothers," said Darlington. "They would call and say some other kid from their hometown had been allowed to walk on and their little Johnny was a much better player.

"It was almost like it was a divine right to walk on at Nebraska. But we don't want to encourage a youngster to walk on unless he has a reasonable chance to eventually make a contribution."

The elimination of the freshman team meant evaluation was even more crucial, because players went directly to the scout team when they got to Nebraska. But the NCAA rule limiting scholarships to 85 overall makes the walk-on program essential.

"When you think about 22 positions plus kickers, you get to 85 pretty quick," Darlington said. "The main reason the walk-on program is so successful is that there's no negative stigma. In fact, it's almost a badge of honor."

Turman, who is now a history teacher and assistant football and basketball coach at Millard West High School, said that contributes to the walk-ons' sense of well-being.

"Almost everyone has in them the idea of rooting for the underdog and that's what people see the walk-on as—an underdog," he said. "People like to see you succeed when the odds are stacked against you. And I guess as a walk-on, they are. Everybody said I was too small or not quick enough."

Another reason for the success of the walk-on program is the way players are treated.

"Once the walk-ons get here, everyone's in the same boat and may the best man win," said NU assistant Ron Brown. "Everyone is on equal footing. Tom Osborne has been extremely faithful holding back scholarships for deserving walk-ons. With that hope financially for the family, they feel better about their lad's dream to play at Nebraska."

Many walk-ons eventually receive a scholarship, but not all do. Jacques Allen of Kansas City, Missouri, walked on at Nebraska after catching 73 passes for 1,350 yards at Raytown High School. He redshirted his first year and then stayed in the program for four years without a scholarship. He graduated from Nebraska in December of 1996.

"Coming from a program where you're the star, you have to learn that everyone at Nebraska was his school's star," said Allen. "One thing I learned is that you have to mature and realize that your roles are going to change in life and this is good preparation for that.

"It was an honor to play under Coach Osborne. I had scholarship offers at other schools, but I wouldn't trade the experience I had with him and Nebraska for anything."

One of the things that makes the program successful is that all players are treated equally.

"Once you're in the program, you'd never know who was on scholarship and who was a walk-on if they didn't put it in the paper," said Turman. "They give you the shoes, warmups, T-shirts and stuff and treat you all the same."

It's not like that everywhere. Darlington and Milt Tenopir were asked some time ago by Louisiana State University to observe its walk-on program and make suggestions so it could be as successful as Nebraska's.

"First, they needed to remember they have a lot of colleges in Louisiana," said Darlington. "Second, the practice field is quite a ways away from where they locker. The scholarship players were bused to practice and the walk-ons had to walk. Third, the scholarship players had their names on their jerseys and the walk-ons had blank jerseys. Fourth, when practice was over, the scholarship players all circled around the head coach and assistants and the walk-ons went over to the side of the field with a graduate assistant.

"We thought it was amazing they thought that was productive. We have a lot of pride in our walk-ons."

That's because the Nebraska football program wouldn't be what it is without the walk-on program, according to Brown.

"In many ways, the walk-on program is the bread and butter, the meat and po-

I.M. Hipp was one of Nebraska's most famous walk-ons. He finished his career in 1979 as NU's fourth-leading career rusher. (Journal Star Library)

tatoes of the program," he said. "Because of the philosophy of play, a lot of players are getting maximum repetitions in practice, so we need the numbers the walk-on program gives us.

"History has a way of being fairly accurate in supporting the worth of the walk-on program. In 1995, a national championship team, our top four wide receivers were Reggie Baul, Brendan Holbein, Clester Johnson and Jon Vedral. Three of the four came in as walk-ons and Clester came in at another position (quarterback)."

Not all walk-ons go through the same experience. Jeff and Joel Makovicka both came to the university as walk-ons from East Butler High School. Jeff was the first of the brothers to play at NU.

"Jeff's experience probably had everything to do with my deciding to walk on," said Joel. "He had it a lot different than I did. He came to visit in April or May after they'd signed everybody and an undergraduate assistant showed him around. At first, the coaches didn't know him and he really had to prove himself.

"If I had to do it first like he did, I don't know if I could do what he did. He kind of paved the way for what I did. I was guaranteed a scholarship when I came down here, so I knew what was going to happen.

"Nebraska doesn't look at it as a walk-on program so much as they just don't have enough scholarships." ∎

Solich: The Chosen Successor

by Steve Sipple
Lincoln Journal Star

Jan. 12, 1998

isconsin almost had him in January of 1990.

It seemed an almost perfect fit when new Badgers Coach Barry Alvarez offered Frank Solich the positions of assistant head coach and offensive coordinator.

Alvarez and Solich were teammates at Nebraska, and they coached against each other in high school when Solich was at Lincoln Southeast and Alvarez at Lincoln Northeast.

Solich, who had recently completed his 11th season as a Nebraska assistant coach, eventually wanted to be a head coach, and he thought he could help his chances by proving himself as an offensive coordinator at Wisconsin.

Solich flew home late on a Saturday night with the job offer. He called Alvarez on Monday to decline. Alvarez had missed by inches.

Nebraska saw this and responded by promising to promote Solich to assistant head coach. The promotion became official in July of 1991, and ever since, it was generally assumed Solich would replace Tom Osborne as head coach when Osborne decided to call it quits.

The moment came December 10, 1997. The longstanding assumption became reality. The handoff from Osborne to Solich was made cleanly. If there had

been any roadblocks to Solich taking over, Osborne, 60, wouldn't have resigned.

So the deal was sealed. After 19 seasons as an assistant at Nebraska—including the past 15 as running backs coach—Solich would become Nebraska's 26th head coach after the Orange Bowl.

Osborne actually had approached Solich early in the 1997 season to discuss the possibility of Osborne's resignation. Solich said he received assurance from Osborne he would be the next head coach—Solich just didn't know when it would happen.

"But (Coach Osborne) said when he was sure the university would go along with his choice for a successor, the decision was made," Solich said. "It was hard to keep it a secret. I told my wife, Pam, and told her not to tell anybody, not even our children. Then, Tom picked the time that he felt would be least disruptive for the team (to announce his resignation)."

Solich had always dreamed of being a college head coach.

"There are a lot of anxieties about taking over," he said. "Tom has done what no other coach has done. I am filling unbelievable shoes."

Solich calls Osborne the greatest

college football coach of all time.

"But as Tom said, no one person is bigger than the program, and I just want to keep the program going," Solich said.

Osborne said "not one (Nebraska assistant) coach had any qualms about Frank taking over."

Solich's coaching resume is indeed impressive.

The 53-year-old helped produce at least one all-conference running back in 13 of his 15 seasons coaching players at the position.

Since Solich began directing the ground attack, Nebraska has captured nine NCAA rushing titles. The Huskers have won 11 straight conference rushing crowns and have never finished worse than second in the league rushing race under Solich.

Solich also has developed a solid reputation as a recruiter. Assigned mainly to the Northeast, he has lured such players as Jason and Christian Peter, Doug Colman, Jeff Mills, Brian Washington and Mike Croel.

With his new job comes an enormous expectation level.

"We will do our best to meet those expectations," he said. "I'm sure some of the fans and some in the press will question me, and I understand that. I just hope the opinions don't get me fired."

Few jobs at the college level are as high-profile as the Nebraska head football coaching position. Solich, however, is no stranger to limelight. In September

1965, *Sports Illustrated* pictured him on the cover of its college football preview issue. The headline: "Nebraska Goes For No. 1."

The magazine made a big deal of Solich's stature. Author Dan Jenkins referred to the 5-foot-8, 157-pounder as being "the size of an underdeveloped cheerleader" in reporting his status as the smallest fullback in major college football.

Jenkins recounted the story of Solich taping a five-pound weight around his waist before weigh-ins to try to avoid being listed as the lightest player on the team. It didn't work; Larry Wachholtz was still a couple pounds heavier.

Solich—who remains close to his college playing weight—has never had a problem with his size.

"People don't look very big to me in general, and never have," he said. "(But) the move that made people conscious of my size was when Coach (Bob) Devaney moved me from halfback to fullback. But size was never a big deal to me."

Solich was born in Johnstown, Pennsylvania, and lived in nearby Smokeless, a small mining town, until the sixth grade.

That was when Solich's father, who entered the mines at age 16, contracted black lung disease from the coal dust. It forced Frank Solich Sr. to leave the mines and eventually move his family to Cleveland, where he worked for Ford Motor Co.

The younger Solich began playing organized football in a Catholic youth league. He went on to play high school ball at Cleveland Holy Name, which featured an elaborate weightlifting program and offseason workouts—virtually unheard of at that time in high schools.

Solich worked hard in the weight room, and his work paid dividends. As a senior, he was an All-American and his team was undefeated and ranked No. 1 in Northern Ohio. He received scholarship offers from Iowa State, Northwestern, Xavier, Cincinnati and Kent State.

NU Coach Tom Osborne and his successor, Frank Solich, spent long hours getting the 1997 Husker football team ready for its matchup with Tennessee in the 1998 Orange Bowl in Miami. (Journal Star Library)

Nebraska, meanwhile, had its eye on Solich's backfield mate at Holy Name— 5-foot-8, 203-pound Mike Worley.

But as Devaney watched Worley on film, he noticed the other fireball in the backfield, and Nebraska eventually offered Solich a scholarship

"But we really recruited Frank to get the other kid to come," Devaney said in 1990.

Worley's career at Nebraska ended in his first practice. It had rained the previous night, and Worley ran a pass pattern on the slippery grass and tore up his knee. He eventually underwent three surgical procedures on his knee.

But Solich became a star.

"Fearless Frankie" — as he was called in the Nebraska media guide—was a three-year starter, a co-captain, earned All-Big Eight honors and ran for 204 yards against Air Force in 1965, a single-game school record that stood for a decade.

But injuries slowed Solich throughout his college career. He broke his ankle as a sophomore and suffered a shoulder injury as a junior that required surgery following the season. And in his second-to-last regular-season game as a senior, he injured a knee running back a kickoff against Oklahoma State.

Nebraska was 10-0 entering the Orange Bowl. A victory against Alabama would have given the Huskers the national crown. But they lost 39-28 with Solich on the bench most of the second half because of his bad knee.

Solich underwent surgery after the season, scaring away professional teams.

"That's when I decided to try coaching," Solich said.

Solich's first coaching job was at

Omaha Holy Name in 1966. The team went 2-6 and 6-2 in two seasons. He then moved on to Lincoln Southeast, leading the Knights from 1968-78.

After the 1977 season, though, he applied for the head coaching position at the University of Nebraska at Omaha. The Mavericks hired Sandy Buda instead.

Osborne called after the 1978 season to offer a part-time job at Nebraska. Solich said the chance to join one of the nation's top programs without having to move his family led him to take the head freshman coaching job at NU. After four full years, he became full-time running backs coach in 1983.

Wisconsin was one of many schools that have tried to hire Solich since the early 1980s. The Badgers, though, came the closest to luring him away. ∎

Running backs coach Frank Solich applauds a Husker touchdown. (Journal Star Library)

Darlington Along for the Ride

by Curt McKeever
Lincoln Journal Star

Jan. 12, 1998

Talk about a wakeup call! George Darlington was sleeping on the floor of a cheap Chicago hotel room (his roommates got the beds), never suspecting that he was about to take a trip to the penthouse.

It was early January 1973, and Darlington, having been the defensive coordinator on a staff at San Jose State that had just been fired, was in the Windy City attending a college football coaches convention.

The ringing of the phone stirred him to semi-consciousness. Darlington picked it up and put it to his ear—the wrong way.

"It sounded like the guy was calling from Europe," he said.

Actually, the guy also was in Chicago for the convention. His name was Tom Osborne, and he was putting the final touches on assembling his first football staff at the University of Nebraska.

Osborne had a life-changing proposition for Darlington.

How do you think you'd like coaching in Lincoln, George?

"I had a wife, three kids, no money and no job," Darlington recalled. Of course he would listen to Osborne, who had contacted him on a recommendation from San Jose State's former head coach.

Darlington interviewed for the defensive ends coaching position the next morning, and when he was done, Osborne told him to hold off on other job opportunities until he had a chance to get back to him.

"I didn't tell my wife because I didn't want to get her hopes up," Darlington said. "But Tom also called her. I phoned her later to check in and she had talked to him. It all worked out. About a week later he hired me."

Darlington, now 58, is the only assistant who was along for every mile of Osborne's incredible 25-year ride as the Cornhuskers' head coach.

A graduate of Rutgers (where he played football and lacrosse) who then got his master's degree at Stanford, Darlington began his coaching career with a two-year stint at Johnson Regional High School in Clark, New Jersey, From there, he went to Lebanon Valley (Pennsylvania) College, followed by a year at Dartmouth and then four years at San Jose State.

Shortly after being hired by Osborne, the Charleston, West Virginia, native explained his reasoning for accepting the offer.

"The opportunity to coach at Nebraska as an assistant is better than being the head coach at some other college," Darlington said. "Some people have the habit of knocking the successful programs. But if Nebraska is a football factory, other institutions ought to try real hard to be a football factory, too. I've found a friendly atmosphere and an honest concern for the well-being of the athlete at Nebraska.

"My big reason for coming is that I believe it is the No. 1 program in the United States. And I'm looking forward to being a part of making it stay that way."

Darlington replaced Jim Walden, who left to join former NU Coach Pete Elliott's staff at Miami. He was the last of three outsiders hired by Osborne.

Jerry Moore, from SMU, came on board as the quarterbacks and receivers coach, and Rick Duval, from Colorado, was added to coach the offensive linemen. Osborne kept Bob Devaney assistants Jim Ross, Mike Corgan, John Melton, Cletus Fisher, Monte Kiffin, Warren Powers and Bill Myles.

"There are no better coaches in the nation than the ones we have retained from Coach Devaney's staff, and the new members of the staff are outstanding young coaches who can contribute a great

37

deal," Osborne said at the time.

Darlington kept his end of the bargain. In 13 seasons coaching the defensive ends, he helped develop four All-Americans (George Andrews, Jimmy Williams, Derrie Nelson and Bob Martin). He then moved over to become the secondary coach.

In each of the past 10 seasons, Nebraska has had at least one defensive back named first-team all-conference. Often, Darlington has been in the position of having to play freshmen and sophomores. Despite that, he's usually bluntly honest about his players' performances.

Before Nebraska's appearance in the 1998 Orange Bowl, Darlington appeared more concerned than normal. The Cornhuskers, with a starting secondary of one senior, two sophomores and a true freshman, were preparing to face Tennes-

see and the all-time leading passer in Southeastern Conference history, Peyton Manning.

"I'm constantly thinking about changeups and when to call what coverages and how to adjust," Darlington said. "It's the same every week, it's just that there has been more time to think about this game."

Whatever he was thinking worked. Nebraska held Manning to his second-lowest passing day in three seasons and went on to post a 42-17 rout.

Darlington had to have been smiling.

But even after poor performances by the Nebraska secondary, he's usually managed to keep things in perspective.

In 1992, Nebraska was getting ready for a big game against Colorado, which followed a contest in which the Cornhuskers had given up 424 yards pass-

ing to Missouri.

"I did get up about 5 a.m. and took some Maalox on Monday morning," Darlington said. "But seriously, we don't feel completely lost."

That's because Darlington is like the mad scientist of defensive football. He understands pass coverages as well as anyone in the country.

Sometimes sarcastic, Darlington is quick to note if something has been tried in the past, and he can remember if the outcome was good or bad.

He's also been prone to take a few jabs whenever someone or something raises his ire.

After Nebraska's 27-24 win at South Carolina in 1986, Darlington was infuriated by the officiating.

"That's the biggest screw job we've gotten in my years at Nebraska. They (the

Husker defensive assistant George Darlington shows diagrams of Texas A & M plays during NU's preparations for the Big 12 championship game in 1997. (Ted Kirk, Journal Star Library)

Gamecocks) had some help to stay in the game," he said. At the Extra Point Club luncheon the next Monday, Darlington "apologized" for that statement.

"For a person who claims a faith in Jesus Christ, the choice of words was very regrettable, and I really feel badly about that," he said. "Also, in regards to the comments, they weren't completely accurate because there were at least two other games that maybe were worse."

While Darlington often gets in a parting word, they usually end up making a lot of sense.

Recently, he noted that football goes in cycles. "We saw the near extinction of option football, and now we're seeing a resurgence 15 years later," he said.

This is how he responded in 1991 when asked what he looks at when assessing Nebraska's pass defense:

"The questions I ask myself are: Are we winning games? Are you coaching to the best of your ability with sound techniques? And what can we do to improve? The answers are: We are winning games, lots of them. We have a sound approach that other coaches use and other coaches want to learn. And, we are improving. We assume that we will get beat less as time goes on and that we will work hard to avoid mistakes."

The rest is history. Since then, Nebraska has won three national championships, lost a bid for another in the Orange Bowl and came one win shy of playing for yet another title.

Thanks to Darlington, Nebraska fans should have a better understanding of the Cornhuskers' success. He has spent many of his Thursday autumn nights teaching a six-week football basics course. His students, mostly women, learn the basic rules of the game, and Darlington also leads them through plays, showing how to read them and what plays may be imminent in a given situation.

"One year a woman broke her wrist practicing a blitz—and she thought it was just the greatest thing in the world," Darlington said. "I teach them things their husbands can't know, even if they played football. I like to joke that I average three divorces a year out of this class. But it's exciting to see people learn things and understand what is happening on the field."

The classes also serve him as a great way to relieve stress.

By Thursday, he once noted, "the hay's in the barn and all I'm doing is being nervous anyway."

But make no mistake, Darlington loves the pressure of coaching.

He gladly shows up for 7 a.m. meetings and regularly works 15-hour days during the season.

He gets to take recruiting trips to California, Hawaii, Oregon, Washington and Europe.

After 36 years in the business, Darlington is a coach like Jacques Cousteau was an explorer.

"My family feels they'll cart me off dead either from the field or the press box," Darlington said before the 1998 Orange Bowl. "I think they would be shocked if I died somewhere other than in a football stadium.

"As long as my health is good, I hope to coach and I hope to stay at Nebraska."

If he retired tomorrow, Darlington would be able to feel good about what he's accomplished at Nebraska. Or, more appropriately, what Osborne allowed him to get accomplished with the Cornhuskers.

"It caused me to stop and think about how long I have been at Nebraska, and how fortunate a situation we've been in with such stability on the staff," he said of Osborne's recent retirement. "He's a great model for coaches around the country."

Darlington must have felt the same from his spot on a motel room floor 25 years ago. ■

Osborne is State College Athlete Of The Year

Hastings senior is first repeater for Sunday Journal and Star award

by Del Black

Sunday Journal and Star

1959

hen Hastings College counts its blessings, it starts by counting the athletic and scholastic achievements of Tom Osborne.

Here's what makes Tom Osborne a repeat choice as the 1958 *Sunday Journal and Star* Nebraska State College Athlete of the Year:

Four varsity football letters.

Three varsity basketball letters (another on its way this season).

Three varsity track letters (another due this spring).

Summer participation in baseball.

A-minus scholastic average through 3½ years of college.

Selected three successive years as *Sunday Journal and Star* All-NCC football quarterback.

Selected two successive years (a third possible this season) on *Sunday*

Journal and Star All-NCC basketball team.

Sunday school teaching and regular church and youth work throughout high school and college career.

All-America small college mention for football and basketball teams.

Candidate for 1959 Rhodes Scholarship.

All-State high school basketball and football recognition.

What else could a college senior list as achievements?

Osborne's record leaves little to be desired.

Tom, a senior majoring in history and minoring in English and economics, becomes the first to repeat as *Sunday*

Journal and Star Athlete of the year. Last year he became the initial junior to receive the coveted award. Prior to that only seniors had gained the honor.

Adding color to the achievements of the 6-3, 185-pound redhead is the fact that he's the third generation of Osbornes at Hastings College. His grandfather, Thomas, was football captain in 1900. Charles, the father of Tom, played at HC in the late 1920s. And now, a brother, Jack, is a freshman and played football for Hastings College.

Tom, who turns 22 in February, has been a first stringer on Hastings College football, basketball and track teams for four years.

He's a top-flight T-formation quarterback and a triple threat performer. Osborne-quarterbacked teams won one Nebraska State College title, were second twice and fifth once.

Hastings College's 4-4 grid mark was not indicative of Osborne's play in 1958. The Broncos got off to a fast start in the beefed-up Nebraska College Conference

Tom Osborne was a standout athlete in basketball, football and track and played all three sports at Hastings College. (Journal Star Library)

race and then took a giant tumble after losing to co-champ Kearney in the make-or-break game for both teams.

Osborne lists his greatest football thrill as the 1957 26-6 win over Kearney. Two appearances in the National NAIA Basketball Tournament rank as tops among his cage thrills.

Osborne, as a freshman playing in the national tourney, admits he got a real basketball lesson while guarding Ben Swain, stellar performer of perennial powerhouse Tennessee A&I. Swain, now a member of the Boston Celtics, tallied 32 points against the Hastings club.

Tom, now a seasoned cage veteran, is the key performer on coach Russ Bogue's '59 Bronco squad. He's currently the club's leading scorer. Bogue was named *Sunday Journal and Star* State College Coach of the Year in 1956.

Track season finds Osborne participating as a middle distance runner and javelin thrower.

Osborne, a much-sought after prep athlete, elected to attend Hastings College because it was in his home town and he thought the advantages of going to a smaller college outweighed those of a larger university.

"I believe I've maintained a high scholastic average in school because of the fact that I can do all my studying at home," Osborne commented. "I know a lot of guys that have trouble studying because of the sometimes noisy and restless dormitory life."

Tom's plans for the future are indefinite. He's certain to do graduate work at some university, however, the site is still unknown. A law degree is one of Tom's goals at the present time.

Pro football could figure in Osborne's immediate future, although he

Tom Osborne's prowess on the football field, in addition to his ability on the basketball court and track, earned him honors as the Lincoln Journal Star State College Athlete of the Year in 1958. He also won the honor his junior year at Hastings College. (Journal Star Library)

has had no definite offers. "I'd be very interested in giving the game a try if the opportunity arose," Tom stated. "The try-outs would be early enough in the summer that I could still start my graduate work in the fall if I didn't make a pro club." The likable redhead admits he's not figuring on the pro game in his future plans. ∎

Hastings' Osborne Ready for Real Pro Grid Test

by Del Black
Sunday Journal and Star

June 28, 1961

Tom Osborne is a professional football player who has his sights set on a collection of college degrees, a job as a college administrator and possible coaching duties.

But first of all, the former Hastings College athlete wants to play football—a lot of football.

Tom made another step in this direction Tuesday when he signed his 1961 contract with the Washington Redskins of the National Football League.

It'll be Osborne's second stint with the 'Skins. He started in pro football in 1959 with the San Francisco 49ers. The 49ers traded him to the 'Skins at the start of last season.

"I guess my first game with Washington was the one people around here remember best," relates Tom. "It was on television and at Baltimore. I had just reported to the 'Skins and had only practiced with them once. I went in for a pass play, told the quarterback where I was going to run, got in the clear and then dropped the ball. I didn't know any patterns, and was quite surprised when I looked back over my shoulder and saw the ball right on target.

"It took me about three games to regain the coach's confidence," recalls Osborne.

Tom, now in Hastings for a brief stay at the home of his parents, goes to Omaha next week to begin a two-week Army reserve stint.

"I've been working out every day, playing golf or tennis in the morning and having my brother pass to me for about 90 minutes in the afternoon."

And, his brother Jack, has the talent to give Tom a good workout. He's a quarterback on the Hastings College team.

Osborne, a 6-3, 195-pound end, reports to the Redskins' training camp at Occidental College in Los Angeles on July 19. Their first of five exhibition games is set for August 14.

New coach Bill McPeak has gained Osborne's confidence.

"He knows football and is a good disciplinarian," praises Tom. "I think we'll win more games this season and will be capable of surprising someone. There's nowhere to go but up," quips Osborne, when recalling the 'Skins' last-place finish last season.

During the off-season, Tom attends UCLA where he is working on his master's degree in psychology. He intends on getting his Ph.D. At UCLA he also serves as counselor in the freshman athletic dormitory. ■

Cornhusker Coach Osborne Tells Tales Of His NFL Career

by Mike Babcock

Lincoln Journal Star

April 25, 1990—Tom Osborne joked about his brief career as a professional football player on the final day of the National Football League draft Monday night.

He was a flanker for the Washington Redskins in 1960, and "we were so desperate, things got so tough, we went to what's known as an incentive-pay system," Osborne said at the annual Fellowship of Christian Athletes banquet at the Devaney Sports Center.

According to Osborne, the system worked this way: Players received predetermined amounts of money for touchdowns, pass receptions, outstanding blocks and tackles and they were fined for mistakes, such as fumbles and missed assignments. "To give you an idea of the kind of player I was, at the end of the year they called me in, added everything up and said I owed the team $34.50," he said.

"To give you an idea of the kind of team we had, they said I was the highest paid player that year."

The truth is, Osborne was an 18th-round draft pick of the San Francisco 49ers out of Hastings College, where he was twice named State College Athlete of the Year. The 49ers' director of player personnel was the brother of an official who had worked the Mineral Water Bowl at Excelsior Springs, Missouri, Osborne's junior year.

Osborne was a quarterback at Hastings, but the 49ers switched him to wide receiver—they already had Y.A. Tittle and John Brodie playing quarterback. Osborne spent his rookie season in the NFL on San Francisco's taxi squad, no small accomplishment given the fact he had been selected so late in the draft.

He was traded to the Redskins in 1960, another event about which he made light at the FCA banquet.

"The first recollection I have of being with the Redskins was in New York City," said Osborne. "I joined them there. I can remember standing out in front of the Waldorf-Astoria. Being such a high-class organization, that's where the Redskins always stayed when they went to new York . . . out in front of the Waldorf-Astoria."

Osborne said, tongue-in-cheek, he scanned The New York Times for a story on the "big trade" that sent him from San Francisco to Washington.

What he found, he said, was a paragraph at the bottom the last page, indicating the Redskins had obtained a fullback.

Osborne said he went straight to Mike Nixon, the Redskins' head coach, and the following conversation took place.

Osborne: "This has to be a misprint or a practical joke."

Nixon: "No, Osborne, we want you to be our fullback."

Osborne: "Well, Coach, I'm 6-foot-4 and 185 pounds. Why in the world would you want a guy like that to be a fullback?"

Nixon: "Have you ever seen the Redskins play before? When you see the size of holes our line opens up . . . you're the only kind of fullback who can get through those holes."

Actually Washington acquired him to be a flanker, the position he played for two seasons, as a backup in 1960 and a regular in 1961, when he ranked second on the team in pass receptions.

Osborne wasn't exaggerating about the Redskins' ineptitude. In 1960, the second of Nixon's two seasons, their record was 1-9-2. In 1961, under Coach Bill McPeak, they were 1-12-1.

Osborne was offered a better contract by Washington for the 1962 season, but he declined. Because he was about to be married, "I was interested in something more stable," he once told a writer.

A letter Osborne wrote to Bob Devaney, asking if he had any openings on his staff, would provide that stability. Devaney, who had just been hired to replace Bill Jennings as head football coach at Nebraska, offered Osborne a job as a graduate assistant, for which he would be paid with meals at the training table. Osborne accepted.

That decision, time has shown, benefited both men, as well as Nebraska, the university and the state. ■

Is there anything better

than a Saturday afternoon

in Memorial Stadium?

Thanks Coach.

...for putting magic

in our lives.

Nebraska's BEST selection of unique Husker™ Apparel and Novelty Items.

Westroads	Crossroads	Gateway	Conestoga
Omaha	Omaha	Lincoln	Grand Island
402 343 0650	402 393 2899	402 464 7944	308 384 6891

Booklets May Be Latest Grid Coaching Technique

June 24, 1965

A new approach in teaching football may come about from an experimental program conducted last fall with the Cornhusker freshman football team.

Tom Osborne, as assistant coach at the University of Nebraska and former professional football player, saw a need for a better way of teaching football players their assignments.

A graduate student in Teachers College, he decided to teach 16 freshmen football players their blocking rules by means of specially prepared booklets.

The results of the experiment were outlined in his thesis, written as a partial requirement for his Master of Arts degree, which he received this past month.

The booklets contained questions and answer frames, arranged so that the player had to answer the question before he could see the answer.

Osborne explained that this involved the technique used by teaching machines, in that the student must respond in order to progress and must understand each point before being allowed to move ahead.

This procedure is in contrast to the present widely used method of handing out blocking rules on mimeographed paper and asking the players to memorize the rules.

Osborne compared the 16 players who used the booklets with a control group which used the conventional methods. By means of four written exams, ratings from the coaches, and grading of two movies of actual games, Osborne found that:

—In the written tests, the experimental group received an average grade of about 10% higher than the control group.

—In the coaches' rating scale, the experimental group had a rating average of 8.1 out of a possible 12 points, compared with 5.4 points for the control group.

—In the movie evaluation, the experimental group had 91 percent of their assignments correct, compared with 83 percent for the control group.

—All evaluative procedures were statistically significant in favoring the programmed teaching method.

Osborne also found that the experimental group tended to spend more time in study of the plays than the control group.

Only guards, tackles and centers were used in the experiment "for it was the coaches' opinion that the blocking assignments of these interior linemen were more complex than those assignments of other positions and were consequently the hardest to learn." ∎

Tom Osborne didn't appear to be too anxious about meeting with the Big Eight Skywriters before his first season as NU head coach. (Journal Star Library)

Osborne's Cornhusker Career Started With Letter

by Dan Forsythe
Lincoln Journal Star

Jan. 18, 1972

Tom Osborne, owner of a Ph.D. in educational psychology, says he'd feel uncomfortable if people called him Dr. Osborne.

"Nobody's called me that for five years. A few people kidded me about it at first, but after the humor wore off they forgot it," says Osborne, named Monday by Bob Devaney as "assistant head coach" on the Cornhusker football staff.

Tom admits he also feels slightly uncomfortable with his newest title . . . and the prospect of being the head coach of the Cornhuskers in 1973.

"I'm very pleased that Bob has shown this much confidence in me. But I feel kind of humble about it. There are so many fine assistants on the staff. I hope this in no way jeopardizes our relationship," he says.

Like fellow assistants Jim Ross, Carl Selmer, John Melton, Mike Corgan and Clete Fisher, Osborne has been associated with Devaney during all 10 years of his stay at Nebraska. But he's been a full-time member of the coaching staff for only four seasons.

He started as a graduate assistant, then split time between the coaching staff and a teaching position before deciding his future belonged in coaching.

"Bob had just been named coach at the time I decided to quite pro football," recalls Osborne, who was a multi-sports standout at both Hastings H.S. and Hastings College.

Osborne, 34, winner of four letters each in football, basketball and track at Hastings College, was the first athlete to be named a two-time winner of the *Lincoln Sunday Journal and Star* State College Athlete of the Year Award.

"I wrote to Devaney in Wyoming asking if I might be able to help while I was attending graduate school," said Tom, who at the time thought he was headed into some sort of student personnel work after he picked up his advanced degrees.

"Bob wrote back and said he probably couldn't pay much, if anything, but

he'd like to have me help out," relates Osborne.

Tom wasn't salaried at the start; his compensation was getting his meals at the training table.

Osborne received his doctorate in 1965 and for a time carried a dual teaching-coaching load.

"The longer I coached the more I liked it. It got to a decision point. There's no way you can be a half-time coach. You can't do anything half-time and do it well," says Osborne. "So I asked if I could be a full-time coach."

A quarterback at Hastings College who became a wide receiver in his short pro career with the San Francisco 49ers and Washington Redskins, Tom has worked with the Cornhusker receivers and passing game as a Devaney assistant.

Devaney indicated that the immediate effect of Osborne becoming assistant head coach was having Tom coordinate the Nebraska recruiting. Other than that there will be little organizational change in the staff for the 1972 season.

Devaney, as coach of the two-time national champion Cornhuskers, has a heavy schedule of clinic and banquet dates. Osborne will have some added responsibilities and decision-making in recruiting in Devaney's absence.

The Cornhusker staff is gearing its recruiting push toward the February 8 date for the Big Eight letter of intent signings.

"We've had a late start because of the bowl game and the Hawaii game," says Osborne, "But being No. 1 has offset this to some degree."

"Our feeling is that people are more receptive to our initial contact. There's a certain amount of flattery about being contacted by the No. 1 team. But in terms of the long haul I'm not sure being No. 1 makes it that much easier. I think 90 percent of recruiting is letting the athlete know you're interested in him personally." ■

Tom Osborne helped develop Johnny Rodgers (20) into a Heisman Trophy winner. (Journal Star Library)

Continuing A Legacy

by Mark Derowitsch
Lincoln Journal Star

Jan. 12, 1998

What Bob Devaney accomplished on the football field is remarkable.

Devaney came to Lincoln in 1962 to take over a football program that hadn't had a winning season in seven years and hadn't been to a bowl game or won a conference championship in 21 seasons.

All Devaney did was turn Nebraska into a national powerhouse.

It took Devaney nine seasons to bring about a change, turning NU into a lasting dynasty. Devaney's first team went 9-2, and during his 11 seasons as Nebraska's coach, he never had a losing record. In 1970 and 1971, Devaney's teams reached the pinnacle of college football, winning back-to-back national championships.

But what Devaney accomplished as Nebraska's athletic director is even better than what he did on the playing field.

After all, as athletic director, Devaney recommended Tom Osborne as his successor as Husker football coach.

Osborne coached the Huskers for 25 years and retired January 2, 1998 as arguably the best coach in college football history. Under Osborne, Nebraska won 255 games, lost 49, tied three and won three national titles.

More impressively, Nebraska went to a bowl game every year under Osborne and won nine conference championships outright. A bad season for Osborne was a 9-3 record.

Yet he never imagined he'd have that kind of success following Devaney, who hired the young Osborne as a graduate assistant in 1962.

"I felt when I took over for Bob that it would be difficult to last more than five years," Osborne said. "Bob always had a built-in grace factor because he turned the program around. I wasn't going to have that opportunity because I was more of a caretaker."

Osborne turned into the master gardener.

Yes, Devaney set the table. But it was Osborne who took Nebraska to the highest level.

"Coach Devaney opened the door and put together a dynasty, and Coach Osborne improved on it," said former Nebraska center Dave Rimington, who played under Osborne from 1979-82. "When you get to the highest level, it's

Bob Devaney brought the NU football team into the spotlight and Tom Osborne kept the Huskers there. (Journal Star Library)

Bob Devaney and Tom Osborne became just the third coaching duo to record back-to-back 100-win seasons at the same school. They did it in a 22-year span. Devaney won 101 games in his Hall of Fame career, while Osborne finished 25 years at NU with 255 wins. (Journal Star Library)

difficult to maintain, but Coach Osborne did it for 25 years because of his integrity and his stability."

It was also Osborne who likely saved Devaney's job as Nebraska's head coach.

It was 1968, and Nebraska had just come off its second straight 6-4 season. It was then that Devaney decided to revamp his offense, with the help of Osborne.

The results kept Devaney at Nebraska and raised Osborne's value as an up-and-coming young coach. The next year, Nebraska went 9-2 and beat Georgia in the Sun Bowl. The Cornhuskers followed that with back-to-back national titles.

Devaney then announced that the 1972 season would be his last, and that he would recommend Osborne for the top job at Nebraska, much to the surprise of most of Devaney's staff, many of whom had been with him a long time.

"In some ways it was a gradual decision," Devaney wrote in his book, Devaney. "The more I watched Tom coach and the more I was around him, the more I felt he would have the best chance for success. I had known most of the other coaches a long time, and I thought any one of them would have been very satisfactory as a head coach. They would have done a good job, but I thought there was one thing about Tom being the coach—he had a great offensive mind, one of the greatest I've ever seen."

Not that everything was rosy for Osborne as Devaney's successor. In his first six years as head coach, Nebraska won 10 games in a season just once and never played for a national title.

As Nebraska struggled, without much success, to beat rival Oklahoma, Osborne began to feel the heat.

He even went so far as to interview for the head coaching job at Colorado, but one thing helped him stay with the Huskers.

"I was comfortable with Bob Devaney," he said.

When he stepped down as coach, Devaney made sure to give Osborne breathing room. He never second-guessed or offered unwanted advice.

He let Osborne get the job done.

"Bob was always supportive, not just of me or the football staff, but he was supportive of everybody that he worked with," Osborne said at a memorial service for Devaney on May 14, 1997. "And he was kind of a cheerleader-type guy. He expected a lot but he gave you the tools to get it done.

"I think the unique thing in the history of football, people who were coaches and then became athletic directors, the guy who became athletic director couldn't help second-guessing and somehow interjecting himself. Bob never did that, publicly or privately. I think it was an amazing tribute to the kind of person he was."

Osborne succeeded under Devaney, and like his former boss, ended his career on top of the coaching profession.

In Osborne's last five years, Nebraska was 60-3 and won three national championships. Just hours after coaching his last game, a 42-17 whipping of Tennessee in the 1998 Orange Bowl, Osborne learned that the coaches had voted the Huskers No. 1.

He went out on top.

"Most anything I have in football I owe to Bob," Osborne said. "He gave me the opportunity to be an assistant coach, then a head coach." ■

Tom Osborne found out in January 1972 that he was Bob Devaney's choice as his successor to coach the Nebraska football team. (Journal Star Library)

Huskers Ready, Confident and . . . BAM!

UCLA wishbone attack stymied, 40-13

by Virgil Parker

Lincoln Journal Star

Sept. 9, 1973

Nebraska combined a new coach and a second-string quarterback with a mixture of newcomers and veterans to produce a 40-13 football victory over highly touted UCLA in Memorial Stadium Saturday afternoon.

"There was a quiet confidence all day," Cornhusker coach Tom Osborne observed after garnering his first triumph after taking over the reins from highly successful Bob Devaney.

"The entire team showed a tremendously calm determination," Osborne added. "Though this was my first game as a head coach, I've been associated with a lot of great Nebraska teams in the past, and I can't recall ever having a group of kids more ready to play."

The Cornhuskers didn't waste any time justifying that feeling. After kicking off to open the clash before 74,966 red-clad fans and a nationwide TV audience, the Black Shirt defenders stopped the Bruins from the west coast on their first series and forced a punt.

Behind second-string signal caller Steve Runty, forced into action by a leg injury to regular Dave Humm, Nebraska moved 56 yards in 11 plays to take a 7-0 lead.

Tony Davis, the sophomore I-back from Tecumseh, carried on seven of those plays, forecasting what UCLA could expect throughout the grey, overcast afternoon.

Davis ended with 24 carries for 147 yards.

"That doesn't quite equal the 327 yards I gained in one high school game," Davis admitted, "but I'll do that some other day."

Davis felt he would be a key to the Huskers' success or failure.

"I knew we'd win if I had a good game," he explained, "because if I had a good game so would the fullback and the offensive line. And they played just super."

Davis, rattling off his words a mile a minute, admitted he was excited and elated by his debut.

"Steve (Runty) is not only the best second-string quarterback in the country," Davis claimed, "He's the best first-stringer around. There may have been some apprehension on the part of some fans and you writers," he added, "but I can assure you the whole team had full confidence in him."

After Runty sneaked the final yard in the opening drive, the Cornhuskers wasted no time in pushing the score to 14-0. Three plays and a punt after the ensuing kickoff, safety Randy Borg returned a UCLA punt 77 yards for another touchdown.

"I was the 'up' man for Johnny Rodgers last year," Borg reminded. "Usually I'd have to signal for a fair catch if it didn't go far enough for Johnny. But I did return one for a touchdown against Army. But believe me, this was a much bigger thrill."

Borg fielded the punt, headed for the left sideline, picked up a bevy of blockers and raced for daylight.

"I had to slow up about mid-field and

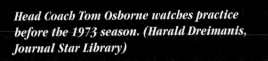

Head Coach Tom Osborne watches practice before the 1973 season. (Harald Dreimanis, Journal Star Library)

wait for a couple of blocks," Borg remembered. "I guess I must have done it about right. Sometimes if you try to go too fast, you'll get tangled up with your own teammates."

Borg said there had been some apprehension while the team waited for the late 3:50 p.m. kickoff, dictated by TV.

"We're usually a fairly loose bunch. This was a good feeling, not a scared feeling. However, you could feel the electricity in the air all day. There was an inner confidence. We were sure ready when game time arrived."

Near the close of the first quarter Nebraska made one of its few mistakes and UCLA capitalized on the miscue to narrow the margin to 14-6.

Second-unit fullback Ralph Powell fumbled at the Husker 14, and two plays later Kermit Johnson slashed 12 yards for the score. But the extra point try by Efron

Herrera, who beat Nebraska with a field goal in the final 22 seconds in Los Angeles in last fall's opener, pulled his boot wide left.

Nebraska roared right back to take a 20-6 advantage, going 77 yards in eight plays. The big gainer was a quick flip in the flat from Runty to Davis for 39 yards and a 13-yard keeper by Runty.

"That's a new play," Runty offered. "And it worked real well several times."

Runty, a walk-on, played his freshman and first varsity season (as a redshirt) without a scholarship.

"I've spent my entire career here preparing myself so I'd be ready when called upon," Runty said, "It's a great feeling to have come through in my first real chance."

Runty said the key was lack of mistakes. "Last year out in LA we fumbled four or five times and made a lot of other

errors. Our first team wasn't called for a single penalty today. We were very consistent. And you can credit Coach Osborne for that. He's a real perfectionist."

Nebraska's seemingly safe lead quickly disappeared just before halftime.

UCLA got the ball in the closing two minutes. A double reverse picked up 18 yards and four plays later Johnson took a pitchout and rambled 43 yards to the Husker three.

The Bruins scored to pull within seven points, 20-13, just 11 seconds before intermission.

"Because it was fourth down we were in a goal line defense," Osborne explained, "Harmon (Mark, UCLA quarterback) barely got off the pitch and then we made some errors. It was our only big mistake, but it looked like a costly one. The play really turned the momentum of the game around to their favor."

Nebraska's Tom Osborne (right) checks with assistant John Melton during Osborne's first game as head coach of the Cornhuskers—a 40-13 win against UCLA on September 8, 1973. (Journal Star Library)

Osborne and Bruin coach Pepper Rodgers agreed on one point. It was Nebraska's sustained drive for a touchdown to open the second half which was the key to the game.

"I told the team at halftime," Osborne recalled, "that we were going to have to take the kickoff and march right down the field or UCLA would have the upper hand."

His Big Red troops responded by moving 80 yards in 16 plays, using up nearly seven minutes on the clock and boosting themselves back to a 26-13 lead.

"That was the key to the whole game," Rodgers agreed. "If we had stopped them and got our offense going, it would have been a whole new game."

Instead the Cornhuskers padded the margin on a 43-yard scamper by Davis and a three-yard burst by Jeff Moran, the latter set up by a Bruin fumble at the UCLA 25.

Osborne felt the outstanding play of his defense might be overlooked in the opener.

"Wait a few games," he advised. "I bet you'll find that UCLA will prove to have one of the best offenses in the nation. Then you'll realize how well our defense performed."

Osborne said that before he had time to savor his first victory, a fan hollered to him on the way from the field, "Just 10 more to go."

The NU mentor admits such an attitude would worry him. "We looked good and had a good game," he admits, "But we've got a long way to go. We certainly can't get the feeling that it's all downhill just because we got by a tough opening opponent."

Borg says the coaches don't need to worry about overconfidence. "The team was accused of having some letdowns last year, especially in our tie with Iowa State. But we have a good balance of veterans and sophomores this time. We have the greatest team unity since I've been here. There's no danger of overconfidence."

Humm says he was frustrated watching from the sidelines. "I'd have played linebacker if they'd let me," he said. "On one extra point play I noticed Steve wasn't out there and dashed onto the field. But the coaches saw me and called me back. They were afraid somebody would fall on my leg."

Osborne said that "Humm should be 100 percent after a two-week rest prior to the next game (North Carolina at home). But Steve did a great job and deserves a lot of credit."

Though Nebraska is known for its nationwide recruiting, the victory had a strong homestate flavor.

Runty and Davis got strong support from fullback Maury Damkroger of Lincoln (8 carries, 41 yards), Ritch Bahe of Fremont (6 carries, 49 yards), Scottsbluff's Frosty Anderson (3 catches, 23 yards and 1 touchdown) and Brent Longwell of Homer (3 receptions for 38 yards).

Even Osborne (Hastings) and defensive coordinator Monte Kiffin (Lexington) are home grown.

Runty and defensive captain John Dutton were named the winners of the Player of the Game scholarships by TV sponsor Chevrolet.

Though Nebraska's defensive play was a key to the Cornhuskers' victory, UCLA became the first team in 31 games to score a touchdown during the first quarter against Nebraska's famed "Black Shirt" defenders.

The Big Red offense more than made up for that, however. The 40 points garnered was the biggest total for Nebraska in an opening-season game since the Huskers swamped South Dakota, 56-0, to begin the 1964 campaign. ∎

1973 Season in Review

Won 9, Lost 2, Tied 1
Big 8: Won 4, Lost 2, Tied 1, 2nd-tie

Date	Opponent	Site	AP Rank NU/Opp.	Result
Sept. 8	UCLA	Lincoln	4/10	W 40-13
Sept. 22	No. Carolina St.	Lincoln	2/14	W 31-14
Sept. 29	Wisconsin	Lincoln	2/	W 20-16
Oct. 6	Minnesota	Minneapolis	2/	W 48-7
Oct. 13	Missouri	Columbia	2/12	L 12-13
Oct. 20	Kansas	Lincoln	11/18	W 10-9
Oct. 27	Oklahoma St.	Stillwater	10/	T 17-17
Nov. 3	Colorado	Lincoln	13/17	W 28-16
Nov. 10	Iowa State	Lincoln	11/	W 31-7
Nov. 17	Kansas State	Manhattan	10/	W 50-21
Nov. 23	Oklahoma	Norman	10/3	L 0-27
Cotton Bowl				
Jan. 1	Texas	Dallas	12/8	W 19-3

Final Rankings: 7th AP (post-bowl), 11th-tie UPI (regular season)

Old Devaney Speech Applies to Present NU Situation

Huskers must now bounce back

by Hal Brown

Lincoln Journal Star

Oct. 14, 1973—Since turning over the Nebraska football coaching chores to Tom Osborne, Bob Devaney has made a conscious effort to avoid any interference with the Osborne program.

But after Saturday's 13-12 heart-breaking loss to Missouri, the former Husker master might provide a needed service by going to his scrapbook and finding a clipping of the speech he gave his Husker team that bowed 17-7 here in 1969.

The essence of that speech in the sad and subdued NU dressing room four years ago was, "You're not dead until they bury you."

Those words so sparked the 1969 Huskers that they didn't lose again until the 1972 opener with UCLA—32 games without another loss.

The situation now facing the Huskers, who went into Saturday's game as the No. 2 team in the country, is almost identical to that 1969 season.

For the Huskers to gain a share of the Big Eight title, they must win the next six and someone must beat Missouri. In 1969, the Huskers did win the next six and someone did beat Missouri—Colorado —and the Huskers and Tigers tied for the league championship.

But Saturday's was an even tougher loss for Nebraska since the Huskers outplayed the Tigers in virtually every category and Missouri never came close to threatening the Husker end zone until re-covering a Randy Borg fumble at the NU 4.

Even after the Tigers drove in the ball on the next two plays to go ahead 13-6 with 2:01 to play, the Huskers rallied on the passing arm of David Humm, who took his team 72 yards in four plays in one

	Neb	Miss
First downs	21	7
Rushes-yards	47-152	53-163
Passing yards	292	7
Return yards	18	29
Passes	20-30-1	2-10-2
Punts	5-36.5	8-39.9
Fumbles-lost	2-2	1-1
Penalties-yards	5-35	5-32

minute and one second.

Humm pitched 31 yards to Ritch Bahe, then hit Larry Mushinskie with a 20-yarder and completed the comeback drive with a 22-yarder to Bahe, setting up a win or tie decision with only one minute left in the game.

Osborne chose to go for the win, but Humm's two-point conversion try, a pass to Tony Davis, was intercepted by Tony Gillick. Missouri fans began celebrating, remembering the Huskers had beaten their Tigers 36-0 and 62-0 in the last two games.

The biggest burden of guilt unfortunately falls on the shoulders of Borg, who, along with his fellow Black Shirts, played a superb game.

Five times in the first half, Missouri started drives at mid-field or in Husker territory and the NU Black Shirts defensive unit kept them out of the end zone.

And Borg was instrumental in stopping two of those drives, intercepting a John Cherry pass at the NU 5-yard line after John Moseley had returned the Huskers' opening kickoff to the Missouri 49.

Missouri started its next drive at the NU 48, but Tom Ruud was the Husker hero this time, stopping Tommy Reamon on a fourth and one play at the NU 39.

After Rich Sanger's 42-yard field goal gave Nebraska a 3-0 lead with 6:23 left in the first quarter, Moseley returned the kickoff to the NU 43. But four plays later the Tigers were back on their own 45.

Then after another Sanger field goal, this one from 29 yards with 15 seconds left in the opening quarter, the Huskers avoided Moseley with an onside kick and Missouri started at the NU 48.

Borg ended that threat by intercepting a Cherry pass at the NU 40.

Borg's mistake was the most obvious to the Faurot Field record crowd of 68,170 as he stood under Jim Goble's punt at the NU 10 with 2:36 to play and the score tied at 6-6.

Missouri's Greg Hill had matched Sanger's two first-quarter field goals with two of his own in the second period, from 35 and 31 yards away.

But other key Husker mistakes also made a difference in this close game.

There was the missed block permitting Missouri's Herris Butler to block a Sanger field goal attempt from the 8-yard line with 4:14 left in the third quarter.

And there was Sanger's field goal try from the 24 that was wide to the left with 6:58 left in the game. Success on either field goal try would have removed some of the tears from Borg's eyes.

While the game was close all the way on the scoreboard, it was far from close in the statisticians booth, with the Huskers owning a 21-7 edge in first downs, trailing in rushing yardage by only 152-163 and leading in passing yardage by 292 to 7 for a total offense edge of 444 yards to 170 yards.

But the scoreboard is where it counts. The score read: Missouri 13, Nebraska, 12. ■

Huskers Hook Horns, 19-3 . . . Runty Out Of Shadow

by Hal Brown

Lincoln Journal Star

Jan. 2, 1974

Steve Runty, who launched Nebraska's 1973 season by directing the Huskers to a 40-13 win over UCLA, came off the bench Tuesday to close that season with a 19-3 Cotton Bowl triumph over Texas.

Runty, a senior from Ogallala who came to Nebraska without a scholarship and who has sat in the shadow of someone throughout his NU stay of five years, directed the Huskers to two second-half touchdowns, breaking a 3-3 halftime deadlock.

The Huskers' second-half scoring surge made what had been a dull afternoon a little more fun for the nearly 20,000 Nebraskans sitting in 30-degree temperatures in the Cotton Bowl Stadium.

But while Runty's entrance into the contest seemed to most of the writers sitting in an unheated press box and most of the 67,500 fans freezing in the stands to spark the Huskers, NU head coach Tom Osborne didn't agree.

"I don't think the fact that we made the quarterback change had anything to do with us winning the game," Osborne told writers as they swarmed around him in a jammed Husker dressing room.

"We had planned on playing both quarterbacks (Runty and David Humm) about an equal amount of time," he added.

However, both Humm and Runty denied they knew of such a plan.

Osborne pointed out that he was more concerned with his Huskers re-establishing who was in charge at halftime than he was in who his quarterback would be.

"Texas was jumping up and down and hollering," Osborne explained, "And we had to show them who was in charge."

The reason the Longhorns were jumping up and down and hollering was that they headed for the halftime intermission just after having held the Huskers out of their end zone on four straight tries from the one-yard line.

The Huskers had taken over at their own 20 after Billy Schott's 44-yard field goal attempt had hit the left upright with 5:14 left in the half.

When Humm found split end Frosty Anderson with a 20-yard pass, the Huskers had a first and goal from the one.

Humm tried to sneak it over, but was stopped by Longhorn linebacker Wade Johnston. Tony Davis tried to dive over a pile, but was stopped by Johnston. Davis tried again and again was met by Johnston. After a time out to discuss the situation, fullback Maury Damkroger was given a chance. But he too was met and stopped by Johnston.

That performance earned Johnston defensive player of the game honors, with the offensive laurels going to Nebraska's Davis, who gained 106 yards on 28 carries.

Despite the halftime emphasis on taking charge, it took the Huskers a while to establish who was in control.

Texas took the second-half kickoff and marched from the Longhorn 29 to the NU 22 for its best drive of the day.

On a third and seven play from the 22, Longhorn Lonnie Bennett had beaten Husker safety Bob Thornton and was waiting in the end zone for quarterback Marty Akin's pass.

It never got there as Akins threw short and Thornton intercepted, giving the Huskers the ball at their own 20.

Runty stepped in under center Rik Bonness for the first time in the game and after three plays, the Huskers were lining up for their first punt of the day, still looking to establish who was in control.

The Huskers finally established that moments later, after Mike Dean's 54-yard field goal effort was short and was returned to the Nebraska 41 by Thornton.

Runty stayed at quarterback and the Huskers began running right at the Longhorns.

Damkroger went up the middle for 11. Davis went up the middle for 12, Runty passed to Bahe for 17.

Then with second and eight at the Texas 12, Bahe took a handoff from Runty on the same inside reverse that had worked so well in the opening win over UCLA.

It worked just as well against Texas as Bahe scored the first TD of the afternoon with 3:05 left in the third quarter and Rich Sanger's extra point kick made it 10-3.

The touchdown broke a six-quarter TD drought for the Huskers, who hadn't crossed an opponent's goal line since the next-to-last game of the regular season against Kansas State.

Osborne's halftime timetable had called for the first five minutes of the second half to be very important to the Huskers in establishing themselves as the better team.

It took the Huskers a bit longer than that.

But once they broke on top by 10-3, it didn't take long to get another one.

Husker All-American tackle John Dutton was wrapping himself around Akins at about the same time Akins was trying to pitch the ball away.

The result was a bad pitch which Husker middle guard John Bell outwrestled Texan Bennett for the ball at the Longhorn 19.

Reserve fullback Ralph Powell moved it to the 13 and Davis put it at the three for a first down.

Rather than the four futile attempts up the middle at the end of the first half, this time Runty handed off to Davis, who followed a block from Powell and went around the right side into the end zone.

Despite the fact that Sanger's extra point kick was deflected, leaving the Huskers with a 16-3 margin, it was now becoming clearly evident who was in control.

Texas now was forced to go to the air, something they hadn't done at all in their season finale with Texas A&M and something they hadn't done successfully for the first three quarters against the Huskers.

When reserve quarterback Mike Presley hit Joe Aboussie with a five-yarder on the next-to-last play of the third quarter, it was Texas' first pass completion in seven quarters of football.

But the Longhorns, who had discovered earlier they couldn't run against the Huskers, found they could not pass, either.

The Husker defense held Texas to just 106 yards rushing and All-American fullback Roosevelt Leaks, who missed part of the game with a bruised knee, gained only 48 yards on 15 carries.

The Longhorns had been the fifth-best running team in the nation, averaging 550.8 yards per game in 10 regular-season contests.

Turnovers and penalties stymied both teams' scoring efforts in the first half, although the Longhorns drove to their opening field goal the first time they had the ball, starting with Johnston's recovery of a Davis fumble at the NU 34 on the fourth play of the game.

Schott's field goal from the 12 gave the Longhorns the lead with 9:30 left in the opening period. When the Huskers came back to win, it stretched the string

to five straight the number of teams that had scored first, then lost the Cotton Bowl Classic.

The Huskers got those three points back on Sanger's 24-yard field goal with 9:05 left in the first half, a field goal set up by Husker defensive end Steve Manstedt's 65-yard return of a fumble by Leaks.

Manstedt's return put the ball at the Texas eight. It also created the biggest controversy of the afternoon.

One official threw his hat down at the point where Manstedt grabbed the ball and signaled the play dead, claiming the ball had hit the ground.

Husker safety Thornton kicked the cap in disgust and Husker Coach Osborne charged onto the field to argue the decision.

Two other officials agreed that Manstedt had picked the ball off in the air and with the vote standing at two-to-one, the Huskers were given the ball at the eight.

CBS-TV's instant replay showed the ball bounced off Leaks' shoe. Had the ball hit the ground, it could not have been advanced by Manstedt.

The victory ended the Huskers' season at 9-2-1, identical to last year when they romped over Notre Dame, 40-6, in the Orange Bowl.

It was Nebraska's fifth straight bowl victory, something no team has ever accomplished. The last bowl loss by Nebraska came in the 1967 Sugar Bowl, a 34-7 drubbing by Alabama, which was the Crimson Tide's last bowl victory.

In the last five bowls, Nebraska has beaten Georgia in the Sun Bowl, LSU, Alabama and Notre Dame in the Orange Bowl and Texas. ■

Nebraska's Tony Davis is stopped in mid-air by the Texas defense in the January 1, 1974 Cotton Bowl. Quarterback Steve Runty rallied the Huskers to a 19-3 win against Texas, Tom Osborne's first bowl victory. (Journal Star Library)

Huskers Rock 'Hawks, Chalk 56-0 Rout

Humm, Westbrook pep Nebraska to big win

by Virgil Parker

Lincoln Journal Star

Oct. 20, 1974

Dave Humm may have lost his memory last week, but he didn't forget how to pass.

The left-hander from Las Vegas had his finest day, breaking three Big Eight Conference records, while guiding Nebraska to a surprising 56-0 victory over Kansas Saturday afternoon.

Adding insult to injury before a partisan sell-out crowd of 52,300—which did include 12,000 rabid red-clad fans from Nebraska—two of Humm's new marks replaced records held by former Kansas great David Jaynes.

Humm, who had a temporary loss of memory after being knocked out early in the second half against Missouri a week ago, rewrote the books when he:

— completed three touchdown passes to bring his career total to 37. The old record was 36 by Jaynes.

—completed his last 15 passes in a row without a miss. Jaynes had the old mark at 14.

—completed 23 of 27 passes for a .852 accuracy average. The best previous was .818 by former teammate Steve Runty who hit 9 of 11 against UCLA to open the 1973 season. So that feat also becomes a new school mark.

Humm's career touchdown total just adds to the Nebraska record he already held, but he and wingback Don Westbrook hooked up to tie another.

All three of Humm's touchdown tosses were aimed at Westbrook, giving the senior from Cheyenne a share of the school record of three TD receptions held jointly by Clarence Swanson (1921), Johnny Rodgers (1971) and Frosty Anderson (1973).

Oklahoma State scout Mark Hatley—the Cowboys, who beat Missouri 31-7 Saturday, come calling to Lincoln next week—observed that "In my opinion Dave Humm has to be as good a passer as there is in the nation."

And Humm dealt the Jayhawks all that damage without playing the last 11 ½ minutes of the game.

The most unbelievable part of the game was the final score. The clash—after Nebraska had lost to Missouri and Kansas was coming off three straight wins, including a 40-9 victory over Florida State which scared mighty Alabama last week (8-7) and a 28-10 win over top-10 rated Texas A&M—was billed as a tossup.

But the 56-0 final count was exactly the same score that the Cornhuskers rolled up their last visit here in 1972.

It was, incidentally, the first time Kansas has been shut out since that other 56-0 whitewashing.

And it could have been more! Two of Humm's four incompletions should have been caught for touchdowns. Chuck Malito was wide open down the sideline on one occasion, and Humm hit Dave Gillespie with a perfect strike on another long bomb that was muffed.

One other pass was tipped by an oncharging defensive lineman, while the other wobbled off target when he was decked as he threw.

Humm, who was sidelined by injury

Husker quarterback David Humm motions that he can't hear on a noisy and muddy field at Ames, Iowa, November 9, 1974. Humm led the Huskers to a 23-13 win. (Journal Star Library)

during Nebraska's only two losses this year, took several hard shots without injury this time. On his second TD toss, Humm took a crushing tackle from KU linebacker Steve Towle.

The NU fans were as shook up as Humm when he appeared injured. "I just had the wind knocked out of me," Humm said. The play came with just 23 seconds left in the first half. After the intermission rest, Humm was ready again.

Was he ever!

But the Nebraska defense certainly came in for its share of glory.

Kansas entered the game as the fourth best offensive team in the nation with a total offensive average of 436 yards.

The Husker "Black Shirts" shut the Jayhawks off with just 71 yards on the ground and 72 through the air.

Kansas sophomore sensation LaVerne Smith, who was the Big Eight's leading rusher, had gained over 100 yards in each of KU's five games this fall. Nebraska allowed him just 25.

In addition, Chuck Jones and Bob Martin blocked KU punts, Tom Ruud and Jim Burrow came up with pass interceptions and Dean Gissler recovered a fumble to aid the Husker offensive cause.

Bobby Thomas made a pitch to win back his punt returning job when he saw

action for the first time in three weeks with a 47-yard runback to set up the final Nebraska touchdown.

Through a scoreless first quarter, the sellout throng watched what they expected—a bruising battle that would likely be decided by a slim margin.

Nebraska had one good march, but it stalled at the KU 23 and Mike Coyle missed a 40-yard field goal try. It was his only miss of the day. He punched through seven straight extra-point shots.

The Huskers got the game's first break at the outset of the second stanza and capitalized on it. After Malito failed to collar the long bomb aimed his way, the slender Big Eight 440-yard dash champ quickly made up for the miscue.

KU safety Bruce Adams muffed a Randy Lessman punt after signaling for a fair catch and Malito made the recovery at the Kansas 39.

Five plays later—including the first three Humm completions—Westbrook caught his first TD toss.

Nebraska was in control the rest of the way, although coach Tom Osborne's troops managed just one more score—Westbrook's second touchdown grab just before halftime.

The telltale sign of what was in store came with the second-half opening kick-

off. Humm directed the NU offense on a 75-yard march. Westbrook and freshman I-back Monte Anthony chipped in with 18 and 12-yard runs and Humm mixed in three passes before Tony Davis powered over from one yard out.

Kansas didn't make a single first down in the second half as the onslaught continued.

The Huskers scored on their next two possessions. The third Humm-Westbrook TD pass made it 28-0. After Martin's punt block, John O'Leary—seeing his first real action since suffering a broken jaw against Wisconsin—tallied the first of his two TDs.

Defensive tackle Gissler then recovered a KU fumble, which led to the first of two TDs for Jeff Moran. His first boosted the score to 42-0, O'Leary made it 49-0 and then Moran capped the afternoon following Thomas' long punt return.

And so the Huskers continue their "roller coaster" campaign. It's either been the depths of despair (Wisconsin and Missouri with Humm on the sidelines) or lopsided runaways.

In the four games in which Humm has been available for fulltime duty, Nebraska has outscored its foes 220-14. ■

1974 Season in Review

Won 9, Lost 3, Tied 0
Big 8: Won 5, Lost 2, Tied 0, 2nd-tie

Date	Opponent	Site	AP Rank NU/Opp.	Result
Sept. 14	Oregon	Lincoln	7/	W 61-7
Sept. 21	Wisconsin	Madison	4/	L 20-21
Sept. 28	Northwestern	Lincoln	10/	W 49-7
Oct. 5	Minnesota	Lincoln	6/	W 54-0
Oct. 12	Missouri	Lincoln	5/	L 10-21
Oct. 19	Kansas	Lawrence	12/13	W 56-0
Oct. 26	Oklahoma St.	Lincoln	9/	W 7-3
Nov. 2	Colorado	Boulder	9/	W 31-15
Nov. 9	Iowa State	Ames	9/	W 23-13
Nov. 16	Kansas State	Lincoln	6/	W 35-7
Nov. 23	Oklahoma	Lincoln	6/1	L 14-28
Sugar Bowl				
Dec. 31	Florida	New Orleans	8/18	W 13-10

Final Rankings: 7th UPI, 9th AP (both post-bowl)

Luck, Davis Lead Comeback

... Goal line stand boosts Husker Sugar Bowl win

by Bob Owens

Lincoln Journal Star

Jan. 1, 1975

A gutty goal line stand by Nebraska's defensive unit midway in the third quarter ignited what had been a lackluster offensive unit and the Cornhuskers rallied to win the 41st Sugar Bowl football game Tuesday evening.

Led by reserve quarterback Terry Luck, the strong running of fullback Tony Davis and I-back Monte Anthony, and the field goal kicking of Mike Coyle, the Huskers roared from a 10-0 deficit to defeat the Florida Gators, 13-10.

The 14,000 red-clad Nebraska fans among the crowd of 67,890 roared their approval as the Huskers did a complete turnabout from what had been a shabby first 37 minutes.

They were within less than a yard of falling behind 17-0 with a little over seven minutes left in the third quarter when they stopped the Gators four times within the five-yard line.

Then Luck, who replaced Dave Humm at this point after Humm had thrown four interceptions, took over and directed a 99-yard drive that completely took momentum away from Florida.

NU receiver Chuck Malito waits for instructions on the sideline as Coach Tom Osborne discusses strategy with his assistants in the press box during the 1974 Sugar Bowl. (Journal Star Library)

Davis, who gained only 12 yards on five carries in the first half, never has played better than he did the rest of the way. The result was his selection as winner of the Miller-Digby Memorial Trophy as the outstanding player in the game.

Davis carried seven times for 50 yards in the touchdown drive and later had a 40-yard run that got the Huskers in position for Coyle's winning field goal.

His figures for the game were 126 yards on 17 rushes.

"Luck did a super job and brought us back in great shape," a happy coach Tom Osborne said. "I'm sorry it had to happen that way to Dave Humm because he's a great quarterback, but he wants to win above all else and he's as happy as anyone else in the locker room."

Osborne said Humm was having a bad night and sometimes a change of quarterbacks gives the team a little lift.

"We ran out of muscle in the fourth quarter," losing coach Doug Dickey said.

Mike Coyle kicks a 39-yard, game-winning field goal with 1:46 left in the December 31, 1974 Sugar Bowl to give Nebraska a 13-10 win against Florida. (Web Ray, Journal Star Library)

"We had a chance to sustain momentum on the play on which James Richards slipped at the Nebraska one-yard line. After that, the momentum of the game turned and Nebraska took it over physically."

Dickey thought the Gators should have gotten more than 10 points in the first half because of the many opportunities with good field position.

"Davis is an impressive runner with tremendous effort," Dickey said. "He had to be the winning edge in the game."

The victory ended Nebraska's season with a 9-3 record and marked the sixth consecutive bowl game victory, tying the collegiate mark set by Georgia Tech in the mid-1950s.

The swing in momentum is clearly shown by the final statistics. After the goal line stand, Florida gained only 50 yards in total offense, 27 of that on passing, while the Huskers rushed for 182 yards and tried only two passes that went incomplete.

Because of the poor first half, Nebraska had only a 320-275 edge in total offense, all but 16 on the ground.

The Huskers couldn't get unwound in a mistake-plagued first half and they went to the dressing room at the intermission trailing 10-0. It marked the first time since last year's Oklahoma game they had been in such a fix.

Humm's first interception came on NU's second series when he aimed a pass at Rich Bahe. Gator cornerback Randy Talbot, however, stepped in front of Bahe to grab the ball at midfield. He ran it 29 yards to the Husker 21.

Then, on the first play, freshman halfback Tony Green went through the middle of the line, veered to his right, and scampered into the end zone for a touchdown. David Posey's kick made it 7-0 with 9:58 left in the first quarter.

The next three times the Huskers got the ball they started at their own 20-, 20- and 22-yard lines.

Early in the second quarter, Humm misfired again and defensive end Preston Kendrick intercepted for Florida. It didn't prove costly, however, because Green fumbled on the second play and Ardell Johnson recovered for the Huskers.

Nebraska got a good drive going, helped by a Florida face mask penalty. It carried to the Gator 29 after a 21-yard run by Don Westbrook. He fumbled, however, and monsterman Wayne Field recovered.

Humm was intercepted again on the next possession as he tried to hit Westbrook, but found Kendrick again instead.

Fortunately, Florida didn't sustain any offensive drives and it was still 7-0 when the Gators took over at their 29 with 1:54 left in the half.

The Gators, getting a pair of big plays, drove to the Husker 11 in six plays, but had the drive thwarted by a combination of the clock and a fine defensive play by tackle Mike Fultz.

Fultz threw Gaffney for a 12-yard loss and the Gators had to settle for a 40-yard field goal with two seconds left in the half. The plays that helped get them in range were a 35-yard pass to Lee McGriff and a 17-yard run by fullback Jimmy DuBose.

The outlook became bleak, indeed, when Humm was intercepted for the fourth time with 9:50 left in the third quarter and the Gators took over on the Nebraska 34. Alvin Cowans nabbed it and returned it 36 yards. Four plays later, they had a first down on the NU 5.

It was the ensuing goal line stand that seemed to ignite the Huskers and they controlled the game the rest of the way.

On the first down from the five, James Richards lost two yards on a tackle by Steve Wieser. Then Green picked up six to the one, but that's as far as Florida got.

Linebacker Bob Nelson smacked DuBose as he hit the center of the line for no gain. Then Gaffney faked up the middle and pitched out to Richards around left end, but Jimmy Burrow came up to stop him again for no gain.

At this point, Luck came off the bench to direct the most fantastic drive of the season for Nebraska. He took the Huskers 99 yards in 18 plays, consuming 8:54 on the clock and picking up seven first downs.

All the plays but one incomplete pass were on the ground with Davis and Anthony carrying seven times each for 72 of the yards. Westbrook had one 18-yard run and Luck carried twice for five and four yards.

The touchdown went to Anthony on a two-yard leap over the center of the line. It came just 1:40 into the final quarter. Coyle's conversion brought Nebraska within three points at 10-7.

The Husker defensive unit, which fired up the offense just before the drive, seemed to be even more determined after the ensuing kickoff when it forced Florida to punt after three plays that gained eight yards from its 11 to the 19.

The punt gave Nebraska the ball on the Gator 49 and the Huskers went to work again. This time it took six plays to get to the Gator 22 where the drive bogged down.

On fourth down, Coyle kicked a 37-yard field goal that didn't get much height, but it was between the uprights and the score was tied 10-10 with 7:12 to play.

Florida picked up a first down before a penalty ruined a drive. But, after punting out, the Gators had the Huskers backed up to their 25. It looked like the fans might be in store for a tie game.

The Huskers, however, weren't to be denied, and on the second play that fact became apparent when Davis blasted through the line, cut to his right and raced 40 yards to the Florida 31.

Three plays left the Huskers a yard short of a first down at the 22 and Coyle again came in to boot a 39-yard field goal for the winning points with 1:46 left.

Nebraska didn't really ice the decision until Mark Heydorf's interception on the last play of the game. ∎

Husker Corner Combo Merits Corso's Plaudits

by Randy York

Lincoln Journal Star

Sept. 21, 1975

When you're the victim, it isn't always easy to cough up the praise. But Indiana football coach Lee Corso believes in recognizing individual excellence.

"I always respect great individual effort and the kid in the left hand corner (of the end zone) and the kid in the right hand corner put our team to sleep with great individual efforts," Corso said Saturday after his Hoosiers absorbed a 45-0 loss to Nebraska.

He was alluding to Nebraska fullback Tony Davis' determined 20-yard touchdown run and split end Bobby Thomas' 12-yard touchdown catch, both in the second quarter.

"Davis broke tackles against two of our best—Donnie Thomas (linebacker) and Willie Wilson (cornerback) and Thomas made a great catch against a great defensive back (Harold Waterhouse)," Corso emphasized.

"Until those two things, we were staggerin', but hangin' in there," Corso said. "Then, all of a sudden, boom . . . then boom again. They just knocked us out.

"I couldn't believe it was 24-0 at halftime," added Corso. "I told my players, this isn't a 24-0 ball game. It's a 10-0 game."

That was more of a short-term analysis. Corso later amended it.

"Darn right, Nebraska compares with the best in the Big 10," he said. "Offensively, they compare with Ohio State and Michigan. And, defensively . . . throw Nebraska, Ohio State, Michigan and Michigan State in there together."

As much of an optimist as Corso is,

he's also a realist. "I think it's safe to say, if we played Nebraska 10 times, we might beat them once," he said, emphasizing the word might.

"Nebraska's good. I mean they're good." Corso said in what was to become a 20-part series saying Nebraska "was good."

Corso, who has said every game is a learning experience, kept his stance despite the lopsided score. "We learned something," he insisted. "We learned what it takes to have 75 straight sellouts of 75,000 people.

"Jesus, Nebraska's got a helluva football program," Corso volunteered. "Nice all around," he assessed. "Good offense. Super defense. Great quickness. Well coached."

Corso went through the motions the rest of the interview. His questions, nervously asked as he mingled through the locker room clapping his hands, became more interesting than his answers.

"How'd Purdue do?" he asked. Informed the Boilermakers had been shut out, Corso said, "Good, good."

He pressed a sportswriter from the *Indianapolis Star*. "Glad you came up.

Tom Osborne puts up a shot over former Husker Bob Nelson during a charity basketball game March 20, 1975. (Journal Star Library)

Glad you came up today. You're going to cover us next week, too, aren't you?"

Corso was equally enthusiastic when he made small talk with an Indiana backer in the corner of locker room.

"They're good aren't they?" he asked. "Boy are they good. This is a good town. Big time. We learned something, didn't we?" ∎

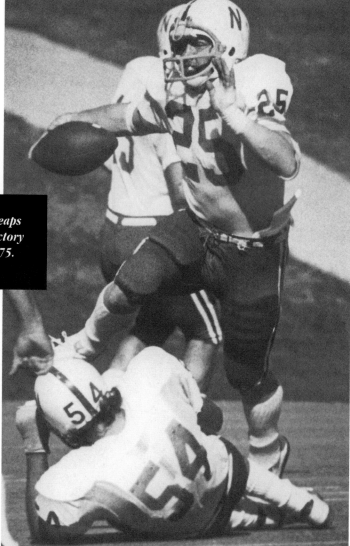

Tony Davis, the Tecumseh Tornado, leaps over a teammate during NU's 12-0 victory against Kansas State November 8, 1975. (Journal Star Library)

1975

Season in Review

Won 10, Lost 2, Tied 0
Big 8: Won 6, Lost 1, Tied 0, 1st-tie

Date	Opponent	Site	AP Rank NU/Opp.	Result
Sept. 13	LSU	Lincoln	6/	W 10-7
Sept. 20	Indiana	Lincoln	6/	W 45-0
Sept. 27	Texas Christian	Lincoln	4/	W 56-14
Oct. 4	Miami, Fla.	Lincoln	4/	W 31-16
Oct. 11	Kansas	Lincoln	4/	W 16-0
Oct. 18	Oklahoma St.	Stillwater	4/	W 28-20
Oct. 25	Colorado	Lincoln	4/	W 63-21
Nov. 1	Missouri	Columbia	3/12	W 30-7
Nov. 8	Kansas State	Manhattan	3/	W 12-0
Nov. 15	Iowa State	Lincoln	2/	W 52-0
Nov. 22	Oklahoma	Norman	2/7	L 10-35
Fiesta Bowl				
Dec. 26	Arizona State	Tempe	6/7	L 14-17

Final Rankings: 9th AP & UPI (both post-bowl)

Ferragamo's Play Draws Osborne's Praise

Self-analysis rejuvenates NU offense

by Bob Owens

Lincoln Journal Star

Oct. 26, 1975—One of the reasons for Nebraska's unexpected success in moving the football early in Saturday's game against Colorado was a scouting report, but it wasn't the one assistant coach Dick Beechner brought back from last week's Colorado victory over Missouri.

The Cornhusker coaching staff did a bit of self-analysis prior to the game, studying films to learn everything their undefeated squad had been doing offensively in the first six games.

Early in the game we tried to go against our normal tendencies," Coach Tom Osborne said after the 63-21 triumph over the tenth-rated Buffaloes. "This time of year you start charting yourself."

As a result of that scouting report, Nebraska did a lot of things differently than it had been doing and just about everything worked. The Huskers scored touchdowns the first three times they had possession of the football.

"We'd get into the power-I and instead of running toward the power set we'd run away from it," Osborne explained. "Or we'd throw out of it. We tried to do some things like that and it worked pretty well.

"Then, as the game went along, we went more and more with our basic I and forgot all the gingerbread stuff. When it counted—the first three or four touchdowns—we were going with a lot of stuff that was a little different."

Osborne thought another factor in the ease of the victory was the play of quarterback Vince Ferragamo, who not only hit 8 of 10 passes for 118 yards and two touchdowns, but who checked off well at the line of scrimmage.

"We mixed things up pretty good and Vince checked off well at the line," Osborne said, "Colorado had some offset line stuff and some stacks and Vince handled it very well. He had a great day. I can't see much to fault. He has gotten a little stronger every game and I was real pleased with his play."

Ferragamo's 42-yard pass for the first Husker touchdown to tie the score after Colorado's Dave Williams had gone 74 yards for the game's first touchdown was the result of a busted assignment by the Buffs.

"It was a variation of what we'd been doing, but it didn't work like we thought it would," Osborne said. "They had a mix-up in their coverage. Their cornerback and safety both went with our wingback and the split end (Bobby Thomas) went right up the middle of the field and caught it at the sideline."

Although there was a lot of good hitting in the game, Osborne didn't think the hits caused all of Colorado's fumbles. "A lot of them were before we got to them. Then they had people who got a little gun-shy.

"Sometimes that kind of thing can snowball. You get to thinking about fumbling. I'm sure it's not a lack of courage, it just is a matter of a domino effect. You lose one and then lose more."

The Huskers had their own "foul-up" on Williams' run that stunned the 76,509 fans.

"Everything possible that could have gone wrong did on that play," Husker safetyman Jimmy Burrow said. "But when you face a quarterback that good those things can happen.

"On the play my assignment was to go from the quarterback to the pitchman," Burrow explained. "When I came up, he cut back and the pursuit was cut off."

Defensive coordinator Monte Kiffin said the "linebacker made a mistake and we missed a tackle and that was it. Their split end cracked on Wonder Monds and Dave Butterfield was up playing the pitch so we lost our pursuit."

Kiffin noted that Colorado ran the same play later on and fumbled the ball to set up one of many easy Nebraska touchdowns.

"The Black Shirts played a heckuva game," he said. "Except for that one play they didn't make anything running against the first defense."

Colorado actually gained just 66 rushing yards from that point until the Husker second team defense took the field with 12:29 to play in the third quarter and the score 56-7.

Just about the only displeasing thing in an otherwise brilliant Husker performance was what Osborne called "a little lack of discipline toward the end of the game.

"I just don't like for a Nebraska team to ever show that—to start talking to the opposition to stir them up and get unnecessary penalties," Osborne said. "We should never have that.

"That was the one negative thing about the ball game. There wasn't a lot of it and some if it was just retaliation, but we don't ever want to do that." ∎

So Much For Hospitality

by Virgil Parker

Lincoln Journal Star

Dec. 28, 1975

Everyone connected with the Nebraska football program spent a week praising the hospitality of the Fiesta Bowl folks. It was great. The best organized and the "most fun" bowl of them all. But the hospitality ended with the kickoff.

Even in this city—its sportswriters and sportscasters, even the fan on the street—is asking, "Why the sudden switch from Ferragamo to Luck?"

In defense of Tom Osborne, if you can remember a year ago, Dave Humm threw four interceptions against Florida before he inserted Terry Luck who brought the Huskers from behind to victory.

The cry then—although not so pronounced since Nebraska did eventually win the game—was, "How come it took Osborne so long to make the change?"

Osborne said he detected some nervousness on Ferragamo's part prior to the start of the game. The first pass was intercepted. It's understandable that he thought, 'Why wait for four bad passes this time? Terry had a good week of practice—better than Vince. Make the change now.'

And though it may not seem to the casual observer that the offense did much of note the rest of the day, Luck engineered two drives for touchdowns and a 14-6 lead going into the fourth quarter.

From then on to the end, Nebraska only had the ball four more times, and two of those possessions started at the one and four-yard lines.

It's tough to get anything started from that deep in your own territory, especially against a swarming defense like that of Arizona State.

Of the other two possessions—each starting at about the Nebraska 30-yard line—the last one was on the move toward a possible winning touchdown or at least a tying field goal, until the fatal fumble.

That wasn't Luck's fault. It wasn't Tony Davis' fault either. No player alive could have held that. Tony didn't have time to bring the ball down from over his head before he was hit by a freight train.

On the other side of the coin, it does seem that if a quarterback knows he's going to be replaced for a single error, he never would be able to pass with confidence.

Osborne said that after the game was tied at 14-all, he was set to put Ferragamo back in. But the next time Nebraska gained possession was following Dave Butterfield's interception and the ball was on the one-yard line. He didn't feel, he said, that it would be wise to put in a guy "cold" facing that kind of field position.

It would have made an easy story to write had he done so and Vince had driven the team the length of the field for a winning touchdown.

Luck came in "cold" from the bench with the ball on the one-yard line and moved the team 99 yards a year ago to win the Sugar Bowl game.

If you want to blame the loss on something, try this. The team didn't go to a movie the night before the game. It was the first time any player could remember missing that tradition.

Seems there was some foul-up and when the team arrived for the show the manager had saved just 20 seats for the 85-man squad.

The loss wasn't the end of the world. It just seemed like it to the seniors who saw the team work hard to gain 10 straight victories and have visions of the Orange Bowl, only to drop the final two.

People were trying to console the players by saying, "The sun will still come up tomorrow." The weather down there was sensational the last two or three days, including game day, so that seemed a good bet.

But it turned out even the weatherman was against us. The sun didn't shine Saturday. ∎

Tom Osborne and his mentor and predecessor, Bob Devaney, look shell-shocked after the Huskers' 35-10 loss at Oklahoma November 22, 1975. (Harald Dreimanis, Journal Star Library)

Huskers Suffer Blues in The Night, 6-6

NU scoring drought lets LSU gain tie

by Virgil Parker

Lincoln Journal Star

Sept. 12, 1976

Football fans across the country won't be making jokes about the Poles anymore. The jokes will be about the polls.

The Nebraska Cornhuskers, ranked No. 1 in the nation by both major wire services in the preseason polls, had to settle for a 6-6 tie against a fired-up band of LSU Tigers in Tiger Stadium here Saturday night.

LSU wasn't even picked to finish in the top half of its own Southeastern Conference race.

Even then the Huskers came out better than a lot of others chosen in the preseason polls to be among the top 10 teams in the country.

On Thursday night, Arizona State, third on one of the charts, was dumped by UCLA. Other victims Saturday were Texas, a 14-13 loser to lowly Boston College, highly regarded Alabama, a 10-7 victim of Ole Miss and Missouri which was picked to finish fourth in the Big Eight, downed USC.

For Nebraska it was shades of the UCLA game of 1972—the last time the Huskers opened on the road and the last time NU was beaten in a season lid-lifter.

In that one, Efran Herrerra sank Nebraska with a last-minute field goal to break a tie and give UCLA a 20-17 victory.

LSU kicker Mike Conway pulled the Tigers into a 6-6 deadlock with fielders from 35 and 18 yards out.

With 40 seconds left, Conway had a shot from a distance of 44 yards. It was long enough, but barely missed to the right.

Nebraska, still trying to pull off a miracle in the closing seconds, saw three futile passes miss the mark. The Huskers were forced to punt with 15 seconds remaining.

That gave LSU one last chance—and as it turned out—a final opportunity for the Huskers.

LSU quarterback Pat Lyons' pass was picked off by Husker defensive end Ray Phillips, who had dropped back into the defensive coverage.

Phillips returned to the LSU 30 and in a desperate attempt as he was tackled, lateraled the ball to linebacker Jim Wightman, who scampered all the way to the end zone.

But the officials ruled Phillips had been run out of bounds before his lateral. The second-largest crowd in Tiger Stadium history—70,746—sank back into their seats, limp from the exciting finish.

"There's no question but what Phillips was out of bounds before he lateraled the ball," NU defensive coordinator Monte Kiffin admitted later. "But I was arguing that he was out of bounds before the clock ran out. We should have had one more play."

Though it was the first time since 1961 that Nebraska has gone three games without a win—counting two season-ending losses to Oklahoma and Arizona State to wind up last year's campaign—Kiffin feels the Huskers have a good chance to bounce back.

"We had an early tie in the 1970 sea-

Running back Rick Berns high steps through the Oklahoma State defense in the Huskers' 14-10 victory November 6, 1976. Berns, who lettered from 1976-78, finished his career eighth on NU's career rushing list with 2,478 yards. (Randy Hampton, Journal Star Library)

son, (21-21 tie with USC in the second game) and still came back to win the other 11 and the national championship.

"I don't want to take anything away from LSU," Kiffin added, "but we didn't play a very good game—certainly not up to our capability. We're going to have to regroup and get better."

Nebraska started out like it deserved its No. 1 ranking. The Huskers took the opening kickoff and moved 65 yards in 11 plays—aided by a 39-yard pass interference penalty against the Tigers—to score on a three-yard pass from quarterback Vince Ferragamo to tight end Ken Spaeth.

But the extra-point attempt by NU kicker Al Eveland went awry when holder Randy Garcia couldn't corral the snap. Garcia picked up the loose ball and tried to skirt left end, but was stopped short and the Huskers then and there settled for their six-point total.

Eveland had two other kicking chances to give Nebraska a winning margin, but his 34-yard field goal try late in the second quarter slithered low and way to the right. At the outset of the final frame he had a 39-yard try blocked. That led to LSU's tying fielder.

Though Nebraska's offense sputtered

in the second half, the Huskers dominated the statistics before intermission, but couldn't get any more points on the board.

Cornhusker coach Tom Osborne, criticized by second guessers in past years for not being daring enough, let his troops go for it twice on fourth down in the first half. Both times they made the needed distance—once during the touchdown drive when fullback Dodie Donnell powered for nine yards and another time when Ferragamo connected with split end Chuck Malito for a 15-yard gain on fourth-and-five.

But the strategy backfired twice. The first time didn't hurt. Ferragamo tried a quarterback sneak on fourth and one from the LSU 35—and appeared to have made the distance—before the officials moved the ball back for the measurement.

The fourth such attempt may have been a case of going to the well once too often. With fourth and three at the LSU 36, a pitchout to I-back Richard Berns resulted in a five-yard loss and gave the Tigers excellent field position on their 41.

Nine plays later Conway kicked his first field goal to close the gap to 6-3.

Later came Conway's fielder following the block of Eveland's try and the deadlocked final score. Not to mention the heartstopping last-second attempt.■

Tom Osborne concentrates on the Huskers' game against LSU September 11, 1976. The game finished in a 6-6 tie. (Journal Star Library)

1976

Season in Review

Won 9, Lost 3, Tied 1
Big 8: Won 4, Lost 3, Tied 0, 4th-tie

Date	Opponent	Site	AP Rank NU/Opp.	Result
Sept. 11	Louisiana State	Baton Rouge	1/	T 6-6
Sept. 18	Indiana	Bloomington	8/	W 45-13
Sept. 25	Texas Christian	Lincoln	6/	W 64-10
Oct. 2	Miami, Fla.	Lincoln	5/	W 17-9
Oct. 9	Colorado	Boulder	6/	W 24-12
Oct. 16	Kansas St.	Lincoln	3/	W 51-0
Oct. 23	Missouri	Lincoln	3/17	L 24-34
Oct. 30	Kansas	Lawrence	9/	W 31-3
Nov. 6	Oklahoma St.	Lincoln	9/13	W 14-10
Nov. 13	Iowa State	Ames	9/	L 28-37
Nov. 26	Oklahoma	Lincoln	10/8	L 17-20
Dec. 4	Hawaii	Honolulu	13/	W 68-3
Astro-Bluebonnet Bowl				
Dec. 31	Texas Tech	Houston	13/9	W 27-24

Final Rankings: 7th UPI, 9th AP (both post-bowl)

Osborne Says Emotion Overrated

by Ken Hambleton
Lincoln Journal Star

Nov. 24, 1976— When they remake the movie "Knute Rockne" Nebraska head football coach Tom Osborne probably wouldn't take the leading role if it were offered.

"A lot of people have been talking about our team's motivation since the Iowa State game," Osborne said following Tuesday's two-hour workout in preparation for Friday's nationally televised game with Oklahoma in Memorial Stadium.

"But I think this business of emotion is a bit overplayed," said Osborne. "People see Pat O'Brien give his speech as Knute Rockne and watch the old team go out and win one for the 'Gipper.'

"But getting a team ready for a game takes all week, not just before the game starts," said Osborne. "If oratory could make a team win there'd be a lot more winning coaches. The worst chewing out I've ever given the team was during the halftime at Iowa State. And that was the worst half of football we've played all year.

"The players are aware of the importance of the game coming up," said Osborne, referring to the fact a Husker win would mean a share of the conference title and a trip to the Orange Bowl. "Emotion is important but I think that at Iowa State, for instance, we were more physically and mentally tired than unemotional."

Osborne carried the point further,

It wasn't until the 1980s that the University of Miami became Tom Osborne's nemesis. Nebraska defeated the Hurricanes 31-16 in 1975, then edged Miami 17-9 in 1976 with the help of plays such as this one by All-America defensive back Dave Butterfield (34). (Journal Star Library)

"Some people say that Nebraska can't win the big games or that I specifically can't win them. But personally, as a coach, I feel that every game and every win is a big one."

"If we were to lose to Kansas State then that game would become a 'big game'," said Osborne. "When we played Iowa State, Oklahoma State, Colorado and Louisiana State we heard that the game with Nebraska was their most important game of the season, and some of the coaches said the game was the most im-

portant game in their history," he added.

Senior Husker cornerback Dave Butterfield said that playing such a tough Big Eight schedule hasn't changed his outlook on Friday's game.

"Both OU and us aren't coming into this game undefeated, but we know we have to win to get the title and the Orange Bowl," said Butterfield. "We aren't preparing for this game much differently than last year except for a few new defensive plays.

"We've had a lot of big games right in a row but this 10 days to prepare make a lot of difference," said Butterfield. "I don't think we'll be flat because we've paced ourselves."

Butterfield's primary defensive concern will be Oklahoma's split end and the OU passing game, which has two completions in its last six games. "I can't get lulled to sleep just because the Sooners don't pass much," said Butterfield. "It's a bit easier covering an end when a team doesn't throw much because when they do pass it's pretty easy to read."

Butterfield said the Huskers have also made some adjustments to defensing the Sooners this year. "We're aware that the past three years the Oklahoma quarterback has hurt us and we're working on containing him this year. Lott (OU quarterback Tom) doesn't have all that much experience but we know he can run very well." ∎

Osborne, Staff Still Wrestling With Oklahoma Downfall

by Dave Sittler

Lincoln Journal Star

Dec. 1, 1976

riday's mindbending 20-17 loss to Oklahoma wasn't the only difficult task Tom Osborne was forced to wrestle with that cold and dreary afternoon.

Trying to unwind in the quiet solitude of his home, Osborne was startled when his children burst through the door with the news that they had heard a national television announcer say their dad might be fired.

Announcer Dave Diles, who was handling the halftime scoreboard show on ABC-TV's telecast of the Pittsburgh-Penn State game, suggested the loss to Oklahoma might cost Osborne his coaching job at Nebraska.

"My kids were watching the game downstairs and heard I might be fired," Osborne recalled Tuesday morning in his office. "I don't know if they were really upset about it, but they wanted to know if it was a fact. I'm sure it had an effect on them."

Having his children subjected to such news is only part of the personal hell Osborne has been going through since the loss to the Sooners.

The mail has been heavy and the phone calls abundant.

"Frankly," Osborne said, "I took the phone off the hook at home for the weekend. The kids took some calls after the game and most of them were not supportive. I don't think the kids should have to heard some of the things that were said."

Osborne knows there has been some adverse mail, questioning his coaching ability and his job status. But he seldom sees derogatory correspondence.

"The first year I used to look at all my mail and sometimes it was depressing," Osborne said. "But my secretaries go though the mail now. I don't look at any of the unsigned ones.

"But I've received a lot of supportive letters which I try to answer."

Nasty letters and crank phone calls are a part of the job and Osborne knows it.

"My wife and I both understood what I was getting into when I took this job," Osborne said.

The Cornhusker coach said his wife, Nancy, has been very helpful during the rough moments.

"It would be very difficult to handle the job if I didn't have a wife like her," Osborne said. "I know some coaches' wives can't even go to the games and they get ulcers. But Nancy is very strong and philosophical. She really seems to have a handle on things and that helps."

Has pressure from the fans and some bad press ever caused Osborne to consider resigning?

"Sure, I've thought about resigning," Osborne admitted. "I've always weighed the pluses and minuses and sometimes it's a pretty thin line between the two."

Obviously, the pluses have so far prevailed for Osborne, who is in his fourth year as head coach for the Huskers.

"I really enjoy football," he explained. "It's a great game. I enjoy working with the players and coaches and respect the sacrifices they make and admire their ability."

Calling the days since the Oklahoma game some of the toughest he's ever spent, Osborne said, "There has been a lot of soul searching going on in this office. No one feels any more disappointed than the coaching staff."

Has he ever worried about being fired?

"No," Osborne said. "Usually when a coach wins 75 to 80% of his games he doesn't have to worry about his job. But maybe that isn't enough here.

"But I've never received any feeling from any University official or the athletic department that they want to get rid of me. But if anyone felt that way, I'd be the last one to fight it."

The cutback on scholarships and coaching staff has made the business of college coaching a precarious one at best, according to Osborne.

"We felt like we had done a pretty good job of coaching last year, when we won our first 10 games," he said. "Then we lost the last two and a lot of people felt like we had a losing season."

Osborne said he thought Nebraska probably had a slight edge over the other Big Eight teams prior to the season. He knew that if a couple of plays went the wrong way it would cause a lot of havoc. His worst fears along that line were realized last Friday.

"The Oklahoma game was a very emotional game and it's tough to live with yourself when you lose," Osborne said. "I've spent a lot of time thinking about that game since and the 20 or 30 different things we might have done to win."

Asked if he has thought a few years down the road about how long he might remain at Nebraska or if he might try pro coaching, Osborne said, "I really just go one year at a time. I just want to do the very best job I can here. Like any coach, I want to win them all, but that is getting to be a pretty tough thing to do." ■

Husker quarterback Vince Ferragamo (15) gets off a pass while under pressure from an Oklahoma defender November 27, 1976. Oklahoma defeated the Huskers 20-17. Ferragamo went on to set the school single-season record for TD passes with 20 in 1976, and his 2,071 yards passing that season were second-most in NU history. (Randy Hampton, Journal Star Library)

Son Of A Buck!
Nebraska "Dazzles" Tide

Huskers triumph in TV thriller, 31-24

by **Virgil Parker**

Lincoln Journal Star

Sept. 18, 1977

If Nebraska's Tom Osborne had a conservative image before, he erased that label with a series of bold coaching decisions on the way to a 31-24 victory over Alabama in Memorial Stadium Saturday afternoon.

The Cornhusker coach dazzled a sellout crowd of 75,899 by ordering three trick plays during a single touchdown drive–an I-back pass, another on which half the NU team seemed to handle the ball, and a fake field goal for the score.

Later, facing a fourth-and-short yardage decision near the 'Bama goal line–and the score tied–Osborne spurned a cinch field goal. Rick Berns responded by diving over a mass of bodies in the line to produce the final margin of victory.

"You'll have your heart in your throat when you call a play like that," the Husker head man admits. "But there was still a lot of time left in the game (Just over seven minutes of the fourth quarter), and I wasn't sure a field goal would produce enough points to hold up.

"It's not that we don't have confidence in our defense, but Alabama has a fine offensive team. They were moving the ball well, too. A touchdown would force them to score and make a two-point conversion to beat us. Even if we didn't get in, they would have had the ball on their own one-foot line."

The strategy paid off. Fabled 'Bama coach Bear Bryant's Crimson Tide was forced into throwing long passes–something wishbone teams don't like to do–and Husker cornerback Jim Pillen picked off two aerials to preserve the victory.

"We gave the passer a pretty good rush," NU defensive coordinator Lance Van Zandt noted," then "Pillen read the quarterback and moved to the ball well. You've got to give the players a lot of credit. They fought and clawed all the way."

The drama, tension and excitement of the game rivaled the classic Nebraska-Oklahoma matchup of 1971 that preceded an Orange Bowl triumph over Alabama and a second straight national championship for the Cornhuskers.

Osborne, who says his "Son of a Buck" reference to The Bear two years ago was "unfortunate, not meant for print and blown out of proportion," felt great and justifiable pride from the win.

"We play them down there next year, but you never know how much longer he'll (Bryant) be coaching. To beat a team coached by Bear Bryant is a great feeling–out of respect for him, not animosity."

Osborne says it is impossible to place enough emphasis on the victory with regard to team morale and the rest of the season–after suffering a stunning upset loss to Washington State in the opening game.

Legendary coach Bear Bryant brought his Crimson Tide to Lincoln September 17, 1977 to take on the Huskers. NU won 31-24. (Journal Star Library)

"The poise our kids showed in this game means a lot," Osborne noted. "If we had come back and played well, but lost, it would have taken a great deal out of our players. This result means a lot for our future. Alabama has as fine an offensive team as we'll face all season."

The game–which surely delighted a television audience seen by 70 percent of the nation–was loaded with "big plays". Despite the high score, many of them were produced by the Nebraska "Black Shirt" defense.

'Bama quarterback Jeff Rutledge completed seven of eight passes last week as the Tide swamped Ole Miss–a team that knocked off No. 3 ranked Notre Dame Saturday while the Huskers were taking care of fourth-rated Alabama.

Nebraska cornerback Ted Harvey set the tempo by picking off Rutledge's first toss–on Alabama's initial play of the game. Before the afternoon was over, the "Black Shirts" intercepted him five times.

That tied a negative 'Bama school record set by Ken Stabler–now the ace passer for the Oakland Raiders–in 1967.

But the biggest play of the game for Nebraska came on the way to the winning touchdown.

Alabama had tallied a touchdown to knot the score at 24-24. The ensuing kickoff sailed into the end zone and the Huskers started out 80 yards from paydirt.

One first down got the drive started, before Nebraska suffered two setbacks. The first was a penalty for delay of game; the second a 15-yard marchoff for illegal use of the hands.

The Huskers faced a third-and-12 situation. Quarterback Randy Garcia, who played brilliantly after starter Tom Sorley reinjured his shoulder, lofted a long pass to fellow Californian Tim Smith down the right sideline.

Smith not only took the pass away from closely covering 'Bama cornerback Don McNeal, but displayed some fancy footwork to stay in bounds to complete a 33-yard gainer.

Seven plays and three first downs later, Berns dived in for the winning touchdown.

"Yes, I called the long pass to Smith," Osborne admitted. "But, I called all the plays, including the ones that didn't work."

Osborne said the call for the touchdown try–while refusing the field goal–was made additionally difficult because his phone to the press box went dead at that moment.

"I really didn't know how far we had to go," he recalls. "But I knew we were down there pretty close."

Harvey's initial interception enabled Nebraska to move within range for a 29-yard field goal by Billy Todd to give the Huskers a 3-0 lead after five minutes of play.

Alabama came right back to take a 7-3 lead, marching 91 yards in 10 plays after the kickoff was fumbled out of bounds at the 'Bama nine.

The drive included some razzle-dazzle by The Tide. The touchdown was set up by a 33-yard gainer after Rutledge handed off to running back Tony Nathan, who then lateraled the ball back to the 'Bama quarterback. He then passed to all-America split end Ozzie Newsome.

Before the first quarter was over, Osborne dug into his bag of tricks.

It started on third and two from the Nebraska 28. Sorley handed off to Berns–who added 128 yards to the 153 he gained in the opener against WSU. The play looked like a sweep around right end. Suddenly Berns stopped and lofted a pass to wingback Curtis Craig over the middle. The gain covered 36 yards.

The very next play produced even more of a flea-flicker.

Against Washington State, the Huskers had given the ball to Berns on a sweep left. But he lateraled back to split end Smith for an end around. It looked like the same play again. But this time Smith tossed a second lateral–back to Sorley–who then threw a forward pass down-field

to tight end Ken Spaeth for an 11-yard gain.

Sorley was smashed just after he got the throw away, injuring the right shoulder he hurt against Washington State.

In came Garcia, who had been rudely treated by Big Red fans in the opener for what they thought had been a subpar performance. When the Huskers faced fourth-and-three at the Alabama seven–and Todd on the field for an apparent field goal try–Garcia took the snap, rolled to his right. Although under heavy pressure from the 'Bama defensive line, Garcia threaded the needle with a pin-point pass to Berns at the goal line. Berns, though well covered by two defenders, took the pass away from both of them and tumbled into the end zone and a 10-7 Nebraska lead.

"A lot of people seemingly gave up on Randy last week," Osborne observed. "Personally, I think it was inexcusable the way they booed him. He led the team right down the field (against WSU) and many of the bad things that happened, he wasn't even involved in. He did a lot of good things today."

Osborne said he was planning to play both quarterbacks against Alabama anyway.

"I hope to use them both throughout the season," the Cornhusker coach added, "I thought we'd lost Sorley for the game when he was hurt. But he was throwing on the sidelines during the second half. He'll be sore tomorrow. But I hope he'll be able to practice and throw the ball this next week."

Nebraska's 10-7 lead didn't last long. Alabama took the next kickoff and drove to a touchdown and a 14-10 advantage.

Two possessions later, Nebraska grabbed the lead again, 17-14. Garcia tossed an outlet pass to I.M. Hipp, who bore a lot of the brunt of the Washington State loss after fumbling on the only play he saw action.

Hipp more than redeemed himself. He grabbed the pass one handed, left his tearaway jersey in the hands of a would-be 'Bama tackler and rambled 53 yards. The very next play, Hipp picked up 13 more and a first down at the Crimson Tide 13.

Monte Anthony, making his first appearance of the year, banged down the middle for nine more, and two plays later Berns scored from two yards out.

But, with just 10 seconds left in the half, Alabama drove close enough for a field goal and a 17-17 intermission stand-off.

Early in the second half, NU linebacker Lee Kunz picked off a Rutledge pass. It took the Huskers just two plays– a 22-yard ramble by Berns and a 17-yard scamper by Craig–to cover the necessary distance and a 24-17 lead.

Alabama came back early in the final frame to produce the last tie–at 24-24–setting the stage for Nebraska's drive to victory.

The 31 points scored by Nebraska were the most recorded against an Alabama team since the Huskers won the Orange Bowl meeting, 38-6.

The results of the weekend will surely scramble the national rankings. In addition to Alabama and Notre Dame, top 10 rated Houston also lost.

Washington State pulled out a close win over Michigan State, 23-21, which will earn the Cougars a spot in the top twenty for the first time in the school's history.

"We just wanted to get Warren (ex-NU aide Warren Powers and new Washington State coach) off to a good start in his career," Osborne joked of last week's game. "We wanted to let him be the Coach of the Week, then come back and beat Alabama."

Osborne admits to one drawback of coaching. "You don't get to savor victory very long. We'll enjoy this for a couple of hours," he observed. "Before the night is over, we'll start working and worrying about Baylor." ■

Nebraska's George Andrews (96) celebrates a big fourth-down stop against No. 4 Bear Bryant-coached Alabama. (Journal Star Library)

Fans Writing To Osborne

by Dave Sittler
Lincoln Journal Star

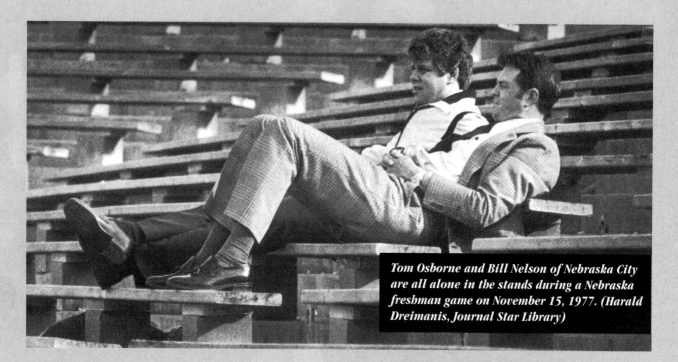

Tom Osborne and Bill Nelson of Nebraska City are all alone in the stands during a Nebraska freshman game on November 15, 1977. (Harald Dreimanis, Journal Star Library)

Oct. 26, 1977—While there was a considerable release of tension among Nebraska fans following Saturday's win over Colorado, no one probably emitted a bigger sigh of relief than Tom Osborne's mailman.

Chatting with sportswriters following Tuesday's practice, Osborne indicated he would never have to worry about joining the Lonely Hearts Club. He receives volumes of mail, especially after a Nebraska defeat.

"It (mail) was pretty heavy after the Iowa State game," said Osborne of the 24-21 loss to the Cyclones. "There's not as much this week."

Most letters are from Monday morning quarterbacks convinced they have the proper solution or a genius idea that will surely bring another national championship to Lincoln.

Osborne said one writer after the Iowa State loss wondered why freshman middle guard Curt Hineline was not promoted to the varsity. The correspondent was convinced Hineline, who is from Bellevue, Wash., could have stopped Iowa State's running game.

"Hineline's a good player," said Osborne of the 6-2, 220-pound frosh who had a fine game against the Iowa State junior varsity. "But (Kerry) Weinmaster (Nebraska's starting middle guard) along with Wightman, (linebacker James) played as well as anyone against Iowa State.

"People don't realize that it's not just the middle guard's job to stop the run up the middle."

Other suggestions Osborne received included throwing the ball more and giving I-back Richard Berns more opportunities to carry the ball.

"No one seemed too dissatisfied that Isaiah (Hipp) ran the ball 25 times," Osborne said. "We'd have to have the ball 100 plays to run everyone that often."

Noting he found many of the letters he receives amusing, Osborne admitted it's hard to swallow all of the ideas, considering the amount of time he and his staff work each football season.

"I think it would be ludicrous for me to walk into someone's business, look around a little bit and then start suggesting who I think should be fired," Osborne said. "The owner of that business probably spends 12-14 hours a day on the job. As coaches, we are spending 16 hours a day here." ■

"Cool Cat" Osborne Fires Up Huskers

by Dave Sittler

Lincoln Journal Star

Dec. 20, 1977

Forget all the passes and penalties, tackles and turnovers. You want to know the real reason Nebraska's football team whipped North Carolina in the Liberty Bowl? The answer takes one word–emotion.

No, to be precise, it takes three words–Tom Osborne's emotion.

Ha, you say. Tom Osborne has about as much emotion as an iceberg? Well, Nebraska's football coach melted this Monday night in Memphis.

The major topic of conversation after the Cornhuskers' thrilling 21-17 comeback win over the Tar Heels, was the emotional lift Osborne provided his players at halftime with his team trailing 14-7 in the 19th annual classic.

"I didn't know Coach Osborne had it in him," senior defensive end Tony Samuel said of Osborne's fiery intermission oratory.

Junior linebacker Lee Kunz said, "I've never seen Coach Osborne quite like he was tonight at halftime. He was so emotional it was unbelieveable. Yelling, screaming, he gave such a great speech. He was fired up, and he fired us up."

Upset by his team's ragged opening half play, Osborne explained to his troops at halftime–in no uncertain terms–what he expected of them the final 30 minutes of the contest viewed by 49,456 fans.

And when his team responded to their coach's plea by producing the dramatic fourth-quarter win, you know what good, ole unemotional Tom Osborne did? He cried.

The tears came later when most of the press had left. But Osborne's eyes were not the only wet ones in the emotionally charged Nebraska dressing room. There were several others.

"I just told the team that they are the greatest bunch of guys I've ever coached," said Osborne of his squad that finished the year 9-3 overall after many predicted a 6-5 finish might be more realistic.

Nebraska junior defensive tackle Barney Cotton, who produced one of the game's biggest plays when he intercepted a North Carolina pass, unabashedly wept after the sizzling game.

"I can't help it I'm crying," Cotton said. "This is the most exciting thing I've ever seen."

Two of the people who provided a huge hunk of the excitement, Randy Garcia and Tim Smith, let their emotions flow in another manner.

Moments after Garcia and Smith cooked up their own version of the California connection by collaborating on a game-winning 34-yard touchdown pass, the West Coast pair savored the moment in a joyful embrace in the hysterical dressing room.

"Hey, way to hang onto the ball," said Garcia, the senior quarterback from Los Angeles as he draped his arm around Smith.

A sophomore split end from Chula Vista, Smith slapped Garcia on the back and happily shouted above the din, "no problem. The way you were putting them (passes) in there, it was easy."

Three quarters a spectator on the Nebraska sideline, Garcia ended his Nebraska career in storybook fashion by coming off the bench to replace the injured Tom Sorley and to quarterback the Huskers to victory.

Garcia was red hot when he got his chance. Throwing just three passes in the final, frantic period, he hit on all three, two of them for touchdowns.

Nebraska Coach Tom Osborne shows his concern as he talks with Brett Moritz (70) in the first half of the 1977 Liberty Bowl. Osborne's fiery halftime speech spurred the Huskers to a 21-17 comeback victory against North Carolina. (Randy Hampton, Journal Star Library)

The first was a 10-yard pitch to wingback Curtis Craig, who made a twisting, diving stab in drawing Nebraska closer at 17-14 with 10:51 remaining.

"I wasn't sure if Curtis had his eye on the ball so I waited and then ended up throwing a bit behind him," Garcia said of the score that saw him execute a nifty fake to the Nebraska I-back that drew in the Tar Heel secondary.

"It wasn't as tough of a catch as it might have looked," Craig said. "I was so wide open because the safety fell down and bumped the monster, who was supposed to cover me."

Nebraska defensive tackle George Andrews, whose 19 tackles earned him most valuable defensive player honors, said, "Barney's interception was the key to this win, no doubt about it."

While Cotton's turnover unlocked the door, Nebraska defensive tackle Dan Pensick's fumble recovery slammed the gates on North Carolina as it set up the Garcia to Smith winning pass.

The ball finally ended up on the Nebraska 43, where Garcia reached into his bag of passing tricks and fakes and performed his magic for the second time. After three running plays, Garcia faked a handoff, spotted Smith streaking across the middle of the field and hit him with a score that completed the comeback.

"I thought it was on the money all the way," said Garcia, whose clutch fireman's job earned him offensive player honors. "But then I heard the crowd groan for a second and I wasn't sure. Then I heard the cheers and I knew."

Reconstructing the play, Garcia said, "I was looking for the tight end first. But when I didn't see him (Ken Spaeth), I looked for Tim. I've been accused of holding the ball too long before, so I wasn't about to hold it too long this time."

Asked about his victory catch, Smith said, "I think the play action fake to the back was the key. "Curtis (Craig) ran a streak and I ran under the coverage and I could tell right away I was wide open."

As he cut across the middle of the field, where Garcia drilled him a moment before being sacked, Smith said he was thinking, "just dig as hard as you can and don't look back."

If he would have glanced back over his shoulder, he would have seen a jubilant Garcia pumping his fist high in the air in victory while jumping for joy.

"This is just super," said Garcia, his voice cracking. "I've been sick all week and my voice was going on me out there tonight. The guys couldn't hear me call signals half the time."

Asked by one reporter how it felt for a great quarterback to go out in such a great way, Garcia, who has suffered many ups and downs in his final Husker season said, "I don't know how great I am, but I can tell you, this win is great."

Emotion has a way of producing such greatness. ∎

1977

Season in Review

Won 9, Lost 3, Tied 0
Big 8: Won 5, Lost 2, Tied 0, 2nd-tie

Date	Opponent	Site	AP Rank NU/Opp.	Result
Sept. 10	Washington St.	Lincoln	15/	L 10-19
Sept. 17	Alabama	Lincoln	/4	W 31-24
Sept. 24	Baylor	Lincoln	14/	W 31-10
Oct. 1	Indiana	Lincoln	11/	W 31-13
Oct. 8	Kansas State	Manhattan	9/	W 26-9
Oct. 15	Iowa State	Lincoln	9/	L 21-24
Oct. 22	Colorado	Lincoln	18/7	W 33-15
Oct. 29	Oklahoma St.	Stillwater	12/	W 31-14
Nov. 5	Missouri	Columbia	11/	W 21-10
Nov. 12	Kansas	Lincoln	12/	W 52-7
Nov. 25	Oklahoma	Norman	11/3	L 7-38
Liberty Bowl				
Dec. 19	North Carolina	Memphis	12/14	W 21-17

Final Rankings: 10th UPI, 12th AP (both post-bowl)

NU Fans Get Wish; Huskers "Barry" Bone

by Virgil Parker

Lincoln Journal Star

Nov. 12, 1978

Nebraska finally put the shoe on the other foot—Billy Todd's left one.

The Cornhuskers, who hadn't scored a fourth-quarter point against Oklahoma since Jeff Kinney's touchdown against the Sooners in the 1971 classic—a tally that propelled Nebraska to a Big Eight Conference title, an Orange Bowl date and an eventual national championship—set up the same three possibilities Saturday in Memorial Stadium after Todd connected with a 24-yard field goal early in the final quarter to earn the Huskers a 17-14 triumph.

Nebraska's defense, which played gallantly throughout the hard-hitting contest between the Barry Switzer-coached, wishbone-wielding offense of the top-rated Sooners and the No. 4-ranked Huskers, this time did the blanking themselves. The Black Shirt defenders held off two furious Oklahoma comeback attempts to preserve the victory.

Oklahoma, which had scored 71 fourth-quarter points in the last six years to none for Nebraska, had the ball twice after Todd left-footed his fielder squarely between the uprights. The first drive started from the Sooner 19-yard line after an officiating error allowed Oklahoma to retain possession despite a fumble on the kickoff that followed Todd's fielder.

OU's Kelly Phelps was blasted by Nebraska's John Ruud and the Huskers recovered at the Sooner 14, but Phelps was ruled down before the bobble.

The Huskers' defense, almost as mad over the call as the Nebraska coaches, stormed in to throw OU quarterback Thomas Lott for a 12-yard loss after the Sooners were first penalized five yards for motion. A delay of game penalty then put the ball back on the one, but Oklahoma fullback Kenny King rambled 47 yards to get the Sooners out of trouble.

Seven plays later, Oklahoma was threatening to take the lead. The Sooners gained the Nebraska 22, but at that point a hard hit by NU tackle Rod Horn caused OU ace Billy Sims to cough up the ball and the other tackle, Dan Pensick, recovered.

The Huskers were far from being out of the woods. Three plays and a punt later, Oklahoma had the ball again—this time at the Nebraska 47.

After just six plays, Oklahoma was knocking at the door again at the NU 21. Again it was Sims, who had gained over 200 yards in each of his last three games. He took a pitchout and circled the right side, skipping to the Nebraska three-yard line, where this time safety Jeff Hansen applied the crunching tackle. Again the ball popped loose and monsterback Jim Pillen, who was named ABC-TV's defensive player of the game, cradled the ball.

Shades of the 1974 Oklahoma State game. In that one, Cowboy quarterback Charlie Weatherbee fumbled on the same yard line in the same southwest corner of the field in the closing moments to enable the Huskers to preserve a narrow 7-3 win.

This time, 3 1/2 agonizing minutes still remained to be played. "It was far from over," Osborne observed later. "We

Jim Pillen (29), Rod Horn (55), and Bruce Dunning (right) celebrate Jeff Hansen's (48) fumble recovery of an Oklahoma fumble November 11, 1978. Nebraska took advantage of six Sooner fumbles to upset the nation's top-ranked team 17-14. (Journal Star Library)

had to move the ball to get away from our goal line and use up some time on the clock, and the offense really came through. Richard (Berns) made some nice runs to take care of that."

Berns, who paced the Husker runners with 113 yards on 25 carries to earn ABC's offensive player of the game honor,

zoomed off right tackle for 13 yards and one first down, then punched out runs of 5 and 9 yards to get another. When Berns carried next, with time running out, OU defensive back Basil Banks took a swing in frustration and was ejected from the game.

The resulting 15-yard penalty moved

the ball near midfield, where Nebraska–since Oklahoma had no timeouts remaining–was able to run out the clock.

Talk about pandemonium. It looked like the entire crowd of 76,015, Memorial Stadium's 99th consecutive sellout, raced onto the field as one. A few minutes later it seemed that all of the 76,000 who weren't busy tearing down the goal posts were in the Nebraska dressing room.

Osborne, wedged into a corner of the room, tried to holler his feelings above the bedlam.

"I'm elated but also relieved," the Husker head man said. "Late in the game, things just weren't going too well for us. It almost seemed like it (a victory over Oklahoma) wasn't meant to be. We thought we had a couple of other fumbles, but the rulings went against us. To stick in there and overcome, that makes me even happier."

His first victory over the Sooners pushed Osborne's coaching record to a sparkling 55 victories against just 14 defeats and two ties. "Of course this had to be my most satisfying win," Osborne observed. "It was certainly the one our fans wanted. And it gives us at least a share of the conference championship and should put us in the Orange Bowl."

Osborne acknowledged that nine Oklahoma fumbles–the Sooners lost six of them–played a big part in the outcome. "Oklahoma runs a high-risk offense," Osborne noted. "The ball-handling required by the wishbone can lead to fumbles. But the real key was the play of our linemen, both offensively and defensively. The offensive line really kicked out. There's no way you're going to blow a team as good as Oklahoma clear out of the ball park. But our kids took it to them.

"And the defense did a great job. Oklahoma is a fine team. And you can't try to stop just one back. We tried to vary our defense, blasting after the quarterback on one play and the fullback on another. I thought the defensive coaches did a super job."

Nebraska defensive coordinator Lance Van Zandt refused to take any of the credit. "The players should get the praise, not the coaches," he insisted. "I could put 100 diagrams on the blackboard, but if the players don't execute properly, no plan is going to win. The main thing is for the players to be aggressive. And I thought our players hit better than in any game this season."

Van Zandt noted that a lot of folks will credit Nebraska's victory to Oklahoma's numerous fumbles. "But they didn't drop it without one of our guys giving them a good hit, did they?" he asked. "Actually, we didn't do much of anything different than we have all year. The biggest mistake we could have made was put in a whole lot of new stuff which might have confused the players. I think we had a good plan, but it was the player's attitude, execution and effort that made it work."

At the outset of the game, Oklahoma didn't take long to ignite its explosive offense. Although Nebraska held the Sooners to three plays and a punt the first time they had the ball, the second OU possession was a different story. Taking over on its own 30, Oklahoma needed just four plays to move the necessary 70 yards for a 7-0 lead.

King rambled for 17 on a pitchout, and though Sims was held for a total of 7 yards on the next two plays, he flashed into the open and rambled 44 yards on third down to score.

Just five plays later things looked darker for Nebraska than the overcast skies. NU quarterback Tom Sorley was on target with a pass to tight end Junior Miller, but the usually sure-handed Miller bobbled the ball twice in midair. It was one bobble too many. Sooner linebacker George Cumby arrived on the scene to make an interception. But that's when the Black Shirts began to assert themselves and turn the game into a stalemate.

Early in the second quarter, after Hansen grabbed the first of his two Oklahoma fumbles, the Huskers started a drive toward a 7-7 tie. Sorley passes of 7 yards to Miller and 17 to Berns, plus a 10-yard run by I.M. Hipp, got the ball in position for Berns' 5-yard blast to paydirt. Todd kicked the extra point to produce the tie with 10:06 left in the half.

Oklahoma didn't threaten again before intermission, but Nebraska did after a 24-yard pass from Sorley to split end Tim Smith put the ball on the Sooner four. But time was running out. Just six seconds remained. Todd came on for a field goal try.

The Huskers were actually too close. The angle was so severe, Todd said later, that he didn't have much room for error. The ball ticked the right upright and caromed away.

"Things were pretty quiet in the dressing room at halftime," Osborne admitted, "but nobody felt we couldn't win. I just encouraged them to keep up the kind of hard-hitting play and all-out effort they had given in the first half."

That kind of play soon paid off. On Oklahoma's second possession, Pensick made the hard-hitting tackle and end Derrie Nelson recovered still another Sims fumble at midfield. The Huskers moved the 50 yards in six plays. The biggest was a 33-yard Sorley to Miller pass. Hipp covered the remaining 17 yards in three carries. His 8-yard TD run came with 9:25 left in the third quarter and Todd made it 14-7 with his conversion kick.

It was the first time this season Oklahoma had been behind!

Oklahoma didn't stay behind long, although the Sooners got one reprieve. Lott fumbled at the NU 35 and Pillen recovered for the Huskers, but Nebraska was ruled offsides on the play. On the very next snap after the penalty, Sims whisked 30 yards and it was a 14-14 tie with 6:47 left in the third stanza.

It wasn't long before Nebraska started the drive that resulted in Todd's successful field goal early in the final frame. Then came nail-biting time for the partisan red-clad crowd as the Huskers thwarted the final two Oklahoma comeback attempts to claim the victory. ∎

Huskers Find Tigers Too Tough To Cage

by Virgil Parker
Lincoln Journal Star

ebraska's dream of a national football championship turned into a nightmare in Memorial Stadium Saturday.

Missouri, so often cast as the giant-killer in recent years, played that role to perfection once again by registering a 35-31 victory over the Orange Bowl-bound Cornhuskers.

In a rare move–and unprecedented in Big Eight history–the Orange Bowl elected to stage a Big Eight championship rematch between co-titlists Nebraska and Oklahoma New Year's night. The one other time a bowl committee scheduled an intra-conference rematch came in the 1960 Sugar Bowl after LSU and Mississippi played to a regular season 6-6 tie. LSU shut out Ole Miss in the bowl game, 21-0.

The biggest Missouri villains were a bunch of ex-Huskers masquerading in Black and Gold parkas as Missouri coaches–Warren Powers, John Faiman, Dick Beechner, Zaven Yaralian, Mark Heydorff, Bill (Thunder) Thornton and Dave Redding.

They had an excellent supporting cast in quarterback Phil Bradley, tight end Kellen Winslow and a bull-like sophomore running back named James Wilder.

It was the second straight year for Powers and his staff to return "home" to Memorial Stadium and sidetrack their alma mater. Powers, who played as a Husker and then coached eight years under Bob Devaney and Tom Osborne, brought Washington State to Lincoln for his head coaching debut last fall and went away with a 19-10 victory. Saturday's game was an even more difficult defeat for the Huskers to swallow. They were No. 2 in the nation and on the threshold of playing top-rated Penn State for the national championship.

"If we could have just slowed them down," Nebraska defensive coordinator Lance Van Zandt lamented about Missouri's relentless offense. "Our offense was moving the ball well enough. But we couldn't stop them. We tried everything we have. We tried our standard 5-2 defense, we tried to blitz, dog, a '59' alignment, eagle–everything. It seemed like the game lasted two weeks. It was a nightmare."

Cornhusker Coach Osborne, fighting back tears–which many of his Husker players could not contain–admitted there wasn't much he could say. "They just beat us. We (the coaches) were worried whether the players could play with the same intensity two weeks in a row. We didn't. We weren't as crisp, not as emotional as against Oklahoma last week.

"We had a chance there at the end," Osborne observed of the final four minutes after Missouri had tallied a touchdown to produce what proved to be the final score. "But the clock was against us as well as a strong Missouri defense. They knew we were going to have to pass and they were able to blitz successfully.

"We didn't want to get into a scoring contest with them," Osborne added, "but that's what happened. They had trouble stopping us, but we couldn't stop them. And they scored the last one."

The score was identical and the game was reminiscent of Nebraska's 35-31 victory over Oklahoma in 1971. An even, see-saw game that went to the team to get the last touchdown.

Missouri won the coin toss and chose to have a strong 25-mph wind at its back. The decision didn't look too smart when Husker I-back Richard Berns scampered 82 yards on the first play of the game to stake Nebraska to a 7-0 lead.

Berns, who was featured on the cover of *Sports Illustrated* this week, didn't let the so-called "*SI* jinx" bother him personally. He finished the day with 255 yards–the most ever gained by a Cornhusker in a single game. The slashing senior first had the record after gaining 211 yards as a sophomore against Hawaii two years ago. But last season, I.M. Hipp snapped the mark with 254 yards against Indiana. Berns exceeded that by a single yard Saturday.

But the personal accomplishment was little consolation to the Wichita Falls, Texas, native, even though he also became Nebraska's all-time career leading rusher in the process. Berns was third on the list going into the game, needing 70 yards to catch previous runner-up Jeff Kinney (2,420 yards) and 95 to catch Tony Davis (2,445). He went by Kinney and almost caught Davis on the game's first play, eventually pushing his total to 2,605 yards with the Orange Bowl game remaining.

Berns' initial touchdown may have been too easy. In any case, Missouri wasn't about to roll over and play dead and the Nebraska defense couldn't handle Bradley's passing or the powerful running of the 220-pound Wilder.

Wilder only gained three yards the first time he carried. It might have been his shortest run of the day. He plowed for 7 yards, steamrolled for 15 more and then capped Missouri's tying touchdown drive of 79 yards in 13 plays by crunching 9 yards to the end zone. It was 7-7. The mood of the day—all offense—had been established.

"They were just blowing our defense off the ball," Osborne said. "And we weren't tackling very well. We just didn't control the line of scrimmage. It was a combination of them having good, big, hard-running backs and us not playing as well as we did last week. That Wilder is as physical a back as we've faced all season."

After the initial tie, Nebraska still seemed to be in control. The Huskers took advantage of a shanked eight-yard Missouri punt and took over on their own 39. With Berns carrying the bulk of the load, Nebraska moved the necessary 61 yards in 12 plays. Stacking against the run, Mizzou was fooled by a two-yard toss from Tom Sorley to tight end Junior Miller for the touchdown. Billy Todd was on target for the second time and it was 14-7 with 2:06 remaining in the first quarter.

Nebraska extended its lead to 17-7 the next time it got the ball, this time moving to a 27-yard Todd field goal. But that also may well have been a turning point in the game for Missouri. The Huskers had a first-and-goal at the two-yard line yet failed to tally a touchdown.

Nebraska got in position for what might have been a clinching touchdown on the game's most sensational play–a 36-yard pass completion from Sorley to split end Tim Smith. The pass was tipped by not one, but two Missouri defenders. But Smith, showing great concentration, made a diving catch at the Missouri four.

On the next play, Missouri was offside. That put the ball at the two. But then Nebraska's offensive line jumped the snap count and the five-yard penalty put the ball back at the seven. A one-yard gain by Berns, an incomplete pass and a draw play that didn't fool anybody forced the Huskers to settle for the field goal.

Now it was Missouri's turn again. The Tigers took the ensuing kickoff and went right down the field–four or five yards at a crack–to move 73 yards in 15 plays to close the gap to three points again 17-14.

The Husker defense almost had Mizzou stopped near mid-field, but Wilder cruised 13 yards on a third-and-eight draw play to keep the march alive. The last 24 yards were covered on a pair of Bradley to Winslow passes of 10 and 14 yards.

Nebraska took the kickoff to open the second half and went 72 yards in 13 plays to take command again, 24-14. A 20-yard pass from Sorley to Brown and a 16-yard run by Brown highlighted the drive. Berns covered the final two yards.

But, it was a case of all offense and no defense by both teams. Mizzou took the next kickoff and needed just nine plays to ramble 76 yards. The Nebraska lead was down to three again, 24-21. Wilder had a run of 21 yards and Winslow caught two Bradley passes for 16 and 29 yards to eat up most of the distance.

The last Winslow catch put the ball on the Husker one. And there the Black Shirt defense made a gallant stand. After three plays the ball was back on the two. But Wilder bulled in on fourth down. ■

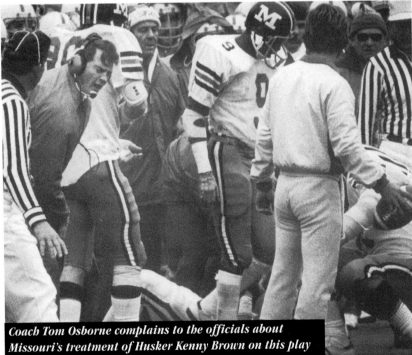

Coach Tom Osborne complains to the officials about Missouri's treatment of Husker Kenny Brown on this play November 18, 1978. The Tigers, with James Wilder running wild, shocked the Huskers 35-31. (Journal Star Library)

"Good Man" Tom Osborne Stays Home

by Randy York
Lincoln Journal Star

Dec. 16, 1978—Tom Osborne decided Tuesday to be a poor businessman—but he's a good man, Charlie Brown.

Nebraska's sixth-year head football coach took his own pulse and decided his heart beats greater for his homestate and the athletes he's recruited than Colorado's generosity and picture postcard scenery.

Speaking via a conference telephone call from Kansas City's International Airport in the midst of a recruiting trip, Osborne admitted he came close to accepting a lucrative offer to become Colorado's head football coach before deciding to remain at Nebraska.

"I guess if it had been a plain business proposition, I'd have gone to Colorado," Osborne said. "The financial opportunity and security are certainly greater ... and there would have been less pressure, at least for awhile.

"But when I thought of the players we've recruited at Nebraska, I realized it would be very, very difficult in the final analysis to tell them I was going to go and coach against them.

"I've been at Nebraska 16 years," the Huskers' 40-year-old head coach said. "It would be very tough to leave a place where I've invested so much time and energy. The Colorado job provided more money and security. But I'm not a mercenary person. I guess, in the final analysis, blood is just thicker than water."

Osborne acknowledged that his three children have reached the ages where "if I was going to make a change, now would be the time."

Since Colorado is one of the few places he was willing to consider, Osborne thought he owed it to himself and his family to investigate.

"Colorado's football program has a lot of potential. That's why I wanted to take a look at it," he said. "I was honored Colorado wanted me and I'm happy the whole thing was handled in such a way as to not embarrass either school."

Osborne, however, felt "somewhat disturbed by all the publicity. In most businesses, a person could fly in and discuss a job without all that publicity. I tried my best to avoid it."

Insisting his interest in Colorado had nothing to do with being upset at Nebraska, Osborne said: "I certainly didn't go there to shake people up" or to strengthen his own negotiating status at Nebraska.

"I have too much respect for both Colorado and Nebraska to play games," Osborne said. "Bob Devaney and I have talked about salary, but I didn't ask for more money or a longer contract. I wanted to look at the Colorado job for other reasons. If finances had been the overriding consideration, I'd have stayed in Boulder."

Osborne's interest to at least look outside Memorial Stadium's walls stems from a number of disappointing developments in recent years.

"People in Nebraska want to win and it takes more than just the coaches and the players to assure that," he said. "I'm told the Oklahoma coaching staff has 60 private airplanes at its disposal (for recruiting purposes). We have two. Maybe that's our fault. Maybe we haven't let people know what our needs are."

Rule changes limiting coaching staffs and scholarships have made winning 11 games progressively more difficult, Osborne indicated.

"We're capable of winning the national championship," he said. "But the only way we can do it is to outwork the other people . . . and that means more people than just the coaching staff. I'm not going to get any smarter. And it's not possible to put any more hours on the job. We have certain limitations. We can have great teams, but it's not easy to win 9,10 or 11 games every year."

Acknowledging that Colorado's approach to football is more low key than Nebraska's, Osborne said "after three or four years, they'd want better results, too."

Eventually, he deduced, the pressure to win would be as great in Colorado as it is in Nebraska.

"In some respects," Osborne said, "the intensity we have at Nebraska helps produce winning teams. It's a double-edged sword."

There was no great feeling among his staff to leave for Colorado, Osborne said, "but they did want me to look at the situation. They were all involved and I suppose most of them would have gone with me."

As serious as he was in his desire to clear the air on the entire issue, Osborne retained his sense of humor.

Noting he was told there would be no trouble selling a much more high-powered television package in Colorado, Osborne quipped: "Maybe they don't know what a dull TV personality I am."

Concerning the tremendous potential to fish in and around Boulder's scenic streams, Osborne admitted if he would have taken the job, "I probably would have been fishing so much of the time I wouldn't have done a very good job of coaching."

With a 55-15-2 record in six years at Nebraska, everyone, obviously, knows otherwise.

Tom Osborne, a poor businessman, but a good man, thrives on hard work . . . and he wouldn't give anyone less than his best. ∎

Husker, Sooner Rematch Official

by Randy York

Lincoln Journal Star

Nov. 19, 1978

Tom Osborne was genuinely stunned.

Nebraska's sixth-year head football coach hadn't even considered playing Oklahoma in the Orange Bowl, but that's the matchup that materialized following the Huskers' 35-31 loss to Missouri Saturday.

The Huskers and Sooners in Miami on New Year's Night . . . as Gomer Pyle would say: "Surprise, surprise, surprise."

The Big Two from the Big Eight will bathe on the same beaches and play in the same bowl in the most shocking development in recent bowl history.

"I'm a little surprised," Osborne admitted in a rather subdued telephone hookup with the Orange Bowl 90 minutes after his second-ranked Huskers had been upset.

"The thought hadn't even crossed my mind," Osborne said. "It came completely out of the blue. I guess life's full of surprises. I certainly didn't think we'd get beat today either."

The line produced some much needed laughter in a telephone conference that linked Osborne, Nebraska Athletic Director Bob Devaney, NU Chancellor Roy Young and Orange Bowl officials Stan Marks and Charles Kimbrell to the Orange Bowl Office in Miami.

Robin White, president of the Orange Bowl, said: "We regret the results of this afternoon's football game, of course. But we are proud to have Nebraska. Please be advised we have asked Oklahoma to play Nebraska in a match unique in bowl history."

White thought he had a first, matching two conference opponents in a postseason game.

But LSU beat Mississippi, 21-0, in the 1960 Sugar Bowl after the two had battled to a 6-6 tie during the regular season.

White said the NU-OU rematch "will be a very exciting game with a tremendous amount of appeal. A week ago, these same two teams played one of the most exciting games ever played.

"Everyone here seems very intrigued by it. We have one of the largest press corps we've ever had."

Osborne, asked if playing Oklahoma twice in such a short time span was too much, admitted "it's a pretty big order. I guess when you beat them one time in seven years, being asked to do it twice in a matter of weeks is asking a lot. But I guess if we can do it, it would be some accomplishment."

As he contemplated the possibility in his office before receiving the official announcement, Osborne expressed misgivings.

"I can see playing them again if we had played them earlier in the season," he said. "But I have to admit I'm surprised by all of this."

Marks and Kimbrell asked Osborne 20 minutes beforehand what he thought about an NU-OU match.

"Do I have a choice?" Osborne asked.

"No."

"Then I guess I don't have a comment," he said.

Kimbrell admitted "personally, I don't favor the game. Tom Osborne has beaten Barry Switzer once on national TV. I can understand how he must feel being asked to turn around and beat him again."

Still, Kimbrell explained the Orange Bowl thinking by pointing out that "historically, we've always gone for the highest ranking team available. This year, OU happens to fall into that category.

"If we had had our wish, of course, we wanted Nebraska to win. We were on pins and needles all day. We had the dream game (Penn State-Nebraska) in the palm of our hand . . . and it just slipped out."

Devaney winced at Georgia's 22-22 tie with Auburn Saturday as much as he winced at Nebraska's loss to Mizzou.

"This is just conjecture," he said, "but I think Penn State would have gone to the Orange Bowl anyway, if Auburn hadn't knocked Georgia out of the Sugar Bowl and put Alabama in. A couple of bad things happened almost at once."

Kimbrell offered another interesting explanation of the Orange Bowl's desire to rematch OU and NU.

"If Penn State should get upset by Pitt next week–which is a very good possibility in a heated rivalry–and if Penn State should go on and beat Alabama in the Sugar Bowl–you still might have the national champion in the Orange Bowl."

He didn't say which team that would be, but it was understood he meant Oklahoma.

The Orange Bowl rematch has one other major feature. The Big Eight Conference now will pocket more than $2 million from both teams instead of the $1 million it would generate from having one representative. ∎

Husker Coach Tom Osborne exhorts his defense during the rematch against Oklahoma in the 1979 Orange Bowl. NU lost 31-24 to the Sooners after beating them 17-14 earlier in the season. (Journal Star Library)

Spies Hurt Nebraska, But Mistakes Decided Game

by Virgil Parker

Lincoln Journal Star

Jan. 2, 1979

Spies. Inside information. Espionage. Intrigue.

James Bond fans would have loved it. Nebraska football coach Tom Osborne didn't.

The stuff of which mystery stories are written may have played a crucial role in the outcome of Oklahoma's 31-24 Orange Bowl victory over Nebraska Monday night.

The plot began weeks ago when Osborne and his staff dreamed up some special plays for the postseason rematch with the Sooners. Top secret!

It thickened two days before the game when the Cornhusker coaches learned that their Oklahoma counterparts knew–in complete detail–all about the plays, right down to the intricate blocking assignment for each player.

The NU staff came in possession of an Oklahoma coach's note pad.

"It had our terminology and other information in it they shouldn't have known about," Husker defensive coordinator Lance Van Zandt says. "The plays,

diagrammed in detail, had never been used in 11 games."

Van Zandt implies–without making a direct accusation–that there is no way Oklahoma could have obtained that material without a spy or an inside informant.

Osborne didn't want to blame the outcome of the game on the "leak" of his special plans, but he was obviously disturbed.

"What concerned me was the fact that we had never even used that formation this season–and never with motion (putting a back in motion prior to the snap)," the Husker head man said. "Yet that note pad not only showed the play–with motion–but how they intended to defense it. They couldn't have learned that from looking at the films of our past games."

Osborne insists he isn't accusing Oklahoma of illegal activity.

"I can't say for sure they watched our practices. Sometimes we sit around in our

coaching meetings and try to guess what the opponent will do and what defensive adjustment we'll make if they actually try such a play. I don't have enough proof to accuse them."

Then the Cornhusker coach observed, "Anyway, based on what I saw out on the field (the number of Nebraska mistakes), I'm not sure it made any difference, anyway."

Husker quarterback Tom Sorley and ace running back Richard Berns were more vocal.

Sorley said even when he audibled (changed the play at the line of scrimmage from the one called in the huddle), the Oklahoma defensive players seemed to know exactly what Nebraska was going to do.

Berns expressed amazement at how well the Sooners seemed to have Nebraska scouted.

Reading the statistics would lead a person to believe Nebraska did very well, despite the apparent espionage. Oklahoma had the nation's most potent rushing offense, averaging 428 yards a game. Monday night, the Sooners managed 292.

In four of his last six games, Heisman Trophy winner Billy Sims of Oklahoma gained over 200 yards per outing. The two times he was held to less? Against Nebraska in Lincoln (153 yards on 25 carries) and in the Orange Bowl (134 yards on another 25 totes).

Nebraska gained 100 yards in total offense more than Oklahoma (437 vs. 339) and a whopping 10 more first downs–27 to 17.

But Sorley threw two pass interceptions and the Huskers were penalized eight times. They all seemed to come at crucial moments.

Oklahoma fumbled 58 times this season and lost 34 of them. The Sooners dropped the ball nine times and lost it on six occasions in the Lincoln game. In this Orange Bowl matchup, OU made only one major mistake–a lost fumble–and that didn't happen until the fourth quarter when the outcome was no longer in doubt.

Nebraska opened the 45th Orange Bowl Classic before a packed house of 66,365 and about 60 million more on national television, like it was going to repeat the victory (17-14) recorded in Lincoln.

The Huskers took the game's opening kickoff and drove 80 yards in 15 plays to take a 7-0 lead. More importantly, they used up 6 1/2 minutes on the clock in the process.

Starting I-back Berns carried the ball on seven of the first nine plays–the other two were Sorley passes–and the march was climaxed by a 21-yard touchdown toss from Sorley to split end Tim Smith.

The Nebraska Black Shirt defense roared on the field to take over. Three plays after the ensuing kickoff, Oklahoma was forced to punt.

But, from then on–at least from a Husker partisan point of view–it was all downhill.

The Sooners tied it 7-7 before the first quarter was over on a two-yard run by Sims that completed a 69-yard drive in 12 plays and held a 14-7 halftime advantage after OU quarterback Thomas Lott danced in from three yards out after throwing a rare Sooner pass (good for 38 yards when Nebraska defender Andy Means slipped and fell).

Oklahoma just about settled the issue by racing 70 yards for a touchdown in just five plays with the second-half kickoff. Sims scored it from 11 yards out after Lott ran 38 and fullback Kenny King another 15.

OU kicker Uwe von Schamann and Nebraska's Billy Todd traded field goals to keep Oklahoma in front by 14 points,

24-10, before Lott tallied another Sooner TD. Sims got that nine-play, 60-yard march started with a 28-yard scamper.

Nebraska rebounded with a touchdown of its own. Sorley passes to tight end Junior Miller and wingback Kenny Brown highlighted the march that covered 86 yards in 15 plays with Berns smashing in from one yard out. That made it 31-17.

That's when Oklahoma committed its only major error, a Lott fumble recovered by NU's David Clark at the OU 42.

I.M. Hipp got thing going with a 15-yard run. But the drive bogged down at the Sooner seven when Craig Johnson, playing at I-back with Berns and fullbacks Andra Franklin and Jim Kotera sidelined by injuries, failed to gain on fourth and six inches.

"That was very crucial," Osborne said. "Our coaches upstairs thought we got a bad spot by the officials. It certainly looked like he made a yard and we only needed a foot. Over four minutes still remained. If we had scored right then and pulled within seven points, it might have gotten pretty interesting." ■

1978 Season in Review

Won 9, Lost 3, Tied 0
Big 8: Won 6, Lost 1, Tied 0, 1st-tie

Date	Opponent	Site	AP Rank NU/Opp.	Result
Sept. 2	Alabama	Birmingham	10/1	L 3-20
Sept. 9	California	Lincoln	10/	W 36-26
Sept. 16	Hawaii	Lincoln	12/	W 56-10
Sept. 30	Indiana	Bloomington	12/	W 69-17
Oct. 7	Iowa State	Ames	10/15	W 23-0
Oct. 14	Kansas State	Lincoln	8/	W 48-14
Oct. 21	Colorado	Boulder	5/	W 52-14
Oct. 28	Oklahoma State	Lincoln	4/	W 22-14
Nov. 4	Kansas	Lawrence	4/	W 63-21
Nov. 11	Oklahoma	Lincoln	4/1	W 17-14
Nov. 18	Missouri	Lincoln	2/	L 31-35
Orange Bowl				
Jan. 1	Oklahoma	Miami	6/4	L 24-31

Final Rankings: 8th AP & UPI (both post-bowl)

Osborne Honored With Game Ball After Win

by **Mike Babcock**

Lincoln Journal Star

Nebraska football Coach Tom Osborne was given the game ball following his Cornhuskers' 42-17 victory over Penn State Saturday.

Offensive captain Tim Smith made the presentation in the midst of a locker room celebration. He praised Osborne for opening up the NU offense against Penn State.

"Joe Paterno is a great coach, but we like to think our coach is a great one, too," Smith said.

But Osborne wanted to make clear that players, not head coaches, win football games. "We just had better players at most positions," he said Sunday afternoon. "You might out-recruit somebody, but when it comes to me out-coaching Joe Paterno, that's not going to happen very often."

"So many times I hear things like Bear Bryant beat Bob Devaney or whatever. Well, that wasn't the case. I don't think I beat Joe Paterno. Our players beat their players."

Prior to Saturday's game, Paterno, the winningest active coach in college football, repeatedly indicated he was concerned that his Penn State team might not be able to stay with the Cornhuskers, that they had too much offense.

"I thought Joe was blowing smoke, but after looking at the films, I could see he was deficient at four or five positions," said Osborne. "I don't know if we could rank Penn State as a national power right now.

"To have scored and moved the ball against some pretty good defensive players should help our confidence, but to be real blunt about it, Utah State and Iowa probably had a little bit better people at the skill positions.

"Even though Penn State had some good athletes, those teams (Utah State and Iowa) had more overall speed," Osborne said.

Nebraska generated 530 yards of total offense, within three of the most ever against a Nittany Lion defense in the school's 92-year history. The loss was Penn State's second in a row, only the fourth time in 14 seasons such a fate has befallen a Paterno-coached team.

The last time an opponent scored 40 points or more against the Nittany Lions was 1970, when Colorado defeated them 41-13 in Boulder.

Nebraska's defense limited the Lions to 183 yards of offense, 82 of which came on their first touchdown drive, their second offensive series of the contest.

When Osborne and Paterno met following Saturday's game, the Cornhusker head coach apologized for the score. "He just said, 'Nice game,' and I said, 'Sorry about the score,'" Osborne recalled. "Really, when you play a good team, you want to win, but you hate to make it embarrassing . . . if that was embarrassing.

"I didn't want to tell our players not to score, though. That would be even more embarrassing," he said.

Osborne said the two schools, which had not played since 1958, will meet three more times in the current series, and "next year we go there.'

"We've got to go against them four times in all, and if we come out with two-of-four, that's not too bad," he said.

The 3-0 start is Nebraska's best since 1975, when the Cornhuskers won their first 10 before season-ending losses to Oklahoma and Arizona State (in the Fiesta Bowl).

"That's really an encouraging start," said Osborne. "But I hope people consider it just that. Sometimes the fans have a tendency to get carried away." ■

Coach Tom Osborne fights off the chill during a spring practice in 1979. (Journal Star Library)

Whew!
NU Finally Breaks Powers' Spell

by Virgil Parker
Lincoln Journal Star

Coach Tom Osborne asks the official for a clarification during NU's 23-20 win at Missouri November 3, 1979. (Journal Star Library)

Nov. 4, 1979—The Nebraska Cornhuskers survived two narrow escapes Saturday. The first was a typical Nebraska-Missouri football cliffhanger. Then, when leaving Columbia airport after a narrow 23-20 victory, their charter plane blew out a tire on takeoff. That required an emergency landing in Omaha before reaching home.

Coach Tom Osborne's Cornhuskers were able to keep their perfect record intact after Mizzou Coach Warren Powers made a last-play decision that will likely be debated and discussed in Tiger Country for some time.

Powers declined the chance to tie the nation's No. 2-ranked Huskers with a chip shot field goal on that final play, instead trying a go-for-broke pass play from the NU 11-yard line.

But NU defensive end Derrie Nelson foiled the attempt by sacking Tiger quarterback Phil Bradley to end the heartstopping action.

"Our football team wasn't ready to play a team like Nebraska for a tie," Powers said. "We needed that win in a bad way to stay in the conference race. I never did consider going for the field goal. I don't think our kids wanted to go for the field goal either. They wanted a win."

Osborne refused to second-guess his ex-assistant coach, who had upset the Huskers the past two seasons with his Washington State and Missouri teams.

"I've been over on the other side of the field when other coaches have second-guessed something I did," Osborne said. "I didn't like it. And I won't second-guess him."

Unlike a lot of Husker faithful in the crowd of 74,575, the second-largest in Faurot Field history, Osborne said, "I was breathing throughout that last play and had both eyes open."

The Huskers had lots of heroes—Nelson was the final one—but as in the Iowa game, when he kicked a winning field goal in the final five minutes of play, placekicker Dean Sukup grabbed the brass ring.

Sukup had three field goals on the day—the last to break a 20-20 deadlock with 3:15 left in the game—and a perfect PAT boot after each of Nebraska's two touchdowns.

"I missed three extra points in six tries in recent games," the Cozad native recalled. "I'm just glad I got that straightened out. I tried not to think how important the last field goal was. You can't put more pressure on yourself than is already there."

Osborne may not question Powers' last-play decision, but he certainly wants to discuss some of the calls made by the game officials with the Big Eight Conference office.

"I usually go over our game films and then talk to Bruce Finlayson (the commissioner of officials for the league) on Mondays. He'll hear from me tomorrow (Sunday) this time."

Osborne was visibly upset over three calls. The first came when NU defensive tackle Bill Barnett appeared to intercept a Bradley pass just before halftime.

Osborne was told the ball belonged to the Huskers, but after referee Dan Foley had a long discussion with Powers, he changed his mind and announced that Bradley had been stopped before he threw the ball. During the confusion, none of the officials knew where Bradley was supposedly tackled.

"That's the first time I've ever had an official tell me one thing and then reverse himself after talking to the other coach," Osborne said. "Warren must have been very persuasive."

More seriously affecting the outcome was a pass interference penalty against Nebraska right in front of the Missouri bench. That kept a Tiger drive alive and helped pull Mizzou from a 20-6 deficit into what turned out to be a sudden 20-20 tie.

The other incident Osborne wants to review on film came early in the second

quarter when NU I-back Jarvis Redwine, the Big Eight's leading rusher, was injured while blocking for an extra point conversion.

"It didn't appear the Missouri player was even trying to block the kick, but instead was going after Jarvis," Osborne said. Redwine, after taking a blow to the back of the knee, was used sparingly and settled for just 36 yards on nine carries after gaining over 100 yards in each of his last five games.

"I hope the film shows the Missouri kid just stumbled into Jarvis," Osborne said, not believing his own statement.

Nebraska appeared to have the game well under control at the outset until Missouri scored two touchdowns in an eight-second span right at the end of the third quarter. That's when Nebraska's 20-6 lead evaporated into a 20-20 tie. ■

1979 Season in Review

Won 10, Lost 2, Tied 0
Big 8: Won 6, Lost 1, Tied 0, 2nd

Date	Opponent	Site	AP Rank NU/Opp.	Result
Sept. 15	Utah State	Lincoln	8/	W 35-14
Sept. 22	Iowa	Iowa City	7/	W 24-21
Sept. 29	Penn State	Lincoln	6/18	W 42-17
Oct. 6	New Mexico St.	Lincoln	5/	W 57-0
Oct. 13	Kansas	Lincoln	5/	W 42-0
Oct. 20	Oklahoma St.	Stillwater	3/	W 36-0
Oct. 27	Colorado	Lincoln	2/	W 38-10
Nov. 3	Missouri	Columbia	2/	W 23-20
Nov. 10	Kansas State	Manhattan	2/	W 21-12
Nov. 17	Iowa State	Lincoln	3/	W 34-3
Nov. 24	Oklahoma	Norman	3/8	L 14-17
Cotton Bowl				
Jan. 1	Houston	Dallas	7/8	L 14-17

Final Rankings: 7th UPI, 9th AP (both post-bowl)

Oklahoma Does It Again– Spoils NU Title Hopes, 17-14

by Virgil Parker

Lincoln Journal Star

Nov. 25, 1979

It happened again. For the second season in a row, the Nebraska Cornhuskers came down to the final game of the regular season ranked No. 2 in the country and with a legitimate shot at the national championship. Only to come up short.

Last year, it was a 17-14 Nebraska victory over Oklahoma that set the stage. The next week, Missouri was the spoiler. This time Oklahoma triumphed by the identical 17-14 count, shoving the Sooners into the Orange Bowl, while the Huskers will settle for a consolation trip to Dallas and a Cotton Bowl date with the Southwest Conference champion.

After the loss to Oklahoma, the Nebraska players, coaches and fans didn't much care who the host team will be. And it's just as well, Arkansas defeated SMU Saturday night, 31-7, eliminating Texas from the Cotton Bowl race, but Houston still has a shot at the berth. If Texas wins its game next week, Arkansas will be the host team in the bowl, regardless of the outcome of Houston's game.

By New Year's Day the Huskers will have a different outlook. First, however, they must recover from the hurts–both physically and mentally–they suffered Saturday before a jam-packed crowd of 71,187.

As though getting bumped from a possible national championship for the second year in a row wasn't tough enough to take, the loss marked the fourth time in 16 years that Oklahoma has spoiled a perfect Nebraska record in a regular season-ending game at Norman, Oklahoma.

In both the 1964 and '66 seasons, Bob Devaney brought perfect 9-0 Nebraska teams to Norman. They lost, 17-7 and 10-9. Tom Osborne's 1975 club had an unblemished 10-0 mark when it came to Norman. The Sooners dominated that game while winning, 35-10.

Husker history buffs aren't going to like this. But in each of the three previous instances, Nebraska then went on to also lose a bowl game–10-7 to Arkansas in the Cotton Bowl following the 1964 season; 34-7 to Alabama in the Sugar Bowl two years later; and 17-14 to Arizona State in the Fiesta Bowl to wind up the '75 campaign.

Ah, yes. There's that score again–17-14.

And Saturday's Oklahoma win by that slim margin gave the Sooners the seventh straight Big Eight championship they have either won outright (4) or shared (3).

Defensive coordinator Lance Van Zandt tried to ease the gloom in the Nebraska dressing room by noting that "there are not too many teams in the country who can lose their last game of the season and be punished by being sent to the Cotton Bowl."

But Osborne, grim-faced and subdued when he met with the press, couldn't find even that much of a bright spot in the outcome.

"Oklahoma just played better than we did," he said flatly. "We had some chances to win, but couldn't get our offense going. You've got to give credit to their offense, however. I never dreamed anybody could gain that many yards (367) against our defense on the ground. And, besides, they hung onto the ball."

The Sooners, who lost six of nine fumbles in Lincoln during last year's meeting, fumbled just once this time. That–and Billy Sims–were the difference Saturday.

Sims, who won the coveted Heisman Trophy last year as a junior, may have become a repeater after gaining 247 yards on 28 carries before a nationwide TV audience.

Though the record books don't supply the answer, it was probably the biggest day for any individual against Nebraska. The best ever against the Huskers by an OU player was 205 yards rushing by Billy Vessels–who was also a Heisman winner.

Nebraska stayed close enough to win with a couple of "intentional" plays. Cornerback Andy Means conned OU wide receiver Freddie Nixon into clipping him while Sims was running for a touchdown. And twice the Huskers pulled an "intentional fumble" play that featured guards John Havekost and Randy Schleusener carrying the ball. Havekost gained 11

yards the time he ran with the ball. Schleusener went 15 yards for a touchdown to produce the final score with 4:43 left in the game, bowling over a couple of would-be tacklers near the goal.

"We'd never used the play before, but had practiced it all fall," Osborne said. "It's not legal for a guard to take a handoff, but he can advance a 'fumble' that occurs behind the line of scrimmage."

Here's how it works. Center Kelly Saalfeld snaps the ball up to the quarterback, who lets the ball hit him on the hands. He "fumbles" it down onto the ground. All the interference and the

backs–except for the one guard–start around one end. The guard picks the ball up off the ground and runs around the other end all by himself.

"It's a risky play," Osborne admitted. "You have to hope the ball hits the quarterback's hands and just drops straight down. I've never seen a major college team try it, although I've seen high school teams work it."

But pulling out all the stops wasn't enough. In addition to the "guard around" plays, Nebraska went for it on fourth-down twice, once when deep in its own territory. ∎

NU Coach Tom Osborne bites his tongue while trying to come up with a play during a 1979 game. (Journal Star Library)

TD Grab Takes Away Huskers' Cotton Candy

Cougar rally nips NU, 17-14

by Randy York

Lincoln Journal Star

Jan. 2, 1980—Tom Osborne is carving a national reputation for successful trickery, but you can bet Nebraska's seven-year head coach would rather be known as his old conservative self. Conservatism, after all, beats losing.

Osborne gave the national television cameras some theatrical things to play with in the 44th Cotton Bowl Tuesday.

But Houston was the team with the encore.

Second-team quarterback Terry Elston hit second-team flanker Eric Herring with a six-yard touchdown pass in the final 12 seconds to give the Cougars a 17-14 win over the Huskers before 64,017 fans on a mail order 60-degree day.

Three minutes and 44 seconds earlier, the euphoria exploded on the Nebraska sidelines when second-team tight end Jeff Finn snagged a six-yard touchdown pass from Jeff Quinn.

"When that guy (Herring) caught his pass," Finn said, "it was like taking a punch right in the gut."

It hurt . . . bad.

The Cougars stung a team that had been stinging their proud veer offense all afternoon.

They did something they had done six previous times this year—came from behind in the fourth quarter to win.

This time, they moved 66 yards in 13 plays to do it and spoiled a script Osborne wishes he'd never had to write.

Nebraska's head coach, frustrated with the results he was getting against a punishing Houston defense, reached into his magic pouch twice in the go-ahead drive.

Bill Barnett's fumble recovery at the Houston 31 with 6:06 remaining set up the opportunity.

The first trick was delivered on a third and two situation from the Houston 23.

I-back Jarvis Redwine took a pitch, then threw back to Quinn, who hustled to the 10 for a 13-yard gain.

Three plays later, on a third and goal at the six, Nebraska tried the old "swinging gate" play where 10 Huskers lined up about 15 yards to the left side of the ball.

Quinn then tried to center the ball in a continuous motion to Redwine, who made the cameras look good by bolting six yards into the end zone behind a convoy of blockers.

Osborne had discussed the play with officials before the game and it would have been legal.

But Quinn picked up the ball, sidearmed it and was called for an illegal snap.

The Huskers, however, got another chance at the six because Houston was offsides on the same play.

Quinn quickly turned disappointment into recovery with the six-yard scoring strike to Finn.

The Grand Island junior was the No. 3 receiver on the play, but benefited from the defensive traffic jam going the other way trying to cover tight end Junior Miller and split end Tim Smith.

Osborne wishes the Huskers could have delivered more in similar situations instead of being forced to play Puff the Magic Dragon.

"I really hate to use those kinds of plays," Osborne said of the pass back to the quarterback and the swinging gate.

"I'd rather go out and execute our basic offensive better, so we wouldn't have to use them, " Osborne said. "We just didn't play as well offensively as I thought we would."

The Huskers went into the game ranked fifth in the nation in total offense, but came out with less than half of their 465-yards-a-game average.

A Houston defense Osborne described as the best Nebraska played this season checked the Huskers to 13 first downs and only 227 yards total offense.

The Cougars were so domineering, they did not allow a Nebraska first down in the third quarter and forced four punts.

"I would guess Ohio State, USC and Oklahoma wouldn't be real anxious to play Houston," Osborne said. "They have a great defense, the kind you need to have a chance at a national championship."

Nebraska's defense battled gallantly, too, until the nation's seventh-best running team beat the Black Shirts with a dangerous weapon on any great running team–the pass.

Elston hit Herring four times in the game-winning drive on plays covering 10,15,11 and 6 yards.

The winning toss came on fourth down with lady luck delivering for Bill Yeoman in his head-to-head battle with Osborne, the now well-known gambler.

"We had two defensive backs in good position," Osborne said of the winning pass. "There was no way it could have gotten in there directly."

NU corner Ric Lindquist tipped the pass and allowed Herring an extra step to juggle the ball.

"It could have bounced down instead of up, but it didn't," Osborne said. "Houston's been known for this all season and it just happened one more time.

"It was a good game for college football," Osborne said, "and I feel different about this one than the one down there in Norman. No matter how the final ratings come out, I'm proud of this team."

■

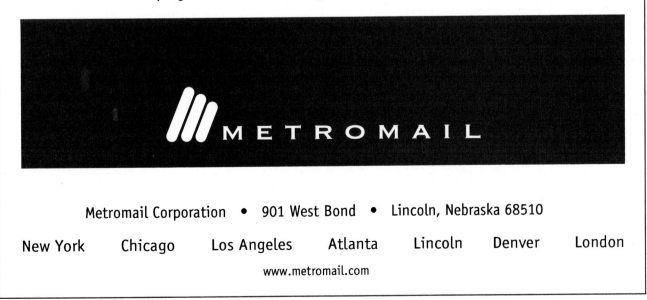

At Metromail, we share your commitment to excellence.

Thank you
Coach Osborne
For leadership by example.

Metromail is a national leader in providing database marketing, direct marketing and reference products and services.

Our team plays to win with insight, information and technology.

/// METROMAIL

Metromail Corporation • 901 West Bond • Lincoln, Nebraska 68510

New York   Chicago   Los Angeles   Atlanta   Lincoln   Denver   London

www.metromail.com

105

NU Black Shirt Raiders Sack Lions' Den

by Virgil Parker

Lincoln Journal Star

Sept. 28, 1980

Nebraska's third-ranked Cornhuskers passed their first major test of the season Saturday. Coach Tom Osborne's Huskers topped the 11th-ranked Nittany Lions of Penn State, 21-7, before the largest crowd in Beaver Stadium history (84,585) and a national television audience of millions more.

It was also the second-biggest crowd before which a Nebraska team ever played. Only Nebraska's 1941 appearance in the Rose Bowl was watched in person by more fans.

But Osborne didn't savor the victory for long. He winced when he found out Oklahoma was beaten by Stanford, 31-14, and was disturbed further to learn that Top 10-ranked Florida State, next week's foe in Lincoln, was edged by Miami, 10-9.

"I guarantee you Oklahoma will be a lot better by the time we play them," Osborne said before discussing the win over Penn State. And he certainly doesn't relish the idea of playing a Florida State team that is looking for revenge after coming off an upset loss.

Osborne did permit himself a moment to reflect on a "hard-fought and well-deserved victory over a very good Penn State team.

"They were certainly a lot better than the team we beat in Lincoln last year (42-17)," he observed. "They were well prepared and really came after us. They presented a lot of different pictures (formations) on defense. Obviously, I'm pleased overall to have won but I certainly wasn't pleased with the number of mistakes we made. Our performance on offense wasn't very pretty, but the defense really did a great job."

Nebraska lost three of five fumbles. Even more disturbing to Osborne were 10 penalties assessed against the Huskers totaling 141 yards.

"We just weren't consistent," the NU coach said. "We stopped ourselves with poor execution and penalties. We need to improve in that department."

Most observers credited the Husker defense with the victory. A fumble recovery (one of four) and a pass interception (one of three) led to Nebraska's first two touchdowns. In addition, Penn State's quarterbacks were sacked seven times for 68 yards in losses.

"I don't consider it a defensive victory," NU defensive coordinator Lance Van Zandt insisted, however. "It was a team victory. Our offense ran 86 plays to just 61 for Penn State. That certainly shows they were doing some good things."

Van Zandt also had praise for his defensive unit. "Our kids were real aggressive. The pass rush was improved. Our philosophy on defense is to make something happen. And I'd say we did af-

Husker defensive end Jimmy Williams celebrates after sacking Penn State quarterback Jeff Hostetler on September 27, 1980. Nebraska stymied the Nittany Lions 21-7 before a crowd of 84,585 at University Park, Pennsylvania. (Humberto Ramirez, Journal Star Library)

ter causing six fumbles (four recovered) and intercepting three passes."

Heisman hopeful Jarvis Redwine's running and quarterback Jeff Quinn's passing made the offensive difference. Redwine upped his nation-leading rushing average by gaining 189 yards on 34 carries. He totalled 179 yards against Utah in the opener, then followed with 153 more against Iowa.

Redwine's performance was the third-highest total ever against a team coached by Joe Paterno, topped only by the 251 yards gained by North Carolina State's Ted Brown in 1977 and the 224 yards Pittsburgh's Tony Dorsett accumulated in 1976.

"Jarvis did carry the ball more than before," Osborne said. "He ran tough to the inside as well as with speed to the outside. And he caught a couple of passes for nice gains (36 and 13 yards). I'm not one to pump up a player for the Heisman, but I've only been around one other back with the talent of Jarvis and that was Johnny Rodgers." Rodgers won the trophy after the 1972 season.

Nebraska never trailed. The Huskers scored on their second possession, then took a 14-0 lead midway through the second quarter. Penn State closed the gap to 14-7 at halftime. Then Nebraska closed the scoring with a sustained 74-yard drive in the third period. It climaxed when Redwine tallied his second touchdown. He's now had two TDs in each of the three games this year.

Nebraska had Penn State in the hole at the outset, but let the Lions off the hook momentarily. Defensive end Derrie Nelson came up with the first quarterback sack to push Penn State back to the nine-yard line. But a third-down, 22-yard gainer on a draw play by tailback Curt Warner gave the Lions some breathing room.

But soon after, the second sack, by defensive end Jimmy Williams forced a punt.

The Huskers couldn't move, but on Penn State's next possession, quarterback Jeff Hostetler bobbled the snap from center and Nelson recovered at the Lions' 30. Four plays later, after a 17-yard dash by Redwine, Quinn sneaked in from the one. Kevin Seibel booted the PAT and it was 7-0 with 5:55 left in the first quarter.

The defense set up the second-quarter touchdown as well. Monster back Sammy Sims picked off a Penn State pass and returned it 27 yards to the Lions' 19.

After fullback Andra Franklin blasted forward for three yards, Redwine caught a Quinn pass in the flat and weaved his way to the three. From there Redwine dived over the line with 6:51 left in the half. Eddie Neil kicked the extra point this time and it was 14-0.

Penn State took the ensuing kickoff and went 74 yards in 8 plays for its only score. The majority of the yardage was eaten up by a 40-yard pass that moved Penn State to the Nebraska five. Two smashes at the line, the second a three-yarder by Warner, produced the TD.

Twice in the first half Neil was short on field goal tries when drives stalled—the last with nine seconds remaining. Both, from 42 and 44 yards, fell short in the stiff wind.

Warner fumbled on Penn State's first play of the second half and Williams recovered at the Lions' 28.

"We had a chance to put the game away right there, but didn't," Osborne said. Three plays gained just five yards and Seibel took his turn into the wind with a field goal try from 40 yards out. His boot was long and high enough, but wide to the left.

Unable to move, Penn Sate quick-kicked on third down. Nebraska took over at its own 26 and put together the final scoring drive.

Passes from Quinn to Todd Brown (12 and 9 yards) and Steve Davies (11 yards) were the big gainers. Redwine dived in from one yard out for the touchdown. The clock read 5:55 left in the third period.

"That long drive of ours in the third quarter was the key to the game," Osborne said. "We had failed to take advantage of some other scoring opportunities earlier. It was good to see that consistent drive."

Osborne said some of Nebraska's offensive problems were caused by Beaver Stadium's big crowd.

"It was not a hostile crowd, but they were enthusiastic," Osborne said. "As a result Jeff (Quinn) couldn't make himself heard when he tried to audible. He did a good job considering that handicap."

Penn State put together the only final frame threat—with the aid of a 26-yard pass interference penalty—eventually gaining the Nebraska 11 before a fumble ended the drive.

Of Nebraska's inability to move the ball in the fourth quarter, Osborne said, "they knew we weren't going to pass at that stage of the game, so they (Penn State's defensive linemen) just pinned their ears back and came at us. We were just trying to stall things out and go home with a win."

Osborne admitted Penn State gave his club "a heckuva workout. I'm going to continue to vote us No. 1 in the poll (he has a vote in the UPI ratings), but you can bet I'll have Penn State among the top 10. Any time you can come in here and win by two touchdowns you're doing a good job. Now we've got to get ready for another tough test. A lot of people figure Florida State to be even better than Penn State." ■

Bowden Praises Nebraska

October 8, 1980

Gentlemen:

I have been coaching college football the past 28 years and have played before some great crowds in this country. I have never seen people with more class than I saw at Nebraska last week. The Nebraska fans, players, cheerleaders, band, officials, coaches etc., gave me a living testimony of what college football should be all about. I actually had the feeling that when we upset the Nebraska team, that instead of hate and spite the Nebraska fans thanked us for coming to Lincoln and putting on a good show. This is nearly unheard of in today's society. Nebraska, you are a great example for Americans to copy. I hope we show half the class your people do.

Sincerely,
Bobby Bowden
Head Football Coach
Florida State University

1980
Season in Review

Won 10, Lost 2, Tied 0
Big 8: Won 6, Lost 1, Tied 0, 2nd

Date	Opponent	Site	AP Rank NU/Opp.	Result
Sept. 13	Utah	Lincoln	8/	W 55-9
Sept. 20	Iowa	Lincoln	6/	W 57-0
Sept. 27	Penn State	State College	3/11	W 21-7
Oct. 4	Florida State	Lincoln	3/16	L 14-18
Oct. 11	Kansas	Lawrence	10/	W 54-0
Oct. 18	Oklahoma State	Lincoln	10/	W 48-7
Oct. 25	Colorado	Boulder	9/	W 45-7
Nov. 1	Missouri	Lincoln	8/15	W 38-16
Nov. 8	Kansas State	Lincoln	5/	W 55-8
Nov. 15	Iowa State	Ames	4/	W 35-0
Nov. 22	Oklahoma	Lincoln	4/9	L 17-21
Sun Bowl				
Dec. 27	Mississippi State	El Paso	8/17	W 31-17

Final Rankings: 7th AP & UPI (both post-bowl)

Osborne: OU Loss Hardest to Swallow

by Randy York

Lincoln Journal Star

Nov. 24, 1980

It's taken almost two days for Tom Osborne to realize it, but Nebraska's head football coach is finally able to see a silver lining in the black cloud of last Saturday's 21-17 loss to Oklahoma.

"Personally, I feel like we're on the right track," Osborne told the season's final Extra Point Club Luncheon Monday afternoon.

"We have gotten it down to a blocked punt, a fumble here, a fumble there or a penalty," Osborne said. "There were about three years there where we got beat kind of bad by those folks.

Now that Nebraska has closed the gap and doesn't need nine fumbles to accomplish the mission, Osborne has to view the situation as progress being an important product.

"If we keep working, keep plodding and keep moving in the right direction," Osborne said, "we're going to beat Oklahoma."

Saturday, Nebraska's eight-year head coach found little consolation with Nebraska's more consistent season than Oklahoma. Monday, he was able to appreciate it and accept it a little better.

"We didn't lose to a Stanford or even a Texas this year," Osborne said. "We probably played more consistently against the better teams, but we still didn't win the big one."

Losing to Florida State and Oklahoma with his best team served to compound the frustration.

"This is the best football team I've had as a head coach. I know that," Osborne said. "It's like Jimmy Carter and inflation. It all comes back to him. The losses all come back to me."

Osborne felt especially responsible for Nebraska's failure in short-yardage situations against Oklahoma.

At the time, "I felt the plays I called were pretty sound," he said. "But I wasn't aware there we were getting whipped at the line. We probably should have trapped, optioned out or even threw the ball. Personally, I should have done a little better job."

Osborne admitted Saturday's loss was "the hardest game we've had to swallow."

Although he felt his team deserved to be favored he also felt it was going to be a tighter game than the public anticipated. Osborne said he tried to play down that fact publicly.

"I figured we were even with us having a little edge on defense," Osborne said, admitting that was somewhat presumptuous.

"If you look at the North Carolina film and the Missouri film, Oklahoma was the best defensive team we've faced," Osborne said. "They didn't give Missouri anything but a meaningless touchdown in the last couple minutes."

Osborne thought Oklahoma's defensive left tackle (Keith Gary) might be a little vulnerable. "But he had a great game against us," Osborne said.

Osborne doesn't like to use a 390-to 275-yard statistical edge as "an alibi or a shoulder to cry on," but he admitted, "I told our team before the game that if we can outrush Oklahoma we're going to win. usually, I don't make a flat out statement like that."

Usually, Osborne isn't wrong on such things either.

Since turnovers did not contribute to Nebraska's undoing, Osborne categorized the loss in the "chance and random factors."

In Oklahoma's winning touchdown drive, for instance, "we had three players in position to recover their fumble and they had one, but they came up with the ball."

NU defensive tackle Henry Waechter "was quite vehement that he had the ball but he reached and pulled it in only part way. He never got it under his body."

Besides short-yardage failures, Osborne figures two other things worked against his team— 1) poor field position caused by poor punts "on a poor day to punt. We punted every time into the wind"; and 2) costly penalties, especially two that contributed to OU's last two touchdown drives.

"You can talk about jinxes, you can talk about emotion and you can talk about reading telegrams," Osborne said, "but to me, stepping with the right foot and preparing are still the most important things to winning."

If Nebraska had played Oklahoma's load option in the first half like it did in the second half, Osborne theorized that the Huskers' defensive end might not have gotten pinned in on Buster Rhymes' 43-yard game-breaking run.

"That was the only time we broke down in the second half," he said. More repetition in the first half might have eliminated that one costly mistake.

Osborne saluted OU quarterback J.C. Watts for completing a 12-yard out pass on the play before the final touchdown.

"He had tried it five times before and the receiver made a diving shoestring catch on his only completion," Osborne said. "Give them credit. He put the ball where he had to on the sixth pass. Great athletes on great teams do that."

Osborne still believes his team fits into that category.

"Now is really going to be the test of our character," he said. "The Big Eight is probably all out the window unless Oklahoma State pulls off a miracle (and beats Oklahoma Saturday).

"It would be very easy to throw in the towel. But we're going to talk about that tonight. I don't want players who don't want to play in El Paso to go. There's only one way to play and that's hard." ■

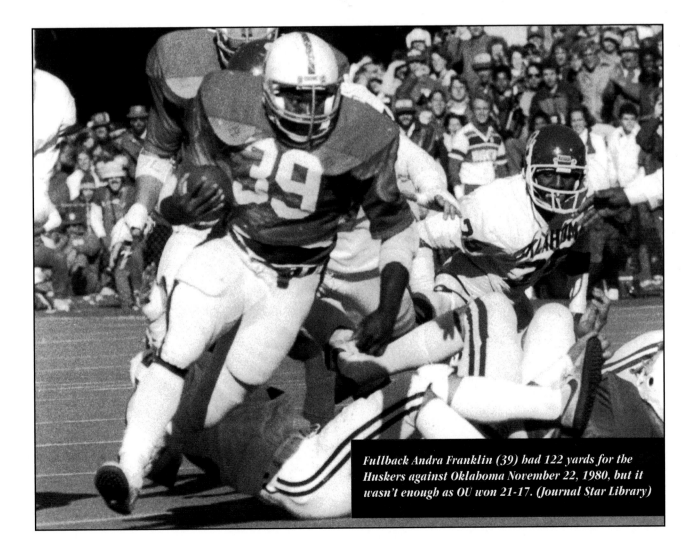

Fullback Andra Franklin (39) had 122 yards for the Huskers against Oklahoma November 22, 1980, but it wasn't enough as OU won 21-17. (Journal Star Library)

Osborne, Tenopir Work On "Air" Game

by Randy York

Lincoln Journal Star

July 5, 1981

In the day-to-day life of a summertime football coach, one thing stands out as a unique experience–Tom Osborne and Milt Tenopir soloed in an airplane for the first time last Monday.

Tenopir, Nebraska's assistant offensive line coach, was airborne at 6:30 that morning. NU's head coach taxied and took off a half an hour later.

"I didn't ask them if they had a bet or not, but I sensed a little bit of competition," offered Lincoln Aire pilot instructor Neal Bloomquist. "Milt told me the day before not to let Tom solo before he did."

Both Husker coaches vowed last winter to get a private pilot's license this summer and both are on schedule to achieve that goal before fall practices begin Aug. 17.

Because Osborne recently vacationed at Lake McConaughy and in Colorado, Tenopir holds a one-week advantage. He'll get his license in about three weeks. Osborne is a month from the same result.

"Both are real good students," Bloomquist said. "Milt took his ground school written test at Southeast Community College and has already passed it. Tom is taking ground school through us."

Originally, Osborne was more interested in an expanded knowledge of aircraft than a private license. He first expressed a desire to land a plane following the bizarre death of LSU Coach Bo Rein on a recruiting flight that ended in tragedy in the Atlantic Ocean 18 months ago.

"I just wanted to get a plane down if I needed to," Osborne said. "There have been a lot of times when I wished I could fly. Situations have developed with ice, turbulence, hail and lightning. Old and young pilots can have heart attacks. I'm not hooked into aviation as a business proposition. But I would like to be able

to get out of a tight situation if one came up."

Tenopir's motives are stronger. Since he recruits states where flying commercial airlines creates hardships, he plans to use his license to recruit.

Tenopir's recruiting territory includes western Nebraska, western Kansas, Wyoming, South Dakota, North Dakota, Colorado and Utah.

"There are so many times when it's impractical to fly commercial," he said, citing this year's successful recruitment of Jeff Bawdon of Williston, North Dakota.

"It took me two days just to see him and get back," Tenopir said. "I had to fly from Denver to Billings (Montana) to Bismark (North Dakota) to Williston. I'd leave at 8:30 in the morning and get there at 4 in the afternoon. I could fly there in three hours myself and get back the same day. Renting a plane would be so much easier and so much cheaper. It would eliminate the lodging and most of the meals."

Tenopir will never forget a 1980 private charter to recruit Doug Herrmann in Custer, South Dakota. He thinks it characterizes his unique problems.

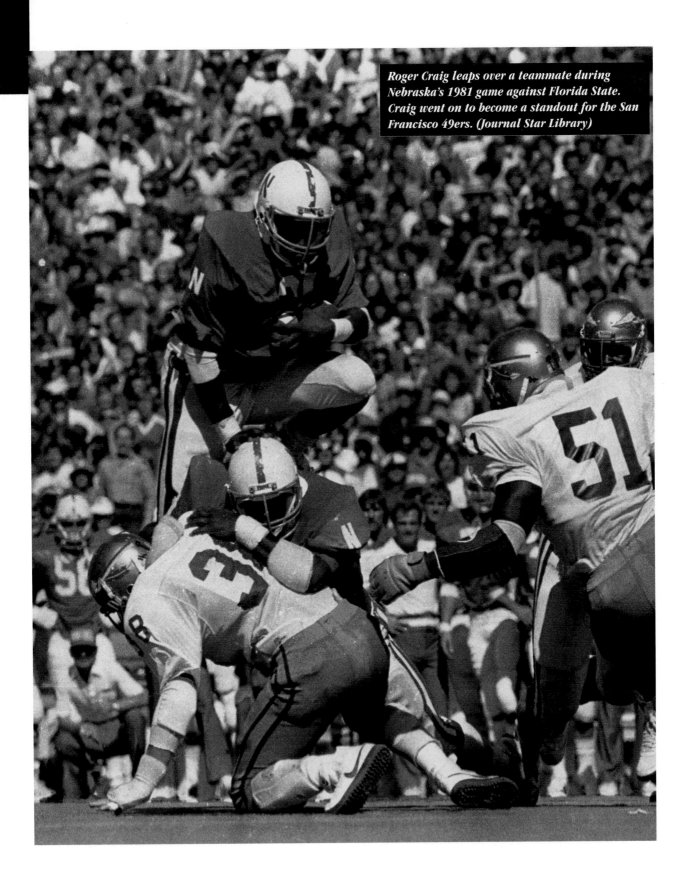

Roger Craig leaps over a teammate during Nebraska's 1981 game against Florida State. Craig went on to become a standout for the San Francisco 49ers. (Journal Star Library)

"It was hairy," Tenopir said. "There weren't any lights on the runway the night we landed."

Custer's unmanned airport is located in the middle of a field. On this particular January evening, all the pilot could see was a plowed strip of black runway between two high snowbanks.

"We taxied around after we landed, looking for someplace to go," Tenopir said. "Finally, we spotted a telephone on a pole by a hanger. We called the State Patrol. A patrolman picked us up and drove us six miles into town to watch Doug play basketball that night."

Osborne wanted to learn how to climb, turn, descent, pitch, roll and bank for security reasons. Tenopir is more serious. He's even thinking of going in with Lincoln grocer Paul Shuster in the purchase of a six-passenger single-engine plane.

"We're in flying for different reasons," Tenopir said.

Still, the competition is there. Tenopir has flown every day for three weeks. Osborne has flown every day that he's been in Lincoln this summer.

"Both coaches take flying very seriously," observed Dick Mickelson, chief pilot for Lincoln Aire. "Thursday afternoon, they were both out here at the same time, doing touch and goes."

Mickelson, sensing the football team resting in Bloomquist's hands, snapped a picture of the two coaches shaking hands with their instructor moments after their maiden solos.

"Milt was clear up on Cloud Nine," Mickelson said. "Tom didn't show it as much, but you could tell he was high, too. He sure was smiling." ■

Osborne Speaks

by Virgil Parker
Lincoln Journal Star

June 6, 1981—The fifth annual convention of the College Football Association (CFA) has not all been devoted to the CFA's squabble with the NCAA over television rights.

The meeting opened with a panel discussion on academics—what the football coach can do to improve the performance of an athlete in the classroom as well as on the playing field. Nebraska Coach Tom Osborne was one of three speakers. And his remarks were extremely well received.

Osborne challenged his fellow coaches. "You are great at motivating your athletes to perform at peak efficiency, to play to the best of their ability," he told the CFA members, which includes 62 of the top football programs in the nation. "That's why you are successful. If you worked as hard at motivating them to perform to the best of their ability in the classroom they would also be successful students."

Osborne noted that several things in recent years—particularly recruiting and grade-tampering scandals— "have cast aspersions on college football and damaged its credibility. Public confidence in college football has been eroded."

The Cornhusker coach blamed a "winning is everything" attitude for much of the problem. Because of that attitude, he said, many feel that anything they do can be justified by the end result (victories).

Sports Illustrated writer John Underwood was scheduled to be a fourth speaker on the academics panel. Osborne said he agreed to appear mainly because Underwood—who didn't show—was going to be there. Osborne was hoping to call Underwood to task for some of the statements he made in a SI article last year.

"He is supposed to be a friend of intercollegiate athletics," Osborne said, "yet he took several isolated instances (of falsified summer school grades for classes never attended, etc.) and made generalizations in his story which simply aren't true or fair.

"I have worked hard—very hard—for the past 12 years on academics,"

Osborne added, "yet the faculty looks out of the corner of their eye at me because of such articles."

Osborne pointed out that the graduation rate for athletes is the same or better than for the general student body, not just at Nebraska, but nationwide. "And that's the way it should be," he said. "We (football coaches) have more control over the athlete than the professor has over the normal student. If the athlete knows we won't let him come out for practice if he is not up on his studies—and he knows we mean it—he'll improve in the classroom."

Osborne did question the NCAA's 30-95 rule (30 scholarship maximum in any one year, 95 overall limit). "If you do a good job in the academic area and achieve a 75 percent retention rate, you'll soon exceed the 95 limit and can't give 30 scholarships each year. If your retention rate is only 50 percent, then you can give 30 grants. So what is the incentive for a coach to do a good job academically? We need to get legislation passed to raise the overall limit." ■

Huskers Win Duel Of Defenses, 6-0

by Virgil Parker

Lincoln Journal Star

Oct. 25, 1981

College football fans love a lot of wide-open offensive excitement. Coaches will tell you it's defense that wins games.

When Nebraska and Missouri clashed in a crucial Big Eight matchup Saturday, the coaches' style prevailed until the final 23 seconds. The action was filled with tough, hard-hitting, swarming defensive play by both teams. Then, the visiting Cornhuskers of Coach Tom Osborne, who appeared to be playing it "close to the vest" in order to win with an "automatic" field goal in the final seconds, handed the ball on a trap play up the middle to fullback Phil Bates.

Bates bulled into the end zone to produce the only points of the game and a hard-earned 6-0 Nebraska victory before a sellout crowd of 72,001 and millions more on television.

The victory enabled Nebraska to remain the only unbeaten, untied team in the Big Eight.

It's a good thing for Nebraska that Plan A wasn't used. After the touchdown, Kevin Seibel missed his first extra-point kick in 57 tries—from the same spot where

he would have tried the "automatic" field goal.

Missouri unwittingly helped the Nebraska cause. Not wanting the Huskers to have a chip shot field goal chance on the final play of the game, the Tigers of Coach Warren Powers called time out just before the touchdown play. They were obviously hoping for a fumble by forcing Nebraska to run one more play before the field goal try. The strategy kept the Huskers from letting the clock run down to the final second before calling time out themselves and bringing on Seibel.

Bates' touchdown prevented Nebraska from being shut out for the first time in eight years—a 27-0 loss to Oklahoma in 1973, Osborne's first season as head coach.

It also prevented Nebraska's first scoreless standoff since a 0-0 game against Indiana in 1938.

The decisive touchdown was set up with three pass completions by NU sophomore quarterback Turner Gill. The Huskers took over for the final time with 2:36 left in the game on their own 35-yard line after the defense had held and forced Missouri's ninth punt of the game.

Gill, who had been bothered throughout the game by a blitzing Mizzou defense, hit wingback Irving Fryar with a 14-yarder. Then came the most crucial play of all. After two aerials fell incomplete—the second was tipped and almost intercepted by the Tigers—Gill faced third-and-10 at his own 49.

He scrambled on a rollout to the right and found split end Todd Brown open along the sideline. The pass netted 24 yards to the Missouri 27.

Two plays later, with just over a minute remaining, Gill threaded the needle to Brown again, this time over the middle to the Tiger four.

That's when the cat-and-mouse game started. Nebraska appeared more interested in not fumbling than scoring as I-back Roger Craig gained one yard on two tries while getting the ball right in front of the uprights.

Then Missouri called time out, forcing the additional play on which Bates squirmed into the end zone.

"We called the trap play up the middle," Osborne said, "but Turner had the option of changing to a pass with an audible if it was open. It wasn't, so he went ahead with the original play. I was disappointed in our lack of scoring more earlier," Osborne admitted, "but I was proud of the way our players held their poise in a tight game and then came through when the chips were down at the end."

Osborne called Missouri's defense, "the best we've faced all year. This was the first game like this for Turner. They had great timing on their blitzes. He just had no time to throw. But this was a great learning experience for him and will really help him. The circumstances were very different than the Colorado and Kansas State games (Gill's only other starts)."

What made the difference in the final drive to the touchdown? "Missouri didn't happen to blitz a couple of times," Osborne said, "and one time, on the completion to Brown along the sideline, Turner managed to run away from the blitz."

NU offensive line coach Milt Tenopir said his troops were also adjusting better by the end of the game. "I'm not saying our offensive line played a great game," he said, "but we made some adjustments at halftime that helped. Turner also read the blitz better in the second half. When they come with eight people on a pass play, you can't block 'em all. Missouri gambled—and a lot of the time they won."

"That makes four games now since we've given up a touchdown," defensive line coach Charlie McBride noted proudly. "This team of ours today played the best defense of any team I've ever been around. I'll tell you what says a lot about our players. Missouri had a broken play in the fourth quarter which resulted in a 37-yard gain. Their quarterback couldn't find the guy to hand it off to and just shuffled a little forward pass behind the line to his tailback.

"That's when our kids had to decide whether to give the game to them or buckle down and play twice as hard. I was really proud of the way they responded. Our defense has improved every week. I just hope it continues to do so in the weeks to come." ■

Nebraska's Phil Bates (43) exalts after scoring the game's only touchdown with 23 seconds left to lift the Huskers to a 6-0 victory against Missouri on October 24, 1981. (Journal Star Library)

At Last! And How!
NU 37, OU 14

by Virgil Parker

Lincoln Journal Star

Nov. 22, 1981

The Nebraska Cornhuskers, Orange Bowl-bound against unbeaten and No. 2 rated Clemson, handed Oklahoma the second Big Eight Conference home-field loss in Sooner Coach Barry Switzer's nine-year career Saturday, completing a perfect conference campaign with a convincing 37-14 victory.

"Even though we had the conference championship clinched a week ago, it wouldn't have been a very happy championship if we hadn't won this one," Cornhusker Coach Tom Osborne said. "We didn't want to back into the Orange Bowl. Now, although I realize our chances are pretty slim, it's a little like 1970 when we went into the Orange Bowl ranked No. 4 and came out with the national title. A lot of things would have to happen for a repeat of that, but we're aware that it's possible."

Osborne noted the victory over the Sooners will be especially sweet to Husker fans.

"I've taken so much guff over this game I'm just pleased to win it," Osborne said. "Our goal each year is to win the conference championship by winning more games than any of the other teams in the league. So, realistically, every win counts one. But in the minds of our fans, a victory over Kansas State counts one, a

win over Colorado is four and a victory over Oklahoma is 10. Even though we had already won the conference title, it would have been a winter of discontent if we hadn't beaten Oklahoma."

Nebraska registered the victory behind "second-string" quarterback Mark Mauer, who, after the Huskers had gotten off to a rocky 1-2 beginning, was replaced by sophomore Turner Gill and had been used sparingly as Nebraska rolled to seven straight wins.

"Mark really had a great day," Osborne said. "Even though he was booed by our fans early in the season and received a lot of nasty letters, he was never bitter. He showed a lot of character and poise–throughout the year–and today.

"I am really happy for him," Osborne said. "People should realize the quarterback isn't the whole team. When the offensive line is performing well, as it did today, the quarterback is going to look a lot better than Mark did in those early

games when the line didn't play as well."

Orange Bowl representative Jim Barker was naturally delighted by the outcome.

"This gives us the best of all bowl lineups," he said. "Clemson is unbeaten and Nebraska has been getting stronger with every game. If Penn State can knock off Pitt, we'll have the No. 1 and No. 4 teams in the country in the Orange Bowl."

Barker and the 4,000 Husker fans on hand at Owen Field weren't thrilled at the outset of the game. Oklahoma took the opening kickoff and zipped 80 yards in just six plays to take a 7-0 lead.

OU full back Stanley Wilson, who led all rushers with 164 yards on 21 carries, bulled his way to a 21-yard gain. Quarterback Darrell Shepard dashed for 18 more and halfback Alvin Ross gained 12. Three plays, three first downs.

"It looked like it was going to be a long afternoon, like we might get blown right out of the park," Osborne said. "Oklahoma has some great offensive players. That's the strength of their team. One of our problems is that it's difficult for us to approximate their wishbone in practice with our scout squad. Their players are just bigger and faster."

Nebraska came right back with the ensuing kickoff to drive from its own 15 to the OU 21 before the drive bogged down. Eddie Neil came on to kick a 38-

yard field goal to pull the Huskers within four at 7-3.

"That might have been the key to the whole game," Osborne said. "If we had been unable to move the ball the first time or two we had it and Oklahoma had scored a second touchdown right away, we may have never been able to get back in the game."

Instead, Nebraska scored four of the five times it had the ball in the first half to take a 24-7 intermission lead. Actually, it was four-for-four. One possession was briefly interrupted when Oklahoma intercepted a pass. But it was promptly fumbled back and Nebraska had a brand new first-and-ten situation.

Nebraska took the lead for good at 10-7 after recovering Oklahoma's first fumble and driving 74 yards in 10 plays, climaxed by Roger Craig's 19-yard TD run.

Craig (102 yards) and alternate I-back Mike Rozier (105) both surpassed the century mark in the same game for the second time this season.

"It is really important to us to have two runners the caliber of Craig and Rozier," Osborne said. "They have more inside and outside ability than any we've ever had. Jarvis (Redwine) could get to

Tom Osborne concentrates while listening to an assistant during the Oklahoma State game November 7, 1981. (Humberto Ramirez, Journal Star Library)

the outside, but he didn't have the inside power of these two. In the middle 70s we had several eight- and nine-yard backs. Oklahoma had guys like Washington and Sims who could break the long run. Now

we've got them. Oklahoma has been good for us. They have forced us to get better. I think in the past they have won because they had the best team. I like to think we won today because we had the best team."

1981

Season in Review

Won 9, Lost 3, Tied 0
Big 8: Won 7, Lost 0, Tied 0, 1st

Date	Opponent	Site	AP Rank NU/Opp.	Result
Sept. 12	Iowa	Iowa City	7/	L 7-10
Sept. 19	Florida State	Lincoln	17/19	W 34-14
Sept. 26	Penn State	Lincoln	15/3	L 24-30
Oct. 3	Auburn	Lincoln	/	W 17-3
Oct. 10	Colorado	Lincoln	/	W 59-0
Oct. 17	Kansas State	Manhattan	19/	W 49-3
Oct. 24	Missouri	Columbia	15/19	W 6-0
Oct. 31	Kansas	Lincoln	12/	W 31-15
Nov. 7	Oklahoma State	Stillwater	11/	W 54-7
Nov. 14	Iowa State	Lincoln	7/	W 31-7
Nov. 21	Oklahoma	Norman	5/	W 37-14
Orange Bowl				
Jan. 1	Clemson	Miami	4/1	L 15-22

Final Rankings: 11th AP, 9th UPI (both post-bowl)

Huskers Can't Cash In On No. 1 Trifecta

by Virgil Parker

Lincoln Journal Star

A national championship was within Nebraska's grasp at the Orange Bowl Friday night. Texas had beaten No. 3 Alabama in the Cotton Bowl. Pittsburgh topped No. 2 Georgia in the Sugar Bowl. But No. 1 Clemson—and many thought a crew of officials from the Southeastern Conference—wouldn't allow the fourth-ranked Cornhuskers to leap-frog the pack to the top.

Nebraska contributed to its own demise by a final 22-15 score. The Huskers lost two crucial fumbles, one of which led to an early Clemson field goal and the other a Tiger touchdown—more than the difference in the final count.

"Clemson has a great team," Cornhusker Coach Tom Osborne said. "But the five or six major penalties which were called against us surely were a factor. Clemson has a great defense. You can't overcome a defense like that when they throw in a big penalty besides."

Osborne said four factors were mostly responsible for Clemson's victory. "We were unable to contain their quarterback (Homer Jordan). They had a great defense, probably the best we faced all year, and they had a superb kicking game. If those three things weren't enough, the penalties finished us."

Three times in the first half, a major penalty was called against Nebraska All-America center Dave Rimington.

"I wasn't blocking any different than I had all season," he said. "But I'm not bad-mouthing the officials. I got called for holding three times in the Auburn game by a Southeastern Conference official. Maybe they call it differently in that league."

Nebraska received the game's opening kickoff, but on the third play, a last-second pitchout from quarterback Mark Mauer to I-back Roger Craig was mishandled and Clemson recovered at the Husker 28.

Although the NU Black Shirt defense dug in to stop the Tigers, Donald Igwebuike came on to boot a 41-yard field goal to give Clemson a 3-0 lead with 11:39 remaining in the first quarter.

Nebraska responded with one of two scoring drives for the night. The Huskers took the ensuing kickoff and drove 69 yards in eight plays to take a 7-3 lead. The big plays were a 13-yard pass from Mauer to split end Todd Brown and a touchdown toss to cover the final 25 yards from I-back Mike Rozier to wingback "Slick" Steels.

But that was it for the first half. The next time Nebraska got the ball, Rimington was called for holding, setting the Huskers back to the six. As soon as the Huskers punted out, safety Jeff Krejci was nailed by a pass interference flag and Clemson soon had another field goal—this time a 37-yarder by Igwebuike to close the gap to 7-6.

Next kickoff. First play. Rimington was holding again. Two plays later he was called for clipping. The ball was back on the Husker six.

The following NU possession saw another clipping penalty push the Huskers back to their own 12. A fumble by fullback Phil Bates occurred two plays later and Clemson managed to gain the necessary 27 yards in seven plays when I-back Cliff Austin tallied a touchdown from two yards out to give the Tigers a 12-7 halftime lead after a two-point conversion pass play try failed.

Osborne tried to collar the referee at the halftime gun, but he went off the field on the Clemson side. "I wasn't trying to give him the devil as much as to get a clarification," Osborne said. "I wanted to know what they were calling so we could correct the problem. The official I did talk to claimed Rimington was grabbing the jersey of the man he was blocking."

On its second possession of the second half, Clemson put together a drive that assured the Tigers of their first national championship. Jordan passes of 12,16,7 and 13 yards–the last to all-America split end Perry Tuttle for the touchdown–gave Clemson what proved to be an insurmountable lead at 19-7.

Just in case that wouldn't be enough, Clemson's Billy Davis soon returned a Nebraska punt 47 yards and Igwebuike tacked on his third field goal, this time from 36 yards out, to push the count to 22-7 with 2:36 left in the third quarter.

Early in the fourth quarter, Nebraska put together its second touchdown drive. Ironically, it also covered 69 yards in eight plays–the identical yardage and number of snaps of the first.

Rozier had runs of 8,8,9 and 12 along the way, while Craig covered the final 26 yards on a nifty scamper.

In order to get within range to win the game, Nebraska had to try a two-point conversion. But confusion reigned.

"We had the wrong center in there," Osborne said, "and we wanted the ball moved to the left hash mark. Mauer didn't understand that. By the time it was taken care of, we were charged with a delay of the game penalty.

"We had a play to the wide side of the field called," Osborne said, "but Mark saw a monster blitz coming and audibled to a play to the short side."

A pitchout to Craig covered the eight yards to produce what proved to be the final score. Nebraska seemed to be in a position to pull it out. The momentum had switched. Over nine minutes remained. And Clemson was unable to move with the ensuing kickoff. It was three plays and a punt and Nebraska was back in business at its own 37.

On the very first play, Rozier burst up the middle for 13 yards and an apparent first down at midfield. But here came another flag. Another holding penalty and it was all over.

The Huskers were forced to punt. The defense never was able to contain Jordan after that. Clemson ran the clock down to just six seconds before giving up the ball. That left enough time for one last desperation play, a "Hail Mary" pass to the end zone that fell incomplete.

"That was the most disappointing loss I've ever had," Osborne said. "There was so much at stake. We had a chance to win it all but let it get away from us. Obviously, we'd have liked to have had Turner Gill available, but I thought Mark played well. If we had better field position, and/or hadn't had so many penalties." Then he paused. "But 'if' doesn't count in football." ∎

Tom Osborne walks off the Orange Bowl field after his Huskers lost 22-15 to national champion Clemson January 1, 1982. (Journal Star Library)

1982

Osborne: Cornhusker Effort Great

by Ken Hambleton

Lincoln Journal Star

Sept. 27, 1982

Nebraska football Coach Tom Osborne agreed with Joe Paterno's statement that "There was enough glory on that field today for both teams" following Penn State's 27-24 victory over the Huskers Saturday at State College, Pennsylvania.

"It was a good game with great plays and great effort," Osborne said in a Sunday press conference. "At times we weren't very good but it wasn't because we weren't trying.

"I thought back to last year and I felt Penn State was the best team in the country at the end of the season. They had all their skilled performers back and with such a good weight program and recruiting program they were able to fill up the holes left by graduation," he said.

"Either they're good—which I choose to believe—or we aren't very good. I think that they are one of the better teams in the country and maybe we will be one of the best in the country," Osborne said.

"It may be hard to anyone to go unbeaten this season. We'd like another crack at Penn State, maybe in the Orange Bowl.

"In some ways we deserved to win and in some ways they did," he said. "There's going to be a lot of attention on the last drive of Penn State. A lot of times you focus on the last plays of the game."

After NU quarterback Turner Gill scored to put Nebraska ahead 24-21 with 1:18 left in the game, Nittany Lion quarterback Todd Blackledge engineered a 65-yard scoring drive to provide the winning margin.

The drive started with a 15-yard penalty for a personal foul on the kickoff following the Husker score, and ended with a 15-yard pass to the NU 2-yard line and a 2-yard touchdown pass from Blackledge to Kirk Bowman.

"The films didn't show the kickoff foul. Dave Ridder threw off a guy who was blocking him. It's normally a call for striking or punching, but at that stage of the game we weren't going to get any breaks and we should avoid anything that looks like a penalty," Osborne said.

On the 15-yard sideline pass to receiver Mike McCloskey to the Husker 2-yard line, Osborne said, "I don't know how they (the officials) could have seen that play like that (inbounds).

"But the 15 yards for the penalty and the 15-yard pass play is 30 yards, and considering they scored with four seconds left, that 30 yards might have been hard to come by in four seconds," Osborne said.

Regardless of the final series, Nebraska's failure to score on its first possession set the tone for the remainder of the game, Osborne said.

"We had the ball fourth-down-and-two, and it looked like we had the play blocked all right," he said. "But we had a problem with the quarterback-center exchange and we didn't get any points. Some score there would have helped."

Turnovers plagued the Huskers throughout the first half, until quarterback Turner Gill engineered an 80-yard scoring drive near the end of the half.

Irving Fryar pulls down a pass from Turner Gill during Nebraska's 27-24 loss to Penn State September 25, 1982. (Randy Hampton, Journal Star Library)

"We didn't play that well in the first half and I was amazed at the halftime stats that showed we had 200 yards. It sure didn't seem like we did that much," he said.

"I thought we'd need 35 points or so to win and we just frittered away too many points in the first half. We needed 14 to 17 points in the first half," he said.

"On our blocking technique, we were a little high in the line and it was so noisy—much more noisy than the last time we were there," Osborne said. "The last time we were there we had a good lead and there wasn't much Penn State enthusiasm. Plus, the lateness of Saturday's kickoff gave their fans time for more celebration before the game."

The noise also forced the Huskers to stop trying to call audible plays at the line of scrimmage, Osborne said. "That meant we had to run some bad plays and that hurt some. Our players were a little jittery because of that and because they couldn't hear the snap count," he said.

Osborne said the ability and the performance of Penn State's offensive line were surprising.

Osborne squelches Patriot job rumor

Jan. 3, 1982—Nebraska head football coach Tom Osborne said Saturday he is not a candidate for the coaching vacancy with the National Football League New England Patriots.

According to The Philadelphia Inquirer, Osborne's name was included on a list of candidates for replacing Ron Erhardt, who was fired after the Patriots' 2-14 season. "I have no interest" in coaching a professional team, said Osborne, who suggested his name appeared on such a list because "people just start drawing names out of a hat."

"In earlier games it was hard to read the strength of their linemen.

"We knew they had great athletes. They had a great recruiting and weight program and had to replace some key people," he said.

"But yesterday, they played much better than they had before. They changed the line of scrimmage—getting six to 10 yards at a crack."

Nebraska failed to get a quarterback sack, and had just one interception of a Todd Blackledge pass.

"Defensively, we didn't slow them down all day. But the biggest problem was they executed so well," Osborne said "We had some poor plays, but Blackledge got the ball off in the nick of time a couple of time and they made some great catches. I don't know if they can throw and catch that well again. If they can, they'll be one of the better teams in the country." ∎

1982

Season in Review

Won 12, Lost 1, Tied 0
Big 8: Won 7, Lost 0, Tied 0, 1st

Date	Opponent	Site	AP Rank NU/Opp.	Result
Sept. 11	Iowa	Lincoln	3/	W 41-7
Sept. 18	New Mexico State	Lincoln	3/	W 68-0
Sept. 25	Penn State	State College	2/8	L 24-27
Oct. 2	Auburn	Auburn	8/20	W 41-7
Oct. 9	Colorado	Boulder	7/	W 40-14
Oct. 16	Kansas State	Lincoln	6/	W 41-13
Oct. 23	Missouri	Lincoln	5/	W 23-19
Oct. 30	Kansas	Lawrence	6/	W 52-0
Nov. 6	Oklahoma State	Lincoln	6/	W 48-10
Nov. 13	Iowa State	Ames	4/	W 48-10
Nov. 26	Oklahoma	Lincoln	3/11	W 28-24
Dec. 4	Hawaii	Honolulu	3/	W 37-16
Orange Bowl				
Jan. 1	Louisiana State	Miami	3/13	W 21-20

Final Rankings: 3rd AP & UPI (both post-bowl)

NU Coaching Staff Lauded For Ethics

One of the nicer Christmas presents received by University of Nebraska football coach Tom Osborne is one of which he is not likely aware—a rather unusual fan letter.

The letter was addressed to this newspaper, arrived virtually on Christmas Eve and gave everyone who read it a genuine lift. Being the Christmas season and all, the editors would like to share the emotion with you, the readers. No further explanation really seems necessary.

"Dear Editor:

"I am a high school football coach from Wisconsin and I have no ulterior motives for writing this letter. Five years ago, the coaching staff from Nebraska recruited two of our young men who were outstanding high school players. One of those players chose to attend Nebraska and the other young man also received a scholarship. However, it was at another major university.

"The young man who was given the scholarship at Nebraska did not develop enough to meet the challenge of an outstanding football program like Nebraska's. He also had a few academic difficulties during his first two years. Tom Osborne and his staff counseled with this young man and encouraged him to concentrate on his academic goals—to graduate. Although he did not continue to play football and directly contribute to the football program, he decided to stay at Nebraska, and was allowed to continue on scholarship and finish his education. He will graduate this year.

"My point is this: In this competitive pressure cooker of collegiate big business football, there are some university coaching staffs what would have made life intolerable for this young man, trying to force him to either transfer or quit, or they would have just used him as a piece of property.

"This young man will be graduating from Nebraska. He loves the university and the community of Lincoln and he has only spoken with the highest regard for the football program and of Tom Osborne and his staff. The people of Nebraska are indeed fortunate to not only have a championship football team to cheer for but also to have ethical coaches with a philosophy of not cheating, and coaches that truly care about the individual boys under their responsibility. Remember that, when Nebraska should lose a few games.

"Good luck Nebraska, good luck Tom Osborne and staff; keep winning and continue to run a class program. Oh yes, the young man who chose to attend another major university started his freshman and sophomore years. However, he had trouble with academics and drugs and has dropped out of school. He will not graduate!

Sincerely,

Ken Biegel
Lincoln High School
Wisconsin Rapids, Wisconsin

Osborne Nixes Offer By SMU

Jan. 16, 1982—Once again, Nebraska football Coach Tom Osborne was the No. 1 choice of another school. This time it was Southern Methodist University. But once again, Osborne is remaining a Cornhusker.

"It's no doubt but what Osborne was SMU's No. 1 choice," said Barry Horn of the *Dallas Morning News*. The Mustangs are seeking a replacement for Ron Meyer, who has accepted the head coaching job with the New England Patriots of the NFL.

"I know that the Nebraska job is a great one," Horn said, "but SMU was 10-1 this year, has everybody coming back and will be off probation next season."

SMU Athletic Director Bob Hitch said Friday he hopes to announce a replacement for Meyer soon.

Although Osborne could not be reached Friday night, Nebraska recruiting coordinator Jerry Pettibone said Osborne has turned down Hitch. "They did talk about the job," Pettibone said, "but I was sitting right with him —as were several other assistant coaches— when he called to turn down their offer."

With Osborne having removed himself from consideration, wire service reports indicate that Dallas Cowboys' quarterback coach John Mackovic is the top candidate. ■

"Simple" Trick Play Not All That Easy

by Ken Hambleton

Lincoln Journal Star

Nebraska football coach Tom Osborne reached into a magic hat Friday afternoon and presto... he pulled out, not a rabbit, but a play one radio announcer called the "bounceroosky."

The trick worked like this:

Quarterback Turner Gill bounced a lateral to wingback Irving Fryar, who relaxed as if it were an incompleted pass, then took the ball on one hop and fired it to tight end Mitch Krenk racing down the field.

That bit of deception produced a 37-yard gain early in the second quarter of the Cornhuskers' 28-24 victory over Oklahoma on Friday afternoon at Memorial Stadium.

What sounds so simple, however, was more complex in its execution. For one thing, Fryar didn't have time to relax.

"Relax? That dude was after my butt," he said of Oklahoma's Gary Lowell, who was applying pressure on the play. "He came flying in there, and I just threw it."

For another, Krenk had to stretch and make a one-handed, juggling catch, the kind of effort for which makers of highlight films search. "If I had more speed, the catch wouldn't have looked that good," Krenk said.

"Irving made a good pass."

The Gill-to-Fryar-to-Krenk razzle dazzle preceded by three snaps Nebraska's second touchdown, a two-yard run by fullback Doug Wilkening which brought the Cornhuskers from behind and gave them the lead for good, at 14-10.

Thought it was hardly the game's turning point or the primary reason Nebraska won, the unusual pass play represented the flair with which the Cornhuskers played offense on Friday.

It was one element in a diversified NU attack. I-back Mike Rozier rushed for 96 yards, all of them in the first half before he reinjured his right ankle and gave way to Roger Craig, who rushed for 56 yards. Gill passed for 74 yards and ran for 65. Wilkening rushed for 58 yards and scored two touchdowns.

Fryar caught four passes for 45 yards and carried three times for 20 yards in addition to his one-for-one passing.

"We knew we could run our offense," Gill said in a chaotic NU locker room.

There were very few things the Cornhuskers didn't try, and almost everything worked—like the trick pass, which, according to Krenk, was called at "just the right time in the game."

Nebraska center Dave Rimington wouldn't have agreed a week and a half ago. When Osborne added the play to the offense, Rimington told him: "I hope you don't use it until we're either 100 points ahead or behind."

"We had a few guys raising their eyebrows when Tom put it in, like 'What's this, a bounce pass?'" said NU receivers coach Gene Huey.

According to Krenk, Oklahoma's defense might have been just as puzzled, but the Sooners reacted quickly and "I couldn't tell for sure.

"It seemed like the defensive backs relaxed for a second, but they were on me awful quick, so it must not have fooled them too much," he said.

Osborne said he got the idea from Colorado; the Buffaloes tried the play against Nebraska "maybe 10 years ago."

The Cornhuskers began practicing it after the Iowa State game, and estimates of its success in practice varied.

According to Osborne, it rarely worked, Gill said it failed more often than not, while Fryar said it worked most of the time. Krenk said it worked maybe "50 to 75 percent of the time."

One thing is certain, under game conditions, the play has been 100 percent successful for Nebraska. The biggest problem in its execution is getting the ball in Fryar's hands. "He's usually the one throwing the pass," said Krenk. "Sometimes the ball takes a bad bounce, and the wingback can't handle it."

Since it's a lateral the ball is in play and can be recovered by the defense.

Fryar said the most difficult aspect of the play is throwing the ball under a rush like the one he got on Friday, not getting the lateral on one hop from Gill.

"That's easy on artificial turf if the quarterback can throw a spiral."

Unlike Gill, however, Fryar sometimes has problems throwing a spiral, "I can't use the laces because my hand's not big enough; I've got to use the back of the ball; otherwise, it goes like a wobbly duck," he said.

Friday, Fryar didn't have time to worry about his grip. "I didn't even see him (Krenk). I just threw it." ∎

Oklahoma's Dwight Drain knocks away a pass intended for NU's Todd Brown on November 26, 1982. The Huskers edged the Sooners 28-24, then defeated Hawaii and LSU to finish the season 12-1 and earn a final No. 3 ranking. (Ted Kirk, Journal Star Library)

Huskers Humble Defending Champions

by **Virgil Parker**

Lincoln Journal Star

Aug. 29, 1983

Nebraska made the pre-season pollsters look good Monday night as Coach Tom Osborne's No. 1-rated Cornhuskers thumped fourth-ranked Penn State, 44-6, in the inaugural edition of the Kickoff Classic.

The convincing victory before 71,123 fans in Giants Stadium at the Meadowland complex and a nationwide television audience, equaled the worst defeat in the 17-year career of Penn State Coach Joe Paterno.

And the Nittany Lions escaped it being his worst setback ever by scoring their lone touchdown in the final 20 seconds. The outcome matched a 38-point loss to UCLA in 1966, Paterno's first year at Penn State.

The result more than avenged a narrow 27-24 Nebraska loss to Penn State last season. It was the only defeat the Huskers suffered in 1982, while Penn State went on to claim the national championship.

"I was genuinely surprised at the final score," Osborne admitted. "I still don't know how good we are. I hope we're that good, but we still have a lot of improving to do.

"A team usually makes its greatest improvement between the first and second games," Osborne added. "I hope we're a lot better a week from Saturday against Wyoming."

Osborne noted that Penn State "had receivers running open during their pass plays. They just didn't get the ball to them, or when they did, the receivers dropped the ball much of the time."

The Cornhusker coach said that the key to the outcome was the play of his defensive unit. "They were the ones who were untested coming into the game," he said. "I was really pleased with their play."

Although neither team was able to move the ball on its first possession, Nebraska moved 78 yards in 12 plays on its second try to take a 7-0 lead with 7:11 left in the first quarter.

The drive was highlighted by a 23-yard pass from quarterback Turner Gill to wingback Irving Fryar and a crucial Gill hookup with second-unit wingback Shane Swanson—on third and 15—which gained the Penn State one.

Gill sneaked the final yard and Dave Schneider added the extra point.

The Huskers scored again on their next possession, going 86 yards in just seven plays.

Fullback Mark Schellen burst up the middle for 34 yards to get the march going. Gill then added 19 more on a keeper before finding tight end Monte Engebritson open on a 19-yard scoring play as time expired at the end of the first quarter.

Schneider's PAT made it 14-0.

"Penn State was up there in an eight-man defensive line much of the time to try and stop our running game," Gill said.

Mike Rozier became Nebraska's second Heisman Trophy winner when he won college football's top honor in 1983. Rozier rushed for an NU and Big Eight-record 2,148 yards that season and finished as NU's career leading rusher. (Journal Star Library)

"We passed a little more than usual and used some option plays—which they don't see much of—to get them opened up a little."

Midway through the second quarter, after Gill hooked up with Fryar on a 17-yard pass play. Nate Mason took over at quarterback for the Huskers.

"That was pre-arranged before the game started," Gill said, assuring that he wasn't sidelined by an injury. "Coach Osborne wanted to get Nate in the game early. That kind of experience in a tight game will be helpful."

After Mike Rozier ripped off a 14-yard gainer, Mason found second-unit tight end Todd Frain over the middle for the final 20 yards and Nebraska's third touchdown. Schneider hit the PAT again, producing the halftime count of 21-0 with 4:23 left before intermission.

"I wasn't yet convinced the game was decided at that point," Osborne said. "Penn State has a lot of pride and tradition. I could see them coming out and scoring a touchdown to open the second half. Then, if we'd turn over the ball to give them another score, we'd be fighting for our lives. I really expected this game to go down to the wire.

Coach Osborne diagrams a play on the sideline during NU's game against Iowa State November 5, 1983. (Gail Folda, Journal Star Library)

"I thought we could win it," Osborne added, "if nothing more, on the leadership and ability of Turner Gill. But I expected something more in the five- to seven-point range."

Neither team moved on its first possession of the second half. On its second chance, Penn State took over on its own 20. Two running plays gained eight yards, but on third down, Husker linebacker Mike Knox stepped in front of the in-tended receiver, picked off the pass and ran untouched 27 yards to the end zone.

"I think that was the play that broke their back," Osborne said. "After that we had the momentum and things just snowballed. I'm sure the game was not a true indication of Penn State's potential strength. They have a good coaching staff and good players. They'll be a good team before the season is over." ■

1983

Season in Review

Won 12, Lost 1, Tied 0
Big 8: Won 7, Lost 0, Tied 0, 1st

Date	Opponent	Site	AP Rank NU/Opp.	Result
Aug. 29	Penn State	E. Rutherford	1/4	W 44-6
Sept. 10	Wyoming	Lincoln	1/	W 56-20
Sept. 17	Minnesota	Minneapolis	1/	W 84-13
Sept. 24	UCLA	Lincoln	1/	W 42-10
Oct. 1	Syracuse	Lincoln	1/	W 63-7
Oct. 8	Oklahoma State	Stillwater	1/	W 14-10
Oct. 15	Missouri	Columbia	1/	W 34-13
Oct. 22	Colorado	Lincoln	1/	W 69-19
Oct. 29	Kansas State	Manhattan	1/	W 51-25
Nov. 5	Iowa State	Lincoln	1/	W 72-29
Nov. 12	Kansas	Lincoln	1/	W 67-13
Nov. 26	Oklahoma	Norman	1/	W 28-21
Orange Bowl				
Jan. 2	Miami, Fla.	Miami	1/5	L 30-31

Final Rankings: 2nd AP & UPI (both post-bowl)

Huskers Survive OSU's Upset Bid

by Virgil Parker
Lincoln Journal Star

Nebraska coaches John Melton (left), Charlie McBride and Tom Osborne look concerned during NU's game at Minnesota September 17, 1983. They didn't need to worry, though, as NU scored 21 points in each quarter of an 84-13 romp. (Journal Star Library)

Oct. 8, 1983—The No. 1-ranked Nebraska Cornhuskers stumbled over their press clippings and a fired-up Oklahoma State defense at Lewis Stadium Saturday afternoon before escaping with a narrow, 14-10, Big Eight Conference victory.

Coach Tom Osborne's Huskers, called the "greatest team in college football history" in the latest issue of Sports Illustrated, had to erase a 10-7 halftime deficit in order to claim the triumph before a partisan crowd of 49,600 that included about 6,000 red-clad Nebraska fans.

Did the famous "SI Jinx" have anything to do with the outcome? "An awful lot of nice things have been written and said about this team," Osborne answered. "You don't think that kind of thing will af-fect the players, but it's hard for them not to at least be affected subconsciously."

Osborne said, however, that Oklahoma State's tenacious defense had a lot more to do with the flow of the game than any jinx.

"They were one determined football team," the Cornhusker coach said of the Cowboys. "It will be interesting to see if they can come back and play that kind of game again next week (against the Oklahoma Sooners). It's usually hard for a coach to get a team up like that more than two or three times a season.

"But we needed a game like that," Osborne added. "I'm just glad we were able to survive and get out with our skin. I hope we learned something and become a better team from this experience. Maybe this will put things in a better perspective for us."

Oklahoma State entered the game unbeaten in four starts and ranked 20th in the nation (UPI poll), while Nebraska was unanimously No. 1 in both ratings. It was the first time since 1975—and only the second time since Nebraska and Oklahoma played the "Game of the Century" in 1971—that two undefeated conference teams have tangled.

"They had beaten some good teams," Osborne said. "They beat up on Texas A&M pretty good and also beat Cincinnati, a team that had beaten Penn State."

Penn State made the Cowboys—and Nebraska—look even better Saturday by topping No. 3-ranked Alabama, 34-28.

The Cowboys came out with a gambling, blitzing defense from the opening whistle. The first time Nebraska had the ball, Mike Rozier was thrown for a rare two-yard loss and quarterback Turner Gill was sacked on two successive plays for 8- and 7-yard losses. It marked the first times Gill had been sacked all season.

"I thought after the way we handled the blitzes of Minnesota, that nobody would try to blitz against us again," Osborne said. "Obviously, Oklahoma State made a liar out of me."

Osborne did allow himself one light moment after the close call against the Cowboys, a victory which made him the winningest coach in Nebraska history—by passing Bob Devaney by a single triumph. "At least I won't have to explain about running up the score," he said. ■

NU's Osborne Would Go For Win Again

by Virgil Parker

Lincoln Journal Star

Jan. 3, 1984

Damned if you do. Damned if you don't. Hindsight usually produces 20-20 vision. But Nebraska Coach Tom Osborne isn't going to be fitted with glasses. He'd do the same thing again.

When Osborne's Cornhuskers bounced back from a two-touchdown deficit to within one point, 31-30, of the Miami Hurricanes in the 50th Orange Bowl Monday night, just 48 seconds remained.

Most press box observers agreed, because No. 2-ranked Texas had lost in the Cotton Bowl earlier in the day, that a tie would retain the No. 1 rating Nebraska had held all season. Although tied, the Huskers would still be the only unbeaten team in the nation.

At a Sunday press conference, his last prior to the game, a remote but prophetic question arose. Osborne was asked if he would play for a tie to win a national championship.

"I suppose," Osborne answered, "if it was fourth and 20 and no time left, and it was a question of doing nothing more than throwing a 'Hail Mary' pass, you might kick (a field goal). But, if it came down to a two-pointer, or if you are inside their 10-yard line, you've got to go for it. It's a one in a 100 question. I hope

it doesn't arise, because if it does, I'm going to be crucified one way or the other."

When the situation did arise, Osborne didn't hesitate a second.

"Football is a game," he said later, "and you play games to win. It never entered my head (to kick the point after to create a tie). Maybe I'm not very smart. But I don't think you go for a tie in that situation. We wanted a undefeated season and a clear-cut national championship."

Miami Coach Howard Schnellenberger expected that decision.

"There was no doubt in my mind, that Nebraska would go for the win and not settle for a tie," Schnellenberger said. "This was a championship game and he went after it like a champion. Osborne is a class guy, a winner, and he did what his type of individual will do it that situation. We would have done the same thing."

Osborne's players also agreed. "I think Coach Osborne did the right thing," said Outland Trophy-winning offensive

guard Dean Steinkuhler, who picked up a deliberate Turner Gill fumble on the old "fumbleroosky" play to score one of Nebraska's touchdowns on a 19-yard run. "He's probably going to take a lot of flak for it. But it was a team thing, I'm sure."

Cornerback Dave Burke, who wore safety Mike McCashland's jersey—name, number and all—throughout the game, agreed. "We played a good season and we wanted to be 13-0. People have been calling us the champions, and when that is happening, you have to end the season like champions. When you are a champion, you don't play for a tie. You play to win."

Although Nebraska won't wind up the champion in the polls, the Huskers went out like one.

Down by two touchdowns in the fourth quarter, Nebraska scored on each of its last two possessions to pull within one point. The last time Nebraska got the ball less than two minutes remained.

After quarterback Turner Gill completed a 29-yard pass to Irving Fryar and a 19-yarder to Ricky Simmons, the Huskers were at the Miami 24. From there, I-back Jeff Smith, who had come on early in the second half after Heisman Trophy winner Mike Rozier was forced from the game with a bruised ankle, took a Gill pitchout to cover the final yards to the end zone.

It was Gill and Smith who tried to combine their talents on the two-point try. But Gill, under pressure, threw a little behind Smith as he broke to the right corner of the end zone. Miami defender Ken Calhoun tipped the ball as it bounced off Smith's shoulder pads.

"It looked to me, from where I stood, that Jeff had a step or two on the defender," Osborne said. "But Turner was under some pressure and he threw the ball a little bit behind Jeff. And somebody might have got a hand on the ball. I really couldn't tell."

Osborne added, "I really feel bad, especially for the players. But I'm thankful for the good things that happened this season. And I'm thankful to God for everything these guys did and for the kind of people they are. I've said it before. Football is a game. And it is. We wanted to win it very badly. But the sun will come out tomorrow. We'll come back. And we'll play well again next year."

With Nebraska losing for the first time in 23 games and because No. 2 Texas lost, Miami—No. 4 in the UPI poll and fifth in AP—is expected to be voted No. 1 when the polls are released Tuesday evening.

"It's all up to the polls," said Miami quarterback Bernie Kosar, who completed 19 of 35 passes for 300 yards—an Orange Bowl record—and two touchdowns against the Huskers. "But in my heart, we're No. 1."

"Miami is a very good offensive football team," Osborne said. "And their defensive unit sure played well, too. Miami deserves to be No. 1. I don't think any of our players would have felt right about backing into No. 1 by going for a tie.

"It was a great football game," Osborne added. "It came down to one or two big plays. And of course the biggest came when we couldn't make the two-point play."

As a result, Nebraska was thwarted in its bid for a national championship for the second time in three years at the Orange Bowl. Two years ago, Osborne's Cornhuskers had the chance to win a national title but fell to Clemson—which was awarded the crown—22-15.

The loss continued the woes Nebraska had encountered in recent post-season bowl appearances.

Although Osborne had guided each of his 11 teams to a bowl game, the Huskers have struggled to a 6-5 record in those games. And four of the six wins have been by a total 11 points, with victory margins of 3, 3, 4 and 1.

In addition to the Orange Bowl losses to Miami and Clemson, Nebraska's only setback of the 1982 season was a narrow and controversial defeat at Penn State, a team that became last year's national champs.

Thus, the Huskers have been narrowly beaten by the eventual national title team three seasons in a row.

The Miami game didn't look like it would come down to a two-point conversion play at the outset. Although Nebraska moved with the opening kickoff to the 'Canes 28—mainly on Rozier runs of 27 and 19 yards—the Huskers had to settle for a field goal try. But it was blocked.

Before Nebraska could recover from the shock, Miami was ahead 17-0. Two Kosar TD passes to tight end Glenn Dennison were sandwiched around a 45-yard field goal by Jeff Davis.

Ironically, Davis had made just one of 10 tries beyond the 40 in his entire career. He missed another of equal distance in the closing minutes which could have iced the game for the Hurricanes. But the one he made was the difference

Nebraska's Outland Trophy and Lombardi Award-winning offensive guard, Dean Steinkuhler, rambles for a 19-yard touchdown on the "fumblerooksy" in the 1984 Orange Bowl. (Ted Kirk, Journal Star Library)

in the game.

That initial Miami scoring outburst had the vast majority of the sellout crowd of 72,549 fans screaming their lungs out. Nebraska, although selling its total allotment of 12,500 tickets, was badly outnumbered.

Nebraska, which had given up just a total of 10 points in the first quarter of its 12 previous games this season—while outscoring those opponents, 139-19—found itself down by 17 before getting untracked.

And, by the end of the game, Nebraska gave up more points than it had to any opponent since losing to Missouri, 35-31, to close out the 1978 regular season.

Early in the second quarter, Burke wearing McCashland's jersey (they had switched in an attempt to confuse Kosar regarding pass coverages and blitzes), picked off a Kosar pass. Nebraska turned

that break into its first score.

But, when the drive started to bog down, Osborne dug into his bad of tricks, and pulled out the "fumbleroosky" play used against Oklahoma for a touchdown by Randy Schleusener in 1979 and later that same season in the Cotton Bowl against Houston to set up another TD.

This time it was Steinkuhler who picked up a deliberate fumble by Gill and rambled around the left side for 19 yards and a touchdown.

Nebraska forced Miami to punt for the first time after the ensuing kickoff and the Huskers moved 64 yards for another touchdown in 10 plays.

A clutch third-down 22-yard pass from Gill to Fryar kept alive a drive which Gill climaxed with a 1-yard quarterback sneak.

Although Nebraska trailed 17-14 at halftime, the Huskers tied the score on a

34-yard Scott Livingston field goal early in the second half.

But Miami, on short running plays which were set up by Kosar's passing, scored twice in the third quarter to take what appeared to be an insurmountable 31-17 lead.

That's when the Huskers staged their last-ditch comeback attempt. Smith scored both touchdowns, the first on a 1-yard plunge after 16 and 12-yard passes from Gill to Todd Frain and Scott Kimball got the ball close.

Then, after Davis missed what would have been a clinching field goal for Miami, Nebraska staged its final drive, climaxed by the heart-stopping two-point try.

As they always said in Brooklyn, "Just wait until next year." With Rozier, Gill and Fryar gone, that may be an empty threat. ■

The 1983 Nebraska football team was considered by many as the best college football team in history. (Journal Star Library)

Profile of Courage

By Randy York
Lincoln Journal Star

Jan. 4, 1984—Call it a wrong decision, a strategic blunder or anything else. But when you do, also call it a profile of courage.

Because that's what Tom Osborne's decision was Monday night in the Orange Bowl... a profile of courage.

When Nebraska's head coach decided to go for two points and a 13-0 season rather than back into a national championship with a tie against Miami, Osborne showed how courageous he is.

"That took a lot of guts," Nebraska Athletic Director Bob Devaney said Tuesday in the lobby of the Fontainbleau Hilton Hotel.

"They ought to give Tom National Coach of the Year just for making that call," Devaney said.

Although he didn't say it, Devaney's voice implied a footnote. Nebraska's athletic director wonders how many other coaches , faced with the same situation, would have made the same decision.

In Devaney's eyes, the courageous decision was the right decision, even though it was an all-or-nothing proposition.

That's one reason why Bob Devaney hand-picked Tom Osborne as his successor. He liked his style. He liked his conviction.

"I've just never seen a guy do so many things right and yet be so unlucky," Devaney said.

Osborne, indeed, is a snake-bitten man when it comes to national championships.

It's happened three straight years. First, Clemson in the 1982 Orange Bowl. Then, Penn State on the movable field. Now this.

If Osborne didn't live on a strong religious faith, he'd have a hard time coping with these things.

Tuesday, six fellow coaches voted Nebraska No. 1, even though the Huskers didn't beat the Hurricanes.

Osborne wasn't one of them. "I voted for Miami," he said. "Maybe I shouldn't have, but I did."

Look at the overall season and Nebraska's 12-1 is better than Miami's 11-1. But we all know the system doesn't work that way.

If, you're going to lose, lose early. If you're going to win, win late. And if you're going to tie, go somewhere besides Nebraska.

I loved Tom Osborne's courage. I can honestly say I prefer the loss to the alternative, even though it still would have meant a national championship.

I can't match too many national champions with the years in which they won. But I do know Notre Dame finished No. 1 in 1966 and Michigan State finished No. 2.

Even though those two team met on November 19 instead of January 2, everyone knew the game would decide the national championship.

Like Nebraska, Notre Dame was in the driver's seat. The Irish were unbeaten entering the season finale. Michigan State was saddled with one loss.

It was a titanic battle between

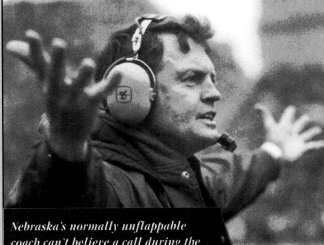

Nebraska's normally unflappable coach can't believe a call during the Iowa State game. (Harald Dreimanis, Journal Star Library)

Michigan State's explosive offense and Notre Dame's stingy defense.

Defense won. Or did it? Ara Parseghian went for a chip-shot field goal and the tie rather than the win.

Parseghian's choice was no greater than Osborne's choice Monday night.

Personally, I admire both coaches. But I still think Parseghian blew that decision that year.

He'll never know if his team was better than Michigan State because he wouldn't put himself on the line to find out.

History says Notre Dame was the 1966 national champion and Michigan State was No. 2 in both polls.

But that national championship was a tainted national championship. In no way does it reflect the true spirit of the sport.

Tom Osborne would not live the rest of his life, asking that unanswerable question. He answered it Monday night. ■

Osborne: Coaching More Than Winning

by Randy York

Lincoln Journal Star

Nov. 15, 1984

On Tom Osborne's state-wide radio call-in show Wednesday night, a minister in Gering made connections with Nebraska's head football coach.

Jim Irwin, the minister, was sitting in his home. Tom Osborne, the coach who once thought about being a minister, was sitting in a radio booth 69 hours before the Nebraska-Oklahoma kickoff.

The two were on the air, live, 400 miles apart.

Irwin had more of an editorial comment than a question. He pinpointed Osborne's Nebraska's roots and named several of Osborne's relatives faster than the head coach could name them himself.

Irwin said he knew all these people and he knew how they related to Osborne's basic character and integrity. But he still couldn't help wondering how a head football coach, in this day and age, could keep winning and winning without sacrificing those old-fashioned principles.

Even though Irwin had the best question of the night—wanting to know Osborne's old-fashioned recipe for modern-day success—it bombed.

It bombed because Osborne was apparently too humble, too shy and too embarrassed to provide much of an answer.

It's hard enough to get that kind of stuff out of him in the privacy of his office.

In this case, though, Osborne's philosophy is self-revealing.

To him, winning is not the truest measure of a successful football coach.

To him, this whole weekend does not depend on whether Nebraska or Oklahoma is listed on the left side of Sunday's scorelist.

"There's always been a certain tension between what's expected of you and what you expect of yourself," said Osborne, who admits it's "really important" to know the difference.

"As coaches and players, our goal is to prepare the best and to play the best we possibly can . . . and to live with the results and accept them with a certain amount of dignity, win or lose. That's what you hope you're about."

If that's too philosophical for those consumed by another quest for a national championship, consider that Osborne probably wants it as much as you do.

Although he insists his primary goal in coaching "is not the win-loss record, is not going to a bowl game and is not being No. 1," he admits that "being human, it is very difficult not to expect to go to a major bowl game and not expect to be No. 1."

Osborne seemingly is willing to pay that price only as long as it doesn't interfere with his honor and integrity.

Remember last January 2 when he could have kicked a simple little extra

Former Husker player and assistant coach Warren Powers gives Tom Osborne a congratulatory handshake after the Missouri Tigers lost 33-23 to NU on October 13, 1984. (Harald Dreimanis, Journal Star Library)

point and backed into his first national championship?

The thought never entered his mind and he has never looked back. He would do it again and again and again.

To him, coaching really does stretch beyond winning. "Coaching is a good business," he said, but the facts puzzle him.

"You go to a coaching convention and look around the room and there are not very many people there over 50 and even fewer there over 60," he related.

"And yet coaching is a profession. You go to a medical meeting or lawyers' convention and you see large numbers of people over 50 and 60. They are respected, men in the prime of their knowledge."

Osborne, 47, said he realizes "coaching is a terminal professional with a high mortality rate" and he has a theory about it—"because we tend to evaluate ourselves the way everybody else does. We think our worth is based on our win-loss record. We think we're unsuccessful because we haven't won enough games."

Even though he is the nation's second-winningest active coach behind Oklahoma's Barry Switzer, Osborne begs to differ.

"Eventually, about as many coaches drive themselves out of the business as much as outside influences—school boards, regents, the press, public pressure, whatever—a lot of it is self-imposed pressure."

Yes, Osborne thinks "it's possible for a team to go 0 and 10 and be successful in terms of having come as close as it can to realizing its potential . . . giving a good effort, preparing well, being intense on the field."

And sometimes, you can't quite pinpoint the whole problem.

"After our loss to Syracuse, naturally I was disappointed," Osborne said. "But I knew it was not because of a lack of effort and I knew in many ways, we had done the best we could on that given day.

"You can't be terribly disappointed," he said. "You can't be terribly up and you can't be terribly down."

That's how Osborne built that bridge over troubled water—from Syracuse to another national championship chance against Oklahoma and possibly, South Carolina in the Orange Bowl.

It seems appropriate that is happening to a man who won a nation's admiration for showing the courage to try and beat Miami with a two-point conversion pass.

It is only appropriate that a man who is considered by his peers to be the best coach in America get another chance.

Last spring, *Athlon* magazine asked 80 major college head football coaches who they thought was the best coach in America and why.

Fifty-nine ballots were returned and 20 voted for Osborne. His stiffest competition came from Michigan's Bo Schembechler and Penn State's Joe Paterno, each of whom received nine votes.

In characteristic fashion, Osborne dismissed the validity of any such poll.

"Those things are cyclical," he said: "That poll may have been taken after the Orange Bowl. I know it wasn't taken after Syracuse. If you did a poll every six months, you'd get a different name every six months." ■

Tom Osborne bows his head as his top-ranked Cornhuskers fall to Syracuse 17-9 on September 29, 1984. Nebraska lost twice as the nation's No. 1 team in 1984, also losing to Oklahoma while ranked on top. (Randy Hampton, Journal Star Library)

Missing Van Brought Tom Back To Earth

by Randy York
Lincoln Journal Star

Nov. 12, 1984—In Lincoln, it was a bee flying up his pant leg and stinging him on the sideline at the Missouri game.

And in Lawrence, it was a policeman having his red and white van towed away.

Tom Osborne's football team may be in line for the nation's No. 1 ranking, but Nebraska's head coach admitted Monday that his personal luck hasn't been all that great this season.

"See this?" Osborne asked, holding up a parking permit at his weekly Extra Point Club Luncheon before an overflow crowd at Miller & Paine.

"A lot of you got one of these last week, but I didn't get one," Osborne said. "A lot of you probably know by now that I got my car towed away at Kansas and I'd like to set the record straight on that. I did not park the car. My wife did."

Nancy Osborne drove the van to Lawrence and parked it eight blocks from the stadium. When the Osbornes returned to the parking place after the game, the van was gone.

"My wife immediately said it was stolen," Tom said. "I pointed out a little sign that said something about 'No Parking.' I said I thought I had an idea of what might have happened."

Osborne said the problem wouldn't have been so bad if John Melton, NU's veteran linebacker coach, hadn't been with him.

"By the time we got to where the car was supposed to be, he was all tired out," Osborne explained. "When I told him we were going to have to walk downtown, John sat down and started crying."

According to Osborne, after a few more blocks of walking, Melton sat down on another curb. "I was just glad his wife was there," Osborne said. "She finally told him how it was, straightened him out and got him going again."

When the Osbornes and Meltons arrived where his van was impounded, "I couldn't see any cars," he said. "There was this little shack that sold fish bait and the guy sitting there said he had my car.

"I still couldn't see where it was. But they had some kind of lot in the back and if you bought a couple dozen minnows, you could get your car back.

"The fishing was slow," Osborne theorized. "So this guy was sitting around and going after Nebraska cars. That was the way he filled in his spare time."

Osborne admitted he twisted the last couple of facs to match his frustration. But the $11 towing fee and $5 ticket were not figments of his imagination.

He did not say if the cab fare and fines were items for the expense account. But Osborne did admit "the game was sort of anticlimactic after that." ∎

1984 Season in Review

Won 10, Lost 2, Tied 0
Big 8: Won 6, Lost 1, Tied 0, 1st-tie

Date	Opponent	Site	AP Rank NU/Opp.	Result
Sept. 8	Wyoming	Lincoln	2/	W 42-7
Sept. 15	Minnesota	Lincoln	1/	W 38-7
Sept. 22	UCLA	Pasadena	1/8	W 42-3
Sept. 29	Syracuse	Syracuse	1/	L 9-17
Oct. 6	Oklahoma State	Lincoln	8/9	W 17-3
Oct. 13	Missouri	Lincoln	6/	W 33-23
Oct. 20	Colorado	Boulder	5/	W 24-7
Oct. 27	Kansas State	Lincoln	4/	W 62-14
Nov. 3	Iowa State	Ames	3/	W 44-0
Nov. 10	Kansas	Lawrence	2/	W 41-7
Nov. 17	Oklahoma	Lincoln	1/4	L 7-17
Sugar Bowl				
Jan. 1	Louisiana State	New Orleans	4/12	W 28-10

Final Rankings: 3rd UPI, 4th AP (both post-bowl)

Osborne Satisfied With Victory

by Virgil Parker
Lincoln Journal Star

Jan. 3, 1985—Game-winning strategy, Booker Brown, the "curse" of coaching at Nebraska and a "thank you" to the Sugar Bowl were a few of the subjects on the agenda when Cornhusker Coach Tom Osborne met with the media Wednesday before he and his Nebraska football team headed back to Lincoln.

Some of the topics were more pleasant than others. The least-palatable to the Cornhusker coach was the subject of Booker Brown.

Osborne ended a week of controversy over Brown's 12-year-old charges of illegal recruiting tactics by taking a lie detector test last Friday.

The polygraph results, Osborne said, proved he was telling the truth when he denied the charges made by the 1972 recruit. Osborne then asked that the matter be dropped until after Nebraska's Sugar Bowl game against LSU.

With the Huskers' 28-10 victory behind him, Osborne said "the university people are still talking to me about some potential (legal) action. As far as I'm concerned, I'd just as soon forget about it for awhile and get on with recruiting. I'm not saying nothing will ever come of it. It may. We'll just have to wait and see."

Osborne admitted the entire episode "was a very disturbing thing to me. The one thing I have tried to emphasize in our program, and to our players, is to do it the right way. So many people out there assume that big time athletics is corrupt, particularly if you win, that any charge like this is given instant credibility.

"The thing that bothered me," Osborne added, "was the amount of attention given to a 12-year-old charge that apparently was not checked out in terms of the track record of the person making the charge."

Osborne got more enjoyment talking about his team's turnaround from a 10-0 deficit to victory. When Nebraska still trailed 10-7 at halftime, several Husker players claimed Osborne "raised his voice" during his halftime talk.

"I don't do that very often," Osborne said. "When I do, I'm more likely to get their attention. We were getting out-hit in the first half. They were pushing us around. Nothing drives a coach crazy quicker than when a team is not playing up to its capability."

After the game Osborne said he "didn't make any special adjustments for the second half. We just played harder and better and things started to fall in place."

Wednesday morning he said one big change was made regarding pass defense. "We thought we could put some pressure on the quarterback by rushing four people," Osborne said. "We tried that in the first half. We not only didn't get to him, we couldn't get in there the few times we blitzed and sent six. So, in the second half we only rushed three—since we weren't getting to him anyway—and defended with eight. We dropped a linebacker back into the middle zone and as a result picked off two or three passes."

Osborne said if Nebraska had lost to LSU "it would have been tough to take. That's one of the curses of coaching at Nebraska. A 9-3 record would not have been very acceptable. Some may not think 10-2 was all that good. But the way the team came back to win gave me a very satisfying feeling for the season."

Osborne had especially high praise for the Sugar Bowl. "We've been to a lot of different bowl games but we've never been treated any nicer than we have during our visit here," Osborne said. "The facilities, the people, the hospitality. It couldn't have been better." ■

Husker Coach Tom Osborne shows his game face during NU's 17-3 victory against Oklahoma State October 6, 1984. (Gail Folda, Journal Star Library)

Heart Surgery For Osborne

by Randy York

Lincoln Journal Star

Feb. 4, 1985

Nebraska Head Football Coach Tom Osborne said Monday that he will undergo heart bypass surgery for a single vessel at Lincoln's Bryan Memorial Hospital on Tuesday.

After Osborne experienced a "fullness or a tightness" in his chest for the past six to eight weeks, Lincoln cardiologist Dr. Walt Weaver gave Osborne an electrocardiogram last Friday.

When the result was abnormal, Nebraska's head football coach underwent a cardiac catheterization at Bryan Monday morning.

"They found a blockage in one artery," Osborne said. "It's not a total blockage and I have not had a heart attack. There is no damage to the heart muscle."

Osborne said he was given three options and he chose single-bypass surgery, which he said should lead to a complete recovery.

Dr. Deepak Gangahar, a cardiovascular surgeon, is scheduled to perform the three- to four-hour operation Tuesday morning.

Osborne said he will be hospitalized approximately a week.

"I guess one thing I am concerned about is recruiting and I don't want this to affect that," Osborne said in an interview from his hospital bed.

"I hope the recruits who have committed and the ones who are considering committing will realize that nothing has changed—other than the fact that I won't be on the road for the next 10 days," Osborne said.

Although he admitted he intends to slow his normal routine, Osborne said he "is in no way contemplating any kind of change. I have no intention of getting out of coaching or changing my lifestyle drastically."

Osborne cited seven things that govern heart disease—obesity, exercise, diet, stress, heredity, smoking and drinking.

"I come out pretty good on all of them except for stress and heredity," Osborne said, citing a mitral-valve prolapse, an inherited heart problem.

"It's a fairly common valve problem that causes your heart to give an extra beat," Osborne said. "Normally, it doesn't cause any concern at all. It's like hay fever. You just get a little discomfort with too much caffeine."

Osborne said he noticed in the last six or eight weeks that "I wasn't running as easily as I normally do. After about three-quarters of a mile, I'd experience a little discomfort. At first I thought it was a virus or a cold. But it persisted, so I got it checked out."

Osborne said he "went hard" in recruiting and travel and "was able to do everything I always did except I got a little more tired and my energy level wasn't what it usually is.

"I guess I was very fortunate I was a jogger. There was no real discomfort that would lead you to believe I had a heart problem. I had no problems driving or walking around. There was no real pain at all. If I hadn't been a runner, the doctor said I would have had a heart attack and keeled over. The jogging enabled me to detect the problem sooner."

NU Coach Tom Osborne talks to members of the media after being released from the hospital. Osborne underwent heart surgery in February of 1985. (Harald Dreimanis, Journal Star Library)

Osborne said doctors gave him three options: 1) "go home, take some medication, slow down and see how I got along"; 2) angioplasty, a non-surgical technique where tiny balloons are inflated and press the blockage against the artery wall to open a passage. "Normally, you would do that," Osborne said, "but this blockage is at the branch of the artery and they didn't recommend it"; and 3) Bypass surgery, if you want to live a normal life and do all the things you've been doing. I'm sure I'll have to slow down for a few weeks. But I'm sure it won't affect me at all by spring ball. They say (after bypass surgery) you can run marathons and do all the things you ever did before. That's the way I want to go."

Osborne said the surgery "will be about like a knee operation in terms of slowing me down. It's not a high-risk type of deal. The odds are 99 percent of pulling through in good shape. So many times when people hear the word bypass, they're thinking about people who have had heart attacks or people who have damaged the heart muscle. I don't have that. I've got a good heart. I just have one artery that doesn't look very good. I imagine (after surgery) I'll feel better than I have." ■

Tom Osborne "In Great Shape" After Surgery

Nebraska Head Football Coach Tom Osborne came out of surgery Tuesday "in great shape," according to his wife, Nancy.

Dr. Deepak Gangahar, a cardiovascular surgeon, performed what was expected to be a coronary bypass for a single vessel.

"Tom's in great shape and the doctor said he has a very strong heart," Nancy said.

The surgery at Lincoln's Bryan Memorial Hospital was completed about 11:30 a.m., after about four hours.

Dr. Walt Weaver, Osborne's personal physician, scheduled a late-afternoon press conference to release more details on the operation.

Nebraska's head coach said he wanted to emphasize that he knew "a lot of fans are supportive. I have a lot of friends. But if they write letters, send telegrams or flowers or call or visit, that's just that many more things you have to acknowledge. I just really would like to have this treated like a head cold—have people forget about it and let it go at that.

"I kind of look at this as a warning," he said. "Nancy has been telling me for years that I'm going to crack up if I don't change. And so maybe this will do it.

"I probably won't go quite as hard in the future," Osborne said. "I probably won't go five days a week from seven in the morning till midnight, then put in 16-hour days on weekends." ■

1985 Season in Review

Won 9, Lost 3
Big 8: Won 6, Lost 1, Tied 0, 2nd

Date	Opponent	Site	AP Rank NU/Opp.	Result
Sept. 7	Florida State	Lincoln	10/17	L 13-17
Sept. 21	Illinois	Lincoln	18/	W 52-25
Sept. 28	Oregon	Lincoln	16/	W 63-0
Oct. 5	New Mexico	Lincoln	13/	W 38-7
Oct. 12	Oklahoma St.	Stillwater	9/5	W 34-24
Oct. 19	Missouri	Columbia	7/	W 28-20
Oct. 26	Colorado	Lincoln	5/	W 17-7
Nov. 2	Kansas State	Manhattan	5/	W 41-3
Nov. 9	Iowa State	Lincoln	3/	W 49-0
Nov. 16	Kansas	Lincoln	2/	W 56-6
Nov. 23	Oklahoma	Norman	2/5	L 7-27

Sunkist Fiesta Bowl

Date	Opponent	Site	AP Rank NU/Opp.	Result
Jan. 1	Michigan	Tempe	7/5	L 23-27

Final Rankings: 10th UPI, 11th AP (both post-bowl)

Operation Seen As Chance For Osborne To Reflect

by Randy York

Lincoln Journal Star

Feb. 8, 1985

One of the most difficult things about coaching is you're always reacting. You never have time to reflect."

Tom Osborne made that statement a couple of months ago, but I'm sure Nebraska's head football coach never thought reality could change so quickly.

Here he is, less than a week from national letter-of-intent day, and he's looking at those antiseptic walls in a hospital.

For such a self-driven man, it has to be the most abrupt change imaginable.

I was not surprised when a secretary in the Nebraska football office said Osborne had called NU recruiting coordinator Steve Pederson Wednesday from intensive care.

The incident fit the personality.

Remember, this is a man who turned on an overhead light and started drawing new pass patterns on the bus ride to the airport after Nebraska lost, 27-24, at Penn State in 1982.

Ursula Walsh, Nebraska's academic counselor, was sitting next to Osborne at the time.

"This is kind of unhealthy, isn't it?" she asked.

"I've got to do something," he told her.

Osborne is the ultimate time-use efficiency expert.

Even though he's recovering from open-heart surgery, he has to be one of the strongest bypass patients in the country.

Few know this, but Tom Osborne not only jogged five miles a day, but also lifted weights three times a week.

"He's been lifting since last June," NU strength coach Boyd Epley said Thursday. "He started lifting when his son and daughter started lifting."

Osborne lifted for fitness more than strength. Still, "he's not your typical 47-year-old," Epley said. "He's very religious about his lifting. He would come in on weekends to get in his third day. Down at the Sugar Bowl, he jumped right on a hip sled and did 510 pounds."

When Osborne starts anything, he goes after it harder than anyone else.

It's his nature. He hates to waste time.

I wonder what he'll do these next few days.

I know he won't be tuning in "the Price is Right" or "Days of Our Lives."

He's probably itching to dial a recruit's telephone number.

One NU football secretary thinks he'll set the world record for being the quickest man to jog after major surgery.

A member of the Husker coaching staff said he wouldn't be surprised if Osborne showed up at the stadium this weekend. More recruits, after all, are visiting.

Type A personalities just don't change after a three-hour operation.

But I'm hoping those close to Osborne are wrong about their leader this one time.

I'm hoping Tom Osborne takes this rare opportunity to reflect rather than react.

There's a sign in the Osborne family kitchen that says it all: "We interrupt this marriage to bring you the football season."

In the Osborne household, everyone understands—wife Nancy, son Mike and daughters Ann and Suzi.

Sure, they spend Easter vacations skiing in Colorado and summer vacations fishing at Lake McConaughy.

But the Osbornes never have had a

winter where they can just hibernate with their own thoughts and without interference from the outside world.

When Tom became a coach, he and his wife made a pact—Thursday nights would always be open.

"We made a decision to always ease off that night," he said. "Even if our sched- ules are full, we make sure we spend a couple hours over a cup of coffee to talk everything over. My marriage is very important to me. It's very easy for two people to go their separate directions. We work at it."

Nancy calls Thursday nights "our sacred time. It's the only time in the whole week where we really touch base during the season. When you're raising teenagers, you need to support each other on decisions."

Well, now the Osbornes have a whole month of sacred time.

And I bet they cherish it more than anyone expects. ■

Nebraska's Dale Klein set an NCAA record with seven field goals in the Huskers' 28-20 victory against Missouri on October 19, 1985. (Humberto Ramirez, Journal Star Library)

Sooners Pop Huskers' Bubble

by Virgil Parker

Lincoln Journal Star

Nov. 24, 1985

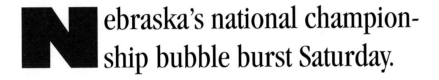 ebraska's national champion-ship bubble burst Saturday.

Before a boisterous hometown crowd of 75,004 at Owen Field, Oklahoma totally dominated the Cornhuskers while rolling to a 27-7 victory.

The triumph earned the Sooners the Orange Bowl berth that No. 2-ranked Nebraska coveted for a chance to play No. 1-rated Penn State.

Instead, Oklahoma will head for the beach, while Nebraska will line up earlier New Year's Day against Big Ten runner-up Michigan at the Fiesta Bowl in Tempe, Arizona.

Nebraska averted its first shutout in 146 games when defensive tackle Chris Spachman picked off a fumble (ruled an interception) in mid-air and rambled 76 yards to score with just 26 seconds left in the game.

The last time the Huskers were blanked occurred in 1973, NU Coach Tom Osborne's first season. And Oklahoma administered that defeat by the same 27-0 count that stood before Spachman's fumble return.

Husker fullback Tom Rathman summed up the Nebraska disappointment. "It seems like Nebraska has a shot at the national championship every year," Rathman said, "but ever since I've been here, we have fallen one game short."

Although it was of little consolation, Rathman noted that Nebraska—with just four starters returning, two on offense and two on defense—was a preseason pick to finish third in the Big Eight.

"A lot of people didn't think we'd win nine games," Rathman said, "so I think we've had a successful season."

"I'm not too proud of the way we played today. We just got a good kicking," Osborne said, "but our guys have had a great year. We knew before we came down here that Oklahoma was a great team. And I saw nothing today to change my mind.

"They have as good a defense, I think, as they have ever had—and that includes when they had the Selmon brothers. They outplayed us badly. And their speed on offense was outstanding."

In past years, Nebraska has been known to pull out a trick play or two against the Sooners, This time the tempo—and the eventual outcome—were set when Oklahoma Coach Barry Switzer came up with a reverse to tight end Keith Jackson that went 88 yards for a touchdown the second time the Sooners had the ball.

OU, aided by a 38-yard pass from freshman quarterback Jamelle Holieway to Jackson, tallied another touchdown on its next possession. Holieway zipped the final 43 yards on a keeper play to complete a 90-yard drive in just six plays. That made it 14-0 midway through the first quarter.

Nebraska never recovered.

"The tight end reverse and our inability to move the ball early took us out of the ball game," Osborne said. "We'd never seen them run the tight end reverse and Jackson is big and fast. But they have a lot of great athletes. (Fullback Lydell) Carr keeps you honest, and the quarterback then does the damage."

Three Huskers had a shot at Holieway on the first of his two TD runs, but nobody could corner the darting 5-9, 175-pounder.

"We did not tackle well," Osborne admitted. "I've got to believe that we're better tacklers than that, but then their

147

talent had a lot to do with it, too. That Holieway is hard to get ahold of."

Nebraska's defense, which went into the game ranked third in the nation against the rush, gave up a whopping 423 yards to the Sooners' wishbone attack.

On the other hand, Oklahoma, second in the country against the run, limited the Huskers to just 161 yards rushing. That was almost 100 yards below the worst previous Nebraska output (256 rushing yards in a victory over Oklahoma State).

And 52 of Nebraska's rushing yards came on one play—a wingback reserve by Von Sheppard. Doug DuBose, Nebraska's all-conference I-back, was limited to just 46 yards on 16 carries.

Nebraska's 10 first downs were five less than against Florida State (the previous low).

Oklahoma extended its lead to 17-zip just before halftime on a 36-yard field goal by Tim Lashar. He then upped the count to 20-0 with a 34-yarder midway through the third quarter.

Holieway followed with a 17-yard scamper later in the third frame to complete the Oklahoma scoring. Then came Spachman's last-gasp effort to avoid the shutout.

Nebraska was not without its chances. Sheppard's long run gained the Sooners 6, but two keepers by Husker starting quarterback McCathorn Clayton didn't gain an inch and his third-down pass was off the mark.

That brought on Dale Klein, who made 13 of 19 field goals this season. But his short 23-yard effort was wide right.

"If we had been able to get that one in for a touchdown," Osborne observed, "we would have cut the score to 14-7 and been back in the ball game."

It wasn't to be.

Neither was it to be when two other Nebraska opportunities arose.

Late in the third quarter, Oklahoma's Derrick Shepard signaled for a fair catch of a Dan Wingard punt. He muffed the catch and NU's Mike Hoefler appeared to recover the ball at the Sooner 20. But one of the officials inadvertently blew his whistle and the play was replayed.

"The official knew he was wrong and was sorry about it," Osborne said, "but that didn't help us any."

Midway through the fourth quarter, after a poor Oklahoma punt, Nebraska took over at the OU 24.

Husker freshman quarterback Steve Taylor, who had relieved Clayton on Nebraska's second possession of the second half, completed a pass to tight end Todd Frain that gained the OU 8.

Taylor gained seven more yards on a keeper to put the ball on the Sooner 1. But after DuBose was thrown for a one-yard loss, Taylor bobbled the snap from center and Oklahoma recovered.

"If it hadn't been for a couple of bad things like that happening to us," Osborne said, "we might have made it a closer game. But I doubt it would have changed the outcome." ■

Oklahoma tight end Keith Jackson (88) breaks loose on an 88-yard end around for the Sooners' first touchdown in a 27-7 win November 23, 1985. (Ted Kirk, Journal Star Library)

Tom Osborne talks with Oklahoma Coach Barry Switzer before the 1985 game between the two schools. Osborne and Switzer came into the Big Eight Conference the same year. (Journal Star Library)

Showdown Overshadows Huskers' Season Of Turmoil

by Ken Hambleton

Lincoln Journal Star

Nov. 21, 1986

For about three hours Saturday afternoon, all that matters in Lincoln is the Nebraska-Oklahoma game.

There will be a game in town. It won't matter that one team is rated higher or one team has won more games from the other team. It won't matter which team has the most yards between television timeouts.

All that will matter to the 76,000 folks in Memorial Stadium and the few million watching on television is the entertainment of a football game.

This has been a football season like no other at Nebraska. And it's not just because no two seasons are alike the same way no two snowflakes and no two fingerprints are alike. This has been the season of the first extensive NCAA probe and first NCAA probation for the Nebraska football program.

Before the season started, Nebraska lost its Heisman Trophy hopeful when Doug DuBose was running along and a minute later was writhing on the Astroturf. A day later, he was out for the season.

Three days before the season started, 60 players started looking for tickets for themselves to get into the Florida State game. A few days later, those players were just looking for tickets to get their parents in the game.

Then, there was another close encounter with the NCAA that ended with the revelations that DuBose had gotten a ride and advice on leasing a car from an academic counselor. He still couldn't play and the academic counselor won't get a raise for a couple of months. The NCAA also graciously accepted the ending of the Lincoln parents program.

The distractions of daily inquiries weighed heavily on each practice, but finally the inquiries ended.

It seemed there were weekly reports of infractions by Nebraska football players. Not much more than usual and no more than a reasonable percentage of the total football player population. The incidents, even minor traffic violations, received the level of attention usually reserved for more important things. Deserved or not, the players learned they are not above the law, nor behind the shield of privacy.

The Huskers almost lost to South Carolina, a team with just one win at the time. Colorado broke an 18-year drought and left Nebraskans bewildered. The victory also led fans of the Buffaloes to believe their team had graduated from the "little six." They were wrong.

There were injuries to offensive players, the likes of which hadn't been experienced before. I-backs and tight ends at Nebraska became an endangered species.

Some recovered. Nebraska bounced back from the Colorado loss and has as good a chance as any team to beat Oklahoma. The Huskers still have concerns about a planned in-depth article in *Sports Illustrated* that has been in the works for

Coach Tom Osborne (left), assistant Charlie McBride and a student manager desperately try to call time out at the end of the first half of NU's game vs. Colorado, October 25, 1986. (Journal Star Library)

at least five weeks. The story is not expected to praise the tradition of success at NU. A *Sports Illustrated* writer in town for the Nebraska-Oklahoma game said that people seem to be nervous around him.

But it appears the sun will shine again. Nebraska has a shot (read: long) at winning the national title. The Huskers will be in a major bowl game regardless of the outcome of the game with Oklahoma. The probation should be lifted within the next seven months. The Huskers have a lot of underclassmen and with a strong recruiting year, could be good again next year.

Saturday afternoon, for about three hours, there will be no bowl bids, television contracts, investigations, allegations, infractions and no sub-committee on eligibility.

There is only the game. Isn't that what started all this business anyway? ■

Tom Osborne doesn't let a little snow bother him during NU's November 1 game against Kansas State. (Journal Star Library)

1986

Season in Review

Won 10, Lost 2, Tied 0
Big 8: Won 5, Lost 2, Tied 0, 3rd-tie

Date	Opponent	Site	AP Rank NU/Opp.	Result
Sept. 6	Florida State	Lincoln	8/11	W 34-17
Sept. 20	Illinois	Champaign	6/	W 59-14
Sept. 27	Oregon	Lincoln	4/	W 48-14
Oct. 4	South Carolina	Columbia	3/	W 27-24
Oct. 11	Oklahoma State	Lincoln	3/	W 30-10
Oct. 18	Missouri	Lincoln	3/	W 48-17
Oct. 25	Colorado	Boulder	3/	L 10-20
Nov. 1	Kansas State	Lincoln	9/	W 38-0
Nov. 8	Iowa State	Ames	7/	W 35-14
Nov. 15	Kansas	Lawrence	6/	W 70-0
Nov. 22	Oklahoma	Lincoln	5/3	L 17-20
USF&G Sugar Bowl				
Jan. 1	Louisiana State	New Orleans	6/5	W 30-15

Final Rankings: 4th UPI, 5th AP (both post-bowl)

"Weird" 4 Minutes Doom Huskers

by Mike Babcock

Lincoln Journal Star

Everything just wasn't enough.

That's what the Memorial Stadium scoreboard said, with numbers.

Prior to Saturday's game with third-ranked Oklahoma, Nebraska head football coach Tom Osborne told his players "we wanted them to go out and play as best they could for 60 minutes, give all they had, and they did that.

"You've got to be willing to live with the result," Osborne said.

What the Cornhuskers must live with is the frustration of a 20-17 loss and the thoughts of what might have been.

Take away the final four minutes or so, and Nebraska had an upset victory.

But those last four minutes . . .

None of the Cornhuskers had the words to express what happened.

Junior defensive tackle Neil Smith, who was credited with 10 tackles, described them as "just weird."

Nebraska lapsed into the Twilight Zone of late-game losses to Oklahoma.

It could've been 1980 or 1976.

But it was 1986, just as plain as the maroon No. 88 on Oklahoma tight end Keith Jackson's white jersey.

And it hurt. A lot.

"We weren't hurting just for ourselves. We were hurting for each other," said Cornhusker linebacker Kevin Parsons. "I don't think I've ever been that emotional about a football game.

"We took everything we had in our guts today and put it on the field today."

It was almost enough. Almost.

Nebraska led until 1:22 remained in the fourth quarter. That's when a 17-yard touchdown pass from Jamelle Holieway to Jackson and a Tim Lashar extra point tied the game at 17.

The pass, which capped an 11-play, 94-yard drive that began with 4:10 remaining, was one of only six the Sooners completed on Saturday. The sixth pass completion was equally dramatic.

Oklahoma faced a third-and-12 from its own 45-yard line with 18 seconds remaining. A tie seemed imminent, at least to anyone unfamiliar with Nebraska's 1980 and 1976 losses to Oklahoma.

Holieway and Jackson teamed up on a 41-yard pass play that took the ball to the Nebraska 14-yard line.

Nine seconds remained.

With six seconds remaining, Lashar kicked a 31-yard field goal.

The game ended on the next play from scrimmage, from the Oklahoma 42-yard line. Nebraska quarterback Steve Taylor was sacked for an 8-yard loss by Sooner defensive tackle Steve Bryan.

The final play was hardly indicative of the Cornhuskers' effort Saturday.

"I really think they played well enough today to at least be Big Eight co-champions," Osborne said.

Instead, Nebraska finished third in the conference, behind champion Oklahoma and second-place Colorado.

As a consolation the Cornhuskers will play in the Sugar Bowl on New Year's Day, against the Southeastern Conference champion, LSU or Alabama.

Oklahoma will represent the Big Eight in the Orange Bowl for the third year in a row on New Year's night.

Except for the late-game efforts of Holieway and Jackson, Nebraska would have gone to Miami. "Oklahoma obviously has a lot of talent, and they were able to get some things done at the end because of it," Osborne said.

Jackson, for example, tipped the ball then caught it on the pass play that set up Lashar's game-winning field goal.

"The (secondary) coverage wasn't all that bad," Osborne said.

At the end it may have been the physical strength of Oklahoma's offensive line that made the difference.

The Sooners' time of possession in the second half was 19:25, which meant they had the ball nearly nine minutes more than Nebraska. And Oklahoma's five interior offensive linemen have a combined weight of nearly one ton.

Even the psychological edge the Cornhuskers may be gotten from wearing their red road pants at home couldn't offset the effects of that line.

"I think our defense got worn down a little bit at the end," Osborne said.

"That was to be expected, being on the field as long as they were. But they played a great ball game."

Oklahoma, which went into the game leading the nation in total offense, rushing offense and scoring offense, came away with 224 rushing yards and 20 points, about half its averages.

Until the Holieway-to-Jackson touchdown pass, the Sooners' only points had come on Holieway's 4-yard scoring run and Lashar's extra-point kick with 2:36 remaining in the first quarter.

Oklahoma's defense came to town with similarly impressive statistics, ranking No. 1 in total defense, rushing defense and scoring defense.

Though Nebraska was limited to 68 yards of offense in the second half, the Cornhuskers did score the first rushing touchdown against the Sooners this season, on I-back Keith Jones' 2-yard run with 6:27 left in the first quarter.

Jones' touchdown capped a 13-play, 85-yard drive. Dale Klein's extra point gave Nebraska a 7-0 lead.

A 32-yard field goal by Klein gave the Cornhuskers a 10-7 lead with 4:46 remaining in the first half.

Nebraska increased that advantage to 17-7 on a 25-yard touchdown pass from Taylor to split end Rod Smith with 10:48 left in the third quarter.

The two-play series, which required only 44 seconds, was set up by Dana Brinson's 48-yard punt return.

Ironically the brief series meant the Cornhuskers' Black Shirt defense had to turn around and go back on the field

The defenders were a weary lot.

"After a while, you run out of whatever you have," Parsons said. "At the end, we were playing solely on desire."

Saturday, that was almost enough.

"Like Vince Lombardi once said, the greatest feeling in the world is to go out and play and afterward, collapse from exhaustion. I did that," Parsons said.

But it wasn't a great feeling.

Even thought he's from New Orleans, Smith wasn't happy about going to the Sugar Bowl. "I wanted a Big Eight championship ring," he said.

"That's something I don't have."

Saturday, Smith almost did. ∎

Nebraska Coach Tom Osborne shows his exasperation about a penalty in the game against Oklahoma. (Journal Star Library)

1987

Osborne: Another 4, 5 Years, At Least

by Don Walton

Lincoln Journal Star

March 16, 1987

Pausing over his lunch of salad and vegetables at the athletic training table complex in Memorial Stadium, Tom Osborne squints his eyes as he ponders the question.

"I don't know. I don't have a plan. I'd like to continue doing this at least another four or five years," he says.

"But if you had asked Bear Bryant at the age of 50, he probably would have said four or five more years too. You just don't know.

"Doing this" is Nebraska's highest-profile job, head coach of the Husker football team.

Bryant did it at Alabama until he was 69.

It's a tough job. In Nebraska, where football is the state's consuming passion and the Huskers have won at least nine games in every one of Osborne's 14 years, the expectations and the demands make it even tougher.

From the first week of last August to mid-February of this year, Tom Osborne had two days off. Now he's getting ready for spring practice.

Over lunch last week, surrounded— and sometimes interrupted— by athletes who were fueling up at midday, Osborne talked about his job and his life, about his joys and frustrations, about what, if anything, might change his mind about staying at Nebraska.

About what's important. And what's not.

And about himself.

"Yeah, I know. There are people who say they wish Tom got excited like that,' the soft-spoken coach says, his mouth curling into the slightest beginning of a smile.

Some head coaches run up and down the sidelines, shouting, celebrating, leading cheers.

"I don't coach that way. I'm on the headphones, trying to think ahead one play. I'm really free to emote because of the way I operate."

But he seems so intense. Does he enjoy it?

"You know, if you watched a surgeon at work, you probably wouldn't have the impression that he was having a great time either," Osborne says.

Not to worry. Tom Osborne enjoys it.

"I like football, the game. I'm intrigued by it. I like the coaching itself."

Especially working with the players.

"For the most part, they're good people, fun to be around. I enjoy seeing people make something out of themselves. Some are disappointments, but you win more than you lose.

"I like people in athletics. They are committed, disciplined. They're risktakers. They know something about paying a price. They're not people who sit back and play it safe."

What doesn't he like about his job?

"The uproar over the indoor foot-

Singer Willie Nelson (left) and Coach Tom Osborne look over Memorial Stadium on July 13, 1987 after signing contracts to hold Farm Aid III at the Nebraska stadium. (Ted Kirk, Journal Star Library)

ball practice facility" jumps immediately to mind.

Osborne is disappointed by the controversy the proposal has engendered.

"Sometimes football can get politicized," he says.

There are also burdens to being such a public figure.

"I do not have much privacy. But it's not all that bad."

No wonder he loves fishing so much.

Is it for the sport or the relaxation?

"Both. And I like it because it's fairly solitary. I go quite a bit in the summer, most every weekend if I can. The farther away, the better.

"Especially when there aren't many people around."

What's most important in his life? "My religious faith, my family, football. And fishing."

Does he feel appreciated by Nebraskans?

"Oh, there are times when everyone feels a little sorry for themselves. But basically I feel people appreciate our efforts even though not many people understand what goes into it."

Are the extraordinarily high expectations in Nebraska every year a burden?

"We've had so many consecutive years, which, by most standards, would be considered highly successful. Those years are treated now very matter-of-factly.

"When Bob Devaney was 9-2 in his first year, that was greeted with great enthusiasm. Now it's business as usual.

"People 35 or younger have a hard time even remembering a losing season.

"I guess a lot is taken for granted, especially when this is not a natural winning situation."

Of all the premier college football programs in the country, Nebraska's is tied to the smallest population base and most requires a successful national recruiting effort.

Steve Taylor, who went to high school in San Diego, drops by the table.

"It's a nice day outside," Osborne tells his young quarterback.

After reviewing last season's films, the coach says, he's convinced that Nebraska needs to throw deep more successfully this year.

"This would be a good day to throw," he says.

Osborne has turned down a number of lucrative financial offers in order to continue coaching where he wants to be.

"There's more to life than money," Osborne says.

It's Osborne's intention to complete his coaching career at Nebraska.

"Unless people decide they don't want me.

"Or if things become so unfavorable here that there is not much chance to be successful."

He's been plenty successful in his 14 years as head coach.

Successful enough that he has received feelers or offers that would pay him far more money from an array of pro and college programs, including the Houston Oilers, the Seattle Seahawks, Colorado, SMU, Arizona State. USC last December. And others.

"Some people simply call to see if you're interested; some call to offer the job.

"I've had plenty of chances to move, but financial inducements won't do it. This is where I like to be."

Some of the offers have been huge.

"One guy called one time and said he would double whatever I was making at Nebraska. Total. TV and everything. He didn't even ask how much I made. I guess I could have told him anything.

"I'd work for him in a personal services contract. I didn't like that approach.

"One pro team offered me at least triple what I make here.

"I've tried not to use those job offers as leverage. I haven't used them to improve my own situation."

Nebraska football has a lot going for it, Osborne says, "good tradition, excellent fan support and reasonably good facilities."

But he says it's falling behind in the third arena.

"We're not in the upper ten percent in terms of facilities as we once were. We're in the upper half."

Nebraska needs an indoor football practice facility if the program is to remain competitive and have the best opportunity for continued success, he says.

Such a facility would compensate for one of the football program's competitive disadvantages: Nebraska's weather.

The most obvious disadvantage is the state's small population base combined with its distance from potential recruits in populous areas of the country. Even more than most schools, Nebraska must recruit well nationally to remain in the top echelon of college football.

"Recruiting is demanding, probably the hardest thing we ever do," Osborne says. "It's a treadmill that lasts about eight weeks."

He visited 80 homes and 75 to 80 schools during the winter's recruiting period.

The competition is enormous.

"It used to be that you could find a great player no one else knew about. Not anymore."

How often is he right in assessing which high school recruits will be great players?

"We're generally right on their physical talent. But it's difficult to measure motivation and tenacity. Some give up easily while some want to play.

"And it's hard to measure maturation. Some continue to get better physically."

Osborne says about two-thirds of Nebraska's scholarship recruits end up "playing some significant role here."

About 50 percent of the top walk-on players do so.

Does Osborne ever worry that some booster may do something to get his football program in serious trouble?

"If it's violations in recruiting, you almost have to have a coach's involvement.

"But I do worry from time to time about an isolated case of some guy taking a player out to dinner after he's gotten here or slipping him $100. There are always a few people willing to bend the rules. And there are always a few who want to be able to say they know a player."

Other than fishing, what's he like to do in his spare time?

"I don't mind golf. But that's a deal where you talk football a lot.

"I play tennis with my wife or daughter.

"I like to read quite a bit. Outdoor magazines, religious philosophy, psychology. I'm not too big on novels. But, once in a while, I read a biography."

Yes, he watches "a little football" on TV too.

No, he doesn't have a favorite baseball team.

He is eating an apple now, finishing his lunch. And that will signal the end of our conversation.

Any game stand out in his mind?

"Maybe the 1978 Oklahoma game.

"And last year's OU game. I've never been around a team that played harder."

Two games—the first a victory, the second a loss.

"The most important thing is to play well," Tom Osborne says.

Not a bad goal for the rest of us, too. ■

1987
Season in Review

Won 10, Lost 2, Tied 0
Big 8: Won 6, Lost 1, Tied 0, 2nd

Date	Opponent	Site	AP Rank NU/Opp.	Result
Sept. 5	Utah State	Lincoln	2/	W 56-12
Sept. 12	UCLA	Lincoln	2/3	W 42-33
Sept. 26	Arizona State	Tempe	2/12	W 35-28
Oct. 3	South Carolina	Lincoln	2/	W 30-21
Oct. 10	Kansas	Lincoln	2/	W 54-2
Oct. 17	Oklahoma St.	Stillwater	2/12	W 35-0
Oct. 24	Kansas St.	Lincoln	2/	W 56-3
Oct. 31	Missouri	Columbia	2/	W 42-7
Nov. 7	Iowa State	Lincoln	2/	W 42-3
Nov. 21	Oklahoma	Lincoln	1/2	L 7-17
Nov. 28	Colorado	Boulder	5/	W 24-7
Sunkist Fiesta Bowl				
Jan. 1	Florida State	Tempe	5/3	L 28-31

Final Rankings: 6th AP & UPI (both post-bowl)

Osborne Says Fun Is In The Pursuit of National Championship

by Mike Babcock

Lincoln Journal Star

Nov. 18, 1987—Winning college football's mythical national championship?

"I've been there before," Tom Osborne said during his weekly news conference on Tuesday.

Nebraska's head coach was an assistant under Bob Devaney when the Cornhuskers won back-to-back national championships following the 1970 and 1971 seasons.

The Cornhuskers had completed a 13-0 season and wrapped up the second of those titles with a 38-6 victory over Alabama in the Orange Bowl. "I remember sitting on the (team) bus in Miami at 1:30 in the morning, everybody was sitting there in a stupor, and thinking, 'Hey this isn't all that big of a deal. So what?'

"It's the pursuit of it that's more important than the winning of it. The process is always more important and more fun than the end results."

Osborne was responding to a question regarding his attitude about winning a national championship, something Nebraska hasn't done during his tenure as head coach.

The No. 1-ranked Cornhuskers almost certainly would be national champions this season if they were to win their remaining three games.

Osborne, who ranks second to Oklahoma's Barry Switzer as the winningest active coach by percentage in Division I of the NCAA, said he isn't driven to win a national title.

"People feel that somehow I'm like Captain Ahab chasing Moby Dick, that I'm obsessed," he said. "It's not that way with me."

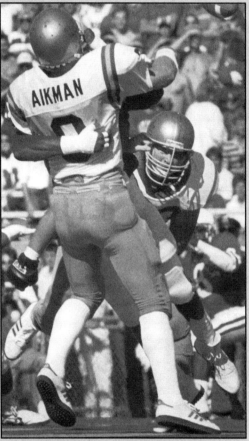

Nebraska's Neil Smith, who went on to a stellar NFL career, sacks UCLA quarterback Troy Aikman in the first half of NU's 42-33 victory against the Bruins on September 12, 1987. (Harald Dreimanis, Journal Star Library)

The national championship is no great white whale to him.

"I feel the most important thing is to play well," Osborne said. "National championships happen. They aren't like the Big Eight championship where you go out and play every team, and if you beat every team, you win it. You've got to be voted the national championship and you've got to have a lot of things conspire . . ."

Osborne has been in position to win a national championship, most notably with his 1983 team, which went into an Orange Bowl game against Miami with a 12-0 record. Nebraska lost the game and the title, 31-30.

After the 1981 season, the Cornhuskers might have been voted national champions if they hadn't lost to Clemson in the Orange Bowl, 22-15.

"It isn't going to drive me crazy if I finish coaching in three years, four years, five years or 10 years and have never won a national championship," said Osborne.

However, he added with a smile, "If I don't do it, I might end my career more quickly because somebody might get me out of here. But it's not something I have to have happen."

Oklahoma has won three national championships under Switzer, in 1974, 1975 and 1985. Competing in the same conference with the Sooners has made Nebraska's task more difficult.

Even so, "it's been fun and it's made us a better football team," Osborne said. Pursuing Oklahoma has been important to us. We've made a lot of changes to try to get to be as good or better than they are. If we didn't have Oklahoma in this league, we wouldn't be as good a team. Maybe it's the same way with them. You have to try to compete with the best.

"In order to be competitive, we've had to be pretty good." ∎

Nebraska defensive end Broderick Thomas takes a break during practice November 20, as the No. 1-ranked Cornhuskers had their last practice prior to their November 21 showdown with Oklahoma. (Ted, Kirk, Journal Star Library)

1988

Cornhuskers Outgun Cowboys

105-point total in game sets scoring record in Memorial Stadium

by Ken Hambleton

Lincoln Journal Star

Oct. 16, 1988

Video games take a quarter or two. A Sunday newspaper costs four quarters.

But it only took Nebraska one quarter to knock out Oklahoma State 63-42 Saturday before 76,432 fans in the highest-scoring game ever at Memorial Stadium.

Nebraska won the game, although Coach Tom Osborne was still worrying about his game.

Sitting around the post game news conference, Osborne compared his Nebraska football team to his golf game.

"This is hard to figure. It's like my golf game," he said. "Every time you've got something fixed, something else breaks down. I still don't know what kind of team we are."

Certainly, the once slow-starting Nebraska offense is fixed.

The Cornhuskers scored six touchdowns in their first 19 plays and clubbed No. 10-ranked and previously unbeaten Oklahoma State to extend the Cowboys' winless streak against the Cornhuskers to 27 years in a row.

But celebrations of Nebraska's offensive success were dampened by the success of Oklahoma State's offense. "Maybe it's just my paranoia, but the rapidity of their scoring and the fact we weren't stopping them had me worried," Osborne said.

Those worries came along after Nebraska teed off on the Cowboys, who were considered to have their best shot of snapping a 0-25-1 non-winning streak against the Cornhuskers and joining the Big Two, Oklahoma and Nebraska, at the top of the Big Eight.

Seventh-ranked Nebraska, 6-1, scored on its first play from scrimmage.

I-back Ken Clark took off around left end and pulled away from one tackler. He then bumped into teammate Todd Millikan, broke another tackle and raced 73 yards for a touchdown.

A little more than two minutes later, Charles Fryar scored on an 86-yard interception return, and after everybody had time to catch their breath, Clark scored again. Then quarterback Steve Taylor added a pair of touchdowns on runs of 60 and 43 yards and Clark scored again.

Less than 20 minutes into the game, Nebraska had a 42-0 lead and Oklahoma State was gasping.

During the 20-minute span, Nebraska had faced just one third down, and Oklahoma State, the NCAA leader in turnover margin, had uncharacteristically turned the ball over twice.

That was enough to convince Oklahoma State Coach Pat Jones that his team would have to wait another year before it could have a chance to beat Nebraska.

"Clark broke a tackle and, after Taylor got loose, by all practical purposes, it was wrapped up then," Jones said.

The Nebraska offense frolicked. The

Tom Osborne shows his disgust after a penalty is called against the Huskers in their October 15, 1988 game against Oklahoma State. (Journal Star Library)

Cornhuskers rolled up big numbers—299 yards rushing in the first quarter, and 570 for the game. Nebraska finished with 662 yards of total offense.

Clark finished with three touchdowns and a near-record 256 yards on 27 carries. He had 106 yards on two carries and 176 on his first eight carries. Taylor had 140 yards rushing, including 103 on his first two carries. He also completed six of 11 passes for 92 yards and a pair of touchdowns to tight end Millikan.

"Taylor, except for one interception, was flawless," Osborne said. "And Clark showed signs that he's the back we thought he could be. He broke tackles, showed balance and was hard to knock off his feet today. I think Kenny (Clark) was almost equal in magnitude to Barry Sanders (the OSU running back who was leading the nation in rushing and scoring)."

But the Nebraska offensive celebrations were dampened by the success of the Cowboy offense.

OSU's 42 points were the most ever scored against an Osborne-coached team.

Nebraska quarterback Steve Taylor (9) gets a block from Bryan Carpenter (29) during NU's 7-3 victory against OU. (Journal Star Library)

1988

Season in Review

Won 11, Lost 2, Tied 0
Big 8: Won 7, Lost 0, Tied 0, 1st

Date	Opponent	Site	AP Rank NU/Opp.	Result
Aug. 27	Texas A & M	E. Rutherford	2/10	W 23-14
Sept. 3	Utah State	Lincoln	2/	W 63-13
Sept. 10	UCLA	Pasadena	2/5	L 28-41
Sept. 24	Arizona State	Lincoln	9/	W 47-16
Oct. 1	UNLV	Lincoln	9/	W 48-6
Oct. 8	Kansas	Lawrence	9/	W 63-10
Oct. 15	Oklahoma State	Lincoln	7/10	W 63-42
Oct. 22	Kansas State	Manhattan	5/	W 48-3
Oct. 29	Missouri	Lincoln	5/	W 26-18
Nov. 5	Iowa State	Ames	7/	W 51-16
Nov. 12	Colorado	Lincoln	7/19	W 7-0
Nov. 19	Oklahoma	Norman	7/9	W 7-3
Orange Bowl				
Jan. 2	Miami, Fla.	Miami	6/2	L 3-23

Final Rankings: 10th AP & UPI (both post-bowl)

Seven Is Enough For Cornhuskers

by Ken Hambleton

Lincoln Journal Star

Nov. 13, 1988

A funny thing happened to Colorado's J.J. Flannigan on the way to the end zone Saturday in Memorial Stadium. And it allowed No. 7 Nebraska to post a 7-0 victory before 76,359 fans in the Cornhuskers' final home game of the season.

Nebraska Coach Tom Osborne called it weird.

Cornhusker safety Mark Blazek said it was freakish.

NU I-back Ken Clark said he was glad it didn't happen to him.

Nebraska quarterback Steve Taylor said he knows the helpless feeling of losing control of the ball on the way to the end zone.

Midway through the second quarter, Flannigan took the ball from quarterback Sal Aunese and burst through the line. As the speedy Colorado halfback streaked toward the Nebraska goal line, nobody was within 10 yards of him.

The ball slipped. Flannigan tried to shift the ball from his left hand to his right. Suddenly, it was rolling on the ground.

He recovered. But 19th-ranked Colorado didn't.

"That was a tight one," Osborne said. "I'm glad it's over with. Our defense played awfully well. At times, we gave them some yards and then we were able to stiffen. It seemed like every time they got inside our 30- or 35-yard line, we were able to hold them and not let them get in good scoring range."

After forcing Colorado to punt when its drive was stymied by Flannigan's fumble, the Cornhuskers then fumbled the ball away at their 39-yard line. But Nebraska cornerback Charles Fryar halted another Colorado scoring threat when he knocked the ball loose from running back Eric Bieniemy and NU safety Tim Jackson recovered at the Nebraska 12. Bieniemy, who had suffered a hamstring injury earlier in the game, didn't return to action after the fumble.

Nebraska couldn't gain a first down and punted. The Buffaloes then drove to the NU 30 but on the last play of the first half, CU kicker Ken Culbertson missed a 47-yard field goal attempt that would have broken a scoreless tie.

After that, the Nebraska defense kept the Cornhuskers in the game. And the offense responded with Clark's 2-yard touchdown run with 4:35 left in the third quarter.

Those were all the points in Nebraska's lowest-scoring game since a 6-0 victory over Missouri in 1981. It also was the lowest point total in Memorial Stadium since Colorado beat Nebraska 7-0 in 1961.

"I think we played well," Osborne said. "I'm hoping we've got a better game in us next week. I don't think we played badly, but I don't think we were necessarily at the emotional pitch that Colorado may have been at."

He said that will not be a problem this week.

Nebraska will finish the regular season in a battle for the Big Eight championship against Oklahoma at Norman on Saturday.

The 10-1 Cornhuskers will advance to the Orange Bowl if they can beat the Sooners. If they lose, the Cornhuskers will probably meet Clemson in the Florida Citrus Bowl.

"We've been through 11 games and this is not the time to choke up," Clark said. "We didn't choke up today, and I can't see it happening next week."

Clark showed a calmness on the scoring drive despite the fact he didn't know where a key fourth-down play was going, he said.

The Cornhuskers faced fourth-and-2 at the Colorado 17 with 5:58 left in the third quarter.

"We had the audible pitch called, where Steve (Taylor) calls which side I'm supposed to take the ball to," Clark said. "I couldn't hear him, so I just waited to see where (fullback Bryan) Carpenter went and I'd go to that side."

Clark, who finished with 165 yards on 28 carries, took the pitch and followed guard John Nelson and tackle Doug Glaser around right end for 10 yards to the Colorado 7. After going around left end for 5 more yards, Clark scored on a pitch play to the right.

"I think I heard the call on that one," said Clark, who moved up to fourth on the Nebraska all-time single season rushing chart. He has 1,330 yards this year, including five games of 100 yards or more.

On Nebraska's next possession, Clark has his longest run of the game when he broke loose for 25 yards to the CU 28 on the second play of the fourth quarter.

Taylor followed with a 25-yard sprint along the sideline. But as Taylor leaped over a teammate at the 3-yard line, CU defensive end Lamarr Gray knocked the ball loose and teammate Tom Reinhardt recovered.

"My first rushing fumble. I hope it's my last," Taylor said. "You try to make something happen. Some days you can. Some days you can't. I just couldn't do it today. But we got a win because our defense played a great game and we got enough to win.

"I was pacing the sidelines, hoping they (the defense) would hold them, and they came through for us. I think that's going to help us next week."

Colorado's only second-half drive into Nebraska territory followed Taylor's fumble. On third-and-7 at the CU 6-yard line, CU quarterback Aunese hit tight end John Perak on a 43-yard pass. The Buffaloes then chipped away to the Nebraska 27.

NU middle guard Lawrence Pete tackled Aunese on consecutive plays. Then, on fourth-and-1, Aunese fumbled the snap, ending Colorado's hopes of its second victory over Nebraska since 1967.

"Overall, this was our best game," Nebraska defensive coordinator Charlie McBride said. "We blitzed once . . . hmmmm. He (Flannigan) just flat dropped the ball on the ground. That was the game. We didn't blitz again. I lost my guts."

The Nebraska defense grew up against Colorado, McBride said.

"You hope a team becomes a team," he said. "And when you hold Colorado out of the end zone, that's a great feat. Confidence becomes a factor in a shutout."

For instance, even though Flannigan recovered his fumble at the Nebraska 19-yard line, NU linebacker Broderick Thomas and a swarm of defenders buried Jeff Campbell for a 19-yard loss two plays later. It was the same split end reverse that burned Nebraska in CU's 1986 victory.

"We emphasized the reverse because Jeff Campbell has hurt everybody we've seen, so we were conscious of him on every play," McBride said.

Some halftime defensive adjustments helped Nebraska all but shut down the Colorado offense. The Buffaloes, who had averaged 278 yards a game rushing, rushed for 62 yards in the second half. Flannigan, who finished with 133 yards rushing, was limited to 42 yards in the second half.

The loss for the 7-3 Buffaloes was hard to take, CU linebacker Don DeLuzio said.

"To play hard and say we fought well doesn't mean nothing." he said. "We came here to win and we didn't and that hurts."

■

Husker lineman John Nelson (76) escorts running back Ken Clark into the end zone for the game's only touchdown during NU's 7-0 victory against Colorado November 12, 1988. (Journal Star Library)

Osborne Won't Save All For OU

by Ken Hambleton
Lincoln Journal Star

Nov. 14, 1988—Tom Osborne said Sunday that he would never sell out a season for one game.

When asked about the approach that Colorado Coach Bill McCartney takes in building his season, Osborne said he wouldn't do it.

McCartney started with a miserable Colorado football program and built it around an annual rivalry with Nebraska. It wasn't much of a rivalry until Colorado beat the Cornhuskers two years ago.

Last weekend, the Colorado coaches and players wore T-shirts with the phrase, "War in Lincoln," emblazoned across the front. The CU locker room was decorated with newspaper headlines that said "War" accompanying a picture of Broderick Thomas appearing to smile as Colorado quarterback Mark Hatcher was taken from the field with a broken leg.

McCartney said last Monday he'd rather beat Nebraska than any other team on the CU schedule. It didn't work, but Colorado came close.

So why doesn't Osborne take that approach with Oklahoma?

There are those fans who find little satisfaction with a 10-win or 11-win season. There are those fans who find little solace in Nebraska beating up teams the Cornhuskers have always beaten because it is expected.

Why not put everything on the line? Work on Oklahoma at least some in every practice at Nebraska. Print the Oklahoma game in big, bold letters on the schedule, talk about Oklahoma each week, and build a win-at-all costs rivalry with Oklahoma.

Why not?

(A) Osborne doesn't think it'll work for Nebraska, and (B) Osborne is the head coach.

"My feeling is my job is to win as many games and to play as close to our potential as possible," Osborne said. "I don't feel that the approach to win one game and put a lot of extra emphasis into one game is a good approach because sometimes it leads you to lose one or two others you ought to win.

"Certainly, this week we'll put a lot of emphasis on Oklahoma. But we didn't talk about it last spring or work on Oklahoma much this summer. We worked on Texas A & M.

"The thing I've understood is that a big game is any game you lose. I was talking at a prison one time and one of the inmates asked, 'Why can't you win the big one?' And I said, 'What game are you talking about?' And he said 'Syracuse.' We had beaten them 63-0 a year before and he remembered the one we lost.

"We lost a couple in a row to Iowa State and that became the big one," Iowa State has since hit the skids. Nebraska has continued to finish in the Top 10.

In other words, a 1-10 season with a victory over Oklahoma is not Osborne's style. If the record of 27 straight winning seasons, 20 years in a row of at least nine wins a year and 20 consecutive bowl games isn't enough, you're in for frustration.

Osborne isn't about to risk the consistency of the most successful college football program to win "the big one."

If Nebraska wins this week, the Cornhuskers will have to face Miami in Miami's Orange Bowl. That'll be an even bigger one because of the heartbreak of a two-point conversion that failed against Miami in the 1983 Orange Bowl. And there is plenty of talk among college coaches that Miami is still the best team in the country despite a one-point loss at Notre Dame this year.

If Nebraska loses this week, it'll play a "big one" in the Citrus Bowl against Clemson, another Cornhusker heartcrusher from the 1982 Orange Bowl and a national championship that might have been for NU.

The problem is the "big ones" are going to be few and far between in the future.

Next season, Nebraska doesn't face a "big one" until October 21, when the Cornhuskers travel to Oklahoma State—a team that hasn't beaten Nebraska since 1961. In 1990, the story is the same.

One side note, though: Nebraska's games might all be big games for the Big Eight. Oklahoma State had its hearing on 62 alleged NCAA infractions with an NCAA committee last weekend in Tucson, Arizona. Oklahoma had already had its hearing. Both schools may be banned from television and bowl games for at least a year. Subtract the loss of revenue from penalties given the Kansas basketball program, and Nebraska football is the only thing left.

■

Cornhuskers' Wish Finally Comes True

by Ken Hambleton

Lincoln Journal Star

Nov. 20, 1988

klahoma quarterback Charles Thompson lie crumpled on the ground as Nebraska's defense left the field for the last time Saturday.

But Thompson wasn't the only casualty. The frustration of four straight losses to Oklahoma, an embarrassing string of losses in the fourth quarter to the mystical "Sooner Magic," and a ton of doubts that had haunted Nebraska since 1983 all disappeared.

The Cornhuskers battled rain, sleet, a 9-degree wind chill and Oklahoma for a 7-3 win before 75,004 fans at Owen Field.

It was time.

Time for a January trip to Miami and an Orange Bowl game against the University of Miami.

Time for an end to Oklahoma's 31-game Big Eight Conference winning streak.

Time for good feelings at season's end.

"Time for a new Big Eight champion," said Broderick Thomas, the Cornhuskers' senior outside linebacker.

And one minute and eleven seconds of time that NU quarterback Steve Taylor

spent dropping to his knee as the clock ran out on the Sooners.

"This time we got the last laugh," Thomas declared as he toyed with a large cloth draped around his neck.

Nebraska's defense answered the bell time and time again and shut off the vaunted Oklahoma wishbone like nobody had in four years. Oklahoma was held to 137 yards of total offense, and only 98 rushing.

"The defense did a tremendous job," Nebraska Coach Tom Osborne said. "There's been some talk this year about our defense and defensive coaches, but I don't know why anyone would talk that way."

Certainly nobody in Norman is talking that way after the Sooners were held without a touchdown for the first time since a 10-0 loss to Missouri in 1983.

"We dominated the line," NU middle guard Lawrence Pete said. "Our defense had to put to rest that about the Nebraska choke and the Sooner Magic and the stuff

that we weren't as good and all that stuff.

"It's a matter of stopping the 'bone. Get them into third down-and-long. If you don't let it click, it won't click," he said.

The Cornhuskers had 14 tackles for 64 yards in losses, including seven quarterback sacks, with six coming when the Sooners faced third down.

None of the sacks of OU's Thompson were more important than the one by Kent Wells for minus eight yards after OU got possession of the ball at the Nebraska 48-yard line with 1:45 left in the game.

After Nebraska linebacker Chris Caliendo corralled OU receiver Eric Bross after a 3-yard pass and Nebraska cornerback Lorenzo Hicks batted away a pass at the Nebraska 30, Pete and teammate Willie Griffin sacked Thompson for the final time.

Thompson, OU's leading rusher and a key figure in Oklahoma's 17-7 victory over Nebraska last year, suffered a broken leg on the play.

"I'm sorry to hear about the broken leg because Charles Thompson is the best wishbone quarterback I've seen since the days of Thomas Lott," said Thomas.

Thompson was OU's biggest threat, and without his net gain of 29 yards rushing, the Sooners would have had even more trouble.

"The quarterback was the responsibility of the tackles—Willie Griffin and Kent Wells," Thomas said. "Lawrence Pete had the fullback. The linebackers had the halfbacks and the options. The rest were for me and the secondary."

And after Thomas and the NU's secondary were done, there wasn't that much left.

"We took a page from Miami's defensive book," Osborne said. Miami handled OU three of its four losses in the last three years. "We call it the Husker defense. It's a 4-3 defense, with the help of an extra linebacker so we got more penetration and better pursuit."

When asked earlier in the week about trying a Miami defense, Osborne specifically said Nebraska didn't want to try something completely new. After Nebraska's win, he revealed the Cornhuskers had worked on the 4-3 defense, specifically for the wishbone, a little bit every Monday this season.

"Our defense flat stuffed them," he said.

Oklahoma's defense, especially two interceptions by Scott Garl, helped the Sooners stay close to the Cornhuskers.

Nebraska got just a 1-yard touchdown dive by Taylor on its first possession of the game.

Taylor and Nebraska I-back Ken Clark helped put the Cornhuskers in position to score more points. Clark gained 167 yards, becoming the first Nebraska player to rush for more than 100 yards against OU since Heisman Trophy winner Mike Rozier did it in 1983, the last time Nebraska won in the series.

Taylor also completed two passes for 48 yards in the first half and rushed for 67 yards in the game, but one drive ended in a missed 41-yard field goal and two others were halted by Garl's interceptions.

Oklahoma's only score followed a fumble by Clark that bounced to the Nebraska 30. Six plays later, R.D. Lashar kicked a 29-yard field goal to close the score to 7-3 with 1:50 left in the third quarter.

"Our line did a heck of a job and we got plenty of yards and had the ball plenty of time, but this was a game for the defense," Clark said. "It seemed like we got what we needed except for the scores.

"Then, I got real nervous when we had to punt the last time. I got that feeling in my stomach that I can't describe," he said.

That feeling was brought about by Jason Belser, who tipped John Kroeker's punt before he knocked the NU punter down. The punt fell dead on the Nebraska 48 with 1:45 left.

"I wasn't worried. We had been having a good time on defense, so what was one more time on the field?" Pete said. "I honestly don't think anybody on the defense was worried. Things had been go-ing too good for us to let up with a minute or so left."

Osborne said it was not a good feeling when Oklahoma got one last chance. "But the day belonged to the defense. We struggled early and came through at the end."

Osborne said there was relief in beating Oklahoma. "The problem is, Nebraska brings such a sense of identity to this game. This is almost out of proportion. So it's good to win it."

Finally, it was time for a phone call from the Orange Bowl Committee, inviting Nebraska.

"Tell Jimmy Johnson we're looking forward to seeing him," Osborne said, referring to the head coach of the Miami Hurricanes. ∎

Nebraska's Andy Keeler signals a Husker touchdown against Oklahoma on November 19, 1988. The Huskers broke a four-game losing streak against the Sooners with the 7-3 victory at Norman. (Journal Star Library)

SO CLOSE

1989

NU's Gdowski Runs Wild In Win

by Ken Hambleton

Lincoln Journal Star

Oct. 29, 1989

Nebraska quarterback Gerry Gdowski perplexed the Iowa State defense, and the Cyclones were kicking themselves as Nebraska rolled to a 49-17 homecoming victory Saturday at Memorial Stadium.

Gdowski ran for a school-record four touchdowns and threw for two more scores to help fourth-ranked Nebraska safely tuck away its eighth victory this season in preparation for the much-anticipated battle against unbeaten and No. 3 Colorado Saturday at Boulder.

"It'll be good to write, talk and practice on the same game," said Nebraska Coach Tom Osborne, who has tried in vain to convince those not involved with the team to pay attention to Nebraska's first eight opponents.

"Colorado? I have no idea. I've looked a little. We were worried about Iowa State today," Osborne said.

Iowa State, now 3-5, outgained Oklahoma 2-to-1 in a 43-40 loss a week ago, and that was enough to concern Nebraska.

"Iowa State has a very good, well-conceived offense and a good quarterback, a good running back and a good line. That's all you need," Osborne said.

Apparently that—and following the pregame plan—was all Nebraska needed, too.

"We thought we could run the options against Iowa State, and we felt the defense would be hard-pressed. And we wanted to win the kicking game," Osborne said.

Gdowski proved Osborne's statement about options correct when he scored on a 74-yard bootleg-option run on the third play of the game.

The senior quarterback took off around the right end and faked a pitch to I-back Leodis Flowers. Gdowski ducked inside blocks by fullback Bryan Carpen-

ter and tight end Monte Kratzenstein and outraced Iowa State cornerback Marcus Robertson to the end zone.

"On film, he doesn't look that fast," Robertson said.

It was the longest run for a touchdown by a Nebraska quarterback, the longest touchdown run by any Cornhusker this season and represented a large chunk of Gdowski's NU quarterback-record 176 yards rushing for the game.

Iowa State then proved Osborne's statement about the test for the Cornhusker defense with an impressive 66-yard scoring drive that ended on a 3-yard run by Blaise Bryant, tying the game 7-7.

"I thought we were going to be in a track meet," Kratzenstein said. "We scored; they scored. It looked like it would be one of those days of a whole lot of touchdowns.

But first, Iowa State proved Osborne's point about the importance of the kicking game.

Facing fourth down-and-9 at the Nebraska 41-yard line, Iowa State lined up for a 58-yard field goal attempt by Jeff Shudak. The center snap, which was bad,

Husker quarterback Gerry Gdowski scampers into the end zone at the end of a 34-yard run against Missouri on October 14, 1989. Gdowski earned numerous athletic and academic honors his senior season. (Ted Kirk, Journal Star Library)

went to Judge Johnston, Iowa State's holder and punter. Johnston stood up and tried to punt the ball for a quick kick.

But Nebraska defensive tackle Kent Wells shoved ISU tackle Gene Williams back and the punt hit Williams squarely in the backside. Nebraska's Mike Croel then smothered ISU's Hussein Warmack, who had recovered the ball at the Nebraska 38.

Four plays later, Gdowski took a circuitous route on a bootleg-option to the right and scored on a 26-yard run to give Nebraska the lead for good.

By then, Nebraska had made changes in its defense. Defensive coordinator Charlie McBride went to the "dime defense," (adding two extra pass defenders), and made adjustments in the four-man pass rush.

"We didn't see an option, an isolation run, or any of the regular offensive stuff," McBride said. "This was the opposite. Passing and draw plays to the quarterback and tailback was what Iowa State was doing and doing it very well."

Bret Oberg, the Big Eight's leading passer who passed for 158 yards and ran for 51, teamed with Bryant, the nation's fifth-leading rusher, to move the Cyclones into field goal position. This time, Shudak kicked a 46-yard field goal against the wind to close the score to 14-10 with 11:21 left in the first half.

The Cyclones managed just 50 yards of total offense in the next 22 minutes of the game, while Gdowski and the Nebraska offense ran wild.

Flowers, subbing for NU leading rusher Ken Clark, who sat out the game because of sore knees, broke away on a 61-yard run to set up what appeared to be a 10-yard touchdown run by Gdowski. The Cornhuskers were penalized for clipping on the play, but Gdowski passed to wingback Tyrone Hughes for a 16-yard score on the next play.

Cornhusker outside linebacker Jeff Mills knocked the ball loose from Bryant on ISU's next possession. Gdowski ran 22 yards on an option and Nate Turner picked up 14 yards on a wingback reverse to move the ball to the Cyclone 25.

Nebraska lined up in the double-tight end formation, like it had on the previous score, and Gdowski hit Hughes in the corner of the end zone with 27 seconds left in the half to give the Cornhuskers a 28-10 lead.

"It was better than 21 points (NU's score), but when we get comfortable is when we are stopping people. And we didn't do that until the final seven or eight minutes of the game," Osborne said.

Nebraska dominated the third quarter. Gdowski capped a 12-play, 80-yard drive to open the second half with a 3-yard touchdown run.

Minutes later, Wells squashed Oberg and knocked the ball loose at the ISU 33. Three plays later, Gdowski added his fourth touchdown of the game on a 4-yard run to give Nebraska a 42-10 lead with 4:29 left in the third quarter.

"We played without four starters and may have lost Mike Grant (backup quarterback) for a while with a separated shoulder and overall, it was still a good day for us," Osborne said.

"We hope we're ready for Colorado."

Gdowski said the team is ready for Colorado.

This is the game everybody dreams about," he said. "Two top teams, national TV and everybody able to concentrate on winning the game. It's Nebraska against Colorado. Nothing else matters now." ∎

1989 Season in Review

Won 10, Lost 2, Tied 0
Big 8: Won 6, Lost 1, Tied 0, 2nd

Date	Opponent	Site	AP Rank NU/Opp.	Result
Sept. 9	No. Illinois	Lincoln	4/	W 48-17
Sept. 16	Utah	Lincoln	4/	W 42-30
Sept. 23	Minnesota	Minneapolis	3/	W 48-0
Sept. 30	Oregon State	Lincoln	3/	W 35-7
Oct. 7	Kansas State	Lincoln	4/	W 58-7
Oct. 14	Missouri	Columbia	4/	W 50-7
Oct. 21	Oklahoma State	Stillwater	4/	W 48-23
Oct. 28	Iowa State	Lincoln	4/	W 49-17
Nov. 4	Colorado	Boulder	3/2	L 21-27
Nov. 11	Kansas	Lincoln	6/	W 51-14
Nov. 18	Oklahoma	Lincoln	6/	W 42-25
Sunkist Fiesta Bowl				
Jan. 1	Florida State	Tempe	6/5	L 17-41

Final Rankings: 11th AP, 12th UPI (both post-bowl)

In Osborne's Mind, This Year's Team Was Great

by Mike Babcock
Lincoln Journal-Star

Nov. 19, 1989—In the locker room after Saturday afternoon's 42-25 victory against Oklahoma at Memorial Stadium, Tom Osborne told the Nebraska football team that it had come as close to fulfilling its potential as any team he's ever coached.

"Coach Osborne doesn't say anything he doesn't mean," said Cornhusker wingback Richard Bell.

"That meant a lot to me."

It meant so much, in fact, that Bell planned to write it down in the notebook he keeps for such comments.

Some day he'll sit down, read through the notebook and reminisce.

In a sense, only seven points stood between Nebraska and its potential. Seven points stood between the Cornhuskers and perfection.

Seven points could have turned their 27-21 loss to Colorado into a victory.

Instead of 10-1, they could have finished the regular season 11-0, with a Big Eight title, an Orange Bowl bid and a shot at a national championship.

As it is, Nebraska finishes second in the conference, with a Fiesta Bowl berth opposite Florida State. The Cornhuskers have a "slim" chance—maybe 10 percent— of playing for the national title, according to Osborne.

Realistically, he'd like his team to finish in such a way that "somebody, somewhere would say, 'Nebraska's pretty good,'" Osborne said.

"I hope we can do a good job and finish it up right."

These Cornhuskers have been pretty good, regardless of what happens at Tempe, Arizona, New Year's Day. They've been good enough to come within seven

Coach Osborne took some time out to watch the Husker junior varsity play on November 3, 1989. He's joined by 3-year-old Aaron Sundberg, son of former NU quarterback Craig Sundberg. (Journal Star Library)

points of being considered great, hardly an adjective most people would have used to describe Osborne's 17th team prior to the season.

Unfortunately, few will use it now, even if Nebraska defeats Florida State in the Fiesta Bowl, but doesn't win the national title.

Greatness has come to mean being ranked No. 1. And as a result, this Cornhusker team probably won't get the respect it has earned.

The same can be said of senior quarterback Gerry Gdowski, who's played a key role in Nebraska's achieving its potential.

"Gerry has played as well as any quarterback I've been associated with," said Osborne. "I think he's deserving of any honors he can receive."

Gdowski has had an outstanding career . . . this season.

He shattered the school record for rushing yardage by a quarterback. He ran for 13 touchdowns to tie Steve Taylor's school record for quarterbacks and passed for 19 touchdowns, one fewer than Vince Ferragamo's school record. And he

finished just 82 yards short of Jerry Tagge's school single-season record for total offense.

Gdowski directed Nebraska's offense with the savvy of Turner Gill. He combined some of the best qualities of some of the best quarterbacks ever to wear Cornhusker jerseys.

Based on spring practice, "I thought he'd be very good," Osborne said during his postgame interview. "I don't know that I envisioned this good. He's certainly matched any expectations I had, maybe exceeded them."

Gdowski has been great.

"He surprised everybody, I think," said Bell. "I take my hat off, my shirt off, everything off to Gerry. He's got to be an All-American somewhere. He's an All-American in my book."

But it's doubtful Gdowski will be first-team all-conference.

Darian Hagan, who directed second-ranked Colorado to the Big Eight championship, seems to be the favorite for an honor Gdowski deserves. Like his team, Gdowski probably will come up seven points short.

Gdowski can look back at this season and know that he played about as well he could play, though. If he didn't reach his potential, he came close.

The rest of the Cornhuskers can remember this, the 100th football season in their school's history, in the same way. Osborne told them so after Saturday afternoon's victory over a respected, and traditional, rival.

Osborne "usually doesn't say things like that," Bell said.

When he does, he means it. And that's worth remembering. ■

Fans Can't Seem To See Changes Osborne Has Made

by Ken Hambleton

Lincoln Journal Star

Jan. 11, 1990

 sampling of the reaction from the Fiesta Bowl game shows that at least some fans haven't lost their sense of humor.

From the "Tastes great, less filling" category there are those critical fans who seem divided between those who blame the Nebraska defense and those who blame the Nebraska offense for the loss to Florida State.

There are some fans who are filled and don't care about the taste. Those fans seem confused. They say Nebraska played a schedule that was too easy but add that Nebraska should have played Arkansas in the Cotton Bowl because that would have been an easier opponent that Florida State.

Some fans claim that Tom Osborne won't open things up on offense. Yet the same fans complain that he called for a fake punt early in the Fiesta Bowl that led to a touchdown.

From those who aren't filled but like the taste there are those fans who want Osborne's head on a platter. Some want defensive coordinator Charlie McBride and defensive coach George Darlington served as appetizers.

Few fans realize just how important the Fiesta Bowl was to Florida State Coach Bobby Bowden. The veteran FSU coach got a lifetime contract and a $350,000 raise after his Fiesta Bowl win. Meanwhile, Osborne remains one of the lowest-paid Division I coaches in the country.

Osborne's immediate reaction to the Fiesta Bowl was one of disappointment and a promise that he would not be changing his approach.

His defense is that the Cornhuskers have won more games than any team in

Tom Osborne shows his exasperation when Oklahoma pulls off a trick play during the November 18, 1989 game, which Nebraska won 42-25. (Ted Kirk, Journal Star Library)

the last decade. They have been in major bowl games the last nine years and have two consecutive victories over archrival Oklahoma.

His detractors say that victories over lesser opponents and a dearth of victories over greater foes prove changes are necessary.

The reality is that Osborne is changing his team. He does every year.

It wasn't until five years ago that Nebraska began recruiting defensive backs in earnest. Since then, the Cornhuskers have signed some of the best in the country.

Nebraska adapted a "dime" pass defense two years ago, and although, it still needs work—obviously—it is a drastic change from the past.

The Cornhuskers installed a number of offensive plays from the "run and shoot," offenses in recent years, and they threw more passes this year for more yards than any time since the mid-1970s.

There are more changes coming.

The recruitment of Matt Jones, a quarterback from Michigan City, Indiana, and other passing quarterbacks show that Nebraska is looking to the skies in the future. Jones is the first "passing" quarterback to sign with Nebraska since Tim Sorley was recruited in 1975.

It's going to take some time. Unless there is some way to move Nebraska closer to the state of Florida, California or Texas—where the players live—it may take a long, long time.

Consider that the teams that have beaten Nebraska in recent years have more players from those states than any other. The players from Florida State and Miami are 90 percent native. Almost 50 percent of Colorado's players are from California. Oklahoma has had as many as 55 percent of its roster filled with players from Texas.

Clicking your heels together three times and repeating, "national championship," will not bring the Cornhuskers their first mythical national football title since 1971.

Adapting, building and growing, plus enjoying a little luck, are the only ways Nebraska will get back on top. ■

1990

Buffaloes Burst NU Bubble

by Ken Hambleton

Lincoln Journal Star

Nov. 4, 1990

Tom Osborne stopped for a moment, looked up at the scoreboard in the southwest corner of Memorial Stadium and shook his head.

It was steam caused by the cold that came out of his nostrils, but it was dreams that drifted away again for the 18-year Nebraska head football coach.

Behind him, Colorado fans and players danced with joy.

Ninth-ranked Colorado scored more fourth-quarter points than any team had managed against third-ranked Nebraska, en route to a 27-12 victory Saturday night. The Buffaloes' victory erased Nebraska's chances for a Big Eight title, an undefeated season and a national title.

CU running back Eric Bieniemy, who fumbled five times and lost three, scored four touchdowns in the fourth quarter to lead the upset before a capacity crowd of 76,464 and a national television audience.

It was Nebraska's fourth straight loss to a Top 10 team and its first and only game against a ranked team this year.

Conversely, it was Colorado's sixth win against a ranked opponent this season.

"When you play a lot of good teams you know what it takes," said Colorado middle guard Joel Steed. "It was to our benefit that we had a tough schedule because we've been through hell."

When asked about Colorado's advantage of playing close games all season, Osborne responded, "They had the one running play we weren't stopping and we had a couple of opportunities in the third quarter," he said. "It's hard, once a team gets ahead, not much time left and they've got the wind at their back. It's hard to pull out of it, particularly when you're not throwing well."

Osborne pointed to a fake punt that failed by a yard when Nebraska faced fourth-and-3 at the Cornhusker 30-yard line with 6:38 left in the game.

"I'll probably catch heck for it," he said. "I'm not second-guessing myself. We talked all week we felt with 10 men on the line they were vulnerable to the fake.

"We came up a yard short. It was worth a shot because we were not stopping them, they had the lead and the wind and we weren't passing well."

Osborne said Colorado's simple, but effective isolation running play with Bieniemy on four scoring drives in the fourth quarter was unstoppable, despite adjustments by the Nebraska defense.

"They ran straight ahead and had good enough blocking and we were just not getting there when they cut back on our nose guard," he said.

Osborne also talked of the frustration of a passing game that never took hold, hitting just 2 of 12 passes for 69 yards.

But most of all, he showed the disappointment of losing.

"I feel very badly about the loss," Osborne said. "I feel bad for our players. I think we probably played the first three quarters well enough to put it away. But at the end of the third quarter and in the fourth quarter they got some things going."

In fact, NCAA rushing leader Bieniemy and the Colorado offensive line of center Jay Leeuwenburg, guards Joe

Defensive end Kenny Walker got a big sendoff at his last home game as a Husker in November 1990. Walker became the first deaf player to play for the Huskers. (Journal Star Library)

Garten and Bryan Campbell, and tackles Mark Vander Poel and Ariel Solomon, got a lot going.

Immediately after Nebraska took a 12-0 lead on a 46-yard touchdown pass from Mickey Joseph to Johnny Mitchell, the Buffaloes took control.

In the next 17 minutes, Colorado scored 27 points and outgained Nebraska 159 yards to minus 4.

"Maybe it didn't hurt us, but it seemed to help them that they had been in so many close games this year," Nebraska offensive guard Jim Wanek said. "They were a confident bunch, very physical and very good. They looked like they knew what they were doing in the fourth quarter."

At the end of the third quarter, Colorado quarterback Darian Hagan hit Rico Smith on a 30-yard pass to the Nebraska 47. Bieniemy, who finished with 137 yards on 38 carries, then ran through the middle of the Nebraska defense five times for 27 yards to move Colorado to the Nebraska 20.

Hagan hit Mark Pritchard on a sideline pass in front of NU's Bruce Pickens at the Nebraska 1. Bieniemy dove over the middle of the line for a touchdown with 14:43 left in the game.

Nebraska never answered.

Three runs by Joseph netted minus 3 yards and caused NU to punt.

Colorado pounced on the opportunity, as Hagan, who hit 3 of 4 passes for 68 yards in the fourth quarter, got the benefit of a leaping sideline catch by Pritchard for a 34-yard gain to the Nebraska 11.

But the Buffs, who lost three of seven fumbles, including one at the Nebraska 2 and another at the NU 20, almost lost another chance to score.

Colorado tight end David Brown caught a short pass but fumbled. Teammate Sean Brown recovered the ball at the Nebraska 2. On fourth down, Bieniemy leaped over the Cornhusker defense to put the Buffaloes ahead for good, 13-12, with 8:37 left.

Nebraska then fell short on the fake punt at its 30 and Colorado pounded its way into the end zone again, with Bieniemy rushing four times for 24 yards, including the final 3 yards for a touchdown.

The Cornhuskers were held to minus 10 yards on their next possession, failed on fourth down again, and Bieniemy capped the victory with his fourth touchdown of the quarter.

Osborne said he was surprised by the fourth-quarter collapse.

"As the game went on, I thought we'd be the stronger team, but they got their running game going and we didn't get it untracked. Once they got ahead they made a couple big plays, a couple of great catches and that was the difference," he said.

Nebraska had chances to expand its lead.

In the third quarter, Joseph sprinted around the right end on a keeper and outraced the Colorado defense to the end zone. He was ruled to have stepped out of bounds at the Colorado 9. The Cornhuskers failed to advance past the CU 3 and Gregg Barrios, who had kicked two field goals earlier to give Nebraska a 6-0 halftime lead, missed a 20-yard attempt.

"I couldn't tell if Mickey stepped out of bounds. He said he didn't," Osborne said. "Then, we didn't get anything out of that, which was really a big play because that would have given us 19 points and then we wouldn't have done some of the things we did at the end."

What the loss will do to Nebraska, Osborne could only guess.

"I'm anxious to see how they (players) respond because after something like this I think you can go different directions. We're hoping we respond favorably and play well this next week against Kansas."

■

1990 Season in Review

Won 9, Lost 3, Tied 0
Big 8: Won 5, Lost 2, Tied 0, 3rd

Date	Opponent	Site	AP Rank NU/Opp.	Result
Sept. 1	Baylor	Lincoln	7/	W 13-0
Sept. 8	No. Illinois	Lincoln	10/	W 60-14
Sept. 22	Minnesota	Lincoln	8/	W 56-0
Sept. 29	Oregon State	Lincoln	8/	W 31-7
Oct. 6	Kansas State	Manhattan	8/	W 45-8
Oct. 13	Missouri	Lincoln	7/	W 69-21
Oct. 20	Oklahoma State	Lincoln	4/	W 31-13
Oct. 27	Iowa State	Ames	4/	W 45-13
Nov. 3	Colorado	Lincoln	3/9	L 12-27
Nov. 10	Kansas	Lawrence	13/	W 41-9
Nov. 23	Oklahoma	Norman	10/	L 10-45
Florida Citrus Bowl				
Jan. 1	Georgia Tech	Orlando	19/2	L 21-45

Final Rankings: 17th-tie UPI, 24th AP (both post-bowl)

Sooners Boom Bumbling Huskers
Seven turnovers, Joseph's injury costly

by Ken Hambleton

Lincoln Journal Star

Unappreciated, unloved, and now, unplugged, Nebraska suffered its worst loss in 22 years Friday at Owen Field.

"I can't explain it. It went dead," Nebraska tight end Johnny Mitchell said after Oklahoma's 45-10 victory. "All those points for them and hardly any for us. The system went dead."

For instance Nebraska ran its famous "fumblerooskie."

Nebraska's other three fumbles and four interceptions were unintentional, but they tore the heart out of the 10th ranked and 9-2 Cornhuskers, who Coach Tom Osborne had claimed were underrated and overlooked this season.

"We called the 'fumblerooskie', where I leave the ball on the ground and Jim Wanek (NU guard) picks it up," Nebraska center Dave Edeal said. "But the ball rolled a little bit and Jim had to fall on it and we got nothing out of it.

"It was somewhat symbolic of the whole game, wasn't it? I mean everything was rolling against us."

Oklahoma, which was unranked, rolled to respectability with 396 yards and the most points scored against Nebraska since the Sooners turned in a 47-0 whipping in 1968.

"I have to say it was one of our poorer performances in my 28 years at Nebraska," Osborne said, "I'm totally embarrassed. I have to take the blame for that performance."

Certainly, Oklahoma can take some credit.

The Sooners held the NCAA's leading rushing team to 118 yards rushing—NU's lowest total since a 41-17 loss to Florida State in last year's Fiesta Bowl.

Oklahoma also rushed through Nebraska's defense for 35 points more than Cornhusker opponents had averaged in 10 previous games.

The Sooners tore through the NCAA's eighth-best passing efficiency defense for 119 yards. Included in those yards was a pivotal 36-yard touchdown pass from freshman Cale Gundy to Adrian Cooper that put Oklahoma ahead for good with 11 minutes 19 seconds left in the first half.

"It seems like we got behind and some of our guys lose the game," Mitchell said. "We lose the lead and that's it, we lose."

Nebraska's offense showed rare glimpses of its previous proficiency after starting quarterback Mickey Joseph was knocked out of the game on Nebraska's sixth play.

Joseph suffered a severe laceration to his right leg when he was forced into the Oklahoma aluminum bench by OU defenders Reggie Barnes and Corey Mayfield at the end of a 13-yard scramble.

Joseph's run was the second-longest play of the first half for Nebraska and NU's fourth-longest play in the game.

"I thought we would make it a positive and 'Win one for Mickey'," NU I-back Leodis Flowers said. "But it didn't happen. We didn't execute on offense, either, and Oklahoma played flawless defense.

"We never overcame the Sooners or the sidelines on our pitches to the outside because we never got much outside. And that's our strength."

The only significant yards the Cornhuskers gained outside came on a 17-yard tight end reverse by Mitchell late in the first half.

Otherwise, most of the scoring was set up by Nebraska turnovers and was realized in Oklahoma touchdowns.

After OU's Cooper caught a floating pass that was over-the-shoulder and over-the-defender (Tyrone Byrd) in the back of the end zone to put Oklahoma ahead, the Sooners never looked back.

Two drives later, Nebraska backup quarterback Mike Grant hit Nate Turner on a short pass, but Barnes immediately knocked loose the ball. It was picked up by Frank Blevins and returned to the NU 12-yard line. Four plays later, Gundy scored on a quarterback sneak.

On Nebraska's next possession, Sooner linebacker Joe Bowden stepped in front of a Grant pass to give Oklahoma the ball.

Gundy hit Cooper on a 40-yard pass that was caught at the same time by Tyrone Legette. Fullback Mike McKinley then scored on a 9-yard run.

"It was like that all day," NU safety Byrd said. "I was there and Tyrone was there and Cooper was there. Tyrone (Legette) had the ball, then we all had the ball. Then, the ref said the offense gets the ball.

"Nate (Turner) didn't have the ball for an eye blink, but they called it a fumble. (Later) I had Cooper covered, too. We were there, but we didn't do our jobs. We didn't get it done."

Nebraska rallied for the last time when Legette recovered a fumble at the Oklahoma 35, and five plays later, Leodis Flowers scored on a 2-yard run to close the gap to 21-10 with three minutes gone in the second half.

"I thought after we scored and got to 21-10 we were still in it," Osborne said.

But Blevins intercepted a Grant pass to give OU the ball at the Nebraska 20. McKinley ran the final 7 yards to put the Sooners ahead 28-10 with 7:41 left in the third quarter.

Nebraska lost a fumble on its next possession. After the Cornhusker defense stopped the Sooners, Nebraska stopped itself with the failed "fumblerooskie" at midfield.

Nebraska seemingly stopped the Sooners again, but were penalized for grabbing Gundy's facemask on what would have been NU's only quarterback sack. Three plays later, McKinley scored on a 48-yard fullback trap to pad the score to 35-10.

A 43-yard interception return for a touchdown by Greg DeQuasie and a Big Eight record-setting field goal by R.D. Lashar ended the scoring.

"Our team never plays with a whole lot of emotionalism, but it didn't seem to me they played with the heart I thought they'd play with," Osborne said. "We did not play good technique, either.

"My goal is to play well. We did not play well. I was surprised. I thought we'd do better on both sides of the ball." ■

To follow the Huskers call 800-742-7315

Lightning Delays Season Opener

by Ryly Jane Hambleton

Lincoln Journal Star

Sept. 8, 1991

A weather-related 19-minute delay in the University of Nebraska football game Saturday was believed to be the first in the school's 102-year football history.

The thunderstorm that halted the game began midway through the third quarter and at 3:24 p.m., referee Steve Usechek of Broomfield, Colorado, announced that the game between the Cornhuskers and Utah Sate would be delayed because of the danger of lightning.

Nebraska was leading 40-20 with 2:10 left in the third quarter when the game was suspended. The Cornhuskers, in the opening game of the season, came back to win 59-28.

The National Weather Service said the temperature dropped 20 degrees between 2 p.m. shortly before the thunderstorm began, and 4:30 p.m., after the storm had passed through the city.

The weather service recorded 0.17 of an inch of rain in the two-hour period. No damage was reported due to the storm, the weather service said.

"It is the discretion of the referee whether the players are endangered," said Bill Jennings of Lincoln, a Big Eight Conference supervisor of officials.

"He went to both coaches and we all agreed up here that it was the right thing to do," Jennings said about the 19-minute delay.

"The rules allow for stopping the game until the lightning passes. They would probably wait at least an hour and then if both coaches agreed, the game could be called," he said during the delay.

The teams returned to the field at 3:40 p.m., and the game resumed at 3:43 p.m.

Both coaches said their teams took the delay in stride.

"The lightning didn't scare me, but Del Weed (University of Nebraska-Lincoln environmental health and safety manager) said we should do it" Nebraska Coach Tom Osborne said of the delay. "The players reacted OK. It was like another halftime.

"I usually call the flight service for a weather report, being a temporary pilot," Osborne said. "I called and they said there was a 20 percent chance of rain after 8 o'clock. So I thought we were out of the woods with no rain today. But I should have gotten an updated report, I guess."

Utah State Coach Chuck Shelton said he has never had a game delayed because of lightning during his coaching career.

Husker players hurry into the locker room to escape a heavy thunderstorm with lightning during the September 7, 1991 game against Utah State. The game was suspended for 19 minutes in the third quarter. (Robert Becker, Journal Star Library)

Nebraska running back Calvin Jones (44) scampers into the end zone on one of his school-record six touchdowns in NU's 59-23 win at Kansas November 9, 1991. In addition to his record six touchdowns, Jones set a school record with 294 yards rushing. (Ted Kirk, Journal Star Library)

"You do what's right to protect kids," he said. "I've never had that happen, ever, but you know what? Nobody cared about us when I was younger. I just didn't worry about lightning. But it was the right thing to do."

Jennings, a longtime Big Eight official, said he was involved in two games that were delayed by lightning, both at the University of Oklahoma.

"The first one, we waited about 45 minutes before we got started, and the second we waited an hour and 45 minutes. That game was with Stanford and it was a close game, so nobody wanted to quit," he said.

On September 29, a game between the University of Southern California and Ohio State was called with 2:28 left in the fourth quarter.

Several officials and players referred to recent lightning deaths at major golf tournaments. One spectator was killed after being struck by lightning at the U.S. Open in the Minneapolis area and another spectator was struck and killed at the PGA Championship in Carmel, Ind.

"I think the trouble with lightning at the golf tournaments has everybody antsy about it now," said Jim Ross, former assistant football coach and assistant athletic director at Nebraska. "I've seen a lot of rain and mud games but I've never seen a game delayed. The ones you have to worry about are the poor spectators—they're not protected."

Connie Wagner, coordinator of the American Red Cross first aid stations, said 11 people were treated for heat-related problems and three were treated for heart problems, all before the rain began. ■

1991
Season in Review

Won 9, Lost 2, Tied 1
Big 8: Won 6, Lost 0, Tied 1, 1st-tie

Date	Opponent	Site	AP Rank NU/Opp.	Result
Sept. 7	Utah State	Lincoln	14/	W 59-28
Sept. 14	Colorado State	Lincoln	13/	W 71-14
Sept. 21	Washington	Lincoln	9/4	L 21-36
Sept. 28	Arizona State	Tempe	16/24	W 18-9
Oct. 12	Oklahoma State	Stillwater	14/	W 49-15
Oct. 19	Kansas State	Lincoln	9/	W 38-31
Oct. 26	Missouri	Lincoln	9/	W 63-6
Nov. 2	Colorado	Boulder	9/15	T 19-19
Nov. 9	Kansas	Lawrence	11/	W 59-23
Nov. 16	Iowa State	Lincoln	11/	W 38-13
Nov. 29	Oklahoma	Lincoln	11/19	W 19-14

Federal Express Orange Bowl

Jan. 1	Miami, Fla.	Miami	11/1	L 22-0

Final Rankings: 15th AP, 16th CNN/USA Today (both post-bowl)

NU Fans Must Face Reality

by Mike Babcock
Lincoln Journal Star

Sept. 23, 1991—This week's Associated Press Top 25 college football poll provides evidence of the national respect Nebraska still commands.

The Cornhuskers are 16th in the poll despite allowing 618 yards, at home, in Saturday night's 36-21 loss to Washington.

Nebraska probably should be no higher than No. 21, and maybe even among the "others receiving votes." But reputation is worth a lot in the polls. And the Cornhuskers have a tradition of success, going back to consecutive national championships in 1970 and 1971.

That tradition also has a downside, which was in evidence in the anger of some Cornhusker fans following Saturday night's loss.

One fan criticized the inability of Nebraska's defense to adjust while he waited for the light to change at 12th and P Streets.

"That's it," he said. His patience was exhausted.

Such an attitude seemed typical. And it's certainly understandable given Nebraska's tradition of success. But it ignores that the Cornhuskers were defeated by a better team Saturday night.

Washington was significantly better, which means Nebraska did well just to hang in with the Huskies as long as it did.

Cornhusker fans have a right to be disappointed about the loss. Angry, though? There's no reason to be angry, unless the belief is Nebraska gave less than its best effort. And you can hardly fault the Conhuskers. They gave it everything they had. But often that's not enough when a team is overmatched by its opponent.

Quarterback Billy Jo Hobert led Washington past Nebraska 36-21 on September 21, 1991. It was Tom Osborne's last loss at NU's Memorial Stadium. (Journal Star Library)

"I don't know if we're clear out of Washington's league," Cornhusker Coach Tom Osborne said after the game.

Nebraska might not be clear out of Washington's class; that's true. But the Cornhuskers apparently are pretty close, which probably is the reason some fans are so angry about the loss. It's tough to admit but Nebraska isn't among the top teams in the country this season and probably hasn't been the last couple of seasons.

These things go in cycles, and the Cornhuskers are in the midst of a downswing, even though Nebraska's downswings would be reason for optimism in a good many major college programs.

The Cornhuskers' slide from the nation's elite, the national championship contenders, has been almost as difficult to see as it is to accept. There are so few times in a given season in which Nebraska's relationship to those top teams is shown—one or two Big Eight games and, of course bowl games have been about the only indicators in recent seasons.

No need to recount those woes.

The Washington game was a painful reminder that Nebraska has to improve if it's going to compete with the nation's best again. That's the reality. There's certainly no disgrace in it.

The Cornhuskers probably aren't that far away, which is why it wasn't unreasonable to think they could have beaten Washington.

But a Nebraska victory would have been an upset. Cornhusker fans shouldn't have gone to the game expecting a victory.

Nebraska played hard, and Washington did some things to self-destruct, thereby enhancing Nebraska's chances.

Still, the Huskies owned the line of scrimmage, offensively and defensively, almost from the beginning. It was apparent, early in the game which of the teams was stronger.

But mistakes, such as the holding penalties on Washington's offensive line, can be significant equalizers, as can the emotion of playing before an enthusiastic home crowd.

As a result, the best team doesn't always win.

It did, however, Saturday night.

Nebraska fans should have been disappointed by the Cornhuskers' inability to seize an opportunity, not angry.

But they've been conditioned by success.

A few, in fact, are still living 20 years in the past. ∎

NU Celebrates 19-14 Triumph

I-back Jones scores game-winning TD with 2:57 Left.

by **Ken Hambleton**

Lincoln Journal Star

Nov. 30, 1991

 own came the rain. Down came the oranges. Down came the stigma of not beating a Top 20 team in three seasons.

And down came the goal posts.

No baloney. Nebraska is headed to the Orange Bowl as Big Eight co-champion after beating Oklahoma 19-14 Friday afternoon to the delight of the 76,386 fans in dark, drenched and delirious Memorial Stadium.

Nebraska I-back Calvin Jones converted a fourth down at the Oklahoma 19-yard line, then scored the game-winning touchdown on a 15-yard run with 2:57 left in the game.

Despite the excitement, Jones kept his priorities in line.

"I thought first to take care of the ball, second to get into the end zone and third to celebrate. And that celebration went right on into the locker room and who knows how long it will last."

Three turnovers in the first 12 minutes of the game left Nebraska trailing Oklahoma 14-0.

The Cornhuskers, ranked No. 11 and now 9-1-1 overall and 6-0-1 in the Big Eight, turned the game around with two field goals by Bryon Bennett, a 10-play, 70-yard scoring drive to open the second half and a dramatic drive in the final minutes.

The win gave NU a share of the Big Eight title with 15th-ranked Colorado. Nebraska was invited to the Orange Bowl because of its higher ranking. The Cornhuskers will play No. 1 Miami on New Year's Day.

"When you make up 14 points in this kind of weather against this kind of defense in this kind of game and win . . . that was excellent," said Nebraska middle guard Pat Engelbert.

There may have been no more important play for the Cornhuskers than the fourth-and-1 situation they faced at the Oklahoma 19 with 3:08 left.

Trailing 14-13, Nebraska chose to forgo a field goal attempt and instead gave the ball to I-back Jones.

The redshirted freshman from Omaha Central took a pitch from quarterback Keithen McCant and ran to the left side of the line, behind pulling guard Erik Wiegert, for a 4-yard gain.

"That's our bread-and-butter play at Nebraska," said Wiegert. "Coach (Osborne) told us it was our season, and asked if we wanted to go for it on fourth down instead of trying a field goal.

"Somebody said, 'Try the pitch play.' We did. And that's that."

On the next play, Jones ran a draw up the middle and raced into the end zone to put NU in front for the first time. For good.

"The linemen didn't give me any opportunity but to get the first down," said Jones. "I've watched so many Nebraska-Oklahoma games for so many years. There was the Sooner Magic with Keith Jackson and other guys. It seemed like Oklahoma guys won too many times.

"This time, I had the run, but it wasn't me, I had no choice with the way our line was blocking," Jones said. On the touchdown, he said, "The linemen blocked a hole that you could have driven a garbage truck through.''

Jones, who finished with 118 yards rushing, and teammate Derek Brown, who had 98, helped Nebraska keep the ball from Oklahoma for all but six plays in the third quarter and eight more in the fourth quarter until the Cornhuskers scored the last time.

Nebraska ground out 227 yards of total offense in the second half (398 total) against OU's defense, which had allowed an average of just 89 yards rushing and 274 yards total offense per game this season.

''They had a good game plan and they wore us down,'' Oklahoma linebacker

Chris Wilson said. ''We have confidence in our defense and Coach (Gary) Gibbs has that confidence in us.''

That led to Gibbs deciding to kick off to open the second half, with the Sooners leading 14-3.

''We couldn't believe that they wanted to make us take the ball first in the second half,'' Wiegert said. ''Maybe they thought they could stop us like they did at the start.

''The thing was, we were getting the yards in the first half, but we had a couple of turnovers and we weren't going to do that in the second half. Maybe they didn't know that.''

Oklahoma scored its first touchdown

after Nebraska's Brown scrambled to pick up the opening kickoff and recovered it at the NU 2. Oklahoma stuffed the Cornhuskers and took over at the NU 33 after a short punt. Five plays later, Cale Gundy scored on a quarterback sneak.

Nebraska followed with turnovers on its next three possessions and OU took advantage. A 1-yard TD run by Mike Gaddis with 12:39 left in the first half culminated a 42-yard drive and gave OU a 14-0 lead.

''When they kicked off to us to start the second half, it was kind of like a dare,'' said McCant. ''We had been doing just fine, moving the ball in the first half but we had turnovers.

''We had no doubts that we could do a better job in the second half.''

Nebraska's Tyrone Hughes, playing with a cast on his left hand, returned the second-half kickoff 30 yards to the NU 30. Brown carried the ball on consecutive plays to the Oklahoma 34. Then, McCant hit tight end Johnny Mitchell on a 23-yard pass. Brown picked up six more yards and McCant scored on a 5-yard run to cut the OU lead to 14-10 with 9:53 left in the third quarter.

The Cornhuskers appeared ready to take the lead when they stopped Oklahoma on three plays, including an 8-yard sack by Travis Hill, to force a punt. NU used 12 plays to move the ball to the Sooner 1.

But Oklahoma's Stacey Dillard stuffed Brown for a 2-yard loss on fourth down to end that threat.

Nebraska's defense stymied Oklahoma on three downs again and, following a Sooner punt, Nebraska drove 35 yards for a 33-yard field goal by Bennett to cut the deficit to 14-13 with 12:20 left in the game.

''I never had a doubt in the second half,'' Mitchell said. ''None of us were scared by Oklahoma's lead at halftime or when they stopped us.

''It takes heart to play on a day like this and we had a lot of heart today.'' ■

Nebraska Coach Tom Osborne uses a referee's microphone to ask the fans at Memorial Stadium to stop throwing oranges onto the field during NU's 19-14 victory against Oklahoma November 29, 1991. (Randy Hampton, Journal Star Library)

Yes, NU Has Orange

Conference clincher "strangest game" for Huskers' Osborne

by Ken Hambleton

Lincoln Journal Star

Nov. 1, 1992

The answer is "Yes, we're going to the Orange Bowl. We accept," a somewhat tired and relieved Nebraska Coach Tom Osborne told a Japanese interviewer.

"It was the strangest game, the most bizarre circumstances I've coached in, but I'm happy to win and happy to win the Big Eight," he said after Nebraska dispatched Kansas State 38-24 Sunday in the Tokyo Dome.

The victory put Nebraska in the Orange Bowl January 1 for the second year in a row. NU shared the Big Eight football title with Colorado last year and won the conference title outright this year for the first time since 1988.

But the bowl game is more than three weeks off and half a world away from Tokyo. Meanwhile, Nebraska was trying to play happy guest to the gracious 50,000 who attended the game.

"We appreciate the interest in American football here, although I'm not sure people here understand all of what went on," Osborne said. "We won. They seemed happy, and they stayed in the stands. That's pretty good."

Nebraska sprinted to a 21-0 lead against a breathless Kansas State team in the first 22 minutes of the game, which began at about 10 p.m. Saturday Lincoln time.

By that stage of the game, Nebraska had 73 yards passing, 142 yards rushing and had run 35 plays to KSU's 10.

"They were sagging on the ropes by the end of the first quarter," Osborne said. "It was warm and humid in there, and they hadn't had a break."

Before Nebraska slammed the door, Kansas State slipped back in the game.

The Wildcats bounced back with a series of four completions by quarterback Matt Garber for 67 yards on a 76-yard drive to cut the score to 21-7 with 6:41 left in the half.

Nebraska lost a fumble and got one back but stalled for the first time since opening the game, and the Wildcats zipped downfield on a 27-yard pass from Garber to Gerald Benton to set up a 40-yard field goal by Tate Wright that cut the margin to 21-10 before halftime.

"I thought we had momentum by going in at the end of the first half at 21-10," Kansas State Coach Bill Snyder said. "Getting those 10 points so quickly seemed to give our defense a chance to catch its breath and give our offense confidence."

That feeling came crashing to an end in the first six minutes of the second half.

Nebraska freshman Tommie Frazier hit two rollout passes—one to Vincent Hawkins and one to Corey Dixon to set up a 42-yard field goal by Byron Bennett.

Kansas State clicked off five first downs in six plays but stalled on downs at the KSU 46 with 5:31 left in the quarter.

The Cornhuskers immediately pounced on the opportunity when Dixon made a diving catch for a 19-yard gain to

Husker quarterback Tommie Frazier dives to complete his 19-yard touchdown run as Kansas State's Tony Williams (74) pursues. Outland winner Will Shields is in the background (Randy Hampton, Journal Star Library)

the KSU 49. Dixon grabbed another Frazier pass for a 9-yard gain, and finally Calvin Jones broke away on a simple sweeping pitch play around the left end for a 38-yard touchdown to put Nebraska ahead 31-10.

Kansas State rallied for a touchdown on an 8-yard run by Garber, but Nebraska clicked off a 10 running-play drive that ended on a quarterback sneak by Frazier with 9:19 left in the game to pad the lead to 38-17.

"We had a nice drive and score, and I thought we were back in the game, but Nebraska had a drive equally as good right after it, and that slowed us down in terms of getting any control of the game," Snyder said.

Nebraska didn't score again, sputtering after reaching the K-State 16 and giving up a long scoring drive to the Wildcats, but the game was never in doubt.

We have to ride back with these guys on the same plane," Osborne said. "We took Calvin Jones out and got in everybody we brought here but Andre McDuffy, who was injured, and there were some letdowns.

"And there was the problem, like when we got the 21-0 lead and again at 38-17, we seemed to relax a bit, and Kansas State kept battling."

Kansas State picked up almost one-third of its 315 yards of total offense after Nebraska's final score with 9:19 left in the game.

"Our game was a little disjointed after we got the big lead early," Osborne said. "We played well to get the lead. We did it again in the third quarter.

"But even with our experience at Iowa State this year (a 19-10 upset), at 21-0 and at 38-10, the guys think, 'Oh, Kansas State,'" Osborne said. "They get up for Colorado and Oklahoma, and they were excited at times in this game. But there were letdowns. I wouldn't think that'd be a problem in Miami, no matter who we play." ■

Husker defenders Trev Alberts (34) and Terry Connealy (99) pressure Colorado quarterback Koy Detmer during NU's 52-7 triumph on October 31, 1992. (Randy Hampton, Journal Star Library)

CU Gives Up Ghost

by Ken Hambleton
Lincoln Journal-Star

ebraska grabbed all the goodies and smashed Colorado 52-7 before a wet and delirious crowd of 76,287 football fans Saturday at Memorial Stadium.

The Cornhuskers bullied their way through a "big one" that many said they couldn't win, shoved aside Colorado's 25-game Big Eight unbeaten streak and rubbed the Buffaloes' passing attack into the turf. It appeared to take more time to tear down the goal posts than the self-appointed archrivals of Nebraska.

"We took the No. 8 team in the country and slammed them," said NU defensive tackle John Parrella. "We didn't win by a fluky field goal, a fifth down, a weird penalty or some lucky deal. We slammed them."

The ferocious attack was part of the plan, according to NU outside linebacker Trev Alberts.

"It was just straight-up, blood-in-your-eyes, go get the quarterback," he said. "Four quarters from the get-go of flying around and going crazy. We could line up in the wrong defense, go the wrong way and still make something happen."

NU freshman quarterback Tommie Frazier, who improved to 2-0 in his second career start, added: "I'm glad I didn't go against our defense today. I wouldn't have gotten up, much less gotten a yard running or passing."

It would be hard to find anything that went wrong for 6-1 Nebraska, which entered the game tied with Colorado for eighth in the Associated Press poll. The Cornhuskers, who had been 0-8 against Top 10 teams since 1988, took away any chance of a close contest with a 428-144 edge in total offense. Nebraska controlled the ball for almost 43 minutes of the 60-minute game.

From the opening play, when Nebraska's Travis Hill intercepted a pass to set up the first touchdown, until the finish, the Cornhuskers controlled everything in the game between 1991 Big Eight co-champions.

"We wanted to be the most dominant, physical team we could be," said NU Coach Tom Osborne. "I didn't see any way we would beat Colorado that badly. Turnovers make you look bad. Colorado is a better football team than what they showed today, but the turnovers just make you look like you're not getting anything done."

By halftime, the Buffaloes were in the bag, trailing 24-7.

Colorado entered the game as the fourth-best passing team in NCAA Division I-A. Nebraska's defense dropped the Buffaloes' average of 334 yards per game passing, allowing Colorado just 136 yards passing and 8 yards rushing.

The Bufs, 2-0-1 in their three most recent games against Nebraska, managed just 7 yards passing on three completions in the second half. They didn't have a first down in the second half until late in the fourth quarter.

Hill, who along with Alberts, Parella, Bruce Moore and Terry Connealy harassed Colorado freshman quarterback Koy Detmer, broke the game open when he picked off a pass on the first play of the game.

Four plays later, Calvin Jones scored the first of his three touchdowns on a 3-yard dive play.

The Cornhuskers sputtered for the first and only time in the game on a drive late in the first quarter when on a fake field goal, a shovel pass from holder Mike Stigge to Cory Schlesinger was dropped.

Nebraska more than made up for that play on its next possession.

Jones, a sophomore I-back from Omaha Central, tore through the Colorado defense—rated 11th in the country—on a 47-yard touchdown blast behind key blocks from guard Will Shields, tackle Rob Zatechka, wingback Abdul Muhammad and tight end Gerald

Armstrong to put NU ahead 14-0 with 13:26 left in the first half.

Minutes later, Steve Carmer, who had almost intercepted two other passes, finally picked off a Detmer pass. Nebraska drove to the CU 1-yard line before Byron Bennett kicked a 24-yard field goal to increase the lead to 17-0.

"The offensive line caused havoc for Colorado," said Jones, who finished with 101 yards rushing.

Colorado answered for the first and only time when Detmer, the younger brother of 1990 Heisman Trophy winner Ty Detmer of Brigham Young, strung together six completions in nine attempts to drive the Buffs 81 yards in 12 plays. James Hill capped the drive when he scored on a 3-yard run.

On Colorado's next possession, Nebraska's Hill made sure his team had one more chance before the end of the half.

He broke through the CU offensive line and grabbed Detmer's hand, knocking the ball loose. Hill recovered at the Colorado 27 with 1:43 left in the half.

Facing third-and-4 at the Colorado 21, Nebraska called on a play out of the past and sent Shields around right end on a "fumblerooskie" to the Buffs' 5. Four plays later, Jones scored from 1 yard out on a dive behind guard Chris Zyzda and tackle Lance Lundberg.

"I had been complaining to the refs about getting held, and I was determined to get in the backfield and do something about it," NU's Hill said of his fumble recovery. "Besides, I knew our offense was doing well enough that one more chance was all they needed to score."

Colorado never had a chance in the second half.

When the buffs stopped Nebraska on downs, NU punter Mike Stigge planted a kick on the CU 2.

Then, Nebraska linebacker Mike Anderson, just back from arthroscopic knee surgery, intercepted a pass at the CU 26 to set up a 5-yard touchdown pass

from Frazier to Armstrong—who has four catches for four touchdowns this year.

The Bufs, after an interception on their second series of the second half, went to sophomore quarterback Kordell Stewart, who has started five games this season but missed too many practices during the week because of leg injuries.

It didn't change a thing.

On Stewart's first play, Hill stopped him for no gain. On his second, Hill and Alberts threw him for a 9-yard loss. On his third play, he overthrew a receiver to avoid a sack. On his fourth play, he barely escaped Alberts again.

Soon thereafter, NU fullback Lance Lewis scored on a 34-yard trap play up the middle. Then Frazier hit Corey Dixon on a 48-yard bomb and connected with William Washington on a 1-yard touchdown pass. Finally, Schlesinger scored on a 5-yard dive that capped a 12-play, 63-yard drive.

"It's just a beginning," Frazier said. "It's not a statement. We have too many games left. But this is a good start." ∎

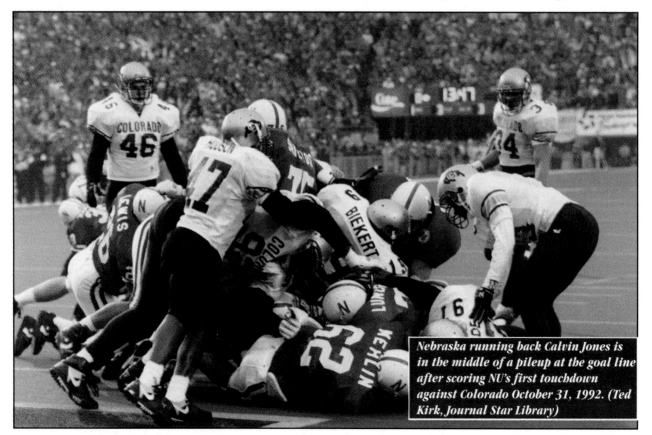

Nebraska running back Calvin Jones is in the middle of a pileup at the goal line after scoring NU's first touchdown against Colorado October 31, 1992. (Ted Kirk, Journal Star Library)

Iowa State fans storm the field at Ames, Iowa, November 14, 1992 after the Cyclones upset No. 7 Nebraska 19-10. The loss was Tom Osborne's final Big Eight Conference defeat and marked the only time in his 25 years as NU head coach that the Huskers lost to a team that finished the season with a sub-.500 record. (Journal Star Library)

1992

Season in Review

Won 9, Lost 3, Tied 0
Big 8: Won 6, Lost 1, Tied 0, 1st

Date	Opponent	Site	AP Rank NU/Opp.	Result
Sept. 5	Utah	Lincoln	11/	W 49-22
Sept. 12	Mid. Tenn. St.	Lincoln	11/	W 48-7
Sept. 19	Washington	Seattle	12/2	L 14-29
Sept. 26	Arizona State	Lincoln	15/	W 45-24
Oct. 10	Oklahoma St.	Lincoln	15/	W 55-0
Oct. 24	Missouri	Columbia	8/	W 34-24
Oct. 31	Colorado	Lincoln	tie 8/tie 8	W 52-7
Nov. 7	Kansas	Lincoln	7/13	W 49-7
Nov. 14	Iowa State	Ames	7/	L 10-19
Nov. 27	Oklahoma	Norman	12/	W 33-9
Dec. 5	Kansas State	Tokyo	11/	W 38-24

Federal Express Orange Bowl

Jan. 1	Florida State	Miami	11/3	L 14-27

Final Rankings: 14th AP, 14th UPI, 14th CNN/USA Today Coaches (post-bowl)

Interestingly Enough, Osborne Deserves To Do Well

by Mike Babcock

Lincoln Journal Star

Oct. 3, 1993

Time magazine once planned an in-depth profile on Tom Osborne, but the project was eventually scrapped, supposedly, because Osborne's story didn't prove interesting enough.

Midwestern values aren't particularly interesting in an often cynical, self-centered society such as ours, where high personal standards tend to be regarded either as suspicious or as character flaws. Unless, of course, the standards are disguised.

They aren't in Osborne, who's in his 21st season as head football coach at the University of Nebraska. They are, however, in Bobby Bowden, the head football coach at Florida State.

Osborne and Bowden are a lot alike, but they're perceived as dramatically different because Bowden is down-home humorous, a good old boy from Alabama, while Osborne is a straight-laced, almost ministerial kind of a guy from Hastings. That's Osborne's image, anyway. Those

who know him well say he has a keen sense of humor.

Undoubtedly, he does. But he's so intelligent, what might be funny to many of us probably seems foolish, if not stupid, to him.

I mention Bowden because he was the focus of the cover story in Sports Illustrated's college football preview issue. The story implied it would be nice if Bowden were to finally win a national championship, not only because he's been so successful and come so close so many times but also because, darn it, he's such a nice guy.

Based on my limited contact with him, Bowden is a nice guy, as nice as you'll find, regardless of occupation or success. I, too, would like to see Bowden be

awarded a mythical national title because I'd like to believe personal goodness is rewarded. Bowden deserves it.

But then, so does Osborne, and I write that knowing it seems to lack the critical objectivity of a serious columnist.

Contrary to what some fans apparently think, my responsibility is not to promote Osborne and his program. I do not look for the nearest open window to leap from the press box when the Cornhuskers lose, nor do I share in their celebration when they win. I rarely wear red, and never at an athletic contest involving Nebraska.

Sometimes, as a result, I fail to give Osborne the same respect I would give Bowden or some other coach. Also, because I'm here instead of in Tallahassee, I'm too close to this situation to see it clearly. The negatives are magnified, the positives blurred.

Osborne's team opens Big Eight Conference play against Oklahoma State at Stillwater Thursday night. The game will be televised nationally on the ESPN cable network. If the Cornhuskers win, the victory would be No. 200 under Osborne.

I say "if" in deference to Osborne,

Tommie Frazier became one of the top quarterbacks in Nebraska history despite being hampered for almost a whole season because of blood clots in his leg. He led the Huskers to two national championships. (Journal Star Library)

who has achieved 199 coaching victories by treating all opponents with equal seriousness. An Osborne-coached team has never lost to Oklahoma State.

Osborne almost certainly will dismiss victory No. 200 as no big deal. As I recall, he used the phrase "hill of beans" following victory No. 100–42-10 against UCLA in 1983.

But it will be a big deal. Only two other active coaches have 200 or more victories: Bowden and Penn State's Joe Paterno.

Despite what reporters who lack the initiative to check the record claim, the majority of Osborne's victories have come against worthy competition–unless the Big Eight doesn't qualify, in which case there is nothing he could have done. On balance, Nebraska's schedules have been no worse than those of any other successful program.

That Osborne has been Nebraska's head coach for 21 years is as impressive as his victory total, not only because it underscores how quickly he has achieved the total (more than nine wins a season, on the average) but also because it's contrary to a trend. Few major college coaches remain at one school

Nebraska linebacker Ed Stewart sacks the UCLA quarterback during NU's 14-13 victory against the Bruins September 18, 1993. (Randy Hampton, Journal Star Library)

that long, by choice or otherwise.

Osborne is a remarkable coach, with a remarkable record, achieved without compromising his values. But those things don't always make for interesting reading, especially if the setting is the Midwest. ■

1993 Season in Review	Won 11, Lost 1, Tied 0 Big 8: Won 7, Lost 0, Tied 0, 1st				
	Date	Opponent	Site	AP Rank NU/Opp.	Result
	Sept. 4	North Texas	Lincoln	9/	W 76-14
	Sept. 11	Texas Tech	Lincoln	9/	W 50-27
	Sept. 18	UCLA	Pasadena	8/	W 14-13
	Sept. 25	Colorado State	Lincoln	6/	W 48-13
	Oct. 7	Oklahoma State	Stillwater	7/	W 27-13
	Oct. 16	Kansas State	Lincoln	6/	W 45-28
	Oct. 23	Missouri	Lincoln	5/	W 49-7
	Oct. 30	Colorado	Boulder	6/20	W 21-17
	Nov. 6	Kansas	Lawrence	6/	W 21-20
	Nov. 13	Iowa State	Lincoln	4/	W 49-17
	Nov. 26	Oklahoma	Lincoln	2/16	W 21-7
	Federal Express Orange Bowl				
	Jan. 1	Florida State	Miami	2/1	L 16-18

Final Rankings: 3rd AP, UPI, and CNN/Today Coaches (all post-bowl)

NU Goes Miles For Coach's 200th Win

by Mike Babcock
Lincoln Journal Star

Oct. 8, 1993—Who says 199 plus one-half doesn't equal 200?

Nebraska found its offense in options and pitches in the second half and discovered its defense in the pit of the line to top Oklahoma State 27-13 Thursday night at Lewis Field and give Tom Osborne his 200th career coaching victory. The go-ahead score came when Barron Miles blocked a punt and recovered it for a touchdown.

"I said, 'Let's go outside,' to Coach Osborne, and we did in the second half," said NU quarterback Tommie Frazier. "Basically, he came up with an offensive package that could get around their defense. We didn't have any doubts. We just had to figure out a plan that would work."

Positive changes for Nebraska's defense were simpler in the nationally televised (ESPN) game.

"We played awful, maybe the worst defense ever in the first half," said NU outside linebacker Trev Alberts. "In the second half, I think it was sheer determination.

"Here is the greatest coach, somebody who has given everything for this team and this program, and we were just playing awful. I think that, more than anything, got us going in the second half."

Maybe that explained Osborne's modesty and reluctance to celebrate joining the group of 12 Division I-A college football coaches with at least 200 victories.

"I take it with some mixed emotion," Osborne said of his 200th win, all of them recorded in his 21 seasons at Nebraska. "You want to see players play up to potential, and in the second half, we did. In the first half, we didn't."

A Husker fan holds up a sign denoting Tom Osborne's 200th victory, which came October 7, 1993. (Randy Hampton, Journal Star Library)

"We were healthier—with Calvin Jones back and Tommie Frazier healed up—but we weren't better."

Frazier contributed 68 yards rushing and 109 yards passing, including a touchdown run, and Jones had 136 yards on 21 carries, including a 44-yard touchdown late in the game.

"In the first half, we had offside calls, missed blocks and missed line calls against a good defense, and that doesn't take much to stop you," Osborne said. "In the second half we played the trap better on defense, and we got away from their defensive strength with our offense."

Osborne emphasized the "we" in talking about the game as well as in talking about the historic victory.

"I'm one-hundredth of the 200 wins," he said. "I'm proud to be a part of an organization that has won 300 games in 31 years. That's gratifying to be a part of a group that works that hard. And that includes our fans, because they don't tolerate anything but winning."

Apparently, Nebraska's football team wouldn't tolerate anything else either.

The fifth- and seventh-ranked Cornhuskers, 5-0 overall and 1-0 in the Big Eight, corralled the Cowboy's offense in the second half.

Oklahoma State managed only 21 yards rushing, two first downs and 59 yards of offense in the second half. By contrast, OSU had 161 yards of offense and 11 first downs while building a 13-6 halftime lead.

Meanwhile, Nebraska's offense more than doubled its first-half output and gave the Cornhuskers the winning margin. The turnaround came quickly in the third quarter.

Frazier finished a seven-play, 56-yard drive with a 4-yard option keeper around the right end to tie the score with 5:24 left in the third quarter.

"We were going outside, and it stopped the effectiveness of Oklahoma State's stunts and blitzes on defense," said NU offensive guard Zach Wiegert.

Frazier gained 28 yards on three options, and Jones picked up 20 yards on a pitch around the left end on the drive.

Cornhusker cornerback Miles then gave Nebraska its first lead when he faked outside, broke free inside and blocked an OSU punt with his chest in the end zone. He fell on the ball for a touchdown, and Nebraska broke away.

"That block by Barron was huge," Osborne said. "He never quits coming. He'll put his face on it, and we won't look away." ■

Osborne Remains A Winner On All Counts

by **Mike Babcock**

Lincoln Journal Star

Oct. 10, 1993

Thursday night, Tom Osborne became only the 12th college football coach in history to achieve 200 NCAA Division I-A career victories.

That total is a standard by which coaching greatness is measured. It is not an absolute, however.

Osborne qualifies by other standards. He reached 200 victories in his 21st season, all at Nebraska. Five others have coached 200 or more victories at one school.

Only two other active major college coaches and 200 victories: Joe Paterno and Bobby Bowden.

Neither Paterno nor Bowden has won as consistently as Osborne, the winningest active Division I-A coach, by percentage. The 200 victories represent a remarkable 80.9 percent of the games he has coached.

But one of Osborne's 46 losses says as much, or more, about his coaching greatness as the 200 victories and the .809 winning percentage.

On the night of January 2, 1984, Osborne solidified his position among the great coaches, by attempting to win when a tie would have been enough.

Osborne's 11th team, undefeated and untied, trailed Miami 31-30 in the Orange Bowl, with 48 seconds left. The Cornhuskers had scored a touchdown, rallying from a 14-point deficit for the second time that night.

A successful extra-point kick would have meant a tie. A two-point conversion would have meant a victory. Either would have meant a national championship for Nebraska.

The circumstances justified a tie. Reason, and the percentages on which Osborne's 200 victories have been based, mandated a tie. But Osborne responded with his heart, refusing even to consider playing for a tie.

He wouldn't have been able to look into the eyes of his players if he had been willing to accept a tie, Osborne said afterward.

Ironically, the play with which Osborne challenged the percentages was a pass–or, at least, ended up as a pass. Turner Gill could have run if there had been an opening.

But Gill rolled out and threw hurriedly to I-back Jeff Smith in the end zone. Miami safety Ken Calhoun deflected the ball, which glanced off Smith's shoulder pad, incomplete. Nebraska football fans can recite that sequence of events by heart.

Osborne has never stood taller than he did that night in Miami, at least not as a football coach. That one decision represents what he stands for: playing to win, being accountable, doing what's right rather than what's expedient, accepting responsibility for one's actions and decisions.

There has been much discussion of Osborne's coaching victories because of his reaching 200. But the relative handful of defeats he has endured also are instructive.

Last year's 19-10 loss to Iowa State, for example, underscores the consistency of Osborne's teams. In 21 seasons, that's Nebraska's only loss to a team finishing with a losing record. The Cyclones were 4-7.

The 45-10 loss to Oklahoma in 1990 was the only time I've seen an Osborne-coached team appear to give up. And I've seen most of Nebraska's 46 losses under Osborne.

It's often difficult to get a good read on someone as successful as Osborne be-cause success can be a mask. Losing builds character, the cliche goes. It also exposes character in those accustomed to winning.

From a writer's point of view, Osborne is best in defense, even though he hasn't had much practice.

That doesn't mean Osborne is a good loser. No one who coaches 200 victories loses well. Osborne is an intense com-petitor, another quality represented by 200 victories.

Osborne doesn't lose well, nor does he accept defeat easily. But outwardly, he responds to losses with the grace and pride that have come to characterize him in victory.

If Osborne's comments about his 200th coaching victory have seemed mun-dane, compare them to what he says the next time his team loses. Those rare op-portunities provide the best insight into one of college football's best coaches, now and for all time. ■

A sellout crowd braved the elements to watch the November 26, 1993 game against Oklahoma, just as fans have for 220 straight games, an NCAA record. (Randy Hampton, Journal Star Library)

No Matter Final Score, Osborne Wins Respect

by Ken Hambleton

Lincoln Journal Star

Dec. 31, 1993

This week, in the glare of national media attention, Tom Osborne tried to dress up his image.

He started his first news conference of the week with a joke about how he took being called a "bowl of Cream of Wheat" as a great insult.

He closed the week with the same joke at a banquet for the Orange Bowl Hall of Fame.

If anything, Osborne is looser, funnier and more open than ever. And that's in spite of the fact his team faces 17-point favorite Florida State Saturday in what is being billed as the national championship game at the Orange Bowl.

Osborne, who is about to complete his 21st season as head coach of the Cornhuskers, has had just one other season finale that decided the national championship. That time, January 2, 1984, his team fell a 2-point conversion short of beating Miami in the Orange Bowl.

"I don't worry about that game. I don't even think about it much," Osborne said. "There's nothing haunting about it or any other game we've played. We just prepare the best we can and hope that's good enough."

In the past six years of bowl games, it hasn't. Nebraska has lost each of those games, including three to Florida State.

In all, Osborne's teams are 8-12 in bowl games. The Cornhuskers have been to a record 25 consecutive bowl games. They also have won at least nine games every year Osborne has coached and helped him become the winningest active coach—by percentage—in the NCAA. Osborne also became the first coach to reach 200 career wins by his 21st season. This year, Nebraska is top-ranked and has a record of 11-0.

And yet, he finds himself bringing up the memories of Buffalo Bills Coach Marv Levy, whose teams have lost the past three Super Bowls, and former Minnesota Vikings Coach Bud Grant, whose teams lost four Super Bowls.

"It's kind of amazing because they've been better than anybody else except for maybe one team, three or four years in a row, which is a very difficult accomplishment, and yet the reaction is if you don't win it all, you somehow don't measure up," Osborne said.

In the eyes of his players, however, Osborne does measure up.

"You're not going to see him dump the water bucket, slam the chalk board and start cussing," said senior defensive tackle Kevin Ramaekers. "He is a guy you respect like you would your dad. I treat him the way I treat my dad. You listen to just about anything he says because you know he's not just talking."

When Osborne posted his 200th victory at Oklahoma State this year, Ramaekers dumped a water bucket on the coach's head, and, on Ramaekers' birthday in early December, Osborne returned the favor at a practice in Lincoln.

Senior inside linebacker Mike Anderson said he wants to win the championship for Osborne as much as he does for himself and his teammates.

"When we win, maybe people will stop looking for the flaws and appreciate him for the great coach and great man that he is," he said. "A lot of people don't know about the scholarship money he provides (more than $20,000 annually to minority students) and the way he helps develop the best academic support program in colleges today.

"He preaches to us about doing well in life and what matters is growing up to be a man and how football is secondary."

Florida State Coach Bobby Bowden said the best compliment he could offer about Osborne was: "He's the kind of man I would like my sons, well, now grandsons, to play for."

Bowden said Osborne is respected as an individual as well as an innovative coach.

"He does what he has to do to win the Big Eight," Bowden said. "He gets in the bowl games. We may have an advantage because we live down here in Florida, closer to the bowl games and closer to

the people who play the game, but there is no finer coach."

Still, Osborne has his detractors.

"One-dimensional offense," said Steve Wieberg of *USA Today*.

"Not willing to change," wrote Michael Wilbon of The *Washington Post*.

"Still hasn't figured it out," said another national writer who asked to remain anonymous.

"They treat Coach Osborne as if he never won a game," said Nebraska tight end Gerald Armstrong. "We're not professionals. It's still a game. And we do win more than our share.

"He keeps the game in the proper perspective and shows that while football is a part of life, that's all it is. It's not like

you live or die on the outcome of the game."

NU All-American and Butkus Award winner Trev Alberts, a senior outside linebacker, said Osborne's loyalty to his players and his staff impresses him the most.

"He stands behind his players, and he stands behind what's best for them," he said. "He may not be the closest friend of most of the team, but he'll be there if you need him."

Said sophomore quarterback Tommie Frazier: "I can talk to him about anything at any time. We have a relationship where I can joke with him–yes, joke with him–and he'll joke with me." ■

All-America linebacker Trev Alberts was among the speakers at a fund-raising dinner celebrating Tom Osborne's 200th victory. The February 3, 1994 dinner raised $250,000 for the Osborne Endowment for Youth. (Gail Folda, Journal Star Library)

Soooooooooooo Close!
NU falls in final seconds

by **Mike Babcock**

Lincoln Journal Star

Jan. 2, 1994

Nebraska's hopes for the mythical national football championship drifted to the left along with Byron Bennett's 45-yard field goal attempt at the end of the Orange Bowl Saturday, but maybe there is something left for the Cornhuskers.

"If there is a moral victory, this is it," NU defensive tackle Kevin Ramaekers said of the Cornhuskers' 18-16 loss to Florida State. "Let's put it this way, a national championship beats the heck out of moral victories, too."

Florida State Coach Bobby Bowden agreed.

"Nebraska deserved to win it as much as we did," he said. "We've lost national championships by missing kicks, and tonight we won with a kick."

The victory put Florida State, 12-1, in position for its first title.

Seminole kicker Scott Bentley kicked his fourth field goal of the game with 21 seconds left to give FSU the win before a record crowd of 81,536.

Florida State's 60-yard drive to set up Bentley's 22-yard field goal took 55 seconds.

Bennett, who hadn't kicked a field goal since October 16, appeared to have won the game with a 27-yard field goal with 1:16 left to give Nebraska a 16-15 lead.

The Cornhusker senior got another chance to give NU its first national championship since the 1971 season, with one second left. But his kick was wide left.

"I think we may have hurried, may have just not gotten the ball right," Bennett said. "All the calls, all the plays and all the game were in that kick.

"It was crazy, and maybe I rushed it a bit."

Nebraska's final drive started at its 43-yard line when Barron Miles returned the FSU kickoff 23 yards.

NU quarterback Tommie Frazier passed to tight end Trumane Bell at the FSU 20, but Bell bobbled the ball as it went out of bounds with eight seconds left in the game.

"That pass to Trumane was still open, so we tried it again," said Frazier, who passed for 206 yards, ran for 77 and was named Nebraska's most valuable player.

Frazier found Bell alone over the middle of the field, and a diving, saving tackle by FSU cornerback Corey Sawyer at the Seminole 28 seemed to win the game.

Fans, Florida State players and coaches flooded the field, while Nebraska players stood in bewilderment.

But officials determined there was one second left when Nebraska called a timeout.

"I was standing next to the ref when I called time out, and I could see two seconds on the clock, so I knew we had some time," Frazier said. "It was all we played for. A chance to win the national championship. That's our whole season, the whole reason for playing.

"We had the chance, and we'll try it again."

Nebraska, which finished 11-1, lost its chance at the national championship on the same field, near the same end zone where a two-point conversion attempt at the end of the game fell short in a 31-30 loss to Miami in the 1984 Orange Bowl.

Coach Tom Osborne said his team played as well as the winners.

"The main thing is playing like champions. As far as I'm concerned, we won," he said. "I'm glad Bobby Bowden got his national championship. I'm sorry we

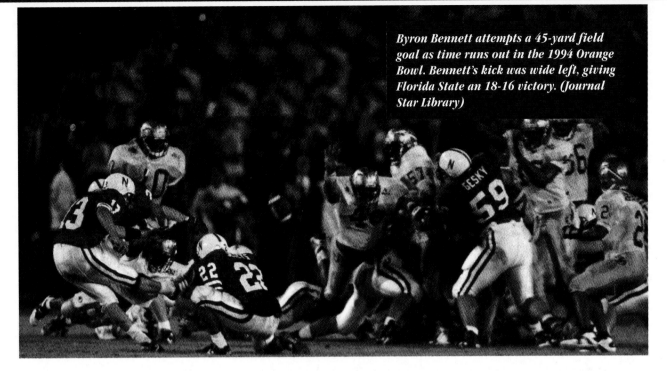

Byron Bennett attempts a 45-yard field goal as time runs out in the 1994 Orange Bowl. Bennett's kick was wide left, giving Florida State an 18-16 victory. (Journal Star Library)

didn't."

The Seminoles began their game-winning drive at their 35 with 1:16 left.

Florida State quarterback and Heisman Trophy winner Charlie Ward hit Warrick Dunn of passes of 21 yards and 9 yards, and Nebraska was called for personal foul and pass interference penalties that moved the ball to the NU 3.

"It was a tough call, but I ran up his heels," and NU rover back Toby Wright. "We played so well all game and they came and got us on that last drive."

Wright then tackled Sean Jackson for a 2-yard loss, and on second down from the 5, FSU chose to kick the field goal.

Minutes earlier, the Cornhuskers drove to the Florida State 22, but facing third-and-9, was penalized for illegal procedure. On third-and-14, Frazier hurried a pass, which was intercepted by Richard Coes.

Nebraska held and forced a punt, but its second penalty of the game for an illegal block in the back forced the Cornhuskers to begin their final drive from their 20 with 4:39 left in the game. NU drove 71 yards and took a 16-15 lead on Bennett's kick.

Nebraska had closed to 15-13 when freshman running back Lawrence Phillips broke through the right side of the line, behind the trapping blocks of Rob Zatechka and Lance Lundberg, to score on a 12-yard run on the first play of the fourth quarter.

The Cornhuskers tried for two points. Frazier sprinted around right end, pump-faked a pass and tried to dive into the end zone but was driven out of bounds by FSU's Ken Alexander and Derrick Alexander.

Florida State scored a touchdown on its first drive of the second half, when fullback William Floyd was ruled in the end zone before he fumbled on a 1-yard dive with the quarter two minutes old.

The Seminoles tacked on a 39-yard field goal by Bentley, the highly recruited freshman from Aurora, Colo., to take a 15-7 lead with 3:06 left in the third quarter.

The Cornhuskers took a 7-3 lead with a dazzling break when Frazier's pass to Clester Johnson was tipped by FSU safety Devon Bush and into the hands of Reggie Baul.

Baul, a sophomore from Papillion, grabbed the ball at the FSU 13 and raced into the end zone to put Nebraska ahead with 5:59 left in the first half.

The Seminoles, favored by 17½ points, bounced back on a 25-yard field goal by Bentley to cut the deficit to a 7-6 with 29 seconds left in the second quarter.

Florida State drove from its 21 with passes of 22 and 14 yards and a 23-yard scramble by Ward. But the march to the Nebraska 5-yard line was stalled on a sack by NU cornerback John Reece, who threw Ward for a 3-yard loss on third down.

The Seminoles took the lead mid-way in the second quarter when Bentley kicked a 34-yard field goal to cap a eight-play, 63-yard drive that was highlighted by a 31-yard pass from Ward to Kevin Knox and pass interference penalty against Reece on third-and-6 that set the ball up for FSU at the Nebraska 15.

Nebraska was a push away from scoring the first touchdown in the game when Corey Dixon grabbed a Florida State punt at the Nebraska 29 and broke four tackles on his way to the end zone. However, apparently Nebraska sophomore Tyrone Williams was called for a push in the back (illegal block) on FSU's Ken Alexander on the return and Nebraska took over at its 23 instead. ∎

Yes, Virginia, There Is An NU

by Ken Hambleton

Lincoln Journal Star

 ebraska's defense ran a lightning quick sideline shuttle service and the Cornhusker offense spent the afternoon touring the field August 28, 1994, in the 12th annual Kickoff Classic at East Rutherford, N.J.

Nebraska picked up where it left off from last year's narrow Orange Bowl loss with a 31-0 thrashing of West Virginia in the most one-sided game in the history of the annual college football season opener.

Junior quarterback Tommie Frazier paced the offensive onslaught as he ran for 130 yards and three touchdowns and passed for 100 more and another touchdown. Frazier's choice of options helped lead Nebraska to 468 yards of total of-

fense and earned him Most Valuable Player honors.

Even though the NU offense had five turnovers, the Cornhusker defense quickly smothered the flames by holding West Virginia to 4 yards in the first half, 89 yards in the game and one fourth-quarter penetration past midfield. Throughout the game, West Virginia, 11-0 in the regular season the previous year, appeared confused, tired and beaten.

"It seemed like our offense couldn't do anything," said West Virginia tailback Robert Walker.

Even though it was an August afternoon in a season that runs until January, Nebraska's victory was so complete, some New York writers were talking about

Frazier winning the Heisman Trophy and the Huskers taking the national title.

"It was just another game for us," said senior offensive tackle Zach Wiegert. "We've got work to do."

NU defensive tackle Christian Peter, who had seven tackles in front of more than 250 family members and friends from his hometown of Locust, New Jersey, suggested the importance of the game could be overestimated. "It could have been a fluke," he said. "We don't know. It was just one game."

Tom Sieler opened the scoring with a 32-yard field goal with 34 seconds left in the first quarter. After West Virginia ended its third series without a first down, Nebraska went to its option game and took control of the game. ■

The Sears National Championship Trophy is one of the most coveted in sports. Nebraska earned three Sears Trophies in Tom Osborne's last four years, including this one after being voted No.1 in The 1994 USA Today/CNN Coaches' Poll. (Journal Star Library)

Excited Opponent Keeps NU On The Run

by Ken Hambleton

Lincoln Journal Star

Standing barefoot on an equipment trunk, Tommie Frazier discussed how unstable Nebraska was in a 42-16 victory against Texas Tech on September 8, 1994, at Jones Stadium in Lubbock, Texas.

At an impromptu news conference, he explained that Nebraska at times had a "shaky" offense, a "shaky" passing game and even a "shaky" defense. But Nebraska found stability in a rock-solid ground game that paved the way for 524 yards rushing and 612 yards of total offense.

"It took awhile to get going," said Frazier, who ran for 84 yards and two touchdowns and threw for 88 yards and another touchdown. "We were not taking it in for the score, and we went back to traditional Nebraska football to fix that."

The tradition was exhibited in the form of Lawrence Phillips rushing for 175 yards and two touchdowns and fullback Cory Schlesinger rushing for 84. Running behind a potent offensive line, Nebraska backs averaged almost 8 yards a carry on 63 attempts.

"It was a combination of things," Frazier said. "I got tired, and the offensive line got tired in the second quarter. But we came in the locker room, rested up and got fired up."

Texas Tech stopped NU's last three drives of the first half. The Red Raiders then scored on an 80-yard drive to open the second half and closed the margin to 14-9 with less than three minutes gone in the third quarter.

"I thought we were going to win, but if we dropped the ball, made a bad play or made a mistake, we were in trouble at that point," Nebraska Coach Tom Osborne said.

"I think they were more excited to play Nebraska than Nebraska was to play them."

Still, Nebraska pulled away with a whopping 370 yards of offense in the second half and put the game away with back-to-back touchdown drives after Texas Tech's third-quarter score. Then the Cornhuskers sent most of the 32,768 fans streaming to the exits when Frazier hit tight end Eric Alford on a 35-yard touchdown pass with 10:56 remaining. ■

The Nebraska defense, including linebacker Clint Brown (45), shut down the Texas Tech offense in NU's 42-16 victory September 8, 1994. (Journal Star Library)

Huskers' Fine Line Keeps Up Grind

by Ken Hambleton

Lincoln Journal Star

ffensive lines do not inspire poetry.

The running game does not lead to artistic interpretation.

Simple, basic running the football deserves simple, basic descriptions.

"Our offense did a great job. They mashed 'em," Nebraska defensive coordinator Charlie McBride said after the Cornhuskers blasted UCLA 49-21 September 17, 1994, at Memorial Stadium.

NU's offensive elan was enough to stymie any hopes of UCLA posting an upset in the Cornhuskers' first home game of the season.

"Their offense is so strong that it helps their defense, because you always feel under the gun to score and that makes you do things you wouldn't otherwise," said UCLA Coach Terry Donahue.

The Cornhusker offensive line started the stampede. Downfield blocks helped extend plays, and NU backs finished the task. Seven Cornhuskers scored TDs, including receiver Brendan Holbein, who had been grazed by a bullet a week earlier.

By the time Nebraska had rolled up a 49-14 advantage with 11:32 left in the game, the Huskers had 15 runs that went for 10 yards or more, including five times for 22 yards or more. NU finished with 484 yards on the ground, an average of 7.4 yards per carry.

NU I-back Lawrence Phillips gained a career-high 178 yards and scored a touchdown, backups Clinton Childs and Damon Benning combined for another 107 yards, and fullbacks Cory Schlesinger and Jeff Makovicka combined for another 100 yards.

"I saw fear in their (the Bruins') eyes," said Nebraska quarterback Tommie Frazier. "It was hard for them to call a defensive front because we kept them off-balance all game."

For the most part, he was right. The Cornhuskers rolled up 555 total yards.

"The offensive line was blowing people up," Schlesinger said. "You know when I can get a 27-yard run, the offensive line is doing it up front and the receivers are blocking downfield, because I'm not the quickest guy in the world." ∎

1994 Season in Review

Won 13, Lost 0, Tied 0
Big Eight: Won 7, Lost 0, Tied 0, 1st

Date	Opponent	Site	AP Rank NU/Opp.	Result
Aug. 28	W. Virginia	E. Rutherford	4/24	W 31-0
Sept. 8	Texas Tech	Lubbock	1/	W 42-16
Sept. 17	UCLA	Lincoln	2/13	W 49-21
Sept. 24	Pacific	Lincoln	2/	W 70-21
Oct. 1	Wyoming	Lincoln	2/	W 42-32
Oct. 8	Oklahoma State	Lincoln	2/16	W 32-3
Oct. 15	Kansas State	Manhattn	2/	W 17-6
Oct. 22	Missouri	Columbia	3/	W 42-7
Oct. 29	Colorado	Lincoln	3/2	W 24-7
Nov. 5	Kansas	Lincoln	1/	W 45-17
Nov. 12	Iowa State	Ames	1/	W 28-12
Nov. 25	Oklahoma	Norman	1/	W 13-3

FedEx Orange Bowl

Jan. 1	Miami	Miami	1/3	W 24-17

Final Rankings: 1st AP, 1st CNN/USA Today Coaches (post-bowl)

Against Pacific, NU Coasts

by Ken Hambleton

Lincoln Journal Star

All those touchdowns. Ten by nine different Nebraska players in a 70-21 dunking of Pacific on September 24, 1994, at Memorial Stadium.

All those yards. The seventh-best all-time total for Nebraska at 699 yards—with 510 of those on the ground—compared to 374 total for Pacific.

All those players. Exactly 104 Cornhuskers got in the game, and a majority of Nebraska's roster was involved in the first half. By the end of the game, even fourth-string quarterback Adam Kucera—a team manager until a month earlier —was being replaced at quarterback by Ryan Held, who had never played the position in his life until two weeks before.

Defensively, the story for Nebraska was similar. Darren Schmadeke, a junior cornerback from Albion, was Nebraska's leading tackler. "Bumps and bruises and I'm tired," Schmadeke said. "I'm not used to feeling like this on a Saturday."

And guess what? Nebraska gets to play Pacific again next year.

Nebraska Coach Tom Osborne was less than excited when asked about the scheduled rematch.

"It was fun to get all the players in, but it was not a fun day," he said. "I don't enjoy the competition."

Nebraska scored four touchdowns in less than six minutes of offense in the first quarter. Two of those scores came after starting quarterback Tommie Frazier was already on the bench.

Frazier played just nine plays, and the first-string offensive line had six additional plays as Nebraska took a 21-0 lead on a touchdown dive by reserve I-back Damon Benning, a 74-yard touchdown run by starting I-back Lawrence Phillips and an 8-yard touchdown run by fullback Cory Schlesinger.

Barron Miles blocked a Pacific punt to give Nebraska the ball on the Tigers' 19-yard line and set up a scoring drive engineered by the second-team offense.

"We designed every drive to end in a touchdown in every game,"

Frazier said. "We got close today."

■

Barron Miles (14) became known as Nebraska's designated punt blocker in 1994. He got a hand on this punt against Pacific September 24, 1994, helping the Huskers to a 70-21 win. (Ted Kirk, Journal Star Library)

NU Offense Shines In Time

by Ken Hambleton

Lincoln Journal Star

The sun didn't come out, but the Nebraska offense did in time to record a 42-32 victory against Wyoming on October 1, 1994, at Memorial Stadium.

Nebraska's Damon Benning recovered a fumbled punt at the Wyoming 8-yard line with 5:32 left in the game, and teammate Lawrence Phillips crashed into the end zone on the next play to give Nebraska its final edge.

At times, Nebraska glimmered brilliantly behind second-string quarterback Brook Berringer, subbing for Tommie Frazier, who was recovering from a blood clot.

At times, the outlook was gloomy, when mistakes were compounded by Wyoming's shining moments. Two NU turnovers led to Wyoming touchdowns, and redshirt freshman quarterback Jeremy Dombek and backup John Gustin ripped the NU pass defense for 344 yards and three touchdowns.

"There is no way we should give up 32 points," Nebraska senior defensive tackle Terry Connealy said. "They got up early, got a lot of confidence, and we just never played all that great on defense. I think this is a real red flag that we ought to pull our heads out of you know where."

The contrast was riveting. Nebraska intercepted two Wyoming passes, scored on four consecutive possessions and dominated the game late in the second quarter and early in the third.

In the first quarter, Nebraska defenders fell down twice, allowing two Wyoming touchdowns. And just before the final flurry in the second quarter, the Huskers lost an interception, suffered through five penalties in six plays and allowed Wyoming to take a 21-7 lead.

"Obviously, when we want to get something done we can," said NU senior offensive tackle Zach Wiegert. "But we all feel like if we had played that well all game and won by 10 points, that's fine."

It's still a matter of perspective.

While NU Coach Tom Osborne talked of disappointments, he said he was pleased his team had been challenged for the first time this year. "We hadn't been tested," he said. ◼

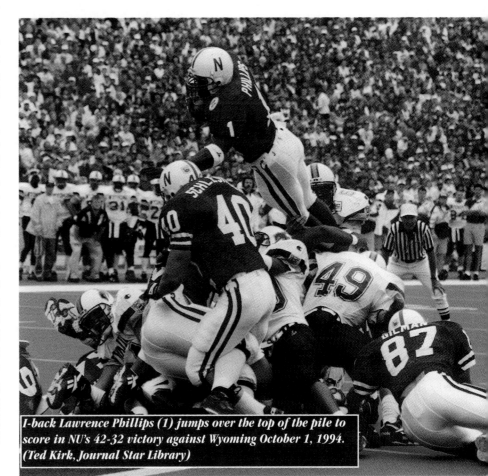

I-back Lawrence Phillips (1) jumps over the top of the pile to score in NU's 42-32 victory against Wyoming October 1, 1994. (Ted Kirk, Journal Star Library)

NU Shows de-Turman-ation

by Ken Hambleton

Lincoln Journal Star

Nebraska's No. 1 quarterback was in the hospital. Its No. 2 quarterback was headed to the hospital.

That left the No. 3 quarterback to help lead the Cornhuskers to a 32-3 whipping of Oklahoma State on October 8, 1994, in their Big Eight Conference opener before 75,453 fans at Memorial Stadium.

"It probably won't sink in for a long time that I was the quarterback in a 9-3 game, quarterback for the No. 2 team in the country," said Nebraska sophomore walk-on Matt Turman. "This is all so strange the way this has happened, but I'm having a good time playing."

Turman enjoyed watching NU's charged-up offensive line blast huge gaps in the Oklahoma State defense as Nebraska I-back Lawrence Phillips ran for 221 yards and three touchdowns and the Cornhusker defense pounded the Cowboys into second-half submission.

Tommie Frazier listened to the game from the hospital while he recovered from blood clots in his leg. His replacement, Brook Berringer, who spent the halftime getting his partially collapsed lung re-inflated, watched the second half from the sidelines. Berringer spent time Saturday night in the hospital for the second week in a row.

That left Turman, whose last major amount of playing time was in the Spring Game and before that in the semifinals of the state high school playoffs when his Wahoo Neumann team lost to Norfolk Catho-

Christian Peter (55) applies pressure on OSU quarterback Tone Jones on October 8, 1994. (Ted Kirk, Journal Star Library)

lic in the fall of 1991.

"Coach Turner Gill told me to get in there, call the play, line up and take a deep breath and pretend like it was just another scrimmage," said Turman, who helped lead the Cornhuskers to three second-half touchdowns and 207 yards of offense. "Then, when I saw the offensive line just blowing people off the ball and the defense play an incredible game, I felt pretty comfortable."

The signs of the problem with Nebraska's quarterbacks didn't register

with the Cowboys either.

"I didn't see any struggle at all," said Oklahoma State running back David Thompson.

The Cornhuskers allowed Oklahoma State two first downs and no yards passing in the second half while holding the Cowboys to 24 yards of total offense. Meanwhile, Nebraska's offense steamrolled for two touchdowns by Phillips in the third quarter to pull away from its 9-3 halftime lead.

The Huskers missed a 39-yard field goal attempt on their first drive of the second half. But 10 consecutive running plays led to a 59-yard scoring drive that ended on a 2-yard leap by Phillips with 4:40 left in the third quarter.

"That touchdown was big for the team," Turman said. "You could see everybody had confidence that we could drive and score whether I was quarterback or not."

Then Turman got a personal boost when he rolled deep to his right and hit tight end Eric Alford on a two-point conversion to increase the lead to 17-3.

"The two-point conversion was a big boost to me," Turman said.

Nebraska backup defensive tackle Jason Pesterfield, a native of Oklahoma, personally stopped OSU's next drive with a tackle and pressure on two incomplete passes to force a Cowboy punt. Turman then hit Abdul Muhammad on a 23-yard pass, and Phillips carried the rest of the way, including a 7-yard touchdown run over right tackle. ∎

NU Defense Pours it On

by Ken Hambleton

Lincoln Journal Star

Heart-pounding, water-splashing, eye-gouging, smash-mouth, in-your-face football was the key to Nebraska's 17-6 victory against Kansas State on the drizzly afternoon of October 15, 1994, at KSU Stadium in Manhattan, Kansas.

"We had our hearts all over the field," said Nebraska senior offensive tackle Zach Wiegert. "It was gut-check time on the touchdown drive in the fourth quarter, and everybody was pounding the defense. And our defense came up big and brought the game back to us."

The Cornhuskers had Tommie Frazier unavailable and Brook Berringer on the bench, giving the start to previous No. 3 quarterback Matt Turman, who had just one half of significant playing experience.

"Coming down here, I thought it (a win) was a 50-50 proposition," said Nebraska Coach Tom Osborne.

Nebraska's offense was altered by choice to protect Berringer's left lung, which had partially collapsed the last two games and forced him into a reserve role against the Wildcats. But the Nebraska offense found plenty to work with in the fourth quarter to pull away from a 7-6 lead.

For most of three quarters, NU I-back Lawrence Phillips and the offensive line were the offense. Phillips carried 31 times for 117 yards and caught two passes for 15 more yards, while the rest of the Nebraska offense accounted for 29 plays and a total of 130 yards. In the first quarter,

Nebraska scored on a 28-yard drive covered in six running plays by Phillips. Darin Erstad added the extra-point kick to give Nebraska all the points it would need to win but not enough to relax.

Previously unbeaten Kansas State responded as expected with a five-play, 62-yard scoring drive that included passes of 21 and 29 yards from Chad May to Mitch Running. Nebraska linebacker Troy Dumas destroyed the chance for a tie when he blocked the extra-point try by Martin Gramatica.

Thereafter, Nebraska's defense held the Wildcats scoreless despite May passing for 249 yards on 22 completions and an edge of 20 more plays than the NU offense through the third quarter.

"We had no big plays at all, and we shot ourselves in the foot with near misses and penalties," said K-State Coach Bill Snyder. "We weren't dominating because we couldn't get the ball off our end of the field. Nebraska is a better team and close don't count."

Nebraska broke the game open on a 15-yard touchdown on a trap play by fullback Jeff Makovicka and a 24-yard field goal by Erstad 10 minutes later.

"There was no doubt we'd win, but we did know we'd be in a dogfight at 7-6," said Dumas, who also intercepted a May pass in the second quarter. "We just didn't have the breakdowns on defense, and our offense took over where we left off."

May hadn't thrown an interception in 148 attempts—a Big Eight record—

until Dumas stepped in front of a pass over the middle at the Nebraska 17-yard line and returned the ball 54 yards to the KSU 29 with 1:43 left in the first half.

"He didn't seem the same after that interception," Dumas said of the KSU quarterback.

Before the interception, May had completed 12 passes for 173 yards. After the interception, May was 10-for-26 for 76 yards. ■

Despite his short stature, NU's Barron Miles played big when challenged by taller receivers. (Journal Star Library)

NU Tames Tigers, Awaits CU

by Ken Hambleton

Lincoln Journal Star

Never has so little variety produced so much for Nebraska as it did in a 42-7 victory October 22, 1994, against Missouri at Faurot Field in Columbia, Missouri.

"It's like Nebraska found one, two, maybe three plays, and kept at it, kept pounding, and we broke," Missouri defensive tackle Steve Martin said. "It's not that wild. You know, Colorado, Nebraska, even without a whole offense, are going to have a great day if you don't stop what they do."

Abdul Muhammad was a sure-handed receiver for the 1994 Nebraska football team. (Ian Doremus, Journal Star Library)

Nebraska limited its offensive options to shield quarterback Brook Berringer, who was in danger of reinjuring the left lung that partially collapsed twice previously. So the junior quarterback was limited to handing off the ball, running bootleg keepers to the sidelines and passing.

Berringer responded with his best passing performance thus far—9-for-13 for 152 yards and three touchdowns. A trio of NU running backs, led by Lawrence Phillips with 110 yards, combined for 330 yards rushing. Those statistics don't include a Missouri fumble at the Nebraska goal line, a pass interception and a return to the Missouri 23-yard line by Barron Miles, three quarterback sacks and the third consecutive stifling total defensive effort.

"Brook can do it all, but we wanted to get through the game without getting hurt," Nebraska Coach Tom Osborne said. "Next week (against Colorado), he'll have to do it all. Next week, we can't sit on anything."

The same is true defensively, according to Charlie McBride, NU's defensive coordinator. "We had one mistake that went for a touchdown, but this was a great game for our defense," he said. "We're developing into a good unit. You just hope you've done enough to be ready for the things we'll see next week."

Nebraska didn't exactly sit on its offense against Missouri, but it took a strong Cornhusker defensive effort to give the Nebraska offense a chance to get started.

After taking a 14-0 halftime lead, Nebraska struggled early in the third quarter. On the opening series after halftime, Berringer's high pitch sailed over Phillips' head, and Missouri recovered at the NU 10. MU tailback Brock Olivio burst off tackle to the 1, and Missouri appeared ready to cut Nebraska's lead in half.

MU tailback Joe Freeman was just about to cross the goal line when Miles slammed his helmet into Freeman's arm, knocking the ball loose. NU linebacker Ed Stewart recovered in the end zone.

"Obviously, we were very fortunate," Osborne said. "That's a key to the second half."

Nebraska was forced to punt, but the offensive frustration ended when Miles' interception set the Cornhuskers up at the Missouri 23. Five plays later, on fourth-and-1, Berringer hit the first of three second-half touchdown passes, connecting with tight end Mark Gilman.

While Nebraska's defense limited Missouri to 24 yards of offense in the third quarter, the Husker offense continued to cash in.

Berringer hit a lonely Brendan Holbein on a 30-yard touchdown pass with 1:36 left in the third quarter and connected with a nearly abandoned Reggie Baul on a 43-yard scoring play to blow the game open.

"The last three touchdowns should not have been scored," said Missouri Coach Larry Smith. ■

NU Has Clout, No Doubt

by Ken Hambleton

Lincoln Journal Star

Nebraska left the field at NU's Memorial Stadium without a doubt.

No more doubts about beating a highly ranked team. Colorado, second in The Associated Press media ratings and No. 3 in the USA Today/ CNN coaches' poll, fell with a resounding thud as Nebraska posted a 24-7 victory October 29, 1994. It was the Cornhuskers' first victory in the last nine tries against teams rated first or second in the AP poll.

"This was a big step," said Nebraska Coach Tom Osborne, whose team was ranked third by AP and second by the coaches. "Now we've got a chance to do some things."

No more doubts about quarterback Brook Berringer, who had been protected in a limited offense the last two games because of injuries to his lung suffered in the two games before that. Nebraska's fill-in for Tommie Frazier connected on 12 of 17 passes for 142 yards and a touchdown and took a number of hits on seven option runs. Berringer also led the Cornhuskers to 345 yards of total offense as Nebraska took sole possession of the Big Eight lead.

"The only reason they (the Huskers) lost ground in the ratings was because they had problems at quarterback, and they satisfied me that their problems are

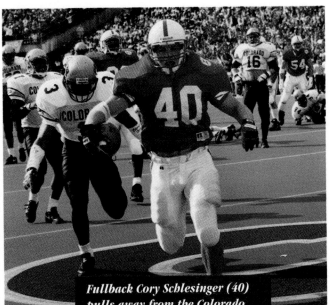

Fullback Cory Schlesinger (40) pulls away from the Colorado defense in Nebraska's 24-7 victory. (Ted Kirk, Journal Star Library)

resolved," said Colorado Coach Bill McCartney, referring to the fact that Nebraska had slipped after spending time at No. 1 in both polls earlier in the season.

Certainly, there were no more doubts about the Nebraska defense, as any one of the 76,131 fans for the 200th consecutive sellout of Memorial Stadium or any of the national television audience could attest.

"Colorado figured it would come in and light up the scoreboard," said Nebraska linebacker Ed Stewart. "There was a great deal of doubt about us. We lost our quarterback, our top defensive back, our second quarterback, our third quarterback. We never had any doubts. Maybe some people will agree with us now."

The Cornhusker defense took the

shine off Heisman Trophy talk for Colorado quarterback Kordell Stewart, who struggled to complete 12 of 28 passes for 150 yards and was held to 24 yards rushing on 14 carries. And national rushing leader Rashaan Salaam was held to a season-low 134 yards, including just 38 in the first half. Colorado's lone touchdown marked the lowest point total for the Buffaloes since a 52-7 lashing by the Huskers two years ago in Lincoln.

"We got this one down deep," said Christian Peter, the Nebraska defensive tackle who had seven tackles, a quarterback sack and a pass broken up. "There were no superstars. Our superstars are out for the season. We're just a bunch of guys nobody knows about and, before this game, nobody really cared much about. And everybody talked and talked about this game, but the fact was Colorado came to our house, and they got rocked."

As soon as the Cornhuskers finished a 51-yard scoring drive with 5:47 left in the first quarter, there didn't seem to be much doubt in the minds of the NU defense as to the outcome.

"Sure, they could have scored from anywhere, anytime and done a bunch of damage in a big hurry because they had all those offensive weapons," Nebraska linebacker Troy Dumas said of the Buffs. "But I don't know if they got anything done on offense when it mattered." ■

Cornhuskers Soar To Victory

by Ken Hambleton

Lincoln Journal Star

Presto chango. In the first nine games of the season, Nebraska almost hypnotized the nation into thinking the Cornhuskers were just another running team.

But in the blink of an eye, Nebraska magically turned into a passing team, then back again in a 45-17 victory against Kansas November 5, 1994, at Memorial Stadium. Brook Berringer dazzled a dizzy Kansas defense for 267 yards passing and two touchdowns—the best passing day by a Nebraska quarterback in 22 years.

Questioned a week earlier by Colorado Coach Bill McCartney as to his ablility to throw to wide receivers, Berringer struck for a 51-yard touchdown pass to split end Reggie Baul and a 64-yard TD pass to wingback Clester Johnson in Nebraska's 38-point first half. Berringer also connected on bombs of 37, 28 and 49 yards.

"I haven't proven anything yet. So don't ask," Berringer said after the game, flashing a smile.

He proved a point to Nebraska Coach Tom Osborne.

"Up until the last few minutes, Brook played flawlessly," Osborne said.

Berringer, who helped post Nebraska's first 250-plus passing game since 1976, had 249 yards passing in the first half. The Cornhusker offense completed the dominance with 201 yards rushing in the second half. I-back Lawrence Phillips, who finished with 153 yards and two touchdowns, gained 118 yards in the third quarter.

"Hey, who would guess? This is Nebraska and the passing opened up the running," Phillips said.

Facing an eight-man defensive front that was designed to stop the run, Berringer took to the air from the outset. He was sacked for an 11-yard loss on the first play of the game.

"You know, that might have been the thing that got us all going on offense," said NU senior guard Brenden Stai. "We'd only given up two sacks all year before that play. And they acted like they were ready for just that play. So we kept passing because we knew they'd have to stop the run to stop us. Only they didn't figure we'd be passing like we did either. Then the passing opened up the runs."

On the Jayhawks' first play of the game, Cornhusker safety Tony Veland in-tercepted a pass at the Kansas 17-yard line. Nebraska settled for a 35-yard field goal by Tom Sieler.

That was the last time the Nebraska offense got less than a touchdown on its next four possessions.

Except for a brief delay when Kansas' Don Davis wrestled the ball from Kareem Moss on a punt return to set up a 41-yard field goal by the Jayhawks' Jeff McCord, Nebraska was soaring.

Berringer found Baul alone on a 51-yard touchdown pass with the game less than five minutes old.

On NU's next possession, Berringer hit tight end Eric Alford on a 28-yard pass and Baul on a 49-yard pass to set up a 4-yard touchdown run by Phillips.

Three minutes later, Alford picked up 17 yards on a reverse to set up a 40-yard touchdown run by fullback Cory Schlesinger.

In the second quarter, Berringer hit tight end Mark Gilman on a 9-yard pass, then watched backup I-back Damon Benning sprint 37 yards with a shovel pass, breaking three tackles along the way. Two plays later, fullback Jeff Makovicka scored on an 8-yard run to boost the score to 31-3 with the game less than 19 minutes old. ■

NU Avoids Redo Of '92

by Ken Hambleton

Lincoln Journal Star

It could be. It might be. It wasn't.

Nebraska was able to flip the calendar and erase the hopes of an Iowa State upset by beating the Cyclones 28-12 November 12, 1994, before 45,186 fans at Cyclone Stadium in Ames, Iowa.

"All I could think about all week was 1992 and what happened over here," said Nebraska defensive tackle Terry Connealy. "When you play against these guys, you can't believe they haven't won a game. And I am not exaggerating."

Nebraska was heavily favored over winless Iowa State. But memories were enough to spark the Cornhuskers to at least a share of their fourth consecutive Big Eight crown.

There were haunting visions of Iowa State's 19-10 upset of Nebraska at Ames in 1992, and there was the reality of the Cyclones' motivation in playing Coach Jim Walden's last game.

More than emotion showed on the scoreboard; Nebraska led a measly 14-12 after three quarters. That was almost enough for the Cyclones to keep going in the fourth quarter.

"Two points, and we had confidence," said Iowa State quarterback Todd Doxzon.

Iowa State scored on a 58-yard touchdown pass that Doxzon lobbed to Calvin Branch, who was beyond the reach of the Nebraska defenders, with 3:42 left in the third quarter. Nebraska bounced right back with a 48-yard pass from Brook Berringer to tight end Mark Gilman and eventually moved to the ISU 27-yard line. But a 20-yard loss on a bad pitch stopped the drive.

Nebraska held Iowa State to 1 yard on its next possession and took over at the Cyclone 41. Two plays later, Berringer broke loose around the right end on a 28-yard run to the ISU 6. On the following play, I-back Damon Benning took the ball on a dive play and sped untouched through the middle of the line to boost the score to 21-12 with 12:09 left.

"I knew something would happen on that drive because the offensive line was all fired up, socking each other around the sidelines," Benning said.

Still, Iowa State refused to surrender. From the Nebraska 32, Doxzon threw a sideline screen pass to Geoff Turner. Turner slipped two tackles, dodged another and broke into the end zone. But the play was called back because of a holding penalty.

"One big play could have changed this game dramatically," Doxzon said. "I think that was the one. We didn't have the gas to hold up much after that."

He was right. After the apparent touchdown was called back, Iowa State managed 12 yards of offense and gave up 139 yards on defense.

Midway through the fourth quarter, Nebraska threatened to score again when Lawrence Phillips—who had been limited to 62 yards on 23 carries—exploded through the line on a 61-yard run to the Iowa State 5. But ISU linebacker Matt Nitchie, a graduate of Lincoln Southeast, ripped the ball away from Phillips. The ball went into the end zone and was recovered by the Cyclones for a touchback.

That didn't halt Nebraska's momentum, however, as NU outside linebackers Dwayne Harris and Donta Jones slammed Doxzon for losses of 7 and 8 yards, respectively, to force a punt. The Cornhuskers then marched 60 yards in four minutes to score on a 21-yard run by Phillips and drown the hopes of an upset. ■

Nebraska Gets Another Shot
Win against OU sends 12-0 NU back to Orange Bowl in search of national title

by Ken Hambleton

Lincoln Journal Star

ebraska completed the full circle to go back to where it started the previous New Year's Day.

At Norman, Oklahoma, on November 25, 1994, the Cornhuskers wrapped up a fourth straight Big Eight title, a fourth consecutive trip to the Orange Bowl and a second consecutive shot at the mythical national title with a 13-3 victory against Oklahoma at Owen Field.

"We're back to the start of everything, baby," said Nebraska outside linebacker Dwayne Harris, referring to Nebraska's 18-16 loss to Florida State in the Jan. 1, 1994, Orange Bowl.

"Not everybody gets a second chance, and we've got one now," said NU senior linebacker Ed Stewart. "We played a tough team in a physical game under tough circumstances and we won it. We won it all the way to get a chance to win it all."

The Cornhuskers struggled to a 3-3, first-half tie and rarely made a dent in the Oklahoma defense. Nebraska gained just 63 yards of total offense in the half compared to 132 for the Sooners. The near-deadlock was enough to make Nebraska Coach Tom Osborne glance over his shoulder.

"I looked at Tommie a few times," he said.

Quarterback Tommie Frazier was in uniform and on the sidelines, available to play for the first time since NU's fourth game of the year.

But in the second half, Nebraska outfought, outslugged and outgained Oklahoma 239 yards to 47 and, more importantly, tacked on a field goal and a touchdown to pull away.

Oklahoma was held to minus 4 yards in the fourth quarter, including five incomplete passes and an interception.

"A game like this comes down to a few good plays, and Nebraska is the one who made those plays," said Oklahoma Coach Gary Gibbs, who had announced his resignation four days before the game.

Those few plays were enough to break the halftime tie and allow Nebraska to dominate the second half. The biggest play may have been a 44-yard pass from quarterback Brook Berringer to Abdul Muhammad on third-and-10 at the NU 43-yard line on the second play of the fourth quarter. Three plays later, Berringer scored the only touchdown of the game on a 1-yard sneak with 13:25 left.

"Oklahoma was in the perfect defense for a deep pass for us—man-to-

man coverage—and Muhammad was wide-open on the option pass," Berringer said.

"That was such a good feeling to get the time (to throw) and get the pass off with the right amount of everything."

The other big offensive play for the Cornhuskers came in the second quarter on third-and-4 from the Oklahoma 38, when Berringer lined up in the shotgun formation and sped 9 yards through the left side of the line. That set up Nebraska's first field goal. Nebraska's defense carried the game much of the rest of the way.

"We figured three points, OK, six points, would be enough with the way we've been playing defense," Stewart said.

Osborne said he thought it would be a defensive struggle.

"The story of the game was the two defenses and our kicking game," he said after the Cornhuskers wrapped up their second consecutive undefeated regular season.

"I felt going in that we had an edge in our kicking game. We had a really long field goal and a couple of long punts." ∎

Nebraska's Terry Connealy celebrates after sacking Miami quarterback Frank Costa near the end of Nebraska's 24-17 victory against the Hurricanes in the 1995 Orange Bowl. Nebraska rallied to beat Miami and win Tom Osborne's first national championship. (Journal Star Library)

Happy NU Year!
Huskers go 13-0
Misery and mystery are over

by Ken Hambleton

Lincoln Journal Star

inished.

Completed. Done. Over. The fat lady is singing, "There is No Place Like Nebraska."

Cornhuskers frolicked on the field and in the locker room at the Orange Bowl for the first time since the end of the 1971 season as Nebraska beat Miami 24-17 in Orange Bowl Stadium.

The victory gave the top-ranked and 13-0 Cornhuskers the mythical national college football title for the first time since 1971—and the third time overall—ending the streak of misery and mystery of playing in Miami.

In the teams' 1984 matchup, Miami tipped away a two-point conversion pass that would have given Nebraska a national title. In 1994, a last-second field goal sailed wide in an 18-16 loss to Florida State.

This time, Nebraska made the two-point conversion after a 15-yard touchdown run by fullback Cory Schlesinger to tie the score with 7:38 left. Then, the Cornhuskers slammed in another Schlesinger touchdown on a 14-yard run with 2:46 left to snap a seven- year bowl losing streak, a 23-year wait for a national title and a string of three straight Orange Bowl losses.

"I don't feel any different or any more vindicated than when we played here last year," said Nebraska Coach Tom Osborne. "I guess I feel a little like sticking around a little longer than usual. But I'm still getting to see my family and see this team play well, and that's all that matters."

For Osborne, the winningest active college coach, the national championship was supposed to lift the monkey off his back after so many close calls.

But he refused to accept that change in perception—of him and of the Nebraska football program.

"The national media put the monkey on my back, not me," he said. "But if this lifts it off, then that's fine."

Quarterback Tommie Frazier said the victory was for Osborne, for Nebraska and for all of the Cornhusker fans.

"We got going in the fourth quarter, and we lived up to what our defense was giving us and we won," he said. "I said all along we could beat them here. They're not unbeatable here."

Frazier, who hadn't played since Sept. 24 because of recurring blood clots in his leg, started the game but was replaced by Brook Berringer late in the first quarter. Frazier had just thrown an interception at the Miami 3-yard line to end NU's first scoring threat.

Berringer, who started seven of the last eight games, handed off to Lawrence Phillips for a 15-yard gain on his first play. But the drive was stopped by a 12-yard sack of Berringer by defensive player of the year Warren Sapp.

Nebraska then changed its defense, bringing in reserves Larry Townsend and Jason Pesterfield, and stopped the Hurricanes at their 12.

After a punt, combined with a 12-yard return by Kareem Moss, Phillips carried twice for 11 yards. Then, seldom-used receiver Riley Washington, the fastest player on the NU team, took a reverse around the right end for 9 yards to the Miami 20.

One play later, Berringer rolled to his right on a bootleg pass and found tight end Mark Gilman on a 19-yard touchdown pass to cut the score to 10-7 with 7:54 left in the first half. That was Nebraska's last serious offensive threat until Berringer was intercepted in the end zone on a pass from Miami's 4-yard line early in the fourth quarter.

That golden opportunity was set up when the snap sailed over the head of Miami punter Dane Prewitt, who kicked the ball through the end zone. Nebraska was given possession at the Miami 4, but the Hurricanes' Earl Little intercepted Berringer's pass.

"I was trying to throw the ball away," Berringer said. "It's kind of a tough situation, knowing that if you make one mistake you're coming out. But we both have nothing to hang our heads about. We both made some mistakes, we both made some good plays, we both helped our team win."

Osborne brought Frazier back in, and

Nebraska bounced back from the missed opportunity.

"It was our turn. Our time," said Frazier, who, for the second straight year, was named Nebraska's most valuable player in the Orange Bowl. "Last year, we left here wanting more. This year, we got it."

The first drive fizzled, but Nebraska got the ball again at the Miami 40 just two minutes later and scored in two plays. Phillips, who rushed for 96 yards, broke loose on a 25-yard option run to the Hurricane 15.

"We figured it was time for a trap play because they were looking outside for the run, and we got them good with Cory," said NU offensive guard Brenden Stai.

Sure enough, Schlesinger slammed over right tackle as the line trapped Sapp, and the fullback from Duncan scored to pull NU to 17-15 with 7:38 left.

Then, in the same end zone where NU's two-point conversion was knocked away in 1984, Frazier found tight end Eric Alford crossing from left to right on a short pass to tie the game.

"I thought we had it when we tied it," said Frazier. "We were taking over in the fourth quarter, and our defense didn't allow them anything."

The Black Shirts held Miami to minus 35 yards of offense in the fourth quarter. Quarterback Frank Costa, who passed for 248 yards in the game, had just 8 yards on two completions in the final period.

"I told our guys that we'd have to win the game," NU defensive coordinator Charlie McBride said. "I felt we had to do it to win the game. They had so many big plays, but we were trying to make the adjustments to stop those in the second half."

McBride explained that he changed the blitzes to create problems for Costa and changed the coverage to keep the Hurricanes confused. "Our players have done it all year, and we had to count on them one last time," McBride said. "We changed our defense, yet we didn't. We added some zone coverage, and we disguised some of our other things. But it took good players and good luck in the end, and you can't argue that either one wasn't there for us tonight."

Linebacker Ed Stewart said there were too many turning points to just pick one or two. "That's the sign of a good team and a bunch of guys playing with confidence," he said. "We made plays when we had to. We were confident from the start, and we stuck with our guts all game."

Phillips, one of the offensive leaders, also praised the defense. "Our defense gave us the chance, and we were taking over the game in our hearts and in our bodies," he said.

After allowing Miami 1 yard on three plays, Nebraska took over at its 42 with 6:28 left.

Frazier threw a 7-yard pass to Reggie Baul. On the next play, Frazier raced around the right end on an option play and cut back to the middle for a 25-yard gain to the Miami 27.

"If I'd played the whole game, I might have been tired," said Frazier, slowed slightly by a cold. "I might not have been so fast. But I came back in the fourth quarter, and I was the freshest one out there."

Three plays later, including a 6-yard run by Frazier on third-and-3 and a 7-yard burst by Phillips, Schlesinger slashed over left tackle, behind another trap block on Sapp, and scored to give Nebraska its first lead of the game.

"We kept banging away at them, and our defense had done so much, we owed it to them and ourselves to start getting something done on offense," Schlesinger said.

Miami had one last try from its 18. But Costa could only complete a 4-yard pass before he was sacked twice, then intercepted by Kareem Moss at midfield.

Frazier kneeled down two times to run out the clock.

"That felt good to be in control, to have the ball and the lead and the national championship," said Frazier. "We knew their defensive front was tired and that all we had to do was pound the ball at them. Pound them with some options, then pound them inside with Schlesinger.

"When I signed here, one of the things I wanted to do was win the national championship. I think it's something we'll savor for a lifetime."

Berringer, who handled the delicate quarterback situation with grace, agreed. "Obviously, I would've liked to have been in there at the end, but you've got to credit Coach Osborne for the decision he made. He looks like a genius," Berringer said.

"I feel good," he added. "We wanted to win it for him (Osborne) as bad as we wanted to win it for ourselves."

Frazier said he and his teammates jumped and hugged and screamed in the locker room, while his coach was reserved about what many people will call his most important victory.

"He's the type of coach who really doesn't show his emotions much, but I'm sure once he gets the chance to think about it, he'll shed a couple of tears and get pretty excited about it."

Osborne said he'd think about it. ∎

Huskers Trample Cowboys

by Curt McKeever
Lincoln Journal Star

About 1,000 Big Red fans lined the way as the Nebraska players filed into the locker room after smashing Oklahoma State 64-21 at Lewis Field in Stillwater, Okla., on Aug. 31, 1995. There was quiet applause, a few handshakes, a few hugs. But mostly, it was quiet. Almost as if the crowd was in awe after its first look at the 1995 version of the NU football team.

After watching senior quarterback Tommie Frazier race through the Big Eight opener with two touchdown passes and a touchdown run, maybe the fans were comfortable.

After watching I-back Lawrence Phillips fumble on his second carry, but rebound for three touchdowns and 153 yards rushing, maybe the fans were overwhelmed.

Certainly, Oklahoma State was beyond the realm of whelm.

Taber LeBlanc, Oklahoma State's freshman linebacker, may have said it best. "The coaches tried to tell us how fast Nebraska was. But this was awesome, you can't believe how fast they really are," he said. "I took hits, we all took hits that we have never taken like in our lives."

Nebraska exploded with big plays and ground out long marches to open the Big Eight Conference season with a victory and extend its conference win streak to 17 victories in a row. NU opened its season against a Big Eight foe because of the opportunity to play a televised evening game on ESPN. Despite the early evening start, the temperature was 99 degrees at kickoff.

After losing the ball on Phillips' fumble at midfield three minutes into the game, Nebraska's defense slammed OSU for minus 15 yards and Jared Tomich slapped down a pass to force a punt.

The Huskers ground out 72 yards in 12 plays, including three option runs by Frazier for 29 yards and two Frazier passes to tight end Mark Gilman for 20 more yards to set up a 3-yard scoring run by Phillips with 6:20 left in the first quarter.

That was all Nebraska needed to take control of the game.

The Huskers scored 30 points in the second quarter and tacked on two more scores in the first six minutes of the third period.

Reserve linebacker Terrell Farley scored on a 29-yard interception return to increase the lead to 16-0.

Then, after Oklahoma State finally broke into positive yards—with a 79-yard run by tailback David Thompson—and finally scored on a touchdown by Andre Richardson, Nebraska showed its big-play potential.

Phillips broke through the line for the longest touchdown run of his career, an 80-yard score immediately after the OSU kickoff.

"I think they were overpursuing, a little overanxious, and they were protecting the option," Phillips said. "They went one way and I cut back the other way. It may have looked like I made some great moves, but I was just plain running all-out."

Phillips scored again on a 27-yard touchdown run just five minutes later to cap a 71-yard drive, then, just before half-time, Frazier scored on a 1-yard dive that was set up by a 20-yard run by reserve fullback Brian Schuster.

It took just one play in the second half before Frazier hit Reggie Baul on a 76-yard touchdown pass, and six more plays for Frazier to find Jon Vedral on a 5-yard touchdown pass to make the score 50-7.

"I'm not sure what defense they were playing, but our blocking scheme was perfect for anything they tried to do," said Frazier. "We were in better condition. You could tell that by the end of the first quarter. And I think when Lawrence made that big run in the second quarter, they (OSU) were deflated," he said. "It was like they gave up and didn't want to play anymore. We gave up a long run and we didn't quit."

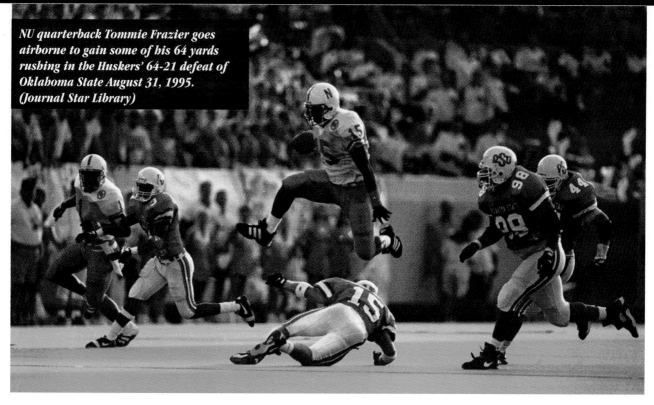

NU quarterback Tommie Frazier goes airborne to gain some of his 64 yards rushing in the Huskers' 64-21 defeat of Oklahoma State August 31, 1995. (Journal Star Library)

Aside from the 79-yard run, the Cowboys managed just 65 more yards on the ground and 138 yards passing. In all, Nebraska gave up 282 yards and was forced to punt just once.

"The first team defense played very well," said NU Coach Tom Osborne. "It was pleasing to see them come up with stops for all the different things Oklahoma State did. Oklahoma State has good backs, and their fine quarterback, Tone Jones, is a fine player, too."

Osborne said it was almost a relief to get the first game completed and with some sense of success. "We gambled on moving the game to the start of the season, but it will pay off," he said. "We hope that we came across well on TV. That's a

terrible thing to say, but you've got to look good on TV these days to have a chance."

Osborne said most of the answers to questions he had before the game were also positive. "I thought the offensive line played very well and I thought we got plenty of plays for a lot of young people. We need that depth because one of our concerns is our depth," he said.

Frazier said almost the same thing. "Most of us would have loved to play more than a half, but we've got to get those people in there who will be playing in case of an injury or something. And we all know about injuries," he said. Frazier hadn't started in a regular-season game since September 24, 1994—before he was sidelined because of blood clots in his leg.

"I think we have the offense that can score and can execute," Frazier said. "We have a great offensive line, too. But the challenge is to do it all season, every game just like this."

Oklahoma Coach Bob Simmons, in his first year with the Cowboys, said he was impressed with Nebraska but upset with his team. "Nebraska did not do anything we did not prepare for," he said. "It just disappoints me the way our defense played. The last half we tried to get it up, and I don't think we did.

"We faced a good football team. They won the national championship, and we knew what we were in for. But we missed tackles, and if you miss tackles like that, you can't win. Especially against a good football team like that." ■

Cornhuskers Run Roughshod Over MSU

by Ken Hambleton
Lincoln Journal Star

You've heard it all before. Tommie Frazier, Nebraska's starting quarterback, goes down in the second quarter. Michigan State quarterback Tony Banks appears to be having a great day on his way to 290 yards passing. The Cornhuskers stumble at times in the first half, with two turnovers, give up 123 yards passing and commit four penalties.

Still, No. 2-ranked Nebraska rose above the chaos on September 9, 1995, to stomp Michigan State 50-10 before 73,891 fans at MSU's Spartan Stadium and a regional television audience.

"Sometimes it wasn't pretty, but it was a pretty good score," said NU safety Tony Veland.

Nebraska was composed enough on defense to hold Michigan State to a touchdown in the first half and a field goal in the second half. Meanwhile, the Cornhusker running game chewed up 552 yards and produced six touchdowns, including four by I-back Lawrence Phillips, and three field goals by freshman Kris Brown.

All that running, including 206 yards by Phillips, came against a defense formed by new Michigan State Coach Nick Saban. A year ago, Saban was a defensive coordinator for the Cleveland Browns, one of the best defenses in the NFL.

Clinton Childs rushed eight times for 83 yards. Freshman I-back Ahman Green carried four times for 74 yards, including a 57-yard touchdown. Nebraska's fourth I-back, James Sims, carried just once, but it turned into an 80-yard touchdown. Frazier and Brook Berringer rushed nine times for 50 yards combined, and fullback Jeff Makovicka added 38 yards on nine carries.

"It just shows that no matter who the quarterback is, no matter who the running back is, there are going to be holes to run through and chances to score," said Phillips, who scored on three 1-yard runs and one 50-yard burst.

Berringer, who started in Frazier's place most of last season, came in during the second quarter after Frazier left the game with a deep thigh bruise. Berringer completed 6 of 11 passes for 106 yards, but most of Nebraska's offense came on the ground.

At times, Michigan State seemed to move at will through the air, as Banks hit Muhsin Muhammad on a 16-yard touchdown pass in the first quarter, followed later in the game by completions to Scott Greene on a 56-yard pass, Derrick Mason on a 22-yarder, Muhammad on a 32-yarder and Luke Bencie on a 21-yarder.

In contrast, the Spartan offense managed just 45 yards rushing on 34 carries. Michigan State squeezed out more than three yards only 10 times and lost ground 13 times. Banks was sacked three times for 16 yards in losses.

Still, there was nothing that diminished NU Coach Tom Osborne's belief in his team. "This is a good road team. The chemistry is good, the play is good. I'd take them anywhere. I'm not saying they'd always win, but they are not going to be intimidated by anybody, anywhere." ■

Husker rush end Jared Tomich corrals Michigan State quarterback Tony Banks on September 9, 1995. The Husker defense stymied the Spartans in a 50-10 victory. (Journal Star Library)

Big Red Answers Challenge

by Ken Hambleton
Lincoln Journal Star

NU Coach Tom Osborne's face shows the strain as he talks to the media after suspending Lawrence Phillips in September of 1995. Osborne later reinstated the I-back to the team. (Ian Doremus, Journal Star Library)

Before the Huskers played Arizona State on September 16, 1995, Coach Tom Osborne challenged his players with a question: "Can you be that great team?"

Quarterback Tommie Frazier answered, "Just watch. That's all I can say," after No. 2-ranked Nebraska scored at a record pace in a 77-28 blowout of Arizona State before 75,418 fans in Memorial Stadium who wondered whether Nebraska could recover from the preceding week of accusations, arrests and innuendoes.

"A couple of incidents don't ruin the whole program," Frazier said. "This is not a whole team of people who did something wrong or were accused of something wrong. From the first play to our last, we showed we can concentrate on the field and get the job done."

Frazier had evidence. On the first play of the game, I-back Clinton Childs ran around the left end on a power sweep, picked up key blocks from tackle Eric Anderson and fullback Jeff Makovicka, and raced 65 yards to score.

After the first score, Nebraska's inventory of touchdowns—on eight of its next nine possessions—left Arizona State's defense reeling.

All of those touchdowns came before Nebraska was forced to punt, and even then the punt was a spectacular 74-yarder by Jesse Kosch, which was downed at the 2 after a diving save by Jared Tomich.

For the most part, Nebraska players and coaches begged off questions about the arrest for assault and indefinite suspension of leading I-back Lawrence Phillips the Sunday before, as well as similar charges brought against backup I-back Damon Benning, who did not play in the ASU game because of injuries. (Phillips would later plead no contest to those charges; the charges against Benning were thrown out when the complainant was discredited by witnesses.) "We put that behind us and we got to play football today," said Frazier, who threw for two touchdowns and ran for two more. His 191 yards passing helped Nebraska to 292 yards passing—the sixth-best passing day ever for the Cornhuskers.

"They're the best team I've ever faced in my whole life," said Arizona State re-

ceiver Keith Poole, who caught six passes for 200 yards and three touchdowns. "They're awesome. That offense is amazing. They're unstoppable, basically."

Osborne's only other concern was the Husker defense—for giving up three long passes for scores—and questions about a lackluster second half. "We didn't play with the same intensity throughout the game, but that's understandable," he said.

Still, Nebraska powered its way to 686 yards of offense—10th-best all-time—and showed that it had recovered from a week during which the players avoided the press and the head coach braced for a hurricane of criticism.

"It was nice to have a game," said Osborne, who had six press conferences during the week to address the charges against his players. ■

NU Shows Mercy, Wins 49-7

by Ken Hambleton
Lincoln Journal Star

No sooner had Nebraska linebacker Doug Colman clipped on a microphone at the postgame news conference September 23, 1995, than he was taking it off.

"Guess there weren't a whole lot of questions," Colman said, smiling.

Nebraska tight end Tim Carpenter goes high to snag a pass against Pacific (Randy Hampton, Journal Star Library)

What does one ask about the second-ranked Cornhuskers after they throttled Pacific 49-7 in front of a hometown crowd of 75,360?

Against a game-but-outmanned opponent, Nebraska was in total control—and 49-7 was about as good as it could have gotten for the Big West Conference Tigers.

Despite playing all 102 players who were healthy and in uniform and despite throwing away its normal game plan (NU passed 36 times, the most in a regular-season contest since heaving that many against Wisconsin in the third game of the 1973 season), the Cornhuskers rolled up 731 yards of offense. That's the fifth-highest total in school history.

"It's sad to say, but I think Coach (Tom) Osborne may have been limiting himself in his play-call selection this week for the fact that everybody was talking about running up the score," said Nebraska center Aaron Graham. "I don't know if that's right or not, but last week we ran a lot of plays that would pretty much ensure big gainers and touchdowns, and this week we were a little bit more concerned.

I think if we would've run the big plays, we would've been just as successful, if not more successful. . . . It could've been probably worse than it was."

The Cornhuskers, with junior I-back Damon Benning rushing for a career-high 173 yards and scoring three touchdowns on just 10 carries, scored touchdowns on five of their first six possessions to take a 35-0 lead into halftime.

By then, Nebraska had piled up 446 yards of offense and had limited the Tigers to just 73.

Pacific running back Joe Abdullah, who entered with the nation's 21st-best rushing average of 123.7 yards, managed 25 against the Cornhuskers.

Asked what he thought it would take for a team to beat Nebraska, winner of 17 straight games and a national-leading 29 in the regular season, Abdullah said, "A professional offensive line and a professional defensive line. I don't know if there is such a thing as a perfect team, but for college football, they're the closest thing to being perfect."

Perfect? Hah.

Although the Huskers had a big offensive day, they threw two interceptions, allowed punts to hit the ground and fumbled twice. Even kicker Kris Brown missed a 30-yard chip-shot field goal.

"Our players responded about as well as they could have, under the circumstances," said Osborne, whose club was such a prohibitive favorite that Las Vegas oddsmakers kept the game off the betting lines. ∎

NU Simply Tough Enough

by Ken Hambleton
Lincoln Journal Star

I-back Damon Benning (21) takes advantage of a block by Aaron Graham (54) during the Huskers' 35-21 win against Washington State September 30, 1995. (Ted Kirk, Journal Star Library)

Nebraska answered the question "Tough enough?" in more ways than one on September 30, 1995.

Crashing head-first into one of the best rushing defenses in the nation, Nebraska bullied its way to a 35-21 victory against Washington State. In doing so, the Huskers hung up 428 yards on the ground and 527 yards overall at Memorial Stadium.

"This was football. This was great," said Grant Wistrom, Nebraska outside linebacker. "They came out talking, it was a great atmosphere for football. The weather was different—cool and cloudy. The fans were different—in it the whole game. And this felt different than anything we felt all year. We loved it."

Washington State charged from the start. On the second play after Nebraska lost a fumble at the Cougar 10-yard line, tailback Frank Madu tore past a blitzing safety and raced 87 yards to score with 8:44 left in the first quarter.

Nebraska had never trailed until Madu's shocker. "I didn't have any doubt we'd come back, but that was tough to give up a big play like that at the start," NU Coach Tom Osborne said.

And the Washington State defense was the stingiest Nebraska faced in 1995. Previously in the season, Nebraska had failed to score only five times out of 26 opportunities inside opponents' 20-yard line. But the Cougars cut off Nebraska drives at the WSU 14-, 16-, 2- and 3-yard lines.

"We've finally beaten Washington State," Osborne said, referring to Nebraska's 0-3 record against the Cougars, with losses in 1977, 1957 and 1920. "It wasn't easy. It was a good game. I was proud of Washington State and, I guess overall, I was proud of us."

Nebraska fought into the lead with two touchdowns by quarterback Tommie Frazier, two field goals by Kris Brown, a spirited touchdown run by I-back Ahman Green and a touchdown pass from Frazier to tight end Mark Gilman midway through the fourth quarter.

Frazier made the highlights videos in an unusual way for a quarterback—by throwing a crushing block that took out Washington State's standout defensive end Dwayne Sanders.

Nebraska found some answers on defense, as well. After giving up the 87-yard touchdown, the Huskers held Washington State to minus 23 yards rushing the rest of the game.

"You want the blitz, you got the blitz," said Charlie McBride, Nebraska defensive coordinator. "We blitzed on that play (the long touchdown run) and they went on a short count. We didn't get the safety around, and when he did, he was way wide and we just weren't ready to play. I thought, except for one play, our rush defense was as good as we've ever played it." ∎

NU Strikes Quickly, Finishes Off Missouri

by Ken Hambleton
Lincoln Journal Star

The No. 2-ranked Cornhuskers fizzled, flopped and foundered more than in any previous game before flashing to a 57-0 victory against Missouri at Memorial Stadium October 14, 1995.

Nebraska had its lowest offensive output of the season against the Tigers, fumbling six times and committing the first offensive penalty for the top units in the last of the laughers of the season.

After the game, Nebraska Coach Tom Osborne warned that the Huskers had some tough games ahead: "From here on it's different. There's nothing easy left and that's good. I enjoy that challenge. The players are looking forward to tough games and we are going to get them."

Nebraska faced No. 8 Kansas State next, No. 9 Colorado the following week and No. 10 Kansas the week after that. Then, Iowa State and No. 12 Oklahoma. "Those will be solid football teams," Osborne said.

Missouri, though, was not. Despite the bobbles, the Huskers churned out 475 yards of offense. Tommie Frazier scored three touchdowns and passed for two more to boost his career total to 64 to break the school record for career total offensive TDs set by quarterback Steve Taylor from 1985-88.

The Huskers had plenty of opportunities to score. Nebraska started six drives in Missouri territory and on average started its 16 drives at its own 44-yard line. Missouri started three drives inside its 5-yard line and did not cross midfield

until the game's final five minutes—and even that drive ended with an interception.

Despite the dominance, there were some questions in the Nebraska postgame interviews. "It could have been real ugly if we clicked on offense like we had in the first five games," Husker center Aaron Graham said. "Our offense could have played better. This was not our best performance. You look at 57-0 and think we got the job done, but there's room for plenty of improvement."

Osborne said the lack of yardage was partially due to the fact that the Huskers rarely had to drive far to score.

Still, what Nebraska lacked on offense was more than covered by the Husker defense. Missouri managed just 122 yards. This time there were no big plays, as the Tigers managed just five plays longer than 10 yards and none longer than 15. "Defensively, this was our best performance," Osborne said. "The only disturbing thing was that we did have two or three (Missouri) guys running open, but they just couldn't hit them."

One reason the Tigers struggled was poor performances from their three quarterbacks, who completed only 9 of 24 passes for 83 yards and two interceptions. Nebraska's defense tossed Missouri's quarterbacks for four sacks and slammed Missouri running backs for minus 45 yards with nine tackles behind the line. The Black Shirts broke up four passes and hurried Tiger quarterbacks four more times.

Further evidence of the Nebraska defensive dominance included a blocked punt by Terrell Farley that turned into the Huskers' first safety of the year, Tony Veland's first interception of the year, and fumble recoveries by Doug Colman and Jared Tomich.

"We turn it up when we play the Big Eight," Husker defensive tackle Christian Peter said. "I don't know why exactly, but it could be because we feel this is our conference. The defense picked it up last year when we got into the Big Eight. We're going to have to play like this and better to win the conference."

The same goes for the offense, Frazier added. "Every game is meaningful. How well you play depends on how you go out on Saturday and execute." he said. "We'll have to play better next week and the week after and the week after that."

Frazier said Nebraska picked up momentum against Missouri after stalling on the Tiger 3 on the first drive of the game. Missouri stopped Nebraska on fourth-and-1 when freshman I-back Ahman Green tried to power through the middle of the line. Nebraska scored quickly when the Huskers started their next drive at the Missouri 31. Frazier ran for 2 yards, then 29 on an option around the left end behind blocks by tight end Mark Gilman and wingback Brendan Holbein.

Three possessions later, Tomich recovered a Missouri fumble at the Tiger 27, and four consecutive runs by Green

Wingback Brendan Holbein celebrates after catching a 29-yard touchdown pass that was tipped by teammate Jon Vedral on the last play of the first half of Nebraska's 57-0 win against Missouri. (Ted Kirk, Journal Star Library)

moved the ball to the 1. Frazier tried to sneak in and was stopped on third down. He flew over the line on the next play to give Nebraska a 14-0 lead.

"That time they stopped me, I saw the defensive line was diving low, so I figured I just had to get up in the air," Frazier said.

Two minutes later, after two runs for 28 yards by fullback Jeff Makovicka, Frazier hit Gilman on a 33-yard pass. That set up a touchdown by Frazier on a 1-yard keeper.

Frazier completed the first-half romp with a 29-yard touchdown pass to Holbein, intended for teammate Jon Vedral, who deflected the ball into the end zone and Holbein's hands as time expired.

Offensive efficiency was much improved in the second half, as the Huskers stalled on their first possession of the third quarter but scored on the next four drives. Green, who ran for 90 yards in his first collegiate start, scored on a 9-yard run,

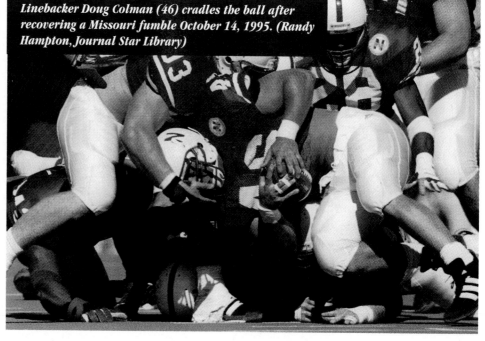
Linebacker Doug Colman (46) cradles the ball after recovering a Missouri fumble October 14, 1995. (Randy Hampton, Journal Star Library)

and tight end Sheldon Jackson took in a 6-yard touchdown pass from Frazier. Backup quarterback Matt Turman scored on a 1-yard keeper, and Damon Benning scored on a 16-yard run to complete the demolition.

"Just think if our offense and our defense play at the same level what we can do in this conference," Graham said. ∎

1995

Season in Review

Won 12, Lost 0, Tied 0
Big Eight: Won 7, Lost 0, 1st

Date	Opponent	Site	AP Rank NU/Opp.	Result
Aug. 31	Oklahoma St.	Stillwater	2/	W 64-21
Sept. 9	Michigan St.	East Lansing	2/	W 50-10
Sept. 16	Arizona State	Lincoln	2/	W 77-28
Sept. 23	Pacific	Lincoln	2/	W 49-7
Sept. 30	Washington St.	Lincoln	2/	W 35-21
Oct. 14	Missouri	Lincoln	2/	W 57-0
Oct. 21	Kansas State	Lincoln	2/8	W 49-25
Oct. 28	Colorado	Boulder	2/7	W 44-21
Nov. 4	Iowa State	Lincoln	1/	W 73-14
Nov. 11	Kansas	Lawrence	1/10	W 41-3
Nov. 24	Oklahoma	Lincoln	1/	W 37-0

Tostitos Fiesta Bowl

Jan. 2	Florida	Tempe	1/2	W 62-24

Final Rankings: 1st AP, 1st CNN/USA Today Coaches (post-bowl)

Frazier, Black Shirts Answer Call

by Ken Hambleton
Lincoln Journal Star

Nebraska answered every time opportunity knocked on October 21, 1995, and that meant the doorway opened often for the Cornhuskers to barge through and flatten the Kansas State football team.

Second-ranked Nebraska blasted away at No. 8 Kansas State with 14 points from the Black Shirts and four touchdown passes by quarterback Tommie Frazier to post a 49-25 victory before 76,072 fans at Memorial Stadium and a regional television audience.

Frazier's dazzling performance and Nebraska's smothering defense combined to dismiss Kansas State and set up a Big Eight showdown next Saturday at Colorado.

"You can't make some of the mistakes against a team like Nebraska and expect anything to happen but what happened," Kansas State Coach Bill Snyder said.

But who could have predicted Nebraska's first punt return for a touchdown in seven years or wingback Jon Vedral falling on a fumble for another touchdown? Who could guess that Nebraska would twice score on shovel passes from Frazier to Ahman Green, then score again when Kansas State tried the same play as hard-charging Nebraska reserve outside linebacker Chad Kelsay tipped the ball into the hands of teammate Luther Hardin?

The Huskers opened the scoring with a 79-yard punt return by Mike Fullman. Nebraska then hammered home four straight touchdowns to erase any question of whether Kansas State could end a 27-year losing string to Nebraska.

"It was unusual," Nebraska Coach Tom Osborne admitted.

By the time the dust cleared at the end of the first half, Nebraska led 35-6 and had 210 yards of offense against the top-ranked total defense and scoring defense in the NCAA.

Kansas State managed one scoring drive in the first half and wasn't heard from again until a quick 19-point burst in the fourth quarter after the Huskers led 42-6.

Still, Nebraska struggled at times, Frazier said, "They held us to our lowest totals of the season, but we only had about 60 plays and in other games we got 80 or 90." Nebraska had a season-low 19 first downs, 46 rushing attempts, 190 rushing yards, 63 total plays and 338 total yards.

Nebraska's defense made up the difference. NU's blitzing linebackers and stunting defensive linemen smothered any dreams of an KSU upset, as outside linebackers Grant Wistrom and Jared Tomich batted KSU quarterback Matt Miller around, and defensive tackles Christian and Jason Peter caved in the Wildcats' offensive line.

"He (Miller) wasn't moving so good after Wistrom got him on that first sack," Tomich said of the second play of the game, when Wistrom dropped Miller for a 4-yard loss. "He was hurting. He was getting up slow. I may have asked, 'How ya doing?' and he did not respond too much."

Miller didn't have much of a chance to respond.

Nebraska's pressure defense impressed Osborne. "That has to be a little bit unnerving when you are hit almost every play, whether you release the ball or not," he said.

Miller left the game after the next-to-last play of the third quarter. "I could have stayed out there, but I was a little woozy," Miller said. "Defensively, they put their licks on me. I got dinged up a little bit."

Nebraska finished with nine quarterback sacks for 82 yards in losses. The Huskers held Kansas State to minus 19 yards rushing, giving the Wildcats a total of minus 26 yards rushing the last two years against NU.

Meanwhile, Frazier was hypnotizing the Kansas State defense. He converted three key third-down plays—on an 9-yard option run, a 19-yard screen pass to Green, and a scramble for 3 yards on a broken play to set up Nebraska's first touchdown. The Huskers scored when Clinton Childs fumbled at the goal line and teammate Vedral pounced on the ball after it squirted out of the hands of KSU's Mario Smith.

After Christian Peter stuffed one play and Nebraska's Terrell Farley and Tomich broke up another two, the NU offense took over again. The Huskers scored on an eight-play, 61-yard drive that included two runs for 27 yards by Frazier and an 11-

yard touchdown pass from Frazier to tight end Sheldon Jackson.

Two minutes later, Frazier passed to Damon Benning on a 23-yard play and two plays later shoveled the ball to Green for a 10-yard score.

"Tommie Frazier is every bit as good as you or I or everybody thought he was," Snyder said. "He's a difference-maker."

By the end of the game, Frazier had two shovel passes out of the shotgun formation to Green for touchdowns, the touchdown pass to Jackson and another to Vedral, but Nebraska was held without a rushing touchdown for the first time in a regular-season game since a loss at Iowa State in 1992.

"Some games we've had way more yards than points and today we had way more points than yards," Osborne said. "We didn't run the ball as well as I'd have liked to. Maybe it was a combination of Kansas State has a very fine defense and maybe we didn't execute quite as well as we should have."

The Husker reserves had plenty of trouble against the Wildcats in the fourth quarter. Things became desperate enough that the NU starters on offense and defense had to return to the field for the final 5:56 after Kansas State scored on a 73-yard passing drive, tacked on another 63-yard passing drive and blocked a Nebraska punt for a touchdown in an eight-minute span in the fourth quarter.

"I really would rather not have had to do that (put starters back in)," Osborne said. "On the other hand, I guess it's really nice to play a good football team and be able to pull your first team out for a bit. Usually you play a game like this and you never take them out at all.

"We may have just substituted a little too early and it backfired on us," he said.

■

NU cornerback Tyrone Williams was named an All-Big Eight player in 1995. He went on to star for the NFL Green Bay Packers. (Ted Kirk, Journal Star Library)

Frazier Paints Masterpiece

NU nearly flawless in flattening Buffs

by Ken Hambleton

Lincoln Journal Star

Flawless? Well, sure there are some chips in the Pyramids. OK, Michaelangelo may have missed a spot on the Sistine Chapel. Tommie Frazier even threw a few incomplete passes and got caught behind the line once or twice.

But Frazier and his Nebraska teammates came as close to a football masterpiece as possible in a 44-21 blasting of Colorado before the largest crowd ever at Folsom Field in Boulder, Colorado, October 28, 1995.

"Tommie Frazier is our leader and he is going to take us to the promised land," Nebraska split end Brendan Holbein said.

Frazier split the Colorado defense with the best passing game of his career —14 completions for 241 yards and two touchdowns. He also ran for 40 yards, with most coming after contact, and another touchdown and jumped into the Heisman Trophy race, according to many Heisman voters in attendance.

Nebraska's offense was flawless in terms of no turnovers, no penalties, and the Husker defense was a close second in Nebraska's fourth consecutive victory against the Buffaloes and second against a No. 7-ranked team in two weeks.

"Oh, it can get better than this," Frazier said. "I think there are a lot of things to work on. But this was pretty good."

It never looked better for Nebraska than it did on NU's first play of the game. Freshman Ahman Green took an option pitch from Frazier around the left end, picked up big blocks from Holbein and fullback Jeff Makovicka and raced 57 yards to score. "I don't know what was different about the play, but there weren't a lot of people for me to dodge because we had everybody blocked," said Green, who finished with 97 yards and two touchdowns.

Nebraska had 76 more plays in the game, including a Green touchdown after Husker linebacker Terrell Farley intercepted a pass and returned it to the Colorado 13-yard line. That score gave Nebraska the lead for good at 14-7 with 2:52 left in the first quarter.

Another one-play scoring strike, on a 52-yard pass from Frazier to Clester Johnson with 1:47 left in the first quarter, and a 10-play, 72-yard scoring drive that ended in the first of Kris Brown's three field goals put NU ahead 24-14.

Frazier, who is 28-1 as a starter in regular-season games, may never have looked better than he did on that drive. He was smacked hard in the middle of the back by Colorado linebacker Mike Phillips and still hit Green on a 35-yard pass down the sideline.

"That's the kind of play that gets defensive guys going," said Farley. "Can you believe that he even got that pass off and got up right away? That's a tough play and I know it can rattle a defense. But our guys were getting yards after they got hit all day long."

The key drive of the game may have been the 83-yard, nine-play scoring march that ended with 10 seconds left in the first half when Frazier hit Jon Vedral on a 7-yard pass to put Nebraska ahead 31-14. "That was big for us to get the momentum going into the locker room," Frazier said. "It fired everybody up."

But Nebraska stalled on its first second-half possession, and the Buffaloes came crashing back into the game. Sophomore quarterback John Hessler hit James Kidd on a long, high fadeaway pass for a 49-yard touchdown on fourth-and-2 to cut the Husker lead to 31-21 with 8:18 left in the third quarter.

"It always bothers you when that happens," Nebraska Coach Tom Osborne said. "It rejuvenated the crowd and gave them a lot of momentum. You've got to credit our team because things could have begun to crumble. But we were able to regroup."

Frazier hit Makovicka on a 10-yard pass and tight end Mark Gilman on a 9-yarder, while Clinton Childs picked up 19 yards on two carries to set up a 36-yard field goal by Brown with 2:01 left in the third quarter.

Nebraska's defense, which had struggled trying to get to Hessler all day, finally grounded the Colorado quarterback. NU outside linebacker Grant Wistrom slammed into Hessler just as he

Mike Minter (10) and Jamel Williams (28) anchored Nebraska's defensive secondary in 1995. (Journal Star Library)

was throwing the ball, and Nebraska linebacker Doug Colman fielded the wobbling pass at the Colorado 21. Four plays later, Brown added another field goal.

"This team rises to the challenge and plays as well on the road as it does at home," Osborne said. "This group was not intimidated at all. Frazier is a great player and held things together. Colorado did some things that were different and to execute as well as we did, when it was difficult to hear—and I don't know how they (NU players) knew what the play change was—and play error-free is hard to do."

The fact Frazier was able to slice through the Colorado defense for 14 completions in 23 attempts was pivotal, Osborne said.

"We knew Colorado would be committed to the run," he said. Nebraska was held to 226 yards rushing, the second-lowest total of the season and almost 200 yards below its nation-leading rushing average.

"We didn't throw as much as we might have," Osborne said. "They crowded us and moved a lot of players to the run. So we passed and passed well. Once we got up 16 points, we weren't going to throw a lot. If we had wanted more yards, I think we could have gotten them. But we wanted to run some time off and we got conservative."

Colorado linebacker Matt Russell expressed the frustration with Frazier's passing. "We felt confident that we could stop them and when we started to stop the run, they went to the pass. We expected them to pass, just not as well as they did."

Nebraska's victory eliminated any chance of Colorado earning a national title, but it extended Husker hopes for a second straight title.

The victory also brought a smile to Osborne's face.

"I like the chemistry of this team. I like being around them, like the way they play, the way they practice and how they approach the game," he said. "Just to win on the road against a very good team is special to me." ■

NU Dazzling Vs. Cyclones

by Ken Hambleton
Lincoln Journal Star

Hurry, hurry, step right up and see the eighth wonder of the world. Watch the Nebraska football team justify its new No. 1 ranking with a tantalizing, yet workmanlike 73-14 victory against Iowa State at Memorial Stadium November 4, 1995.

Nebraska's football circus presented the stupendous Tommie Frazier and the high-flying Cornhusker offense, the monstrous Nebraska defense, as well as spectacular feats by dozens of other players while entertaining 75,505 fans and the Iowa State football team.

In the center ring, the colossal Nebraska offensive line displayed its power for 89 plays that produced a dazzling 10 touchdowns, 776 yards of total offense (fifth-best all-time) and 624 yards rushing (second-best all-time) by 15 different fleet-footed ball carriers.

The master of ceremonies, senior quarterback Frazier, battled a sore leg all week but still made Cyclone defenders and Heisman Trophy pretenders seemingly disappear. He rushed for 62 yards and two touchdowns, and threw for 118 yards and two more touchdowns in playing just over half of the game.

The young, the talented, the flashy freshman I-back Ahman Green startled the audience with his 176 yards rushing and four touchdowns to become NU's all-time leading freshman running back.

For suspense, Iowa State back Troy Davis, the nation's leading rusher at 190.7 yards per game, managed 121 yards against a Nebraska defense that intercepted two passes, recovered a fumble and a kickoff, and three times threw ISU backs for losses.

For drama, Nebraska fans, facing criticism from CBS News, warmly welcomed back I-back Lawrence Phillips, suspended for the past six games for assaulting his ex-girlfriend on September 10.

The immediate reviews were positive.

"I've been in college football for 25 years, and that's as fine a team as I've ever coached against," said Iowa State Coach Dan McCarney. "And I've coached against No. 1 teams before. They're a totally, totally dominant football team, just outstanding in every way. Not only do they have great talent and outstanding players, but they also do a great job of coaching. Once the score got away from us, it was the men and the boys."

The score got away in swift fashion.

Frazier ran to his left behind fullback Jeff Makovicka and tight end Mark Gilman for a 4-yard touchdown run to end an opening eight-play, 69-yard drive. Nebraska kicker Kris Brown accidentally chipped the ensuing kickoff, but teammate Eric Stokes recovered the ball and the Huskers scored again in 11 plays, when Frazier shoveled a short pass to Green for a 6-yard touchdown.

Iowa State finally got the ball, with the game almost nine minutes old, but had to punt after six plays, and Nebraska scored again, this time on a 17-yard run by Green to boost the score to 20-0 before the end of the first quarter.

Nebraska scored on every one of its next seven possessions—10 in a row—before taking a break and then scoring one final time with 7:23 left in the game.

Iowa State, 3-6, had a nice drive of 75 yards to score in the second quarter and tallied again in the fourth quarter, but Nebraska didn't give the Cyclones a glimmer of hope, as Green scored on a 26-yard run, Frazier hit Reggie Baul on a 36-yard touchdown pass and Brown added a 38-yard field goal before the end of the first half.

Frazier hopped into the end zone to cap a short scoring drive that started when Iowa State fumbled the opening kickoff of the second half. Green then tacked on a 64-yard touchdown run, Phillips added a 13-yard scoring run, and Clinton Childs scored on a 13-yard run—after fullback Brian Schuster scampered 55 yards—to increase the margin to 66-7 with 3:41 left in the third quarter.

"They're playing well right now and I've been very pleased with them," Nebraska Coach Tom Osborne said. "They seem to hang together well. I was a bit apprehensive, because when you play K-State and Colorado back-to-back, sometimes there's a little tendency to have an emotional letdown and I didn't think we did that.

"I think we played with consistency and good effort. I don't think it was inspired, but it was a solid football game."

The Husker players show their unity with a pre-game huddle before the Iowa State game November 4, 1995. (Randy Hampton, Journal Star Library)

Solid in the sense that Iowa State couldn't even get a chip at Nebraska's win streaks of 34 regular-season games, 22 in all games, and 29 games at home.

"We love to play the game and I think we showed it today," Nebraska safety Mike Minter said.

Frazier spoke for the offense: "It was pretty much business as usual for us. We had to go out there and win, because we knew if we go out there and stumble, we wouldn't be playing for the championship. Coach Osborne just asks us to go out there and be consistent."

The consistency showed, as Nebraska totaled more than 450 yards of total offense in eight of nine games, and hovers close to an average of 600 yards a game. It showed in another four quarters without a turnover, stretching the string to 16 quarters in a row. It also showed in the fact Nebraska did not punt once.

"We didn't play a perfect game," Minter said. "We had some mental breakdowns and they got a couple of touchdowns on us. For the most part, we played all right. But nobody on this team is going to listen to anything but talk about the next game and talk about playing better.

"Why should we listen to people compliment us and relax? The same reason we don't listen to the negative stuff," he said. "We feel we have the best program, the best team and we want to prove that. We'll know all about if we're right after the next two games and then in January. Anything before that, like getting too high about this game, is just not the way we do things around here." ■

It Ain't Pretty, But It Counts

by Ken Hambleton
Lincoln Journal Star

If it doesn't look like a blowout and doesn't feel like a blowout, is it still a blowout?

No picture explained Nebraska's 41-3 victory against No. 10 Kansas on November 11, 1995, better than record-setting Nebraska quarterback Tommie Frazier leaving KU's Memorial Stadium on crutches.

"We did what we had to do," Frazier said. "Our goal was the win the Big Eight. We have one more victory before our main goal: the Fiesta Bowl and a chance at getting another national championship. We could have done worse."

Nebraska senior defensive tackle Christian Peter added: "We felt like we were in the toughest dogfight of the year in the first half."

Nebraska, 10-0, clinched a tie for the Big Eight title with the win, but the Huskers didn't appear headed anywhere in the first half. NU slip-slided into a 14-0 lead despite a stunning short-passing display by Kansas quarterback Mark Williams. In the third quarter, the Huskers rambled for 178 yards of offense, holding Kansas to 40 yards and iced the game with scoring drives of 58, 60 and 60 yards by the time the fourth quarter was less than two minutes old.

Jon Vedral recovered a fumbled punt in the end zone to open the scoring. Nebraska punted again and Jared Tomich ripped the ball loose from Kansas back June Henley and teammate Tony Veland recovered at the Jayhawk 30-yard line.

Frazier ducked, danced and stepped his way on a 25-yard run, and sneaked in from the 1 to put Nebraska ahead 14-0 with 1:10 left in the first quarter.

The Jayhawks, 8-2, still seemed to have the answer to Nebraska's fortune.

Kansas constantly stymied the Nebraska offense and, behind the passing of Williams, moved at will through the Nebraska defense.

It didn't matter. Kansas rolled up almost 200 yards of offense in the first half on 22 pass completions. It

Few Husker opponents were able to contain Tommie Frazier and I-back Lawrence Phillips (1) during the 1995 season. (Randy Hampton, Journal Star Library)

added up to one field goal. The rest of the drives fizzled harmlessly.

Nebraska linebacker Phil Ellis tipped away a fourth-down Kansas pass at the Nebraska 33. Another drive ended with an interception by Nebraska's Tyrone Williams at the Nebraska 11.

A late Kansas drive to the Nebraska 22 proved inconsequential when time ran out as the Jayhawks lined up for a field goal at the end of the first half.

In the second half, Frazier threw passes of 16 and 14 yards to Clester Johnson and ran for 5 yards to set up a touchdown. Frazier lobbed a short pass to tight end Vershan Jackson to give Nebraska a 21-3 lead with the second half just over three minutes old.

Frazier threw his first interception in 100 passes on Nebraska's next possession, but Ellis intercepted a Williams pass and returned it to the Nebraska 40 four plays later.

Frazier scrambled for 28 yards and handed off to Lawrence Phillips three times for 23 yards, including a 6-yard touchdown run to make it 28-3.

Tomich, Christian Peter and Grant Wistrom applied pressure, and Williams threw two incomplete passes and was sacked by Tomich for a 3-yard loss on Kansas' next possession.

Frazier completed passes of 12 and 10 yards, kept on an option for 11 yards, handed off to Phillips for 15 more yards, and scored on a 5-yard run to the right to give the Huskers a 35-6 lead with 13:46 left in the game.

To add to the Jayhawks' frustration, Nebraska cornerback Mike Fullman intercepted a pass by former Husker Ben Rutz and returned it 86 yards to score.

"To beat Nebraska you have to play near-perfect, errorless football," Kansas Coach Glen Mason said. "They're too good a team to spot a 14-0 lead. We didn't do enough with the things we got. Nebraska did plenty." ∎

NU Slams Sooners In Finale

by Ken Hambleton
Lincoln Journal Star

The final game of the storied Big Eight Conference ended without quarterback wizardry and without dazzling and daring running. It was a day of brutal defensive domination.

No sirens for long touchdown passes. No bells for reverses and flea-flickers. Just the loud thuds of Oklahoma quarterbacks and running backs hitting the turf as Nebraska slammed a 37-0 conclusion on the Sooners at Memorial Stadium November 24, 1995.

Nebraska's touted offense was slowed and quarterback Tommie Frazier's performance was merely mortal in the midst of hyped competition for the Heisman Trophy. The Cornhusker defense provided the solution—domination in Nebraska's first shutout of Oklahoma in 53 years in the legendary series.

Nebraska outside linebackers Jared Tomich and Grant Wistrom raced through the Oklahoma backfield with a vengeance, and Husker defensive tackles Jason Peter and Christian Peter mauled the Sooner line and wrestled their way into Oklahoma's offensive plans. Tomich had two quarterback sacks and rushed Oklahoma quarterbacks for at least four hurries, resulting in harmless passes. Wistrom had two sacks and a number of hurries, while the Peter brothers combined for nine tackles.

"These kids are confident for a good reason—they're very good," said Nebraska defensive coordinator Charlie McBride. "We had great pass coverage, great leadership on the field and our best defensive effort in years. There was a lot of head-banging in there and I think our kids were having a lot of fun."

Top-ranked Nebraska, 11-0, received an unofficial invitation to the January 2 Fiesta Bowl at Tempe, Arizona, to play in its third consecutive national championship game for a chance to win a second straight national title.

Coach Tom Osborne said the victory was almost expected by his team. "It's interesting that a lot of times a team goes undefeated and wins the Big Eight. There's a huge amount of emotion and everybody gets excited," he said. "It wasn't real quiet, but the team was like it expected to win, and the real major focus is the whole ball of wax."

It didn't take long for the Huskers to establish their supremacy over Oklahoma for the fifth year in a row (the longest Nebraska win streak against Oklahoma since 1930-36). The Sooners, who finished with a 5-5-1 record—Oklahoma's worst since 1965—never threatened to score and were limited to 241 yards of total offense.

"Their defense gave us trouble, too," said Nebraska center Aaron Graham. "But our guys on defense were outstanding, and Oklahoma had trouble breathing—not just moving the ball."

NU's freshman kicker, Kris Brown, who booted three field goals, ended the first Nebraska drive with a 31-yard kick. That was the last time Nebraska's offense was heard from until the final second of the first half, when Brown added a 27-yard field goal. In between, Nebraska linebacker Jamel Williams intercepted an Oklahoma pass and returned it 36 yards for a touchdown with 8:36 left in the first quarter, and the rest of the Nebraska defense stifled all but a few Sooner passes.

By the end of the first half, Oklahoma had minus 7 yards rushing and had been in Nebraska's half of the field just once. Even that Sooner penetration, to the Nebraska 38-yard line, ended back at the Sooner 44 after Tomich chased Oklahoma quarterback Garrick McGee into an intentional-grounding penalty, then sacked him for a 4-yard loss.

Nebraska showed more of the same in the second half, holding the Sooners to minus 1 yard on their first possession as the Peter brothers hounded McGee into submission. On Oklahoma's second possession, Tomich ripped the ball loose from tailback James Allen, and Husker safety Tony Veland scooped up the fumble and returned it 57 yards for a touchdown to give Nebraska a 20-0 lead.

"Oklahoma shut down our running game until the end, but we played so well everywhere else, we were unstoppable as usual," said Nebraska linebacker Terrell Farley. "When I saw Tony Veland's rear end (on his fumble return for a touchdown) and when I saw Jamel Williams streaking on the sideline (on his interception return for a touchdown), I knew we had some answers to them stopping our offense."

Nebraska linebacker Phil Ellis, Tomich, Farley and safety Mike Minter punished the Sooners again and, after a 48-yard punt return by Mike Fullman, Brown added his third field goal of the day.

Michael Booker (20) gives Husker teammate Jamel Williams (28) a hug after Williams returned an interception for a touchdown against Oklahoma on November 24, 1995. (Ted Kirk, Journal Star Library)

Finally, Frazier who hit just 12 passes for 128 yards, connected with wingback Jon Vedral for a 38-yard touchdown—the first offensive touchdown of the game for the Huskers—to boost the score to 30-0 with 14:12 left in the game.

"Eventually, we knew the offense would break through even though Oklahoma was the best defense we played all year," Vedral said. "They shut down our running game, our option game and yet we still got 407 yards, three field goals and two touchdowns to go with our two defensive touchdowns."

"Pretty much a complete team win. Sounds like a No. 1 team to me. Defense wins championships, plain and simple," said defensive lineman Christian Peter. "We stopped them on first downs, on second downs, on third downs and even on that fourth down, when Grant Wistrom got them at our 25 late in the game. Our backers were flying around and everybody on the line was in there for the whole fight."

The Huskers also won in the kicking game, with 110 yards in punt returns.

"I was very proud of the way our defense played today," Osborne said. "I

thought they played a great ball game. We got some turnovers, obviously, a lot of field position, and kept them out of the end zone. I was very proud of the overall effort they gave.

"It wasn't easy, and I don't think the difference between the two teams was 37 points in terms of ability or anything else."

But Osborne reminded everyone that he believed in his team. "I never felt today that we were going to get beat," he said. "That took some of the pressure off. Fourteen points on defense did, too." ■

Huskers Take A Bite Out of Woeful Gators

by Ken Hambleton
Lincoln Journal Star

There was nothing left. A few days after the January 2, 1996, Fiesta Bowl, they sold the turf, in preparation for Super Bowl XXX. A few minutes into the second quarter of the Fiesta Bowl, Florida and the largest crowd in Sun Devil Stadium history was sold, too.

Nebraska took the game 62-24, took the national title for the second year in a row and took any doubt about a consensus repeat championship for the first time since Oklahoma won back-to-back titles in 1955-56. The Cornhuskers earned their 25th consecutive victory, to go with five straight Big Eight crowns and a record 36 wins in three years.

Like a cold wind from the north, Nebraska blew in across the desert, ripping the life out of the potent Florida offense and destroying a Gator defense that had been more than adequate for 12 victories, a Southeastern Conference championship and the No. 2 rating.

Nebraska left nothing to the imagination.

The emotion was gone and the Nebraska locker room didn't have nearly the celebration of the 1994 national championship. "This wasn't as emotional as last year," Nebraska Coach Tom Osborne said.

The excitement had been exhausted in the third quarter. "They played and reacted like they expected this," Osborne said of the Huskers.

The victory was complete.

The top-ranked Cornhuskers frolicked in a blowout of No. 2-rated Florida in the Fiesta Bowl—the biggest college game ever in terms of a $26 million payout, a special Bowl Alliance matchup of two undefeated teams, and—supposedly—the two best teams in the country.

More than 30,000 of the record crowd of 79,864 fans wore red, and one coach was red-faced after the game. "If they are the best, and they are, I don't think we come even close," said Florida Coach Steve Spurrier. "They were better in every phase and we weren't good enough. We just got clobbered and I'm embarrassed."

Nebraska's defense completely dismantled Florida's Fun 'N' Gun offense, leaving it sad and outgunned with three interceptions—one returned for a touchdown by Michael Booker, and one each by Eric Stokes and Tony Veland—a fumble recovery, a safety on a blitz by Jamel Williams, seven quarterback sacks and minus 28 yards rushing.

"We were ready for this game to go down to the wire," said Nebraska outside linebacker Jared Tomich. "After a while, you could see in their eyes that they were done playing. The fire was gone."

Florida took the lead early on, lost it and regained it 10-6, marking only the second time all season Nebraska had trailed.

The Huskers quickly bounced back when Lawrence Phillips, who gained 105 yards in the first half, tore through the middle of the line, then juked two would-be tackles and outran the rest on a 42-yard touchdown run with the second quarter just 35 seconds old.

Phillips finished with 165 yards and three touchdowns and became the first Nebraska back in 11 years to gain more than 100 yards in a bowl game.

Nebraska's defense, which limited Florida to 124 yards in the first half, then tore through the Gator line for back-to-back sacks by Terrell Farley from the left and Williams from the right—the latter for a safety and a 15-10 Nebraska lead.

The Huskers took the free kick and, with a 34-yard return by Clinton Childs, set up another quick scoring drive.

On the second play of the drive, quarterback Tommie Frazier, lining up in a three-point stance similar to a fullback, then walked to the line. Nebraska, with five wideouts for the first time, then spread the field, and Frazier took off on a 32-yard run that included breaking three tackles on his way to the Gator 16-yard line.

Frazier got the ball to freshman Ahman Green on Nebraska's first option pitch of the game, for a 7-yard gain to the 5. Brian Schuster burst through the middle for a 4-yard gain and Green finished the drive with a 1-yard dive to give the Huskers a 22-10 lead with 9:13 left in the first half.

Nebraska's defense, which had five sacks for 24 yards in losses in the first half, stuffed Florida the next two times, and Kris Brown added two field goals sandwiched around a 42-yard interception return for a touchdown by Booker to put Nebraska ahead 35-10 at halftime.

Linebacker Phil Ellis helps douse Husker Coach Tom Osborne after NU's 62-24 trouncing of Florida in the 1996 Fiesta Bowl. The win gave NU its second consecutive national championship. (Journal Star Library)

"Last year, we wore Miami down in the fourth quarter," Nebraska defensive tackle Christian Peter said. "This year, we may have worn them down in the second quarter."

Florida quarterback Danny Wuerffel, who set an NCAA record for passing efficiency in 1995, was constantly on the run. In the first quarter, he found favorite receiver Chris Doering for four passes for 56 yards and led the Gators to a field goal and a touchdown. In the next quarter, Florida had zero yards of total offense and one completion to Doering, and found itself wallowing in the Nebraska defense.

"A couple of times we didn't have enough blockers, but other times they just picked the right places. We were ready for it. We just didn't stop it," Wuerffel said.

While the Husker defense was tearing up the Florida offensive plan, the Nebraska offense was partying in a series of successful plays.

Nebraska's opening touchdown, a 16-yard pass from Frazier, rolling to his right and hitting Phillips on the left, was a new play. Frazier's quarterback draws for a 35-yard touchdown and his impressive seven-tackle-breaking, 15-second-long, 75-yard touchdown option run were commonplace for the senior quarterback ù but spectacular on the field.

"I think Frazier showed there is still a place in college football for a running quarterback," Osborne said. "Our offensive line did a great job and the option still works pretty well, I think."

Frazier gained a quarterback-record 199 yards rushing and threw for 105 yards and a touchdown but was subdued after his performance and the impressive victory. "One score just kind of rolls into another for us," he said. "We always give 100 percent, but some days things just click better. Once this offense gets rolling, I think it's pretty hard to stop. We're thinking about keeping moving—just playing hard—and if something bad happens, move on."

Quarterback Tommie Frazier made sure that the Huskers would repeat as national champions, helping Nebraska to a 62-24 thrashing of second-ranked Florida in the 1996 Fiesta Bowl. (Ted Kirk, Journal Star Library)

Frazier threw two interceptions, one in the end zone and one that led to a Florida score. Phillips missed a wide-open halfback pass to Reggie Baul in the end zone. And Nebraska ran out of time on the Florida 1-yard line at the end of the game.

I didn't think it would be a blowout," Osborne said. "We made some mistakes, but they didn't hurt us much, and they made some mistakes that hurt them. We matched up better on defense than I thought we would, and we got bigger chunks of yardage than I thought we would."

The Huskers found almost all the answers to solving the Gators' attack.

Nebraska's defensive coaches cooked up a new zone blitz to bewilder Wuerffel, and the offense simply pounded the Gator defense. In the end, there were no questions.

"This may be the biggest game of all time and we were huge," said Nebraska defensive back Tyrone Williams. "A win here means no question—no Penn State, no question. We are No. 1 again and again."

Osborne repeated he was overwhelmed by the outcome.

"We'll take it," he said as he dripped and shivered from his drenching in the on-field celebration. "We thought that maybe they hadn't see a defense like ours and maybe they hadn't seen a running game like ours."

Spurrier agreed: "We were embarrassed because so many people were watching—early—and we could not make it a contest. We've been on the good end of these scores and now we're on the bad end.

"We just were not good enough. Obviously, they were."

About the only thing not in Nebraska's favor was a strutting, long-striding run by defensive tackle Christian Peter that was ruled down before he made his march in the Florida end zone late in the game.

"Oh, this is great," Peter said as he was swept away by the fans that swarmed the field following the game. "But they called back my 98-yard run (after Ne-braska stopped a point-after try by Florida, and Peter scooped up the ball), and I almost had a heart attack at the 10-yard line.

"Maybe we can check the tape," he said with a laugh.

Osborne completed the postgame news conference the morning after with a sobering thought:

"This has been a terrible year and a great year. It's taxing and gratifying to work with a group of players with that focus and drive. And at times, it's been very hard." ∎

Coach Tom Osborne kids Christian Peter during a January 3, 1996 rally at the Bob Devaney Sports Center celebrating Nebraska's second straight national championship. (Robert Becker, Journal Star Library)

1996

Berringer Embraced Life, Faith, Osborne Says

by **Curt McKeever**

Lincoln Journal Star

April 19, 1996

Brook Berringer embraced life like there was no tomorrow and sacrificed individual stardom to become a champion.

That's how a teary-eyed Nebraska football coach described the Cornhuskers' former quarterback, who died Thursday afternoon in a plane accident near Raymond.

"I think if you had somebody that you wanted your son to be like, Brook would be a good place to start," Tom Osborne said after speaking at the annual Fellowship of Christian Athletes banquet in Devaney Sports Center.

Berringer, 22, was supposed to be one of five current and former NU players to speak at the assembly.

"It's so hard to take. It's such a loss," said Doug Colman, who, like Berringer, was a senior on the 1995 national championship team. "He was quality as a person, a man and a player. He wore this whole thing here, with being a starter and being on the sideline behind Tommie, and

he handled the whole thing better than I could or anybody I know could."

Berringer, who was born in Scottsbluff but grew up in Goodland, Kansas, played backup to Tommie Frazier for most of his career. But whenever he was called upon, Berringer performed in stellar fashion.

In 1994, when Frazier was sidelined by blood clots, Berringer started seven games. The Huskers won them all en route to the team's first national championship since 1971.

He played the second half of a game against Wyoming with a partially collapsed lung, missing only one start because of the injury.

His best game statistically at Nebraska was during the 1994 season, a 24-7 victory over Colorado, ranked second in the nation at the time. He completed

12 of 17 passes for 142 yards and one touchdown. His 30-yard scoring strike to tight end Eric Alford gave the Huskers a 24-0 lead.

"Brook was a good guy, one of those people who stood for all the right things," Osborne said. "He handled a tough situation about as well and with as much dignity as anybody ever could with his playing situation. I was very close to Brook personally.

"He was just one of those guys that it's very hard to find anything bad to even think about him. I have tremendous sorrow and empathy for his mother."

Last season, Berringer played sparingly as Frazier led the team to a series of runaway victories that propelled Frazier to a second-place finish in Heisman voting. But Berringer was still expected to be selected in this weekend's National Football League draft.

"I know he was a guy in the spotlight, out of the spotlight and always the same guy," said Mark Gilman, a senior tight end for Nebraska in 1995. "He always took time to sign autographs, visit the hospital, visit schools, talk with kids and never once made any noise about it.

"I remember he came to get me, and

Quarterback Brook Berringer died in a plane crash April 18, 1996. The 1996 NU team dedicated the season to Berringer. (Ted Kirk, Journal Star Library)

he'd get other guys, to go to the hospital to visit kids or sick people. I went with him once to see this kid who was in a car accident. The kid had casts all over his body. We visited, and the kid fell asleep. Then a nurse asked if we'd visit another kid, and Brook said, 'Sure.' And before the night was over, we saw another kid."

Kasey Shields, assistant manager of the Cowboy Loop restaurant in Goodland, Kansas, and a former high school teammate of Berringer, was heartbroken over the news.

"The whole town can't believe this thing happened," Shields said. "He was a hero around here."

Nebraska's "Night of Champions" program, which was to honor the Cornhuskers' national champion football and volleyball teams tonight, was canceled.

The musical group Sawyer Brown was scheduled to perform at the celebration. Nebraska was able to book the country-rock act mainly because of Berringer's friendship with band members. Berringer had even been practicing to do a song with the group.

Osborne said refunds would be available to fans, "but those that don't (want them), we'd like to put them into something that his family would like to remember Brook by. We'd like to do something for him. He was a great guy, and he deserves to be remembered."

Gov. Ben Nelson echoed that thought.

"Brook touched our lives with his skill on the field, but he was much more than a football star," Nelson said in a press release. "He was a respected role model and a natural leader."

Osborne detailed to the FCA banquet crowd how he spent nearly four hours a day with Berringer for five or six months of the year. He said they both enjoyed hunting, fishing and flying.

"There may be a somber note to it, but at the same time I know Brook would want this event to go on as planned and would want it to be done in the spirit in which it was intended, which is to honor God," Osborne said. "Brook honored God with his life. Brook was a guy who enjoyed life to the fullest."

Osborne then offered a word of prayer.

"Our heavenly father, we thank you for who you are and we trust you and we put our wills and our lives in your hands. We pray that you'd be with Brook and his family, and we pray that this evening might be dedicated to his memory . . ."

Osborne said his regular practice of faith would help him get through the loss.

"When the events of today happen, it's not like you're unprepared, to some degree. . ."

Art Lindsay, a financial planner for Security Mutual Life who wrote NU assistant coach Ron Brown's book, *I Can*, was moved to deliver an unrehearsed speech to the crowd. Lindsay recalled a visit he had with Berringer after the 1995 season had ended. When he asked Berringer what he wanted to happen in the coming months, Lindsay said, the player responded, "Art, all I really want is to grow in my relationship with Jesus Christ. This is the greatest thing that's ever happened to me."

Berringer graduated from Nebraska in December with a degree in business administration and was a first-team Phillips 66 Academic All-Big Eight recipient. He is survived by his mother, Jan, and two sisters, Nicoel and Drue. He was preceded in death by his father, Warren.

"He loved life," Osborne said. "He did what he wanted to do. He had a lot of enthusiasms and he enjoyed every day, so I'm sure he had no regrets." ∎

Husker quarterback Brook Berringer stepped in and helped the Huskers to the 1994 national championship after Tommie Frazier was sidelined because of blood clots. (Ted Kirk, Journal Star Library)

Remembering Brook

by Curt McKeever

Lincoln Journal Star

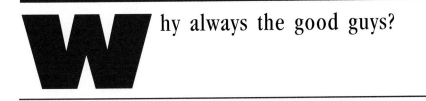

hy always the good guys?

Brook Berringer's untimely death on April 18, 1996 had anyone who knew the popular 22-year-old asking that question.

You could try to characterize Berringer, but you'd probably leave out something good.

He was smart, balanced, talented, handsome, bright, caring and understanding.

He wanted and battled to be the best quarterback at Nebraska, but accepted with class the likelihood that his teammate, Tommie Frazier, probably was going to end up being the one to claim that role.

But in terms of commitment to youth, community outreach programs and conservation groups, Berringer was second-to-none.

"I've coached some 2,000 football players at Nebraska, and I've gotten to know about 700 intimately. And I can honestly say nobody had better character than Brook Berringer," said Nebraska Coach Tom Osborne, speaking to the 3,000 mourners who attended Berringer's funeral service in Goodland, Kansas.

Osborne, eight of his assistant coaches and about 20 current or former NU athletes were among those who at-tended the services for Berringer and his childhood friend, Tobey Lake. Both were killed when the small airplane Berringer was piloting crashed shortly after takeoff from a private airstrip near Raymond, Nebraska.

"There are two questions you have to ask yourself," Osborne continued. "One: What did you do with what you had? If that counts, Brook was a great success. As a student and as an athlete, he got as much as he could out of himself.

"Second: Did you honor God with what you gave? Again, I think Brook did a great job with that."

For many Nebraska fans, Berringer "arrived" after the fourth game of the 1994 season, when Frazier was sidelined by a blood clot in his leg. Berringer went on to engineer eight victories, starting seven of those games, in the Cornhuskers' drive to their first national championship since 1971.

After directing NU to a 31-0 victory against West Virginia in the 1994 Kickoff Classic, Frazier was considered a Heisman Trophy candidate. But the blood clots in his leg sidelined him, opening the door for Berringer.

In his first start, the 6-foot-4, 220-pound Berringer rallied Nebraska to a 42-32 win against Wyoming. He did so playing with cracked ribs and a partially collapsed left lung, injuries he suffered late in the first half. After being hospitalized, Berringer came back to play the next week, but suffered a second lung collapse during a 32-3 win against Oklahoma State.

Nebraska's biggest game of the season—at Kansas State—was the following week. Although Osborne opted to start walk-on quarterback Matt Turman, he called on Berringer late in the first half. Berringer, wearing a specially made flak jacket to protect his ribs, then directed the Cornhuskers to 10 second-half points in a 17-6 win.

Two weeks later, Nebraska faced second-ranked Colorado, and Berringer came through with another clutch performance. He completed 12 of 17 passes and threw a touchdown to spark a 24-7 victory. By the end of the game, NU fans had regained all of their early season optimism.

"I think they've got a good defense. I don't think it's anything that we're not going to be able to move the ball against and put some points up against," Berringer said prior to the game against the Buffaloes. "We're going to be able to get some things done.

"I think I've developed well. I came in in a tough situation, when a lot of people maybe had some questions as to whether I'd be able to get it done. To most people who know anything about football,

Nebraska Coach Tom Osborne speaks at the funeral of former NU quarterback Brook Berringer April 22, 1996 at Goodland, Kansas. (Gail Folda, Journal Star Library)

as if Frazier might not have a chance to earn his second straight Orange Bowl MVP award. But in the second half, Berringer gave way to Frazier after successive drives in which he made a bad exchange that led to a lost fumble and threw an interception in the Miami end zone. Frazier then marched Nebraska to two fourth-quarter touchdowns in its 24-17 triumph.

"Obviously, I would've liked to have been in there at the end, but you've got to credit Coach Osborne for the decision he made," Berringer said after the game. "He looks like a genius.

"I feel good. We wanted to win it for him as bad as we wanted to win it for ourselves."

Frazier returned the next season and successfully led Nebraska to another national championship. Berringer—who threw for 1,574 of his career 2,141 yards and 10 of his 12 touchdowns in 1994—became the reliable backup.

He did come in to lead the Cornhuskers to a 50-10 win against Michigan State after Frazier was sidelined with a deep thigh bruise. But thereafter, he came in in the second quarter, then mopped up in the second half.

If he was disappointed, Berringer hid it well.

He remained committed to his community activities.

"When I was a little kid, I would have died for something like this," Berringer said after talking to Sheridan Elementary students in 1995.

"Every time he was back here, Brook was always mobbed by little kids, and I don't remember him turning down an autograph request," said Mike Johnson, Berringer's high school football coach. "He gave an awful lot back to the people here."

A first-team Academic All-Big Eight honoree, Berringer graduated with a degree in business administration in December of 1995. His focus then turned to getting ready for the 1996 NFL Draft.

Many experts had Berringer pegged

I think I've proved that we can move the ball and put points up."

From that point on, Berringer's accomplishments received the attention they deserved. He provided a remarkable story in a remarkable season, coming off the bench to put Nebraska into a position to play for the national championship.

In the process, he captured the imagination of Cornhusker fans and many of his teammates.

The next week at Kansas, Berringer threw for 267 yards, the most for a Nebraska quarterback in 22 seasons.

"A perfect day for football," he said after the 45-17 win. "The only thing I think it would be better for is quail hunting, and I'll take care of that tomorrow."

Berringer developed a deep appreciation of the outdoors through his father, Warren, who was stricken with cancer and died when Brook was 7.

On the day Brook was born, Warren bought him a fishing license. He pulled his son out of kindergarten to go on a

hunting trip in Montana. By the time Brook was 7, the two were shooting pheasants.

"I still think about him every day. I believe in my heart that he sees what I'm doing and that he's proud," Berringer said before the 1995 Orange Bowl.

It was a time when Berringer could have been bitter. After all, Osborne had named Frazier the starter for the game against Miami.

But there were no gripes.

"Whatever it takes to win the Orange Bowl and the national title is what it takes to make me happy," Berringer said. "I've been through a lot of good things and a lot of bad things. Hopefully, that made me the kind of person able to handle this."

In Miami, against the hometown Hurricanes, Berringer relieved Frazier after the second offensive series and guided NU to a touchdown—a 19-yard TD pass to tight end Mark Gilman to draw the Cornhuskers to 10-7 at halftime.

He was playing so well that it looked

to be the fifth or sixth quarterback taken in the draft. Berringer held out hope of becoming a Kansas City Chief, so he could be near his girlfriend, Tiffini Lake.

The first day of the draft was April 20—two days after the fatal plane accident. It opened with a moment of silence for Berringer.

Nebraska had planned a "Night of Champions" celebration in Memorial Stadium for April 19 to honor the football and volleyball teams' national championships. The event was canceled. Later, because few people requested refunds for their tickets, the university handed over almost $100,000 to the Brook Berringer Memorial Fund, which went to help pay for his sister Nicoel's medical school expenses. Brook had planned on giving the NFL signing bonus he received to Nicoel.

On April 20, Nebraska went ahead with its annual Red-White spring football game. A crowd of 50,000 sat in silence before kickoff as the giant video screens displayed a tribute to Berringer. In it, he was shown visiting with school children, reading Dr. Seuss' book *Green Eggs and Ham*, hunting and playing football.

"He's gone in body but he's here in our hearts," Nebraska quarterback coach Turner Gill said. "He deserved to live 50 or 60 more years. We'd all have been better off if he had. But the one thing that keeps me going is that we know he lived a full 22 years, and we know there is a way we can join him."

Art Lindsay, who wrote a biography of Berringer titled *One Final Pass*, had become spiritually close to Berringer during the 1995 season.

"I can honestly tell you, Brook was exactly the same on the inside that he was on the outside," Lindsay said. "I'm going to miss the arm on my shoulder. A lot of kids are going to miss his visits and care. His friends and fans will miss his presence. But he is still with us and will always be with us.

"His faith kicked in and carried him through the ups and downs of college football. When our faith kicks in, it will carry us through trying to make sense of Brook's death. That's the only way we can get by this. God has taken care of this and he will take care of Brook."

Four days after Berringer's funeral, his sister Nicoel and brother-in-law Kevin Nasseri welcomed Ellen Brook Nasseri into the world.

The 1996 Nebraska football team voted to dedicate the season to Berringer.

To honor his commitment to youth and the community outreach projects sponsored by the NU football team, the university started The Brook Berringer Citizenship Team to annually recognize Husker players who have contributed to their community through volunteer work and community service, and displayed strong personal character and high ideals.

Mark Miller, the lead vocalist in the country-rock group Sawyer Brown, wrote and released "Nebraska Song" as a tribute to Berringer, who had gotten to know members of the band. The band later performed a benefit concert at the Nebraska State Fair to raise funds for a $150,000 Brook Berringer Endowment Scholarship for future NU football players.

In his book, *On Solid Ground*, Osborne wrote: "Although we have grieved for Brook and his family, we have been sustained by the quality of his life, the love he shared with his family and friends, and his faith in our Lord."

Like all the good guys before him, Brook Berringer deserves to be remembered.

"I learned from Brook you have to use what you have and make as much difference as you can— while you can," Nebraska split end Lance Brown said. ■

Quarterback Brook Berringer gets instruction from Coach Tom Osborne during a 1994 game. (Ted Kirk, Journal Star Library)

Sun Devils Scorch Huskers

by Ken Hambleton
Lincoln Journal Star

Sept. 22, 1996— Thud. That's the sound of the biggest upset in college football this year and maybe the biggest victory in Arizona State history. It was the sound of the goalposts at Sun Devil Stadium hitting the ground.

It was the sound the ball made when Scott Frost, sitting in the end zone after ASU's third safety, threw the ball at the goalpost.

It sounds a lot as if 19-0, Arizona State over Nebraska on Saturday night, is the biggest upset of the year and maybe the last few years.

Nebraska's amazing streak of dominance in college football, sometimes called the best team ever, melted in the hot desert night at Arizona State September 21, 1996.

"A great chapter in college football ended tonight, and we're going to start a new one with a big party next week at home," said Nebraska senior safety Eric Stokes. "Nobody is quitting. Nobody says it's over. We lost. Tennessee, Texas and some other folks lost. We'll pick it up. That's the attitude we had with winning. It's the same attitude with a loss."

Certainly the loss, as well as the frustration, was something new for Nebraska football in the last three years.

Oddly, Nebraska never had a chance Saturday night before a capacity crowd of 74,089 fans at Tempe, Arizona.

National champions for the last two years, Nebraska had even as-

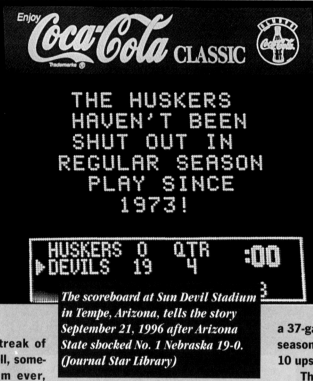

The scoreboard at Sun Devil Stadium in Tempe, Arizona, tells the story September 21, 1996 after Arizona State shocked No. 1 Nebraska 19-0. (Journal Star Library)

sumed the mantle of best team ever after its last appearance in Sun Devil Stadium. That time, on January 2, 1996, Nebraska blasted No. 2 Florida 62-24 in the Fiesta Bowl.

It capped a 1995 season that included Nebraska's 77-28 victory against Arizona State.

Because of that score, many believed that No. 1 Nebraska would easily handle No. 17 Arizona State a second consecutive year.

That confidence wasn't relayed in the stunning first half during which Nebraska gave up two safeties for the first time in school history, allowed two field goals and got stung repeatedly by ASU quarterback Jake Plummer.

Plummer passed for a whopping

292 yards and completed 20 passes, including a 25-yard touchdown pass on the Sun Devils' opening drive. He hit favorite receiver Keith Poole completely alone in the end zone to give ASU a lead it never relinquished.

Nebraska had not been rated No. 1 in the preseason ratings since 1984, a season in which the Huskers were upset at Syracuse. Coincidentally, Nebraska hammered Syracuse 63-10 in 1983.

Nebraska had the nation's longest winning streak at 26 games. It had a 37-game winning streak in regular-season games, dating back to a 19-10 upset at Iowa State in 1992.

The Huskers were outgained, outmanned and out-everythinged by Arizona State.

Nebraska junior quarterback Frost completed just one of his first seven passes, and the Huskers had 133 yards in total offense by the end of the third quarter on the way to finishing with 226. Meanwhile, the Sun Devils had a total of 371 yards of offense after three quarters and finished with 401.

The Huskers were never able to mount a threat after the first quarter, when they got as close as the ASU 5-yard line. But even that drive ended in disarray when Frost missed connections on a pitch to Damon Benning and ASU recovered the ball at the 22.

Meanwhile, Arizona State counted on two field goals by Robert Nycz and a series of Nebraska mistakes to notch the upset. ∎

Brown Makes Huskers Believers
Longhorn QB back ups bold words with bold play

by Ken Hambleton

Lincoln Journal Star

Texas players said their 37-27 upset of Nebraska in the Big 12 Conference Championship Game at St. Louis was unbelievable.

Nebraska Coach Tom Osborne said the Longhorns were uncanny. The Cornhuskers' dreams of a third consecutive national championship are now unreachable.

The play of the game was unreal. Facing fourth down-and-2 inches at the Texas 28-yard line, Longhorn quarterback James Brown bedazzled Nebraska one last time.

While the Huskers geared up for a head-to-head quarterback sneak, Brown rolled to his left, dodged the rush of Nebraska's Ryan Terwilliger and lobbed a pass to tight end Derek Lewis, who raced 61 yards to the Nebraska 11.

The play was so unreal that Lewis said he looked at the big screen TV in the end zone and saw he was being chased by Nebraska linebacker Jamel Williams. "It was like a dream," Lewis said. "I thought I was all alone and saw him, so I covered up and protected the ball."

Texas reserve tailback Priest Holmes scored on the next play—his third touchdown of the game.

The upset by the three-touchdown underdog and unranked Longhorns ended Nebraska's conference championship string at five and clipped NU's hopes of playing in a fourth consecutive national championship game.

Texas finished with 503 yards total offense—the 11th-best effort against Nebraska and the most since Kansas State in 1993.

"It probably isn't supposed to happen against Nebraska," said Texas wide receiver Mike Adams. "They thought they were better than that—stop the running game, get the sacks, beat us up—too bad."

Osborne was philosophical about the loss. "You pick it up and go on and say that Texas played better than we did," Osborne said. "Fourth and a foot (inches) was a tremendous call. It's a gamble but it worked."

Plenty of things worked for Texas that hadn't worked for any Nebraska opponent since the start of the 1993 season—including Arizona State, which beat the Huskers earlier this year.

"We didn't feel they'd be able to run on us as well as they did," Osborne said. "That was the difference. We felt they would get some yards by the pass. A lot of times they had second-and-3s and a lot of those kinds of things. We didn't get them into long-yardage situations." ■

1996 Season in Review

Won 11, Lost 2
Big 12: Won 8, Lost 0, 1st, North Division

Date	Opponent	Site	AP Rank NU/Opp.	Result
Sept. 7	Michigan St.	Lincoln	1/	W 55-14
Sept. 21	Arizona St.	Tempe	1/17	L 0-19
Sept. 28	Colorado St.	Lincoln	8/	W 65-9
Oct. 5	Kansas State	Manhattan	7/16	W 39-3
Oct. 12	Baylor	Lincoln	5/	W 49-0
Oct. 19	Texas Tech	Lubbock	5/	W 24-10
Oct. 26	Kansas	Lincoln	5/	W 63-7
Nov. 2	Oklahoma	Norman	5/	W 73-21
Nov. 9	Missouri	Lincoln	5/	W 51-7
Nov. 16	Iowa State	Ames	5/	W 49-19
Nov. 29	Colorado	Lincoln	4/5	W 17-12
Big 12 Championship Game				
Dec. 7	Texas	St. Louis	3/	L 27-37
FedEx Orange Bowl				
Dec. 31	Virginia Tech	Miami	6/10	W 41-21

Final Rankings: 6th AP, 6th CNN/USA Today Coaches (post-bowl)

It Wasn't Perfect, But . . .

NU shows flashes of old form

by Ken Hambleton

Lincoln Journal Star

 ebraska did not lay claim to the national championship in the August heat and humidity August 30, 1997, in Memorial Stadium.

The Huskers made mistakes—not many. They had trouble stopping Akron's offense—not that often. Nebraska even struggled on offense when the third and fourth teams finished off the mismatch.

"I guess that's getting picky if the scout teams didn't play that well," Nebraska Coach Tom Osborne said. "They (the scout teams) really haven't run our plays except for just the five days of practice they've been here."

Nebraska pummeled Akron 59-14 before 75,124 sweaty fans for the start of Osborne's 25th year as head coach.

It's only natural that the Huskers are a bit picky. The sixth-ranked Huskers were 56-point favorites against the 109th-ranked team named for rubber boots.

The complaints: "If I don't have their attention it's going to be a 9-2 season and we're going to the Slippery Bowl," said Nebraska defensive coordinator Charlie McBride.

"It was pretty hot," quarterback Scott Frost said after posting 190 yards of total offense and running for touchdowns of 26 yards and 5 yards. "I thought that playing was probably just as bad as sitting in the stands, though. I think people were hot up there."

"If we go to Washington (September 20) and play like this, we'll get our butts kicked," said defensive tackle Jason Peter, who helped hold Akron to 82 yards and three first downs in the first half.

"These kind of games don't give me great joy," Osborne said. "But we have to play whoever's on our schedule. We did everything we could to do better in terms of strengthening it."

"No sacks and we were not physical, kind of soft, kind of vanilla," said McBride.

Nebraska actually stalled and Kris Brown missed a field goal attempt on its first drive.

A quick fix and a switch on the bewildering option play allowed Nebraska to score on its next nine possessions.

By the end of the game, Nebraska rolled up 644 yards of total offense, including 472 yards rushing, with 123 yards by Frost on options and 79 by backup QB Frankie London on similar plays.

Even freshman quarterback Bobby Newcombe, with a unique style of option, picked up 32 yards rushing.

To add to Nebraska's joy, fullback Joel Makovicka decided he wasn't going to be tackled on a 20-yard touchdown run that involved five collisions with Zip defenders and hitch-hiking linebacker George Cameron. I-back Ahman Green scored on a 45-yard option run, Makovicka added an 11-yard burst through the middle, and freshman I-back Correll Buckhalter scored on scampers of 8 yards and 3 yards.

"The offensive execution was crisp," Osborne said.

Akron Coach Lee Owens, a former assistant at Ohio State, was more impressed. "I told Coach Osborne that seeing this up close and personal, I have not seen a better team than Nebraska," Owens said. "He said, 'I hope you're right.'"

Tom Osborne holds up the Bowl Alliance trophy after his Cornhuskers defeated Tennessee 42-17 in the 1998 Orange Bowl. (Ian Doremus, Journal Star Library)

Game Not Too Golden For Huskers

by Ken Hambleton

Lincoln Journal Star

Boos for Scott Frost and a second-half comeback against a team from the Sunshine State looking to make a statement in Memorial Stadium—just what you'd expect of a Nebraska-Florida State matchup, right?

In retrospect, maybe a game against the powerful Seminoles September 13, 1997, would have been better for No. 3 Cornhuskers.

Instead, against the unheralded Central Florida Golden Knights and flashy quarterback Daunte Culpepper, Nebraska struggled to a 38-24 victory before turning thoughts to next week's game at third-ranked Washington.

"Because of the newness of their being in Division I, and lack of recognition, I don't think very many people realized they're very good," Nebraska Coach Tom Osborne said of UCF, a second-year NCAA Division I-A team that stunned the crowd of 75,327 by taking a 17-14 half-time lead. "On the positive side, we didn't seem to lose our poise."

Much of that credit goes to senior quarterback Frost. Booed as he returned to the field in the second quarter following a touchdown drive led by backup Frankie London, Frost marched the Cornhuskers to 17 points in their next five possessions. The only two that ended up scoreless came when I-back Ahman Green fumbled and kicker Kris Brown missed a 27-yard field goal on the final play of the first half.

"I thought Scott responded well," Osborne said. "Other than maybe one or two plays, he played flawlessly . . . . If the fans are disappointed, I hope they'll temper that disappointment a little bit with the realization that we played a good team."

Culpepper, a dangerous thrower and at 6-foot-4 surprisingly elusive, had Central Florida in position to become the first unranked team since 1978 to beat NU at home. He threw for 186 yards and a touchdown in the first half, and drew his team to 31-24 with another TD strike with 7:17 left.

But NU countered with a multitude of offensive stars—including freshman I-back Correll Buckhalter, who had his second straight two-touchdown game—to wear out the Golden Knights en route to a 38th straight home win.

"I kind of liked it (when they scored to make it 31-24) because it gave us a challenge," offensive guard Aaron Taylor said. "I definitely didn't like it for the fact they'd took it down on our defense again, but we just kind of said, 'Look fellas, it's in the offense's hands. We've got to keep plugging away and get first downs, and we did that.' I think that showed a lot of character."

Anything less and maybe as Florida State did in Memorial Stadium 17 years ago, Central Florida would have been celebrating a benchmark victory. ∎

Coach Tom Osborne had belief in his starting quarterback, Scott Frost, despite fans' opinions. Frost led NU to a share of the national championship. (Ted Kirk, Journal Star Library)

NU, Frost Put Freeze on Huskies

by Ken Hambleton
Lincoln Journal Star

Nebraska proved the establishment of college football wrong again in a 27-14 spanking of No. 2-ranked Washington September 20, 1997.

The Cornhuskers established once again that: The running game in football is not the Rambler against a Ferrari of a passing game. Nebraska's 384 yards rushing proved more valuable than Washington's 299 yards passing.

That quarterback Scott Frost can manage with or without the support of the crowd. He scored two touchdowns and led the Huskers to 472 yards of total offense against the defense that led the country in rushing defense.

That not all games against higher-ranked teams automatically mean a loss. The Huskers were 1-11 against higher-rated teams since 1981 but now have won four straight against teams ranked in the top three.

That perceptions of performances against Akron and Central Florida were wrong.

That the Big 12 Conference leadership is not dead and there can be a national championship game outside the Rose Bowl.

Seventh-ranked Nebraska, now 3-0, upset a higher-ranked team for the second time in 10 tries in the last nine years. It also stopped a two-game losing streak to the Huskies stemming from losses in 1991 and '92.

"There were doubters this year just like there were doubters last year," said Frost, who startled Washington with touchdown runs of 34 and 30 yards in the first quarter. "We just played the physical game, the way we know best and won.

"If we can run the ball down your throat, then we've got a good chance of winning."

The Huskers put a season's worth of running the football into the Washington defensive throat in the first quarter.

"It was a shotgun approach that threw us off—and inside-outside attack running game that was very much a changeup," said Washington Coach Jim Lambright. "The changes they made in formations we charted are totally different. They totally went away from what they did in the past."

Nebraska Coach Tom Osborne grinned and paused, and explained that preparations for the game were extensive.

"We held a lot of things back against the first two opponents," he said. "A week ago we weren't sure in the fourth quarter if we would be able to hold them. But there were a few things that we had worked on with Washington in mind that we hadn't had to show."

For instance, Frost's first touchdown run was a fake to fullback Joel Makovicka. Frost took off on an angle to the left and scored from 34 yards out.

The next time Nebraska had the ball, after eight running plays and a pass for 3 yards, Frost took off from the shotgun position, ducked one tackler and raced to the end zone on a 30-yard run.

"The first one (touchdown) we hadn't run yet," Frost said. "We were kind of saving it for today. I faked to the fullback, and the I-back led me up the hole. I kind of got hit a little on the line, but we knew that if we could get it by the initial surge that we would have a big hole."

Nebraska force fed Washington another 55-yard scoring drive that Frost sparked with a 14-yard pass to Matt Davison and a 21-yard pass to Shevin Wiggins. Green ran 4 yards untouched into the end zone to give Nebraska a 21-0 lead.

By then, the Husker defense knocked Washington's heralded quarterback, Brock Huard, out of the game with a sprained ankle. His replacement, Marques Tuiasosopo, came in and completed a 36-yard pass and a 12-yard touchdown pass to cut the score to 21-7 at halftime.

Nebraska stalled on its first two drives in the second half and botched a 41-yard field-goal attempt.

The Huskies cut the score to 21-14 with a touchdown pass from Tuiasosopo to Mike Reed that capped a drive that included passes of 54 and 15 yards.

Washington then tried an onside kick, but the ball went out of bounds at the Huskies' 47 and Nebraska ground out enough yards to set up a 20-yard field goal by Kris Brown.

Washington had one final chance to close the score, when the Huskies pinned Nebraska on its 5-yard line with 8:17 left in the game.

On the second play, Makovicka, who finished with 129 yards, broke through the line for a 47-yard run and Nebraska drove for another Brown field goal.

There was no holding back the Husk-ers' feelings after the game. "We've got a bunch of little stumps but they block pretty good, don't they," said Nebraska offensive line coach Milt Tenopir.

"We changed the schemes a bit, got to the outside and plugged away on the inside. We probably did more things right than I can remember."

For some Huskers, there was vindi-cation in the upset.

"We've had faith in the offense throughout the year," said Nebraska rush end Grant Wistrom. "I think some people are really going to have to eat their words, especially our fans who booed us last week at home. Washington was giving up minus 2.5 yards a game and man, we came out and put it to them and just stuffed it down their throats all day." ■

Scott Frost proved his mettle against No. 2 Washington September 20, 1997, with two rushing touchdowns in NU's 27-14 spanking of the Huskies. (Ted Kirk, Journal Star Library)

Nebraska Rushes To Decision

Cornhuskers pass yet another test

by Ken Hambleton
Lincoln Journal Star

The only question left for the Nebraska football team is "What's left?"

The third-ranked Cornhuskers destroyed their second straight ranked opponent.

This time, NU handled No. 17 and previously unbeaten Kansas State 56-26 October 4, 1997, under the lights at Memorial Stadium.

Before the crowd of 75,856 drifted into the night, Nebraska soared behind the four touchdowns of Ahman Green, who rushed for 193 yards, and a stifling defense that held Kansas State to just 11 yards of total offense between early in the first quarter and late in the third quarter.

Nebraska crushed Washington at Seattle two weeks ago and declared Kansas State as the biggest challenge left on its schedule.

That was before Nebraska's offensive line dominated the line of scrimmage and the Husker defense smothered the Wildcat offense through most of the game.

It's a proven formula.

"We think we can run the ball against most people and we don't think many people can run on us," Coach Tom Osborne said. "So far this year, that has been the case and we hope it stays that way."

For almost nine minutes, the promised shootout to open the Big 12 Conference schedule for the two teams lived up to its billing.

Nebraska traded touchdowns with Kansas State but scored six of the next seven times it had the ball and limited K-State to 11 yards of offense during the scoring explosion to lead 41-6 with 5:30 left in the third quarter.

Kansas State Coach Bill Snyder said he didn't have any questions about the strength of Nebraska, which has ended K-State unbeaten strings the last five years.

"I think this game goes to prove that Nebraska has an extremely fine football team offensively and defensively," he said.

Kansas State quarterback Michael Bishop kept the Wildcats alive with 162 yards passing that included one touchdown pass. But he was sacked twice, intercepted twice and thrown for 38 yards of losses.

As Husker defensive back Eric Warfield explained, "They are a good team, they will score some. It's nothing to panic about. We'll get better."

The same goes for the Nebraska offense, which gained 473 yards against a team that gave up 56 to Bowling Green a week ago.

Nebraska quarterback Scott Frost, who rushed for 98 yards and threw for 94 more, said the Huskers were simply enjoying themselves.

"We were having fun," Frost said. "I think we're a good team. I'm not afraid to say that. I think we're as good a team as there is out there."

The Black Shirts also celebrated, with a safety and a 71-yard interception return by freshman Joe Walker.

Nebraska raced to a 20-6 halftime lead behind the touchdowns by Green and Frost and two field goals by Kris Brown.

"I'm glad we came through this as well as we did," said Osborne. "I don't know if these were our two toughest games (Washington and KSU) but this is nice to have this hurdle behind us." ■

Grant Wistrom became Nebraska's fourth Lombardi Award winner. (Journal Star Library)

NU Gets Limit Early, Calls Off Hunt

by Ken Hambleton

Lincoln Journal Star

Baylor is not going to build any shrines to Nebraska football.

After Baylor's 49-21 loss to Nebraska October 11, 1997, not many opinions changed in the Bears' locker room.

"Those guys are something else in college football," said Baylor quarterback Jeff Watson.

"We're not going to bow down to them as gods or anything. But they have talent, depth, speed and they hit like nobody else."

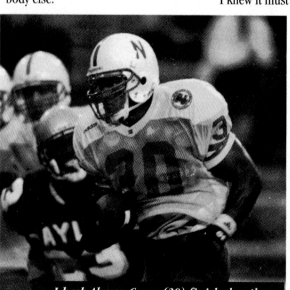

I-back Ahman Green (30) finished as the second-leading rusher in the nation in 1997. He rushed for 158 yards and scored four touchdowns in NU's 49-21 victory against Baylor October 11, 1997. (Journal Star Library)

Watson hit 7 of 19 passes for 66 yards. He was sacked four times for 36 yards in losses. He almost lost his jaw.

"Grant Wistrom hit me on a play when I dropped back to pass and I thought he broke my jaw," Watson said of the play midway in the second quarter. "He put his helmet in my earhole and that was the hardest hit I've ever had in football.

"I knew it was something else and I could still hear the crowd go 'Ooooo'. So I knew it must have looked awful, too."

Baylor scored on the first play of its second possession, when Jerod Douglas outraced Nebraska defenders on an 80-yard touchdown run.

The Bears didn't have a play that netted positive yardage again until there was 10 minutes left in the second quarter. They finished the first half with just 15 yards more than the touchdown run gave them.

"We hoped to run the ball better," said Baylor first-year coach Dave Roberts. "We were struggling in the first half to do anything, run, pass,

hold onto the ball, stop them.

"They had a lot to do with it. Their defensive end (Wistrom),the defensive tackle (Jason Peter), and the other defensive tackles (Chad Kelsay and Mike Rucker) had a lot to do with all our offensive troubles," he said.

Watson and Roberts said the Cornhuskers also showed a strength in pass coverage.

"We thought we might do better passing, but their coverage is the best I've seen," Watson said. "They had a freshman back there who is pretty darn good, I thought."

After Baylor tied the score 7-7 on Douglas's long run, the Bears stopped Nebraska on fourth down at the Baylor 22-yard line.

On Baylor's second play, Douglas was supposed to step in front of a shotgun formation snap to Watson. "I wasn't accounting for the wetness of the ball and I just couldn't handle it," Douglas said. Nebraska's Jason Wiltz recovered the fumble and Nebraska scored on the next play.

Less than two minutes later, Nebraska scored again. Only two minutes after that, the Huskers scored to take a 28-7 lead. Another three minutes later it was 35-7.

"Four or five plays can make a big change in momentum and in how you are playing a game," said Roberts. ∎

Black Shirts Sack Tech

Huskers stake claim to No. 1

by **Ken Hambleton**
Lincoln Journal Star

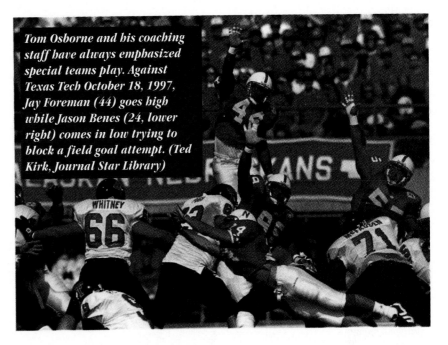

Tom Osborne and his coaching staff have always emphasized special teams play. Against Texas Tech October 18, 1997, Jay Foreman (44) goes high while Jason Benes (24, lower right) comes in low trying to block a field goal attempt. (Ted Kirk, Journal Star Library)

Nebraska shut down Texas Tech and started up talk of a No. 1 ranking.

Unlike current No. 1-ranked Penn State, the Huskers remained undefeated and unruffled with a 29-0 unanimous decision against Texas Tech October 18, 1997.

Penn State scraped out a 16-15 victory against unheralded Minnesota.

No. 2 Nebraska was dominant in every phase of the game played before a Homecoming crowd of 75,764 fans, who couldn't keep their eyes and hopes off the scoreboard that showed Penn State's struggles.

If today's polls show Nebraska on top, it is a matter of debate to some. To others, there is no question.

"This sure looks like a No. 1 team to me," said Jason Peter, Nebraska defensive tackle. "We did what we were supposed to do—beat everyone we played and look better each week. What should happen? Of course, I feel we should be No. 1.

"If we keep playing like this, things will fall our way eventually with the polls and we won't even have to talk about it."

Nebraska Coach Tom Osborne said he wasn't so sure. "What do we deserve?," he said. "We have a good team and I think we are playing well. We are not unbeatable."

Nebraska slammed the door on any discussion about Texas Tech.

The NU defense allowed just 17 yards rushing and 127 yards of total offense. Nebraska's offense struggled to score touchdowns at times but still ground out 400 yards rushing, with Ahman Green rushing for 178 yards and a touchdown.

Nebraska completed the sweep by winning the kicking game, too. Kris Brown booted three field goals and Nebraska averaged starting on its 31 with the help of strong punting by Jesse Kosch.

It was more than enough to convince Texas Tech Coach Spike Dykes.

"They've got the kind of football team that's really, really hard to beat," he said. "When you've got a great defense and you've got an offense that's like the German army coming at you, they just keep coming. And the kicking game—that guy hasn't missed a field goal. He just kicks everything right through the middle. Those things are all momentum-boosters and they all add to the issue." ∎

Top-Ranked Nebraska KOs KU

by Ken Hambleton
Lincoln Journal Star

It was a dark and stormy night.

And to add to the cliché, Nebraska notched a 35-0 victory against Kansas October 25, 1997, before 42,000 rain-soaked, wind-blown fans at KU's Memorial Stadium.

The No. 1-ranked Huskers posted their 29th straight win and ninth shutout against Kansas since 1968.

When Nebraska punches the time clock for playing Kansas, the result almost seems inevitable:

The Huskers' seventh win of the season;

Guaranteed another in Nebraska's string of 36 consecutive winning seasons;

Gave Coach Tom Osborne his 249th victory;

Extended Nebraska's conference regular-season winning streak to 35 games; and

Marked the 19th time in NU history under Osborne that Nebraska is 4-0 in the conference and 10th time in 25 years that his team is 7-0.

Those items are repeated often enough and often at the doorstep of the Kansas football team.

For many, it would be a resume of gallant achievement. For Nebraska it's just another day, another win and another week at No. 1 in the polls.

"It was not spectacular but solid," said Osborne. "Is 35-0 enough to stay No. 1? I don't know. I'll never understand the polls."

Osborne was defensive about his offense, saying, "This was not an easy night to play offense, and we figured that our defense should stop their offense.

"All together, that's a good win. But like I said, nothing spectacular."

Nebraska earned its second consecutive shutout without ever backing into its half of the field on defense.

Kansas finished with just 48 yards in offense—only 15 more yards than Nebraska quarterback Scott Frost threw for with just four completions.

The problem for the Jayhawks, who have been felled 29 times in a row by Nebraska by an average score of 46-7, was that a third-quarter defensive stand was sandwiched by Nebraska's 21-point burst to start the game and a 14-point flurry in the fourth quarter. ■

Fullback Joel Makovicka (45) made up the final part of NU's backfield triumvirate in 1997. The junior from East Butler High School was one of three Huskers named to Sports Illustrated's 1997 All-Walk-On Team. (Randy Hampton, Journal Star Library)

OU-CH!
Huskers Romp, Give Osborne Milestone Win

by Ken Hambleton
Lincoln Journal Star

It's hard to tell whether it was a raindrop or a teardrop that ran down Tom Osborne's cheek.

It could have been a tear of joy after watching his 25th Nebraska football team speed light years away from Oklahoma, 69-7, to end the teams' series, which often was decided by seconds, inches and so many great moments.

If it was a teardrop, it could have been gratitude for the players and fans who stood in the rain and wind to celebrate Osborne's 250th coaching victory November 1, 1997, in Memorial Stadium. Knowing how Osborne down-played the milestone victory all week, it was probably a raindrop after all.

"It's not me. I have played a very small role in this. I haven't won a game," said Osborne after he accepted a plaque from Nebraska defensive tackle Jason Peter commemorating Osborne's 250th victory in 25 years of coaching.

"Today we played for Coach Osborne," said linebacker Brian Shaw. "The captains in their pregame speech said he deserves the 250th and he deserves one with style and our complete effort. We weren't going to let his other 24 teams down today."

There was some doubt for almost a minute-and-a-half.

Top-ranked Nebraska lost a fumble on its first possession, and Oklahoma had the ball 47 seconds before giving it back.

The Cornhuskers, with the No. 1 rushing offense in the country, managed just 1 yard in four plays, but picked up a Kris Brown field goal to take the lead.

The Huskers scored on four of their next five possessions. Nebraska had just 171 yards of total offense but efficiently produced a 34-0 halftime lead on a 5-yard run by Joel Makovicka, a 42-yard Brown field goal into the wind, a 15-yard run by Correll Buckhalter, a lightning-quick 40-yard touchdown pass from Scott Frost to freshman wingback Bobby Newcombe and a 12-yard run by Frost.

After the opening drive, the Huskers started drives at the Oklahoma 8, 27, 23, 28 and 40. Three of those drives were started by Oklahoma fumbles from three different quarterbacks. Not J.C. Watts, Thomas Lott and Jamelle Holieway of the gloried Sooner past, but Eric Moore, Justin Fuente and Brandon Daniels of the struggling team of the present.

The Huskers' other two jump-starts in Oklahoma territory in the first half were the result of a 43-yard fumble return by Nebraska's Octavious McFarlin and a 57-yard punt return by Newcombe.

"I was uneasy early and we went through the first quarter and part of the second quarter without many yards but plenty of points," Osborne said. "Turnovers obviously had a big impact.

"Maybe after a few bad things happened they (the Sooners) may have lost heart a little bit."

By the time a double-rainbow arced across the sky and pelting rain sent many fans scrambling for the exits, Nebraska had a string of remarkable and very un-Sooner-Husker-like results, including:

—Rush end Grant Wistrom and defensive tackle Jason Peter personally tore through the Oklahoma defense. The two seniors enjoyed what Nebraska defensive coordinator Charlie McBride said was, "The best day by two players as good as Nebraska has had on defense. They got it done like no two others I can remember."

—552 yards of offense, "And it was after we sputtered early, if you can say sputtered," said Nebraska center Josh Heskew.

—142 points in two seasons against Oklahoma.

—A fullback record of three touchdowns by Makovicka, who gained 101 yards and said, "It was nothing really special. We were just running right at them and the linemen did a good job all day."

—A seventh straight game of 100 yards for I-back Ahman Green. "It was a good day for the offense. I think the Big 12 has changed a lot of things," he said.

—The biggest day for freshman receiver-returner Newcombe, who had 88 yards in catches, 19 yards rushing and his first touchdown.

—It evened Osborne's career record against the Sooners at 13-13.

—Ended the legendary rivalry with Oklahoma for at least two years —except a possible meeting in the Big 12 playoff in 1998 —with a resounding thud, punctuated by fireworks after Osborne was honored. ■

Husker quarterback Scott Frost leaps over a teammate and an Oklahoma player on November 1, 1997. Frost led Nebraska to a 69-7 win, Tom Osborne's 250th as NU head coach. (Ted Kirk, Journal Star Library)

Missouri: WOW!

A little luck helps NU halt Mizzou

by Steve Sipple
Lincoln Journal Star

They say you need a little luck to win the mythical national football championship.

Well, the luck top-ranked Nebraska experienced during its 45-38 overtime victory against Missouri November 8, 1997, was magical and mythical and downright unbelievable.

Most of the crowd of 66,846 at Faurot Field stood in utter amazement at the end of what will go down as one of the most scintillating games of the 1997 college football season.

"I don't know what you'd call it— I'd call it the best there is," Nebraska defensive coordinator Charlie McBride said.

"I can never remember one quite like this," said Tom Osborne, celebrating his silver anniversary season as the Cornhuskers' head coach.

"We had a lot of good things happen to win it. I thought we were pretty much done for at one time."

Osborne couldn't have been feeling overly confident with seven seconds left in regulation. Nebraska quarterback Scott Frost, facing a third-and-10 from the Missouri 12-yard line, dropped into the pocket, looked to his left and saw nobody open.

So Frost glanced toward the middle and zipped a pass to wingback Shevin Wiggins in the end zone. Wiggins dropped the ball but somehow managed to pop it into the air with his foot. Matt Davison, a true freshman from Tecumseh and NU's third-string split end, made a head-long

dive and scooped up the ball inches off the turf.

"The ball was floating like a punt, end-over-end," Davison said. "I guess the Lord was watching over me, because I was at the right place at the right time."

Davison said he has "no doubt" he caught the ball before it hit the ground.

"But I wanted to see the ref make the call before I got too excited," he said.

Davison's monumental brush with good fortune helped tie the score 38-38, setting the stage for Nebraska's first brush with overtime, during which the teams get equal and alternating possessions 25 yards from the opponent's end zone.

Missouri won the coin toss and elected to defend in the overtime. Nebraska I-back Ahman Green—who finished with 189 yards on 30 carries—arried twice for 13 yards, moving the ball to the Tiger 12.

Frost kept it on the ground, sprinting to his right before turning it upfield along the sideline. At the 3, he left his feet and landed in the end zone, giving him his fourth touchdown of the day. Kris Brown nailed the extra-point kick and Missouri took over.

Tiger junior quarterback Corby Jones —who ravaged the Cornhusker secondary for a career-high 233 passing yards— sandwiched a 3-yard run between two incompletions, leaving Mizzou with a fourth-and-7 at the Nebraska 22.

On fourth down, Nebraska rush ends Grant Wistrom and Mike Rucker—both

of whom are Missouri natives—sacked Jones, and the Cornhuskers somehow escaped.

"We're just happy to win," said Frost, who rushed for a career-high 141 yards. "I still think we're No. 1, but we'll have an opportunity to prove that down the road."

Missouri turned in a performance reminiscent of the 1970s and early '80s, when it made a habit of remarkable upsets.

"When something is within your grasp . . . you're one play away and you can see it," said Missouri Coach Larry Smith, referring to the moments before Davison's miracle catch. "That's what makes this tougher. One stinkin' play— that's what it was."

Actually, this was a game that will be remembered for much more than Davison's catch.

Let's start with what Missouri accomplished. You have to go back 82 games, to the 1991 Citrus Bowl, to find the last time a team scored as many as 38 points against Nebraska. Georgia Tech defeated NU 45-21 in that game.

Missouri racked up 386 total yards against a Nebraska defense that entered the game ranked third nationally after allowing only 217.8 yards per game through eight contests.

"During the pregame (warmups), it seemed like we were ready to roll," Nebraska rush end Chad Kelsay said of the Black Shirts. "But it was one of those days

Matt Davison's miracle catch of this bobbled pass as time ran out against Missouri was considered the college football play of the year. NU's Shevin Wiggins (5) managed to kick the ball before Missouri's Harold Piersey (2) could get it, and Davison caught it just off the ground to help Nebraska tie the game. The Huskers went on to win 45-38 in overtime. The flea-kicker propelled the Huskers to an undefeated season. (Ted Kirk, Journal Star Library)

where we weren't clicking and they were. We just didn't play up to our potential.

"It was ironic that we could win the game after how well the offense played," Kelsay added. "They kept us in the game all day long."

Frost led a Nebraska attack that totaled 528 yards, including 353 on the ground. The senior from Wood River completed 11 of 24 passes for 175 yards and one touchdown, with two interceptions.

His 141 rushing yards gave him his third 100-plus day this season. His 316 yards of total offense were 3 short of the NU record set by Jerry Tagge at Missouri in 1971.

Frost was asked if he had any doubts in the game's final minutes.

"Are you kidding?" he asked. "Down seven with (1:02) left, there's a lot of doubts."

But Frost kept Nebraska alive with sideline passes on a 10-play, 67-yard drive that ended with Davison's catch.

"I'm very proud of the players," Osborne said. "I thought we showed great poise. We had some bad breaks and some good breaks—our good breaks came at the end of the game.

"It was just kind of one of those days where someone was going to win at the end, and we're just fortunate it was us." ■

NU Runs Wild On Cyclones

by Ken Hambleton
Lincoln Journal Star

Nebraska football was frozen in time with The Catch in The Game last week at Columbia.

Only the fans and the Iowa State defense froze November 15, 1997, as the Cornhuskers flashed into warp speed and burned Iowa State 77-14 before 75,613 shivering fans at Memorial Stadium.

"After last week, we needed a day like this," said Nebraska senior defensive tackle Jason Peter.

Nebraska led 21-0 less than five minutes into the game.

Instead of calling plays to save precious seconds on the clock to set up a daring, wacky play like he did last week against Missouri, Coach Tom Osborne debated whether his quarterback should kneel down or simply dive up the middle at the end of the first half in Nebraska's demolition of the Cyclones.

Nebraska led 63-7 at halftime.

"Both games were fun," said Nebraska I-back Ahman Green, who frolicked in rushing for 209 yards and three touchdowns.

"Last week, nobody knew. It was a teeth-grinder. This week, we got things rolling and you can't stop us when that happens."

Quarterback Scott Frost ran for 88 yards and two touchdowns and hit 8 of 9 passes for 111 yards and another touchdown in the merriment of Nebraska's last home game of the season.

There was no contest between 10-0 Nebraska, winner of the Big 12 North Division, and 1-9 Iowa State, victim of a vengeful Husker team. Nebraska locked up a berth in the Big 12 playoff December 6 in the Alamodome at San Antonio.

The Huskers seemed in a hurry to get there. They had 35 points in just 16 plays in the first quarter.

"We beat them up," said senior guard Matt Hoskinson. "We were mad about a close game last week. We were bigger, stronger and faster. They were weak. They are trying to build a program. We've already got one. We took it to them and they gave up."

Iowa State Coach Dan McCarney didn't argue.

"We were absolutely ineffective on both sides of the ball in the first half," he said. "When people are putting up that many points and we're that ineffective, then it's our fault—not theirs."

The Huskers had six players account for nine rushing touchdowns, scored on a 53-yard punt return by freshman Bobby Newcombe and could even afford to have two drives stop at the Iowa State 2-yard line. Nebraska had three one-play scoring drives.

Osborne patiently waited for the few questions he faced after the game.

"This is the quietest I've ever heard you guys," he said at the postgame press conference.

McCarney didn't have any questions either.

"We feel like that is the best football team in America," he said. "There is just no doubt in my mind that that is the finest college football team in the country. They are a great, great football team." ∎

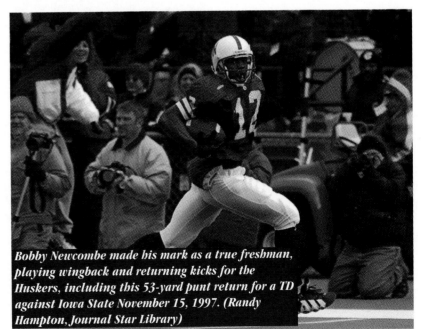

Bobby Newcombe made his mark as a true freshman, playing wingback and returning kicks for the Huskers, including this 53-yard punt return for a TD against Iowa State November 15, 1997. (Randy Hampton, Journal Star Library)

A Rocky Finish In Boulder

by Ken Hambleton
Lincoln Journal Star

Colorado almost spun out of Nebraska's grasp in a dizzying finish that had the No. 2-ranked Cornhuskers gasping and confused.

Nebraska freshman cornerback Erwin Swiney spun Colorado receiver Phil Savoy out of bounds, just 3 yards short of a first down with 21 seconds left to preserve NU's 27-24 victory at Folsom Field on November 28, 1997.

Colorado appeared out of the game and headed for its first losing season in 11 years without so much as a yelp when Nebraska took a 27-10 lead into the fourth quarter.

"It (the end of the third quarter) was like the end of the game for our concentration," said Nebraska fullback Joel Makovicka.

The only problem was that Colorado wasn't finished yet.

The Buffs, 5-6, scored two touchdowns with ease in a span of 39 seconds and stuffed Nebraska's offense to get one final shot at the undefeated Huskers.

Colorado quarterback John Hessler, cheered by the crowd only when he went to the bench with a thumb injury with 8:10 left in the game, returned to the field and hit Phil Savoy on a 16-yard pass. He missed on his next two passes, and with an offensive pass interference penalty against Savoy, faced fourth down-and-25 with 21 seconds left.

Savoy sprinted 15 yards and turned to the sideline to catch Hessler's last pass. Swiney grabbed Savoy's arm and spun him out of bounds to save the game for NU.

Nebraska players and coaches were shaking their heads.

"I think we made them look better than they are," said Nebraska quarterback Scott Frost, who went over 1,000 yards passing and 1,000 yards rushing in a season, just the 11th time in NCAA Division I history that a player has accomplished the feat.

"We kept having little things happen. We'd miss on a couple of blocks, had a few penalties and fumbled the ball."

Nebraska's near self-destruction started when Colorado safety Ryan Sutter stripped the ball from NU I-back Ahman Green and Colorado's Ryan Black recovered at the Buffs' 23-yard line with 4:59 left in the game.

Hessler guided Colorado on a 77-yard scoring drive in just less than two minutes, cutting the score to 27-17 with 3:16 left.

The Buffs recovered an onside kick that bounced off the hands of Husker T.J. DeBates, and needed just four plays to cover 55 yards. Hessler found Robert Toler in the back of the end zone to close the score to 27-24 with 2:37 left.

Nebraska, which finished with 442 yards—43 in the fourth quarter—managed just two first downs in the final quarter and gained just 8 yards compared to Colorado's 165 in the final five minutes of the game.

"This was a terrible performance," said Nebraska All-America guard Aaron Taylor. "We need to get a lot better before anybody around here can be talking about

Nebraska senior Eric Warfield (3) had a stabilizing influence on the Huskers' young defensive secondary in 1997. Among his plays was this interception against Colorado November 28. (Ted Kirk, Journal Star Library)

the polls again. As of right now, forget the polls."

"It wouldn't be wise to talk about the polls before the Texas A&M game," said Nebraska Coach Tom Osborne. "The bottom line is we won the game. But we almost lost to a team with five losses (now six)." ∎

12-0! NU Puts Agony And Misery On Aggies

Huskers look to Miami

by Ken Hambleton
Lincoln Journal Star

This time, the South will not rise again.

Nebraska made sure there would be no insurrection in the Big 12 Conference championship game. The No. 2-ranked Cornhuskers quelled any outburst from Texas A&M in a 54-15 victory December 6, 1997, in the Alamodome.

The victory gave Nebraska a 12-0 record, its first Big 12 championship, and a berth in the January 2 Orange Bowl.

It also served as redemption for losing to three-touchdown underdog Texas in the first conference playoff game the year before.

"This was sweet revenge," said Nebraska All-America guard Aaron Taylor. "We seniors talked all week, actually since last winter, that we were going to get it back and make a statement."

Nebraska erased any doubts among the 64,824 fans in the Alamodome and the rest of a national television audience with seven scores on seven possession in the first half.

"We felt like we were representing all the teams in the Big 12 South and we're a reflection of how strong the South is," said Texas A&M quarterback Branndon Stewart. "I'm kind of embarrassed for the South."

Representing the North champion, Nebraska quarterback Scott Frost, playing perhaps his best game, according to Nebraska Coach Tom Osborne, threw for 181 yards and ran for another 40 and two touchdowns in the first half.

What Frost left, Ahman Green picked up, with 104 yards and two touchdowns before halftime. Green finished with 179 yards and three touchdowns and had three catches for 16 yards.

"It was just too much for us to stop," said Texas A&M linebacker Dat Nguyen. "Scott Frost is such a great competitor and he's so smart. He knew where our weaknesses were every time they lined up."

There were even some weaknesses Frost didn't discover. Nebraska freshman Bobby Newcombe blew through the Texas A&M "Wrecking Crew" defense for 108 yards of offense in the first quarter. He rushed twice for 27 yards, caught a 26-yard pass and returned two punts for 55 yards.

And remember, Nebraska's offense wasn't as spectacular as the defense, Taylor said.

"Our defense was just pounding those guys," he said. "It was phenomenal because they were just blasting those guys. It got our offense up."

Even with captain and defensive tackle Jason Peter limited to one quarter of action because of back spasms, the Nebraska defense allowed just two first-half first downs. Except for a 63-yard pass, the Huskers allowed just 15 yards of offense by A&M and that was all in the air, because the Aggies had minus 5 yards rushing in the first half.

"We were playing for everybody who saw what happened with Texas last year and we were playing for ourselves and our goal to get to the Orange Bowl," said Nebraska rush end Mike Rucker. "We had to prove ourselves after the letdown at the end of the Colorado game last week and for Missouri a couple of weeks ago.

"I think we proved the point today."

Nebraska's offense sputtered a bit in the first quarter. After Frost scored on a 6-yard touchdown run, the Huskers settled for Kris Brown field goals of 27, 26 and 31 yards.

Brown added another first-half field goal after Green scored two more touchdowns—on a 25-yard option run to the right and on a 1-yard leap to cap a 67-yard drive.

"We didn't want to get knocked out early," Texas A&M Coach R.C. Slocum said. "We didn't get knocked out but we had some knots on our head and we were reeling.

"I was not shocked. I knew that their pressure would be good and I was disappointed with some of our pass plays in the first half and our lack of execution."

Osborne, a strong opponent of the playoff game, said he was pleased with his team's victory.

Husker defensive tackle Jason Peter celebrates a sack in the Big 12 championship game against Texas A & M December 6, 1997. NU coaches say Peter was one of the best to ever play the position at Nebraska. (Randy Hampton, Journal Star Library)

"Last year, against Texas, we didn't get that excited and looked ahead to the Sugar Bowl and we goofed up.

"This time, we wanted to get it done. The players wanted another chance at a national championship and they have done their part by getting to 12-0," he said.

"This is a great team, any way you stack it. We won't spend a lot of time talking about the polls. It's all in the eyes of the beholder and anything you say sounds self-serving."

Some others weren't so shy about talk of a national championship. "We must have made some impression on somebody," said Taylor. "I don't know how much better we could have played, except at the end.

"But we'll just go to Miami and play our best and let the rest take care of itself."

The victory puts Nebraska a step closer to a ninth perfect season.

Osborne has coached two of those— both national championship teams. "We played well against the good teams in big games—Washington, Kansas State and when we were cranked up, we played awfully well," the coach said.

"When they face the challenge, they get going pretty good. I'd like to see us finish the job." ■

The Run To No. 1

Huskers flatten Vols, get one title

by Ken Hambleton
Lincoln Journal Star

Nebraska uncorked a famous vintage in honor of Coach Tom Osborne.

The dizzying celebrations included the reliable blocking by Nebraska's offensive line, bubbly runs by Ahman Green and the effervescence of Scott Frost's passing.

The result was a giddy 42-17 Cornhusker frolic in the Orange Bowl at the expense of No. 3-ranked Tennessee.

"Nebraska was simply wonderful," said Tennessee Coach Phil Fulmer. "They handed us our butts."

The Huskers were also wonderful in the eyes of the coaches who vote in the ESPN/USA Today poll. Nebraska finished ranked No. 1 int the coaches' poll, receiving 32 first-place votes to 30 for Michigan. The Associated Press voters chose Michigan 51 to 18.

The win was good enough to give Osborne his third perfect season in the last four as he ended a sterling 25-year career as coach of the Huskers.

Tennessee Coach Phil Fulmer led the charge for Nebraska.

"They are everything a No. 1 team should be," he said. "They got my vote."

There was little doubt that Nebraska's players were trying all they could to give Osborne his third national title.

"There is no doubt who is No. 1 in my mind," Nebraska defensive tackle Jason Peter said. "Let's get together at 16 San Paulo Drive in Jersey next weekend. That's my backyard. If you guys want to

go there, no problem. We'll play Michigan."

After a few minor adjustments—the same kind that gave Osborne a 255-49-3 record in 25 years—Nebraska rushed for 227 yards and three touchdowns in the third quarter to crack the game wide-open.

The Huskers finished with a dominating 534 yards of offense, including 409 rushing.

"It looked like something would give," said Nebraska running backs coach Frank Solich, who took over for Osborne as head coach after the game. "They had so many people committed to the run, and it worked early. We had to change something, so we passed.

"Then, they back off and we ran some dives, some options and some isolations and did well," said Solich. "It was a classic Coach Osborne game and the players did it real well all game long."

Nebraska's defense shackled Tennessee quarterback Peyton Manning, holding the Heisman Trophy runner-up to 134 yards passing and the Vols to 315 yards of total offense.

"We beat the snot out of No. 2 Washington on the road, the snot out of No. 3 here and the snot out of No. 20 Texas A&M in the Big 12 championship," said Husker Grant Wistrom.

Nebraska seemingly locked up the game when the Huskers opened the second half with a bone-crunching, 12-play, 80-yard drive that ended with Scott Frost

squeezing into the end zone from the 1-yard line.

Nebraska served meat and potatoes again on its second possession of the second half, as Green broke loose for 57 yards on four carries and Frost scored on an 11-yard keeper around right end to extend the score to 28-3 with 5:07 left in the third quarter.

Tennessee finally countered with a touchdown pass from Manning to Peerless Price that ended a nine-play, 72-yard drive that included four completions by Manning for 37 yards and a 23-yard run by Jamal Lewis.

It wasn't nearly enough.

Green scored on a 22-yard run to cap a four-play, 80-yard drive, and Frost scored again on a 9-yard run to boost the score to 42-9.

"When you run four plays and go 80 yards and run nine plays and go 80 yards and just keep pounding away, the other team tends to give up," Nebraska center Josh Heskew said. "I don't think they had anything left on their defense."

Osborne agreed, to a point.

"We didn't do anything special," he said. "We saw a few things as the second quarter unraveled. Scott made some exceptionally good throws and that got them off our backs and we began to get a few things working.

"I think we got them off-balance and wore them down. It's a physical style of football—just knocking people down. Eventually that takes a toll."

The Huskers were unconventional in the first half in taking a 14-3 lead. Frost outpassed Manning 109 yards to 96 yards and Tennessee outrushed the nation's top rushing team 80 yards to 69 yards.

The difference was a new play, a wingback isolation play to Shevin Wiggins that he turned into a 10-yard touchdown run. The score followed a fumbled Tennessee punt that Husker junior Lance Brown recovered at the Vols' 15-yard line.

Nebraska's first touchdown came on a 1-yard run by Green to cap a 78-yard, eight-play drive.

"You could hear those guys on their defensive line breathing real hard," said Nebraska All-America guard Aaron Taylor. "You can't keep getting up and taking a beating like we were giving them all day.

"You can't tackle Ahman Green or Scott or Joel Makovicka when you can't catch your breath," he said. "They eventually rolled over."

Then it was time for Osborne to give his final postgame speech.

"He got a little emotional and told us thanks for everything," Taylor said. "He was a little emotional but it was typical postgame speech."

Nebraska played the same way, Nebraska defensive coordinator Charlie McBride said.

"The players were emotional and played a typical game in what is a typical Tom Osborne game for the last 25 years. It was as good as you can get, just like Tom was as good as we could get." ∎

Scott Frost lets everyone know who he thinks is the best team in the country after NU's 42-17 victory against Tennessee in the 1998 Orange Bowl. (Journal Star Library)

Frost, Teammates Can Celebrate Title

by Mark Derowitsch
Lincoln Journal Star

Immediately following the Orange Bowl Friday night, Nebraska quarterback Scott Frost began lobbying for at least a share of the national championship.

It worked. At least in part.

Three hours after they took apart Tennessee 42-17 in the Orange Bowl to cap a 13-0 season, the Huskers learned the ESPN/USA Today coaches poll gave Nebraska a share of the national title. Michigan, which went 12-0, was named winner of The Associated Press media poll.

"I didn't know how it would turn out," Frost said Saturday at the Bob Devaney Sports Center, shortly after he returned to Lincoln from Miami. "I don't know if it made any difference or not."

Actually, Frost didn't spend much time thinking about his last-minute pleas for recognition. He had other things on his mind, like beating Tennessee and sending retiring Coach Tom Osborne out a winner.

Frost, and the rest of the Huskers, did most of their talking on the field. With Frost running the option, Nebraska rushed for 409 yards and finished the game with 534 yards of total offense.

Nebraska entered the day ranked second in both national polls, but its performance was enough to sway the coaches to move the Huskers up. The Husk-

ers earned 32 of a possible 62 first-place votes in the ESPN/USA Today poll, while 30 coaches voted for Michigan.

While Frost was busy preparing for the Orange Bowl, his older brother, Steve, put together some remarks he could use following the game.

"I said what I had to say," the NU quarterback said. "I had other things to worry about, so my brother prepared a speech for me to use after the game."

Frost was eating a late supper at the team's hotel early Saturday morning when he heard his efforts paid off. Because of the roar of the crowd, Frost didn't hear the news first-hand.

"I didn't even hear it—I heard the crowd that had gathered around the TV go nuts and I kind of figured we won it," he said. "It was an exciting moment for everybody."

Nebraska I-back Ahman Green was stepping out of the shower in his hotel room when he found out the Huskers earned a part of the national championship.

Like Frost, Green heard the reaction of Nebraska's players and fans before he heard the news himself. Green's room was located on the ninth floor of the hotel while most of the Huskers were in a dining room on the first floor.

"I got dressed and went down

and started yelling and hugging people," said Green, who rushed for an Orange Bowl-record 206 yards. "It was great to be a part of it."

Nebraska deserved the No. 1 ranking, according to Green.

The Huskers held Tennessee quarterback Peyton Manning to just 134 passing yards and one touchdown to win their second consecutive Orange Bowl.

Nebraska gave Osborne his third national crown in four years and won the title for the fifth time in school history.

"We went 13-0—you can't get any better than that," Green said. "We deserved to win it."

Jay Sims, Green's backup, didn't immediately hear the news, either. But, like Green, he heard the commotion and ran toward it.

"The room just exploded," he said. "Everybody had their hands up in the air when I looked up. I just saw a bunch of No. 1s."

Tight end Tim Carpenter said he's glad two teams were able to celebrate Saturday morning. While Nebraska deserved its share of the title, Carpenter said, it's hard not to support Michigan's claim to the national championship.

"You can't deny Michigan the championship, or at least a share of it," he said. "But they can't deny us one, either." ■

Say It Isn't So!

Osborne: Orange Bowl to be last game as coach

by Ken Hambleton

Lincoln Journal Star

Dec. 11, 1997

Tears welled up in Tom Osborne's eyes and lumps filled the throats of 150 players and thousands of Nebraska fans.

Even Nebraska's new head football coach, Frank Solich, felt the sadness when the football legend announced his resignation.

Osborne, who will step down after the Orange Bowl, said his health, his faith and his belief in the strength of continuity in the Nebraska football program led to his decision a day after he "soft-shoed" retirement talk at his weekly news conference.

"The hardest thing is talking to the players," Osborne said as he teared up. "I tried to say things I thought were funny, but nobody laughed and I felt bad. I care very much about those guys.

"But it is better this way now than for a guy from the outside who comes in and treats the players differently."

Osborne bowed his head.

He looked up.

His face reddened and tears welled again when he stepped back from the podium and heard Nebraska Athletic Director Bill Byrne announce by phone that Solich would be promoted to head coach after the January 2 Orange Bowl. Bad weather stranded Byrne in Chicago.

Solich, who was in Toronto visiting recruit Dahrran Diedrick Tuesday, also battled the weather, but he made it to Lincoln in time.

"This is a tough day for people in Nebraska and a few will be in shock," Solich said. "This is a day of mixed emotions for me. I am sad because Tom is so close to us all. I am excited to be named the head coach of the Nebraska football team."

Osborne, too, had mixed emotions.

"This has not been a fun day for me," he said. "My future, I don't know. Usually, you leave these jobs when you get fired or get a better deal. I don't have a better deal, but I have nothing in mind other than to finish this out and then take some time."

Osborne discussed his emergency trip to Bryan Memorial Hospital early on the morning of November 16. At the time, Osborne reported the problem was a "heart flutter" that required only new medication and some monitoring.

Wednesday, he said the heart problem "put me under and I had to be shocked to get back (a regular heart rhythm). It will go out again and might mean a pacemaker if life goes on."

Osborne said he was still in reasonably good health.

"I'm not going to keel over on you right now," he joked. But he added that the demands of a 15-hour day, seven days a week, were too much.

"This is what I enjoy doing, but I'm positive to make the adjustments you have to do your homework and there are no shortcuts. To call the plays and make the adjustments, I realized that in the last

Tom Osborne was quick to point out on December 10, 1997, that he was not going to give up the reins of the Huskers until after the January 2, 1998 Orange Bowl game against Tennessee. His team sent him out on a winning note, defeating Tennessee 42-17 and earning a share of the national title. (Ted Kirk, Journal Star Library)

three months I could not sustain that for any great length of time, and I don't want to be in the position where somebody tells me I'm not getting the job done."

Additionally, Osborne said he was calling it quits because naming Solich now would assure the continuity of the program.

"The third reason was that I take my faith seriously, and I feel for me to continue beyond this time that I would not feel good about the spiritual aspect of life," he said.

He said he was leaving the program in the best shape possible and offered to help with recruiting through the national letter of intent signing day February 4. Most of the 10 recruits who have com-

mitted orally to the Huskers said they would honor their commitments.

Osborne said he contacted his eight assistant coaches, six of whom were out of town recruiting. Each said he supported Solich.

"Not one coach had any qualms about Frank taking over and that is unusual," Osborne said. "There is usually some jealousy and some back-biting."

When Osborne took over for Bob Devaney, the Nebraska coaching staff was shaken with the departure of five assistants over the next three years.

"I was 35 years old and some of those coaches had been with Bob for 20 years," Osborne said. "I didn't know which end was up."

He said this time should be different.

"We tried to make sure what the order of staff was and everybody has been supportive," Osborne said. "I appreciate that."

Emotion surfaced again when Osborne said he would spend more time with his family and his faith.

"I appreciate my wife Nancy's stance in all this. She had to raise three children single-handedly, and I did not realize until recently how difficult some of that was," he said.

In almost a whisper, he added, "I don't know if you can ever make up for lost time, but maybe a few things will make up for some times we maybe should have had that did not happen together."

Osborne told his coaching staff of his decision Tuesday. Assistant coaches Charlie McBride, NU defensive coordinator and assistant for 21 years, and Milt Tenopir, offensive line coach for 24 years, said they would stay with the program.

"This is not a one-man operation," Osborne said. "What the people of Nebraska can't afford to lose is the coaching staff. Some of what I'm doing is for continuity and consistency. This decision has been in the process for a few months. There have been a few things that happened with my stamina and cardiovascular problems.

"But at some point in the next two years I might have to call a halt. It would be wise to back off before I had to leave feet-first." ∎

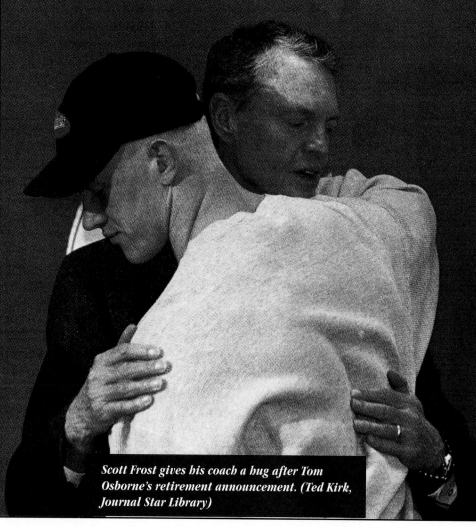

Scott Frost gives his coach a hug after Tom Osborne's retirement announcement. (Ted Kirk, Journal Star Library)

IT WASN'T ANOTHER MUNDANE MEETING

by Steve Sipple

Lincoln Journal Star

Dec. 11, 1997—Nebraska junior fullback Joel Makovicka badly wanted for it to be just another mundane team meeting December 10, 1997.

It began that way, with Tom Osborne discussing preparations for the Orange Bowl game against Tennessee.

Eventually, Makovicka said, the 60-year-old head coach began easing into the subject nobody wanted to hear. The speculation was accurate: Osborne was retiring after the bowl game.

"He wanted to downplay the emotion and try to have a sense of humor about it," Makovicka said. "He told a few stories and tried to keep it light. But nobody took it lightly.

"It was stunning silence when we realized what he was getting at. It was like people couldn't believe what they were hearing."

Freshman I-back Dan Alexander said the players' silence was overwhelming.

"You could hear a pin drop when Coach Osborne was talking," Alexander said. "Everybody left the room in the same, quiet way. It was almost morose. Some of the players were crying. Some wouldn't talk to anybody.

"There was a lot of emotion in that room."

Matt Hoskinson, a senior offensive lineman, said he fought to avoid looking at his teammates for fear of breaking down.

"It would have led to a domino effect," he said. "This team is close, and it's close to Coach Osborne."

Osborne addressed the players at 2 p.m. in the auditorium where the team regularly meets. Shortly after he met with the players, Osborne told the media the news that sent shockwaves throughout the college football world.

Some Nebraska players said they were in shock during the team meeting. Some were somber afterward, others upbeat.

A few players said they expected the announcement in the wake of rumors that spread like wildfire beginning Monday. Even so, they were saddened by the finality.

Makovicka was among more than a dozen players who watched Osborne address the media. Afterward, the players expressed support for his decision and optimism about the future under new head coach Frank Solich.

Many described Osborne as a father figure.

"He gives you words of encouragement, not only about football, but about life," said freshman cornerback Erwin Swiney, a Lincoln Northeast graduate. "He gathers us all under his wing and keeps us together."

Senior quarterback Scott Frost said the coach made him a better man.

"We don't learn just football here," Frost said. "We learn how to become grownups, how to be mature, how to become men."

Osborne's eyes welled with tears during the news conference when he mentioned the players.

Alexander understood; he said the coach makes it a point to know all the players, from the stars to the obscure walk-ons.

"I've heard of other head coaches who don't know all their players' names," Alexander said. "Coach Osborne knows everybody's name, and when the players come back (after they graduate), he still knows them."

"It's going to be on us (to beat Tennessee)," junior split end Kenny Cheatham said. "We don't want Coach Osborne to go out a loser; we want him to go out the way he came in—a winner." ■

Making Sacrifices

by **Ryly Jane Hambleton**

Lincoln Journal Star

Jan. 12, 1998

Nancy Osborne knows better than the rest of the Osborne family what sacrifices were made for husband, Tom, to be the University of Nebraska head football coach for 25 years.

There were birthdays and anniversaries that were celebrated early or late. And 29 straight bowl games meant a lot of Christmas parties in hotel suites and ballrooms. Family outings were difficult because the red-headed coach was so recognizable. Nancy and Tom would slip into gymnasiums to watch their children compete in athletics, but try as they might to blend in, fans would always flock to their sides to talk or get an autograph.

It will take a little adjustment for the family to have Tom around. Nancy said having her husband of 36 years at home will be similar to when he would return from the end of recruiting season.

"In the past, when he came home and suddenly wanted to be in the discussions of making adult decisions for the children, you'd wonder, 'Where have you been?' That takes awhile to adjust to," she said. "We'll have plenty of time to adjust to a lot of new things now."

Now, the Osborne's children—Mike, Ann and Suzi—are grown up with families of their own. Mike and his wife, Emily, have a son, William, and a daughter, Catey. Ann is married to Bob Wilke and they have a daughter, Haley. Suzi is married to Kevin Dobbs, who is a high school coach.

"A frequent topic of discussion the last few weeks has been the grandkids," said Mike. "I know he (his dad) would like to spend some time getting to know them better."

Being the child of Nebraska's head football coach wasn't always easy. But Mike, who played basketball and football in high school and football at Hastings College, his father's alma mater, said it was always memorable.

"A lot of kids have dads who travel or are very busy and can't attend their sporting events," said Mike. "My dad wasn't able to be at most of my games. He came as often as he could and I understood. Now I'm past my game-playing age, but maybe he'll come to my YMCA basketball games or something.

"People ask me if it's hard being Tom Osborne's son. I guess the only thing I can tell them is that I don't know anything but that. I've seen things up close at a major college football program that a lot of kids would like to see and that was a lot of fun. On the other hand, there were pressures I perceived, like being under a microscope, and that wasn't fun. But overall, it's been a lot of fun."

The football staff at Nebraska also became an extended family for the Osbornes.

"I think the hardest part about this will be not seeing all of them every Saturday and as often as I did," said Ann. "It will seem weird not yelling with them at games like I have been since I was 2 years old."

That tradition will continue in the Osborne family. Just like her mother before her, Haley Wilke has been immersed in football and she's only 18 months old.

"She understands the word touchdown and puts her hands up. And when she sees the football stadium, she says 'Grandpa,' " said Ann. "With her being so young, we will just tell her what Grandpa did for 25 years."

Ann and Mike were on hand the day Tom announced his resignation, offering moral support to each other. Tears marked the event for both of them until

Tom and Nancy Osborne pose for this 1984 Christmas portrait with their son Mike and daughters Ann (back) and Suzi. (Ted Kirk, Journal Star Library)

Tom persuaded their mother to join him at the front of the room. Watching on a tiny television monitor, both immediately beamed.

"I knew when this day came, the neatest thing about it would be that now my dad and mom would get to spend time together they probably never got," said Ann. "At first, my dad won't know what to do with his time, but I know they'll be able to catch up on a lot of lost time together."

For Nancy Osborne, keeping it secret was the hardest part of knowing for months that her husband would resign at the end of the season.

"It never really came close to slipping out, even though I knew about it since he made the decision to resign at the beginning of the season," she said. "The whole season was hard because I knew it was going to be the last time going to the Colorado game or going to any of the other road games. It was difficult to not share that feeling with anybody."

Osborne told her children so they would know that road trips this season would be the last of their dad's career.

"This has been quite an experience," Nancy said. "It is amazing the heartwarming response to Tom's announcement. We have felt nothing but care and love for Tom and our family. I've even received messages from wives of recently retired men with some advice."

She never expected such a reaction.

"Sometimes in the football family," she said, "you learn to keep closed up because you know that three wins and you're out because that isn't enough wins, and three losses and you're out because that's too many losses."

Can a man who has worked 15-hour days for most of the past 25 years make the transition to a life of leisure? Not likely, and Nancy wouldn't expect that.

"Tom and I both see this as resigning and not retiring," she said. "He has a lot of energy and talent in a lot of areas, and he will work as long as he can. And honestly, we do not know what that (future work) is going to be."

Nancy and her husband will continue to work with the growing Teammates Program, which matches Husker football players and business leaders with junior high school students. The Osbornes will raise money for the University of Nebraska-Lincoln's Love Library, St. Mark's United Methodist Church and the Osborne Legacy program, including $15 million for Hastings College.

Jack Osborne said initially he had mixed emotions about his brother's resignation.

"I'm both happy and sad. It's been a tremendously enjoyable thing to be a part of and now it's over," he said. "But I would think being as close as the family has been, they are looking forward to spending more time with him (Tom). We were all concerned about the pace he had to keep and the stress and what he put in the program."

That stress sometimes reached the family. Phone calls to the house or people yelling in public are bound to have an effect.

"It's amazing how the number of knuckleheads has diminished with Tom's success," Jack said. "In general, the news people in this state knew Tom about as well as you can know him and treated him pretty well. But there were some, especially nationally, who didn't know the truth. They attacked his morals and his decision-making and had no basis or grounds to make those attacks."

Time with the family was one of the reasons Tom cited for his resignation.

"He likes fishing and seeing the grandkids and traveling," said Mike. "I like golf and he likes fishing, so we'll probably argue about what we do. But we'll manage to compromise." ■

Nancy Osborne stood by her husband during his years as Nebraska football coach, and was at his side when he announced his resignation December 10, 1997. (Ted Kirk, Journal Star Library)

Praise From His Peers

by Jeff Korbelik

Lincoln Journal Star

Jan. 12, 1998

Bobby Bowden knew when he took over the Florida State football program in 1976 that the road ahead of him building the school into a college powerhouse would be difficult.

Then he saw four road dates at Nebraska in the next 10 years, and the road became really rocky.

"It nearly made me want to change jobs," Bowden said, laughing. "I thought I would be out of here by '81."

That was the kind of respect Bowden had for Nebraska and its coach, Tom Osborne, who at age 60 retired from coaching after 25 seasons at Nebraska.

"It was a sad day for me and college football," Bowden said. "I put Tom and Joe Paterno, Lavell Edwards and Hayden Fry in that 'icon' category. You sit and wonder who'll be next and I guess I thought Tom would be the last of those to retire."

Bowden, Penn State's Paterno, Brigham Young's Edwards and Iowa's Fry are all older than Osborne. Fry, 66 and a 45-year coaching veteran, was stunned when he found out his close friend had decided to retire.

"I thought Tom would be coaching forever," Fry said.

Even Osborne's biggest rival was taken aback, but former Oklahoma and Dallas Cowboys Coach Barry Switzer said he understood.

"I'm as surprised as everyone would be, but when I reflect on Tom's career and what he accomplished at Nebraska, you have to ask what else can he accomplish?" Switzer said. "He accomplished it all. No one won as consistently as Tom did. He won every year and a lot of times he was undefeated. What more could he do?"

Osborne was 255-49-3 in 25 years and won national titles in three of his last four years. He had winning records against 53 schools and losing marks against just six: Georgia Tech (0-1), Houston (0-1), Clemson (0-1), Florida State (2-6), Michigan (0-1) and Washington (1-2).

Four of the Florida State losses were in bowl games, as were the losses to Georgia Tech, Houston, Clemson and Michigan. Osborne was 12-13 in bowl games, but won his last four, including a 42-17 victory against Tennessee in the 1998 Orange Bowl, his last game. The victory secured a share of the national title.

Bowden was 2-2 in his first four games against the Cornhuskers. He said

his teams easily could have been 0-4.

"When you played a Tom Osborne-coached team, you knew you would play as fine a team fundamentally as there is," Bowden said. "They have always blocked and tackled better than any team we played."

Osborne's 255 wins trail only Paul "Bear" Bryant (323), Amos Alonzo Stagg (314), Glenn "Pop" Warner (313), Paterno (298) and Bowden (281) among NCAA Division I-A coaches. Only Penn State's Paterno and Bowden are still coaching.

Paterno was 2-3 against his friend and said he enjoyed competing against Osborne's teams.

"I've got some mixed feelings," he said. "Good news, bad news. If that's what he wants to do, great, I wish him the very best. The bad news is we're really losing one of the most outstanding people who has ever coached the game."

Colorado Coach Rick Neuheisel called Osborne legendary.

"He is one of the legends in the business and has certainly earned the right to be mentioned in the same breath as the all-time greats," said Neuheisel, who coached and played against Osborne's teams. "Colorado, like most others, couldn't beat Nebraska very often."

Osborne was 21-3-1 against the Buffaloes. He never lost to former Big Eight foes Kansas (25-0), Kansas State (25-0) and Oklahoma State (22-0-1).

He was 13-13 against Oklahoma. The Huskers' rivalry with the Sooners was one the most rabid in the 1970s and '80s.

Osborne and Switzer both broke into college coaching in 1973. Osborne's first win against Switzer came in 1978, one of the NU's coach's most memorable moments.

"I was a rookie coach taking over for Chuck Fairbanks and he was a rookie coach taking over for Bob Devaney," Switzer said. "It was amazing how our careers started. We (the Sooners) won early and he started winning late.

"I guess right now he's looking at the fourth quarter of life and wants to spend it with his family."

Fry said Osborne's success on the field can be tied to his relationship with his players. Osborne was known for giving troubled student-athletes second chances because he believed in them.

Osborne was at times criticized for his compassion. He came under fire nationally when he reinstated I-back Lawrence Phillips after an eight-game suspension. Phillips was arrested for assaulting his girlfriend.

"He was always trying to help the student-athlete," Fry said. "That was why he was such a successful recruiter. The student-athlete read into his personality a sincere, genuine person, as well as a great coach."

Bowden noted the same sincerity.

"Tom is himself," he said. "There is not one phony fiber in his body. What you see is what you get." ■

The Final Chapter

by John Mabry
Lincoln Journal Star

You would have thought it was just another game against Iowa State.

From his retirement announcement on December 10 to the last play of the 1998 Orange Bowl, Tom Osborne played down the significance of his final game as Nebraska's head football coach.

After leading the Big Red for 306 games during a 25-year career as head coach, Osborne wasn't going to get all choked up about one more.

The Cornhuskers had a job to do—beat Tennessee in Miami—and it didn't matter to him whether it was game No. 7 or 307.

Osborne ran his last football practice in Lincoln on December 23 and afterward got about as sentimental as a fast-food cook saying goodbye to a burger.

"The last practice in Lincoln?" Osborne said. "Not that big a deal to me right now. No difficulties. No particular emotions."

The players, however, knew that it was a special occasion. Osborne had run thousands of Nebraska football practices

in Lincoln, but he wouldn't be running any more.

"I think a lot of us seniors tried to soak it all in, because to be on Tom Osborne's last team for the last practice in Lincoln is an honor," offensive guard Jon Zatechka said. "It hasn't all started to sink in. It probably won't. But we're enjoying it as much as we can. We're 12-0 and that's pretty enjoyable.

"This has been a great year and everybody wants to make it complete for Coach Osborne. He was the same old Coach Osborne. Down to business. 'Got a job to do.'

"I think the best is yet to come down in Miami."

Miami.

Other than Lincoln, there could be no better final resting place for Osborne's coaching career. Over the years, he got to know south Florida like a Miami cabbie.

Osborne ended up coaching a whole

season of Orange Bowls. The game against Tennessee was his 11th.

In Osborne's 10 previous bowl trips to Miami, the Huskers had experienced their share of heartbreak. But it also was the site of Osborne's greatest triumph.

The University of Miami took a national title away from the Huskers with a 31-30 Orange Bowl victory on January 2, 1984.

After Nebraska scored a touchdown in the final minute, Osborne decided to go for two points rather than a tie, which would have been enough to clinch a national championship. Turner Gill's two-point pass to Jeff Smith was knocked away along with Nebraska's title hopes.

Eleven years later, the Cornhuskers finally paid the Hurricanes back with a come-from-behind Orange Bowl win that gave Osborne his first national championship. The Huskers scored two fourth-quarter touchdowns and beat the Hurricanes 24-17.

Two days before the 1998 Orange Bowl, Osborne maintained his lack of interest in all of the talk about his final game.

"This is not a sentimental journey or anything like that," he said. "I don't think about this being my last game. I think about the game itself. You are always hoping you have covered everything. You're always concerned with playing well and staying focused.

"I don't feel any different than any

QB Scott Frost led Nebraska to an Orange Bowl victory, undefeated season, and a share of the national title in 1997. (Journal Star Library)

touchdown run by Green, a brief preview of what was in store for Tennessee in the second half.

After wingback Shevin Wiggins gave the Huskers a 14-0 lead with a 10-yard run in the second quarter, Osborne brought the troops together for a little pep talk.

The message was simple: Forget about Michigan winning. If we continue to take care of business here, the voters might jump to our side in the polls.

In the second half, the Huskers stated their case quite clearly.

With Green and Frost leading the way, Nebraska scored 21 third-quarter points for a 35-9 lead. Green finished the game with an Orange Bowl-record 206 yards rushing and two touchdowns. Frost had three touchdown runs.

As Osborne watched the final seconds of his coaching career tick off the clock, the scoreboard read: "Nebraska 42, Tennessee 17."

Osborne didn't know it at the time, but the effort would be enough to send him out with a piece of the national championship.

Players came up to congratulate their departing coach. Some with a hug or a handshake. Others with a few kind words.

"We were laughing and giggling because we were having so much fun," Nebraska offensive lineman Matt Hoskinson said. "We played our hearts out for Coach Osborne because he gave his heart for us."

There was some literal meaning to that statement, since Osborne had undergone treatment for heart trouble during the season.

But his health was not an issue as

other game I've coached. Obviously, I am aware of the fact that this is my last one, but it doesn't trigger any special feeling or emotions at this point."

The night before the game, he stuck with the "What's the big deal?" refrain.

The second-ranked Huskers had a brief practice at Pro Player Stadium, but most of the talk was about the Rose Bowl that night between top-ranked Michigan and Washington State. A Cougar victory would mean that the Orange Bowl between Nebraska and No. 3 Tennessee would be for the national championship.

After watching the end of Michigan's 21-16 victory with his players, Osborne showed no signs of being discouraged.

"As far as our team is concerned,"

he said, "we set a number of goals at the start of the season, and I don't think any of those are eliminated at this time."

At about 8:30 p.m. EST on January 2, Tom Osborne led his Cornhuskers onto the bright green field at Pro Player Stadium.

The battle with the Volunteers was supposed to be a showdown between the Huskers' strong ground game and Tennessee's potent aerial attack.

The Huskers had one of the nation's top rushers in Ahman Green and a scrambling quarterback in Scott Frost. The Vols had Heisman Trophy runner-up Peyton Manning at quarterback and several speedy receivers.

Nebraska struck first with a 1-yard

Big Red fans loudly paid homage to their leader after one final triumph.

First it was, "Os-borne, Os-borne!" then "T.O., T.O.!"

Osborne's wife, Nancy, stood close by and laughed as her husband sheepishly took it all in.

She admitted what he wouldn't. That Tom's final game truly was a big deal.

"It was a very big deal," she said. "He couldn't afford to feel it until it was over. He had to keep coaching and keep focused, and it's been difficult."

Tom's brother, Jack Osborne, also made the trip from Nebraska to Miami. He knew how significant the game was and sensed that Tom did, too.

"I think he's probably terribly emotional," Jack said. "He has kind of, just

like always, kept it inside."

Keeping it inside. Just part of the playbook that made Osborne one of the greatest coaches in college football history.

A few hours after the Orange Bowl victory, the news came. One more chance for Osborne to keep it inside. He didn't disappoint.

The Orange Bowl rout, which wasn't enough to get the media voters to go with the Huskers as the top-ranked team in The Associated Press poll, was just enough to convince Osborne's peers that he had the best team in the country. Nebraska was No. 1 in the USA Today/ESPN coaches' poll.

Osborne was in his pajamas packing for the trip home when he heard.

"The coaches' poll was a little bit of a surprise, but a nice surprise," he said. "By that time, I was wrung out enough that there wasn't much emotion left.

"Naturally, I was pleased and gratified."

Osborne always talked about his success in understated terms. But he finished with a record that screamed for attention —255-49-3.

The Cornhuskers won 13 conference titles under Osborne, and the Orange Bowl victory gave him his third national championship.

He really did go out on top.

"I guess from our standpoint," Osborne said, "it couldn't have worked out any better." ■

Ahman Green was a key reason why Nebraska led the country in rushing in 1997. (Journal Star Library)